Foundation iPhone App Development

Build An iPhone App in 5 Days with iOS 6 SDK

Nick Kuh

friendsof

DESIGNER TO DESIGNER™

an Apress® company

Foundation iPhone App Development

Build An iPhone App in 5 Days with iOS 6 SDK

ISBN-13 (pbk): 978-1-4302-4374-8

ISBN-13 (electronic): 978-1-4302-4375-5

Trademarked names, logos, and images may appear in this book. Rather than use a trademark symbol with every occurrence of a trademarked name, logos, or image we use the names, logos, or images only in an editorial fashion and to the benefit of the trademark owner, with no intention of infringement of the trademark.

The use in this publication of trade names, service marks, and similar terms, even if they are not identified as such, is not to be taken as an expression of opinion as to whether or not they are subject to proprietary rights.

While the advice and information in this book are believed to be true and accurate at the date of publication, neither the authors nor the editors nor the publisher can accept any legal responsibility for any errors or omissions that may be made. The publisher makes no warranty, express or implied, with respect to the material contained herein.

Distributed to the book trade worldwide by Springer Science+Business Media New York, 233 Spring Street, 6th Floor, New York, NY 10013. Phone 1-800-SPRINGER, fax (201) 348-4505, e-mail orders-ny@springer-sbm.com, or visit www.springeronline.com.

For information on translations, please e-mail rights@apress.com or visit www.apress.com.

Apress and friendsofED books may be purchased in bulk for academic, corporate, or promotional use. eBook versions and licenses are also available for most titles. For more information, reference our Special Bulk Sales–eBook Licensing web page at www.apress.com/bulk-sales.

Any source code or other supplementary materials referenced by the author in this text is available to readers at www.apress.com. For detailed information about how to locate your book's source code, go to www.apress.com/source-code.

Credits

To my wife and son, Nicole and Finn, who keep me happy and loved.

Contents at a Glance

Contents

About the Author

Nick Kuh is a iOS Consultant and Developer based in the UK with 14 years experience developing mobile, desktop and web applications for clients such as the BBC, ESPN, Channel 4, Pearson and Novartis. He works on large commercial iOS projects as well as helping start-ups to launch on the App Store.

Nick balances his commercial work with the development of his own successful indie apps like *Tap to Chat*, *Poker Royale* and *Portfolio Pro*.

You can find Nick on Twitter as @nickkuh or on his website www.nickkuh.com.

About the Technical Reviewer

Felipe Laso Marsetti is a self-taught software developer specializing in iOS development and currently employed as a Systems Engineer at Lextech Global Services. Despite having worked with many languages throughout his life, nothing makes him happier than working on projects for iPhone and iPad. Felipe has over 2 years of professional iOS experience. He likes to write on his blog at http://iFe.li, create iOS tutorials and articles as a member of http://www.raywenderlich.com or work as a technical reviewer for

Objective-C and iOS related books. You can find Felipe on Twitter as @Airjordan12345, on Facebook under his name or on App.net as @iFeli. When he's not working or programming, Felipe loves to read and learn new languages and technologies, watch sports, cook or play the guitar and violin.

About the Cover Image Artist

 **Corné van Dooren** designed the front cover image for this book. After taking a break from friends of ED to create a new design for the Foundation series, he worked at combining technological and organic forms, with the results now appearing on the cover of this and other books.

Corné spent his childhood drawing on everything at hand and then began exploring the infinite world of multimedia—and his journey of discovery hasn't stopped since. His mantra has always been "the only limit to multimedia is the imagination," a saying that keeps him moving forward constantly.

Corné works for many international clients, writes features for multimedia magazines, reviews and tests software, authors multimedia studies, and works on many other friends of ED books. If you like Corné's work, be sure to check out his chapter in *New Masters of Photoshop: Volume 2* (friends of ED, 2004). You can see more of his work (and contact him) at his website, www.cornevandooren.com.

Acknowledgments

First and foremost I'd like to thank my wonderful wife, Nicole, for her constant support, love and the eternal sense of fun that she brings to our family life. She has always encouraged me to follow my instincts and take chances in life that have attributed greatly to my career success. Nicole helps to keep my geek side nice and balanced by providing creative input and ideas for many of my projects. Nicole is a professional photographer and this is the reason that I've built a number of photography-related apps (Portfolio Pro, Portfolio to Go). Check out her work at www.nicolecarman.com.

My nine year-old son Finn never fails to make me smile and laugh when we hang out. He loves the fact his dad is an Apple developer. He's even taught me a thing or two about iOS having become a mini techie expert himself in knowing his way around iPads and iPods and all the best games of course.

I'd like to thank Felipe Laso Marsetti for his great tech advice and enthusiasm about this book throughout the course of its development.

A special mention of thanks to Douglas Pundick for his expertise and mentorship that have helped shape my book into a manuscript that I'm very proud of.

Thanks to Jill Balzano for keeping me on schedule and always being on hand to advise.

Thanks to Steve Anglin for approving my book proposal and for making this all possible.

Last but by no means least, thanks to my mum and dad for all their love and encouragement throughout my life ☺

Introduction

My programming roots originated with Flash in 1999 when I first started writing object-oriented Games and Applications in ActionScript. More recently, in 2009, shortly after Apple launched the App Store and opened up their exciting new mobile platform to third parties, I decided to jump ship and become an iPhone Developer.

The transition from developing for the Flash Player to the iPhone was not the smoothest ride, but one key factor that helped me more than anything is that the same foundation principals of object-oriented programming for Flash are also at the heart of Objective-C and the iOS SDK.

If you are already working with another object-oriented language then you should be able to apply that knowledge to Objective-C and soon be up-and-running building apps for the iPhone.

Who should buy this book

Are you a Flash or Java Developer? PHP or Ruby Programmer? You're already proficient in at least one other object-oriented programming language and want to extend you skillset to include the hugely popular iOS platform. This book is for you.

Or perhaps you're a beginner iPhone Developer. You've already worked through many of the code examples that other books provide. You're now looking to learn how to build a larger scale app and pooling together knowledge you've gained from working through these example code snippets isn't at all obvious.

If you're completely new to programming then you may find this book quite challenging. However, I've always found that getting stuck in, even at the deep-end, is often a great way to face new challenges. If you're a newbie but also a fast learner then welcome aboard! I'll keep you in mind during our journey.

My book will help you to conquer the challenges of getting up-and-running with Objective-C. I will help you to effectively exploit your knowledge of object-oriented programming to code great iOS Apps. Don't worry if your object-oriented code is a bit patchy though. Throughout this book I will regularly highlight how iOS applies the Model View Controller (MVC) paradigm.

I'll get your hands dirty with Xcode from the off. This is going to be a very hands-on book. After all, we've only got 5 days to build an app!

You can even download the app we'll be developing right now as it's live in the App Store under the title *Birthday Reminder for Facebook*.

What this book with teach you

Other books will provide you with chapter after chapter of code examples for the various frameworks in the iOS SDK but when it comes to building your app you'll then need to figure out how best to combine those concepts together.

This book employs a very different method to learning. I will teach you how to build a professional, custom-designed, object-oriented iPhone App in just 5 days.

We'll start with a Photoshop PSD design and an app idea. Then, throughout the remainder of the book, I will guide you through each stage of building this app. But it's *you* who will build the app. You will learn how to think like an app developer, how to turn an idea into a beautiful iPhone app and a great number of tips and tricks along the way.

You'll learn a development process that I've devised over the last 3+ years that you will be able to apply to your own apps after completing the course.

The App that you'll be developing is quite simple on the surface, but the development principals it introduces are equally suitable for the development of larger, more complex apps.

Over time I've discovered there are often many different ways to solve the programmatic challenges that one faces on a daily basis when building iOS apps. Challenges like:

- The best way to load remote images into a scrolling table view that won't lock up the user interface and keep the app optimized.
- How to persistently store user data such as text and images and facilitate the user to edit and change that data, or cancel their changes.
- How to implement a custom app design without having to build custom iOS view components.

This book will address these kinds of challenges with solutions that I make use of in my own commercial projects. Solutions that will save you days, months, even years of invested time!

The process I'll exercise to teach you the skill of programming iOS Apps will be a step-by-step process. We are going to build an App from conception to completion. *You* are going to build this app! Along the way you'll learn:

- How to capitalize on making your beautiful app design resonate thanks to Apple's high resolution retina displays on all the new iPhone and iPod Touch devices
- How to map out/mock-up all the views of your app very quickly using Storyboards in Xcode and iOS 6
- How to build view controllers with object-oriented inheritance – centralizing core, reusable methods. Less code. Fewer bugs. Easier to make future changes.
- How Core Data will solve all of your app's data persistence needs. Although, this is quite an advanced topic I'll provide you with an easy-to-follow introduction to Core Data that will form the foundation for more complex projects. Stay friends with Core Data. It's worth it ☺
- How to deeply integrate Facebook's Graph API using the very latest Social framework introduced by Apple in iOS 6.
- How to take advantage of in-app social network marketing – get your users promoting your great app to their friends!

There's a lot to cover here!

What this book won't teach you

This is not a reference book for the iOS SDK. I won't be providing examples of every iOS framework. There are many other great books that do this already.

Day 1

Objective C, Xcode and iOS SDK
Foundation Work

Chapter 1

Designing and Planning Our App

Author: Throughout the course of this book, you will build an app from conception to completion!

You: Yes, Sensei!

Author: I expect you to build this app yourself. That's the only way you're going to learn!

You: Yes, Sensei!

OK, enough of *The Karate Kid* references (well, there may be a few more along the way ☺). The point I'm making is that via a step-by-step, chapter-by-chapter process, I will be your tutor—but *you* will have to put in the donkeywork. You are expected to write every line of code for this app. You are expected to create every class and view in this app.

I will provide you with all the design assets for this project. I've even cut them up into the actual image assets that you'll embed into your own app.

If you want to really challenge yourself, don't even look at the staged source code—throw it away! Just work with the exported image asset files and write all the code yourself.

I will also provide the start and finish source code for each chapter of your app development journey. So if you ever get stuck or want to jump ahead to a specific section of the app, go right ahead. How's the Sensei going to find out anyway?

Throughout this chapter, we'll focus on the initial planning and design stage of building a new iPhone app: how to get started once you have your app idea, a look at the competition for your app, and a number of tips and tricks to help your app stand out from the hundreds of thousands of apps in Apple's App Store.

The app idea

We've all forgotten a birthday before, right?

The app you're going to build is a birthday reminder app. *Birthday Reminder* will ensure that our users never forget a birthday again! It's a simple but useful idea and just the sort of thing that makes for a good iPhone app idea.

With *Birthday Reminder*, all of your friends' and family members' birthdays are stored in one place. You'll get a notification reminder on the day of or in advance of every birthday. No more embarrassing late cards and presents. Our app will solve this core problem for our users. It's a single task that the app will do seamlessly—making the user's life a little easier.

A common misconception by some app developers is to think that adding more features to their app will increase its popularity and App Store ranking. Instead, keep your app ideas simple—and deliver a beautiful, intuitive user experience. Focus on doing one thing really well with your app rather than doing ten things badly.

This app is going to stand out from the competition. Its icons and user interface are going to be so beautiful, it's going to make you want to lick your iPhone! The user experience is going to be instantly intuitive to new users. The app will also be zippy and responsive to touch—just what iOS users have come to expect from great iPhone and iPad apps!

Adding and editing birthdays

Users of our app will be able to add and edit an unlimited number of birthdays. We'll include the option to assign a photo to each birthday via the iPhone camera or Photo Library.

All birthdays will be stored offline in a local database on the iPhone. We'll read and write to the database via Apple's Core Data framework (you'll learn more about Core Data in Chapter 8).

Importing birthdays from the Address Book and Facebook

We'll program an import mechanism into our app that facilitates our users to batch-import birthdays using the latest iOS 6 Facebook social integration and native Address Book frameworks. We won't force our users to import every one of his or her Facebook friends, however. We'll allow them to pick and choose. This is one of the great benefits of creating our own custom offline storage solution: we control the data.

Saving selected birthdays persistently in our app also means that we won't lose this data and have to resync our app with the Address Book or Facebook, even if the OS shuts it down—which of course it never will because we're building an optimized app here.

Note taking

We'll include a note-taking option in our app—the perfect way for our user to keep track of gift ideas. Notes will also be saved and stored in our offline Core Data store.

Reminder notifications

Our app will take advantage of local notifications in the iOS SDK. In our app code, we'll schedule these notification alerts, which will fire on the user's iPhone in time for each birthday reminder—even when our app isn't running. We'll also play a little Happy Birthday jingle with our birthday reminders.

Facebook social integration and in-app marketing

We won't stop at just importing Facebook birthdays into our App. We'll learn how to deeply integrate with Facebook's Graph API and Apple's iOS 6 social framework to enable users to post directly to their friends' Facebook Walls without having to exit the app. In addition to this being a useful feature for our users, we automatically gain free advertising for *Birthday Reminder*. Every Facebook post via a third-party app includes a direct link back to the originating app. This helps to publicize *Birthday Reminder* every time any of our users post Happy Birthday messages to their Facebook friends.

We'll also make it easy for our user to call, SMS, or e-mail birthday wishes to friends imported from the Address Book.

The competition

We have our app idea, but before we get into the design and coding stages, now might be a good time to take a look at the competition.

It's always worth looking at your app's most successful competitors at the beginning of a project.

Search the App Store for your target keywords. Which apps regularly come up at the top of the search list? Typically, those are the apps getting the most downloads. What are these successful competitors doing right? It is likely to be a combination of the following:

- They have a great icon.
- They've built a great app.
- They've designed a beautiful UI (user interface).
- Their app is easy to use and has an intuitive user experience.
- They've integrated social networking into their app effectively.
- They've run a strong marketing campaign.
- They've been featured by Apple in the App Store.
- They've got lots of 4- and 5-star ratings.
- They had the idea first and launched ahead of the competition.

The last point in this list is often one of the most likely scenarios. A great number of those app makers who got into the App Store early with a good idea are still holding strong in their category. Being in the top 100 of your category gives your app a great deal of publicity. If you're lucky enough to hit that position, your app gets much greater App Store visibility—and therefore a greater continued chance of success.

As a new app developer, I recommend that you focus on the first six points on that list (the only points that are under your control) and in turn, with good marketing, you may rise up the charts based on your hard work.

At its peak, *Tap to Chat* was in the top 50 free social networking apps in the US App Store—it was getting 4,000+ daily downloads. This remained the case for a good few months. My team then released a better version of our app under a new company. However, the new version never got lucky enough to reach the same chart position as the original. It didn't matter that the second version of our app was totally awesome, it mattered that our first version had reached a powerful position and maintained its popularity.

In preparation for this book, I built the first version of *Birthday Reminder* in only five days. Before doing so, I took a good look at competitor apps. I checked out the search results, and I downloaded and paid for a few of the other birthday reminder apps that stood out from the crowd. I actually discovered 120 competitor iPhone apps in search results for "birthday reminder". This didn't put me off the idea, however. For starters, I was confident that I could implement at least the first five points on my list of what it takes to be successful: I could build a beautiful app with an intuitive user experience that would deliver on its core task of reminding users of all their friends' birthdays. The app would incorporate Facebook social media in a useful way for users, but also be an effective method for empowering peer-to-peer marketing.

I was actually encouraged by the search results. Yes, some of the competitor apps are good, but without pulling any punches, the majority of them were not.

Some of the top results have hundreds of ratings and reviews. This is also encouraging because it shows there's a strong market for birthday reminder apps if you can get noticed.

If you want to check out the app you'll be building from scratch throughout the course of this book, then you can download *Birthday Reminder for Facebook* from the App Store right now.

The App Store title

Registered Apple developers (see Chapter 2) submit their apps to the App Store via the iTunes Connect web site (see Chapter 14). iTunes Connect will not permit you to set an App Store title for your app if it's already taken. You'll see that some developers get around this by adding "+" or "Pro" or other suffixes to get (roughly) the App Store title they want.

Don't confuse your App Store title with the *bundle display name*, which is the title of your app on the iPhone home screen. They are two very different animals. The display name is set in your app bundle's `Info.plist` (see Chapter 3) and is limited to about 12 characters before getting truncated.

Alongside your icon, your App Store title will be your primary entry point to app sales/downloads. Potential customers will only have your icon and the first few words of your App Store title when scrolling through the rows and rows of competitor apps.

Avoid being too obscure with your App Store title. You should include the keywords you'd expect users to search and find your app. The App Store search algorithm gives a good amount of importance to the words in app titles. Unless you already have a strong brand outside of iTunes, you'll need to choose the words in your title very carefully.

The order of the words in the title is equally important. In iOS 6, you have about 40 characters until the App Store truncates your title when browsed on an iPhone. For users still on iOS 5, the App Store title is restricted to a single line and gets truncated after about 18 characters. Make the most of those characters! Make sure that the first word or two in your title, combined with your icon, conveys exactly what your app does.

Don't shy away from using additional relevant keywords in your App Store title; for example, *Portfolio Pro for iPad—Brandable Photo and Video App*. Including a strapline in your title improves your chances of appearing in relevant App Store searches.

I was lucky enough to grab the title *Birthday Reminder for Facebook* when I built the first iteration of this app. Facebook users are a big market on the App Store. They will help promote the app each time they use it to post a birthday message on a friend's wall. It's worth targeting these users.

The icon design

It may be that you're a jack-of-all-trades when it comes to making iPhone apps. You can program well-written object-oriented code *and* have an artistic eye for designing beautiful user interfaces. Lucky you!

For most of us, it's one or the other. This book is aimed at developers, so as a handy hint, if you're looking to outsource the design work of your app to a talented iOS design guru, then I'd highly recommend starting at www.dribbble.com. Dribbble is a wonderful site for finding talented designers. It's a social site where designers share and comment on their latest work. Try a search for **iOS** or **iPhone**, and browse the many pages of related designs. It's a great way to discover designers with a style that suits your app idea.

Using Dribbble, I discovered the designer of the app icon and user interface for *Birthday Reminder*.

As with your App Store title, your icon provides the first impression of your iPhone app. Potential users will decide whether to find out more about your app initially based on its icon. So don't leave the icon until the last minute—it's not an afterthought, it's as important as the app itself!

New iPhone and iPod Touch devices have retina displays. So an eye-catching, beautiful icon that makes great use of the 114×114 pixel icon size on a retina screen is a must.

Figure 1-1 shows the icon for our app. A strong yet fun and colorful design with a subtle 3D effect will stand out against our competitors' icons.

Figure 1-1. *Birthday Reminder*'s icon: simple, colorful, and eye-catching

As with your App Store title, don't try to be too clever with your icon. It's important that your potential users immediately grasp what your app does from the icon design. I chose a birthday cake design for our app icon that also translates into the user interface design for our app.

The user interface design

Most of the designers I work with use Photoshop as their tool of choice when designing for iOS apps. Thanks to the talented folk over at Teehan+Lax, designers have access to a very handy PSD file with all of the native iOS controls mocked up into Photoshop layers in a single iOS GUI (graphical user interface) PSD file. This makes an ideal starting point when designing for iOS. The PSD is free to download from www.teehanlax.com/downloads (see Figure 1-2).

Figure 1-2. iOS GUI PSD by Teehan+Lax

Retina displays, the status bar, and the iPhone 5

The iPhone screen pre-iPhone 5 is 320×480 *points*. This is the same for both retina and non-retina screens. Points are different from pixels. In Objective-C, every reference to the size or the position of a view is measured in points. The iPhone 5 screen is 320×568 points.

Prior to the iPhone 4, each point was made up of a single pixel. With retina displays, however, there are four pixels squeezed into every point (2×2 grid), resulting in the dimensions of an iPhone 4 or iPhone 4s retina display being a total of 640×960 pixels (see Figure 1-3). The iPhone 5 screen packs in 640×1136 pixels (see Figure 1-3). The status bar is 20 points high, and therefore 40 pixels high on a retina display.

I'd suggest always including the iOS status bar in your app design. By default, the status bar in an app is displayed, but in code or via the Info.plist (see Chapter 3), developers can hide the status bar and make their apps full screen. Avoid doing so unless you have a really good reason, such as transitioning into a full screen photo slideshow.

The status bar includes valuable information for our user, such as the current phone and Internet signal level, the time, and the battery life remaining. Without the status bar, you still have a whooping great 320×460 points (320×548 on the iPhone 5!) of screen real estate for your app view— the sort of space Blackberry developers can only dream about!

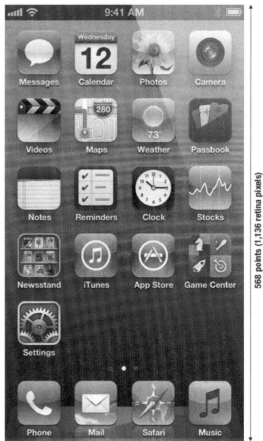

Figure 1-3. Points and pixels of a retina display

Paper prototyping: starting with the design

I strongly recommend completing the design of your app *in advance* of writing a single line of code. I always start with a pencil and paper, sketching out every view of the user interface. This method should result in a good, well-thought-out design layout for each view in your app, and reduce the risk of future code refactoring.

Typically, I'll draw several iterations of each view of my app until I'm happy with the layout. Then I'll photograph the results and e-mail them to my designer with detailed instructions to mock up the final designs in Photoshop. The designer then creates 640×960 pixel retina-ready PSD files for each view of the app.

When working with clients, insist that the design be signed off before you start coding their app. Clients often fight this requirement, claiming that their app is a work in progress, and therefore the design is subject to change. This is just bad planning on their part.

By taking the time to sketch out every screen design before starting code, your clients will save you copious amounts of wasted development time—and, therefore, wasted budget. They will save money if they invest in good planning!

It's amazing how many potential user interface design problems can be solved on paper. This process of sketching out screens in advance of code is also known as *paper prototyping*. It enables individuals and teams to examine each screen and discuss the implications of one type of layout vs. another.

Designing an intuitive and engaging user interface is a process that this book will frequently reference, but if you want to delve in deeper at this stage, then who better to learn from than the gurus of user interface design themselves: Apple.

Let me introduce you to the HIG—Apple's Human Interface Guidelines, which you can read at your leisure on the Apple Developer web site at `http://developer.apple.com/library/ios/#documentation/ UserExperience/Conceptual/MobileHIG/Introduction/Introduction.html`.

The HIG takes you, very clearly, through every aspect of good user interface design for iOS apps. Everything from the minimum hit area of a button (44×44 points) through every finger gesture (tap, slide, flick, etc.), and exactly how your user will expect your app to respond.

People become very familiar with the way apps and the operating system functions on their smartphone. Unexpected user interface behavior results in annoyance from our users. It's not that difficult to keep them happy and enjoy using our app. The HIG provides you with everything you need to do just that.

A walk-through of app designs

In order to get you thinking in the terminology of the iOS SDK, I'm going to refer to each of the screens in our app as *views*. I'll go further into the details of views and view controllers in Chapter 3, but it's good to recognize at this early stage that each screen in our app is a view.

In iOS, each of our main views has a corresponding view controller class.

This is our first introduction to Apple's implementation of the Model-View-Controller (MVC) paradigm in the iOS SDK. Don't worry if you're already getting confused. I'll be fleshing out more details about views, view controllers, and MVC in iOS in Chapters 4, 5, and 6.

Birthday Reminder will consist of the following main views (each controlled by its own view controller):

- Home view (birthday listings)
- Birthday detail view
- Birthday notes view
- Add or edit a birthday view
- Import from Address Book view

- Import from Facebook view

- Settings view and subviews

The home view

When our app first launches, it will have an empty database. There will be no birthdays to display. So rather than display an empty birthdays list, we'll hide the table view and render two big call-to-action buttons to encourage the user to get started by importing birthdays from their Address Book and from Facebook (see Figure 1-4a).

As soon as one or more birthdays have been added to the app, we'll show the populated table view of birthdays. We'll still give the user easy access to the Address Book and Facebook import buttons, but they will take less prominence in our screen design (see Figure 1-4b).

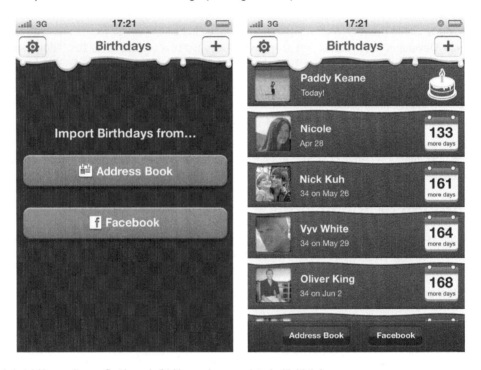

Figure 1-4. (a) Home view on first launch (b) Home view populated with birthdays

Our home view (Figures 1-4a and 1-4b) includes standard control components from the iOS SDK: a navigation bar (UINavigationBar), labels (UILabel), buttons (UIButton), a table view (UITableView), table view cells (UITableViewCell), image views (UIImageView), a toolbar (UIToolbar), and bar button items (UIBarButtonItem). These are not custom-made components. What you'll notice, however, is the extent to which we can re-skin these standard components to make a beautiful user interface design.

In iOS 5, Apple added Appearance APIs, which have continued to evolve in iOS 6. These APIs make skinning Apple's UI components much easier than with previous versions of the iOS SDK. *Birthday Reminder* will exploit these features to full effect.

The design concept of using a birthday cake for our icon is also prominent throughout the main views of our app, such as the home view and import birthdays views, where each of the birthdays will be represented as a layer of a cake. Each of these cake layers will be rendered by a custom-designed table cell (UITableViewCell) in our app.

It is common in iPhone apps for the app navigation to be controlled via a special type of view controller: a view controller that organizes multiple child view controllers. The main examples of these parent view controllers are the navigation controller (UINavigationController) and the tab bar controllers (UITabBarController) that control the flow of child views and view controllers in a manageable way for a small screen device.

The navigation bar at the top of our home view is owned by our app's main navigation controller. When populated with birthdays, the home view displays a table view with multiple table cells to render the details of each birthday.

When the user taps one of listed birthdays in the table view, our app will respond to the tap gesture and create an instance of the birthday detail view. The birthday detail view will be "pushed" onto the main navigation controller. The navigation controller will animate the current home view, sliding it off to the left, and the new detail view, sliding it in from the right. You will have no doubt seen this behavior in many of the iPhone apps you use daily.

The birthday detail view

At the point that the home view controller creates the birthday detail view controller and view, it will also pass data (birthday data) to the birthday detail view controller. The birthday detail view controller will dynamically update its view to display the user details and any birthday notes saved for this entry in the database.

Birthday Reminder will need to aggregate three types of birthdays, but it will display them all in the same detail view:

- Birthdays imported from the iPhone Address Book
- Birthdays imported from Facebook
- Birthdays added manually to the app

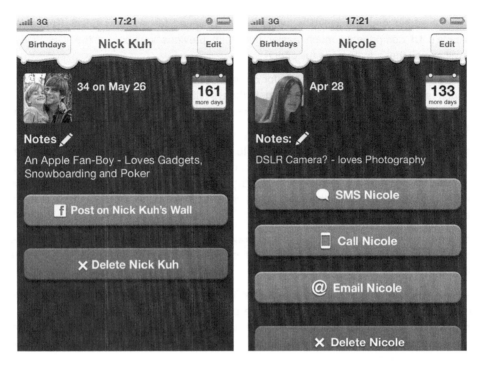

Figure 1-5. (**a**) Birthday detail view displaying a Facebook import (**b**) Birthday detail view displaying an Address Book import

If the displayed birthday is an import from Facebook, then *Birthday Reminder* will enable the user to post a birthday message to the friend's Facebook Wall directly inside our app using Apple's social framework and Facebook's Graph API.

If this birthday was imported from the user's iPhone contacts, then our app will also be able to access the telephone number and e-mail associated with the contact. Adding direct links to enable our user to SMS, call, or e-mail birthday greetings to a friend is a great way to make the most of the native access our app has been granted to the user's Address Book.

Editing birthdays and adding notes: going modal

The birthday data in our app will remain editable. So we're going to include an Edit button in the navigation bar when the user is viewing the birthday detail view. When tapped, our app will present an editable version of the current birthday details, and the user will be able to make changes (see Figure 1-6a).

Do you see the note-taking icon under the birthday image on the screens shown in Figure 1-5? When the user taps on the pencil, the birthday detail view controller will respond to this gesture by presenting our note-taking view (see Figure 1-6b).

Figure 1-6. (**a**) Add/edit birthday detail view (**b**) Edit birthday notes view

Both of these choices enable the user to *edit* the data he is currently viewing in our app. We need to make this very clear to our user. We do this by presenting these editing views modally. Again, it's our parent navigation controller that animates in the modal view(s) from the bottom of the iPhone screen. The user will be presented with Cancel and Save options: two very clear choices for them to manipulate the data model.

We're going to use Apple's Core Data framework for all of the local data persistence in our app. This has a number of advantages, such as making any birthday editable directly in our app—regardless of whether it was added manually or imported from the user's Address Book or Facebook.

Core Data is an Apple framework for object graph management and data persistence. The default backing store used by Core Data is an SQLite database, but there are alternative storage options. Although Core Data is generally considered an advanced topic, I'll introduce you to the basics of adding object, text, and binary data persistence into your apps; in our case, simply by being able to save and edit birthdays between sessions (see Chapter 8).

Native Facebook integration

Because *Birthday Reminder* will keep its own store of birthday data, we will enable users to pick and choose the friends they wish to import into the app from Facebook (see Figure 1-7b), and then save the birthday data, friend names, and profile icon URLs locally into our Core Data store.

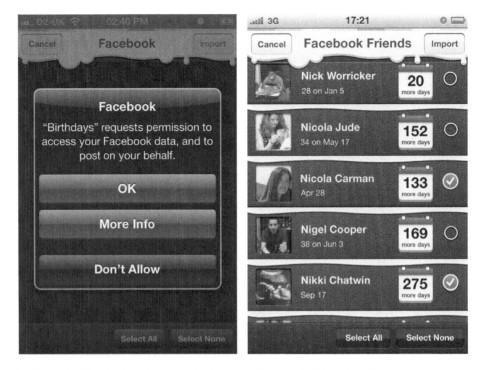

Figure 1-7. (**a**) Handling Facebook authorization (**b**) Preparing to import birthdays from Facebook

Prior to iOS 6, Facebook enabled and encouraged iOS developers to integrate social features into iOS apps. In iOS 6, Apple has now partnered with Facebook to include Facebook's Single Sign-On mechanism directly into the iOS platform.

In iOS 6, Apple has tightened up data privacy to ensure that users need to opt-in when either sharing data from Facebook or their Address Book. We'll learn how to handle the authorization flow (see Figure 1-7a).

The Import from Address Book View will look identical to the Import from Facebook View, with multiple selection and select all/none shortcut buttons. These import views will be presented modally in our app. When a user taps a button to import from a list of Facebook friends or Address Book contacts, they will be making direct changes to the data model by adding new birthdays to the store. It makes sense to present these import views modally and include the option for the user to cancel their import action.

Settings views

Birthday Reminder will fire local iOS notifications for every birthday stored in its data model prior to or on the date of each stored birthday. Via our Settings views, we'll allow our app users to set when they want to get their reminder alerts (see Figures 1-8a, b, and c).

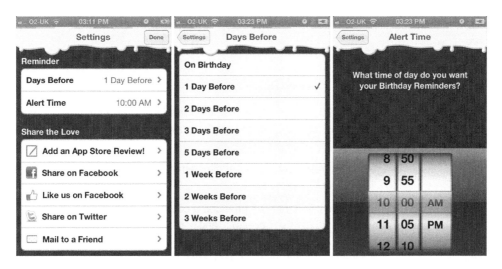

Figure 1-8. (a) Main Settings view (b) Days Before settings view (c) Alert Time settings view

Settings views are also a good place to add promotional links. Goad your user to add a nice App Store review. Increase your Facebook likes and enable users to share your app by e-mail, Twitter, or Facebook. You've done all the hard work of getting your app into the hands of your users, don't miss out on a perfect opportunity to increase the popularity ranking of your app in the App Store and to take advantage of marketing on social networks!

Exporting design image assets

Now that we're 100 percent happy with our design PSD (well, I'm going to assume you're happy!), we can start to break apart and export the icons and background images that will be part of our Xcode project.

Throughout the remainder of the book, I'll provide you with the exported PNG image assets when they are required for each chapter and stage of our project.

Within the Chapter 1 source design/code, you'll also find seven Photoshop PSD files for the retina designs of the main views in our app. The inclusion of these design files gives you a good starting point for what you should expect when commissioning a designer for your own projects.

After completing this book and as you start building your own apps, you will need to go through the process of creating asset PNGs and JPGs for yourself. You won't always be able to predict the best way to slice up your design PSD. It's a process that I often action during development when I need an asset for the view I'm working on.

We're going to create an app that is optimized for retina displays. With four times as many pixels on a retina display to non-retina, all of our retina-optimized images will look smooth and crisp on the user's iPhone.

The trick is to create two versions of every icon and background image: (1) one for non-retina and (2) one twice the non-retina size and of a higher quality for retina screens.

The iOS SDK will automatically detect retina-ready imagery as long as you adhere to the following naming convention:

Standard: `my-image.png`

Retina: `my-image@2x.png`

In this example, if `my-image.png` is 150×100 pixels in size, then `my-image@2x.png` is 300×200 pixels in size and automatically used by retina devices instead of the standard image, making the most of all additional pixels.

Assuming this example image is not stretchable, then the dimensions of the image view that is rendering this image on screen is 150×100 *points*.

In the source code for this chapter, you'll find that I've provided a couple of example exported PNG assets: `navigation-bar-background.png` (320×60 pixels) and `navigation-bar-background@2x.png` (640×120 pixels). Older non-retina devices like the iPhone 3G iOS display the `navigation-bar-background.png` version of the image. On the newer retina devices, `navigation-bar-background@2x.png` is automatically used by iOS, resulting in a much crisper and less pixelated version of the image, but still displayed within the 320×60 point rectangle.

The PSDs for our *Birthday Reminder* app have all been designed for the dimensions of a retina screen—640×960 pixels. So in exporting each asset, I initially exported all of the retina assets using the `[filename]@2x.[fileformat]` naming convention. Then, I flattened and downsized each exported image to half its retina size, and exported the smaller versions without the @2x for the older non-retina screens.

> *Tip: Make sure that your retina assets are an even pixel width and height so that when you downsize them by half, the resulting size is a full pixel width and height.*

A little extra help

Throughout this book, I guide and assist you at every stage of the journey. After the course, however, when you start your own app development journey, you will probably encounter occasional roadblocks. We all do.

Perhaps you won't be able to figure out how to make a certain framework work, or you struggle with provisioning for an App Store submission. Whatever the problem, you're unlikely to be the first to experience it. Help is at hand!

Apple's own documentation is extensive—you can browse through the docs online via the iOS Developer Center. Alternatively, Xcode enables you to jump straight to the specific class, framework, or method that you're struggling with via the ^⌘? keyboard shortcut.

When you come up against specific bugs in your iOS code, there are some very handy reference web sites and blogs to turn to. Stack Overflow (stackoverflow.com) is by far my favorite. It is a geeks' question/answer site for all programming languages. Other geeks vote on the best answers to each technical question posted. If you come up against a problem, you can bet that someone on Stack Overflow has already provided the answer.

In addition, the Apple Developer Forum on the iOS Developer Center is another great resource for developers to post and search for answers to iOS specific questions. Some questions are even answered by Apple's own engineers—answers straight from the source!

Summary

We now know what we're going to build. We've planned all the screens of our app.

We've learned that the best way to start making an app is to sketch out your views with a pencil and pad; work out the best user experience and user interface design on paper; and resolve design challenges before getting into the code. This is the most robust way to build an app and keep future refactoring to an absolute minimum.

But we haven't yet touched Xcode or written any code yet. Unfortunately, we still have a few more core tasks to do before we can start coding.

Let's move on to registering as an Apple developer and provisioning our app for device testing!

Chapter 2

Provisioning Our App for Development

For some, this will be the slow-going chapter. It covers all of the tasks that we need to do before we can really get started developing our app. These tasks are kind of dull, but you won't get very far until they're complete.

The process of becoming a fully paid and enrolled member of the iOS Developer Program is a bit of an uphill battle, but once you're through it, you'll be able to build and submit as many apps to the App Store as you have the time to make!

Once you've completed enrollment in the iOS Developer Program, then you'll be able to return to this chapter and we'll explore the iOS Provisioning Portal in detail. We'll also go through the step-by-step process necessary to prepare your own provisioning environment for on-device testing of your apps.

Download Xcode for free

To start developing apps, we only need one piece of Apple software: Xcode (see Figure 2-1).

Figure 2-1. Xcode: Apple's developer tool for creating Mac and iOS applications

Xcode is distributed by Apple for free via the Mac App Store. The first thing to do is open the App Store on your Mac, and then download and install Xcode straight from the store. You'll need to be working on an Intel-based Mac running Lion or Mountain Lion to install Xcode 4.5 (or greater). While Xcode downloads and installs in the background, you can just keep reading.

Here's a direct link to Xcode in the US Mac App Store:

`http://itunes.apple.com/us/app/xcode/id448457090?mt=12`

When Apple shipped Xcode 4.1, the original download size was a whopping 4GB! There were a lot of impatient developers out there hogging up their Internet connection for hours—or even days—at a time while the mighty Xcode downloaded. The install process also used to be more cumbersome: Apple distributed an installer rather than an app via the store, and once downloaded, developers then had to step through a secondary install process. The installer added files and folders to the Developer directory of your hard drive alongside numerous separate developer tools like Instruments and Application Loader.

Xcode 4.5+ is less than a 100MB download and is distributed as a single application that automatically installs when the short download-time completes. Debug tools like Instruments are now packaged inside the Xcode application bundle. Various versions of the iOS simulator are downloaded in the background as required (for example, if your app needs to support iOS 4 or 5, Apple provides iOS simulators to enable you to run and check your app in older versions of iOS).

Registering as an Apple developer

There are two stages of registration required before we can test our app on an iPhone and submit apps to the App Store:

- Registering as an Apple developer, which is free
- Enrolling in the iOS Developer Program, which costs $99

Registering as an Apple developer is free via Apple's Developer web site:

`http://developer.apple.com/programs/register/`

Registration gives you access to sample code, documentation, and WWDC (Apple Worldwide Developers Conference) tutorial videos.

To register as an Apple developer, you'll need to use an existing Apple ID or create a new one. If you've ever downloaded an app from the App Store to your iPhone, then you used your Apple ID to do so. Alternatively, if you've ever used MobileMe, iCloud, or Game Center, you used your Apple ID.

So what are you waiting for? Go through the Apple developer registration stages and report back when you're done! This shouldn't take too long, and once completed, you'll gain immediate access to the iOS Dev Center. Figure 2-2 highlights the differences between the free registration and the $99 iOS Developer Program.

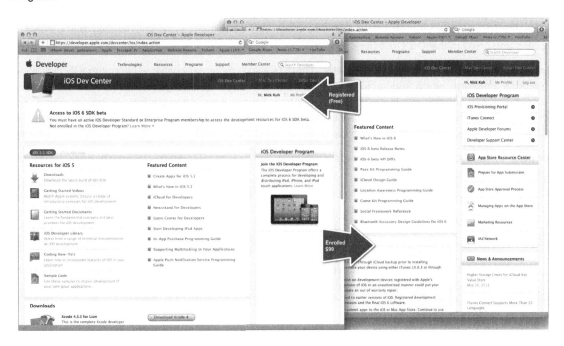

Figure 2-2. The iOS Dev Center: The left screenshot shows the free registration window; the right screenshot shows the enrolled developer window.

In Figure 2-2, you'll see that the right-hand column of the iOS Dev Center is initially populated with a promotional advertisement for the iOS Developer Program. Once you've completed the application to enroll in the Developer Program, this column becomes populated with all the additional resources needed to prepare your apps for distribution (the right screenshot in Figure 2-2 shows a paid member logged in).

> Note: It is not 100 percent essential to become a paid member of the iOS Developer Program to complete the course in this book. You can test your code in the iOS simulator on your Mac.

In order to test our apps on iPhones (and eventually, to submit apps to the App Store), you need to become a paid member of the Apple Developer Program. So, on to the next stage.

Enrolling in the iOS Developer Program

If you plan to develop your own App Store or Enterprise apps, you need to complete the application process and enroll in the iOS Developer Program.

The standard program fee costs $99 per year. There is also a more expensive version: the iOS Developer Enterprise Program, which has a $299 annual fee. The main advantage of choosing the Enterprise Program is that it enables you to distribute apps in-house without having to publish via the App Store. The Enterprise Program is intended for large companies. There's a separate process that companies need to go through to prove eligibility (this is outside of the scope of this book).

For most of us, the standard iOS Developer Program will suffice. Becoming an enrolled iOS Developer gives you access to:

- The iOS Provisioning Portal
- iTunes Connect
- Apple Developer Forums
- The new iOS SDK betas. At the time of writing this book, iOS 6 was still in beta. As you can see in Figure 2-2, until I became a paid member of the iOS Developer Program, I didn't have access to the new beta.

In order to debug directly on your iPhone and distribute your apps, you need to create provisioning profiles. These are files that Xcode bakes into your app when it compiles. The provisioning profile determines which devices your app can be installed on. Once we have access to the iOS Provisioning Portal, we are able to generate and download these provisioning profiles.

iTunes Connect (https://itunesconnect.apple.com) is a content management system for your App Store apps. Submitting new apps and app updates to the App Store is handled by iTunes Connect. In addition, developers log in to iTunes Connect to manage:

- Bank and tax info/contracts
- Sales trends and reports

The Apple Developer Forums provide a great online resource for iOS and Mac software programming questions.

Before you can get access to these iOS developer tools and resources, you'll need to wait for Apple to approve your iOS Developer Program application (see Figure 2-3).

Figure 2-3. Enrolling in the iOS Developer Program

First, go through the enrollment process on Apple's Developer web site:

`http://developer.apple.com/programs/ios/`

That shouldn't take too long. Afterward, however, you'll probably wait for as long as two weeks until Apple accepts your application to the program. There's quite a lot of red tape to get through. Don't worry though. In the meantime, you can skip to Chapter 3. Once you get approved, flip back to this chapter and I'll walk you through the somewhat confusing process of provisioning our app for testing on devices.

iOS Provisioning Portal

Welcome to the iOS Provisioning Portal (see Figure 2-4). We're now going to step through each stage of the process required to generate provisioning profiles.

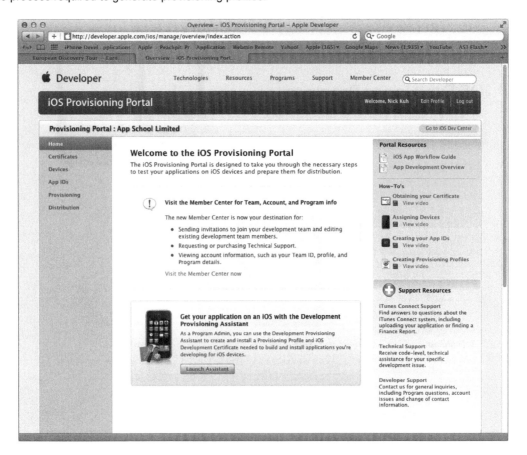

Figure 2-4. iOS Provisioning Portal

Take a look at the left-hand column of Figure 2-4. The menu lists the following stages of provisioning in the exact order we're going to step through them:

- *Certificates*: You'll need to create one developer certificate and one distribution signing certificate for use with this app and all future apps.

- *Devices*: Here's where you will add the Unique Device Identifiers (UDID) of all the iPhones, iPods, and iPads that you wish to test your apps on.

- *App IDs*: Before you can create a provisioning profile for our app, you'll need to create a unique identifier for the app, which Xcode will use to associate your compiling project with the correct provisioning profile.

- *Provisioning*: At this point, you'll finally be generating the provision profile(s) I've been referencing. Each profile ties together the certificate(s), devices, and App ID created in the three preceding stages.

Generating certificates

When you first access the Certificates section of the Provisioning Portal, you'll discover that you don't have any signing certificate by default. You'll need to generate one in order to debug and install your apps on your iPhone or other iOS devices.

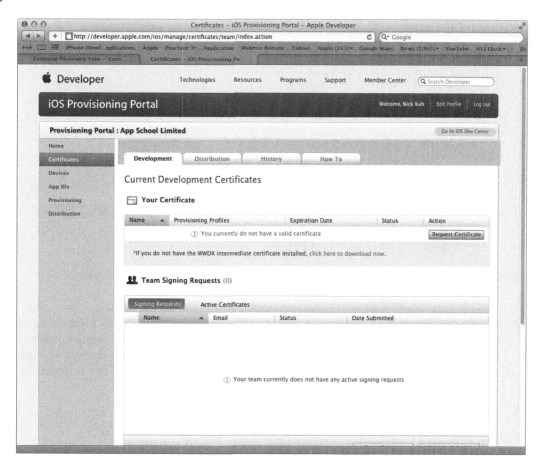

Figure 2-5. The Certificates section of the Provisioning Portal before generating a certificate

To generate the certificate, you'll first need to create a certificate request file. The certificate request file must be generated via your Mac. Open up Keychain Access via Applications   Utilities   Keychain Access. From within Keychain Access, you'll need to select the Request a Certificate From a Certificate Authority... menu option (see Figure 2-6).

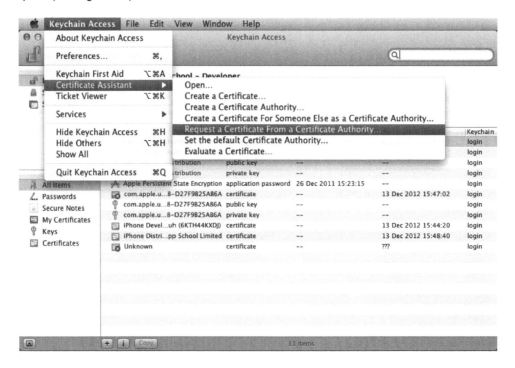

Figure 2-6. Initiating a certificate request from Keychain Access on OS X

Keychain Access will now present you with a dialog box (see Figure 2-7) where you'll need to:

1. Enter your e-mail address.

2. Enter a Common Name. The name you enter is displayed in Keychain Access once you complete the certificate generation process. When you reach the point where you're ready to submit your app to the App Store, you'll need to repeat this certificate generation process to create a certificate for your App Store provisioning. Choose a name that identifies this certificate as the development version.

3. Select the Saved to Disk option.

4. Tap Continue and save the certificate request to your desktop.

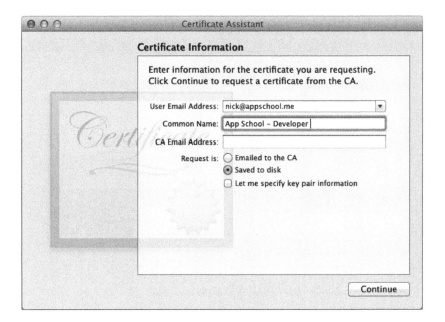

Figure 2-7. Setting options for a development certificate request, still in Keychain Access

The resulting certificate request file on your desktop is titled `CertificateSigningRequest.certSigningRequest`. This is just a temporary file that is only needed for the next step.

Switch back to the iOS Provisioning Portal in your browser. Once you've tapped the Request Certificate button (in the browser window), you'll be asked to choose the certificate request file generated via Keychain Access (see Figure 2-8).

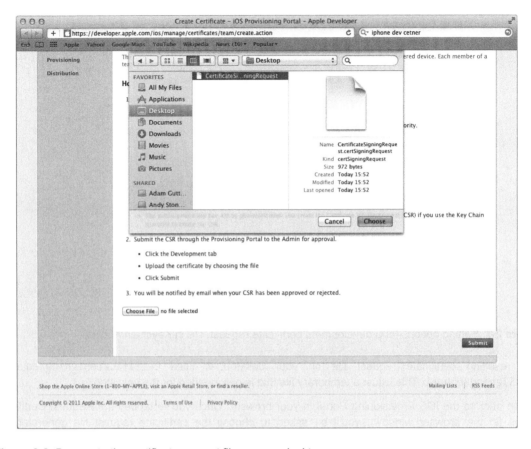

Figure 2-8. Browse to the certificate request file on your desktop

Submit your certificate request. Congratulations! You've just generated your first development certificate. You should now be able to see it listed in the Provisioning Portal (see Figure 2-9).

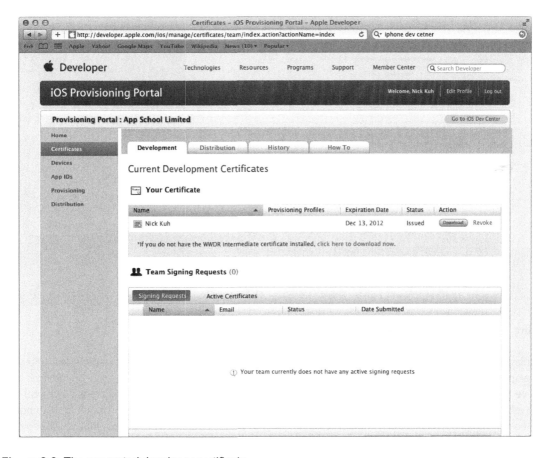

Figure 2-9. The generated developer certificate

Download the certificate from the Provisioning Portal. Double-click the downloaded developer_identity.cer file. You will be prompted by Keychain Access to add the certificate (see Figure 2-10).

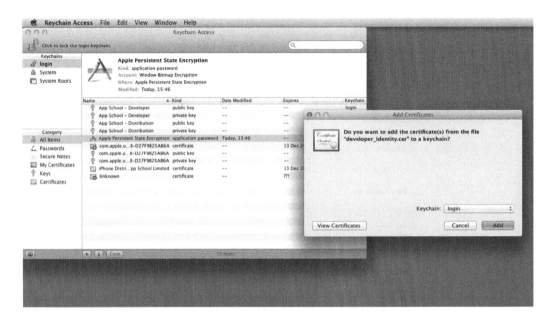

Figure 2-10. Add and autoinstall the downloaded certificate.

At this point, you've completed the certificate generation process for development. Xcode will use your development signing certificate when it compiles debug versions of your apps to run on devices that you've registered in the Provisioning Portal. In order to build release versions of your apps that you can both share with beta testers and submit to the App Store, you'll also need to create a distribution certificate. The process is exactly the same as creating a developer certificate, except that you'll begin by selecting the Distribution tab from the Certificates section of the Provisioning Portal. While it's still fresh in your memory, you may want to repeat the whole certificate generation process for creating a distribution certificate now.

Within the Certificates section of the Provisioning Portal, you see that Apple includes a link to download the WWDR Intermediate Certificate. Download and double-click to install this certificate to your Mac's keychain. The WWDR (Apple Worldwide Developer Relations Certification Authority) certificate simply confirms that your development or distribution profile certificate was issued by Apple.

Adding devices

Every iPhone, iPod, and iPad has a Unique Device Identifier. It is this UDID that you'll need for every device you want included for testing your app prior to App Store submission.

With your iPhone connected to your Mac, open Xcode and switch to the Organizer window (Window ▸ Organizer or ⌘⇧2). Under Devices, you should see your iPhone listed. Select your phone and the detail view will populate to show, among other things, your iPhone's Identifier (see Figure 2-11). The UDID is a 40-character alphanumeric string.

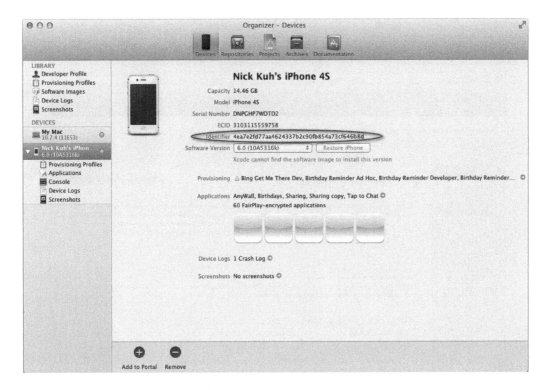

Figure 2-11. Accessing your iPhone UDID via Xcode's Organizer

The process of adding devices to the Provisioning Portal is fairly straightforward. Browse to the Devices section of the Provisioning Portal. Tap Add Devices and then enter your iPhone's UDID. Once a device is saved to the Provisioning Portal, it appears on the list of devices associated with your developer account (see Figure 2-12).

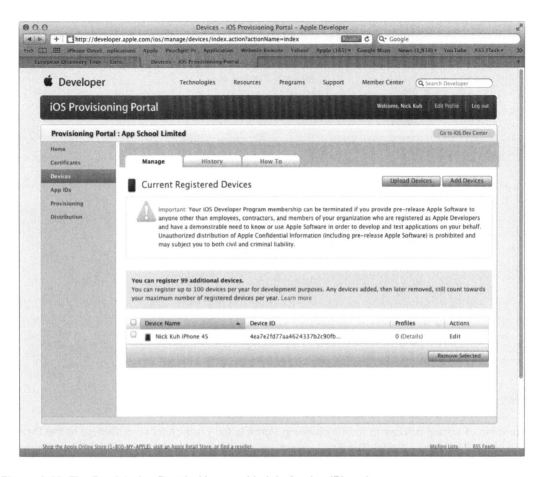

Figure 2-12. The Provisioning Portal with one added device (my iPhone)

> *Note: Device UDIDs can also be accessed in iTunes when your device is connected via USB to your Mac. However, when it comes to requesting UDIDs from clients, I usually just ask them to download one of the numerous free UDID-sending apps listed in the App Store. Try a search on **UDID**.*

Creating an App ID

For each app you develop, you only create a single App ID. You'll create multiple provisioning profiles for each app, but only a single App ID (see Figure 2-13).

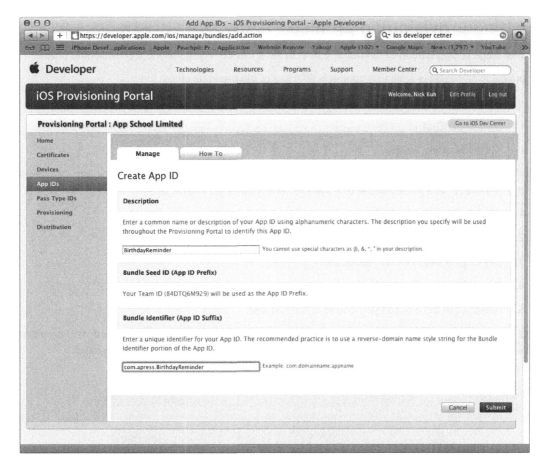

Figure 2-13. Creating an App ID via the Provisioning Portal

To create an App ID, we need to supply the following two inputs:

- *A description.* I've entered **BirthdayReminder**—you can do the same.

- *A bundle identifier.* This must be a unique string that the App Store and iOS devices will use to identify your app from the hundreds of thousands of other apps. As Figure 2-13 indicates, it's customary to provide a reverse domain path of your web site, such as com.domainname.BirthdayReminder. The Provisioning Portal won't permit you to use the com.apress.BirthdayReminder shown in the example because this identifier is already in use by me!

- In your bundle identifier, change the com and the domainname placeholders, but keep the BirthdayReminder (case sensitive) part. This ensures that in Chapter 3, Xcode will be able to automatically detect the correct provisioning profile for our app project, also titled BirthdayReminder (case sensitive).

Generating provisioning profiles

The final stage of preparation to run our app directly on a device is to generate a provisioning profile.

The provisioning profile is a file that connects all three of the previous steps:

- Signing certificate
- Device UDID(s)
- App ID/bundle identifier

With the Provisioning menu option selected, you'll create a provisioning profile that you can use to debug *Birthday Reminder*. You'll need to perform the following steps (see Figure 2-14):

1. Click the New Profile button.
2. Name the profile Birthday Reminder Developer.
3. Select your development certificate.
4. Select BirthdayReminder from the drop-down menu.
5. Select all of the devices you added in the last step.

In the future, each time you create a new app, you'll need to create a new App ID and new provisioning profiles for the development of your app. You won't need to generate new signing certificates.

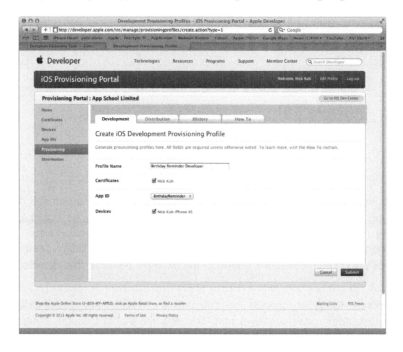

Figure 2-14. Generating a provisioning profile for *Birthday Reminder* development

By default, the iOS Provisioning Portal displays the *development* provisioning profiles (see Figure 2-15).

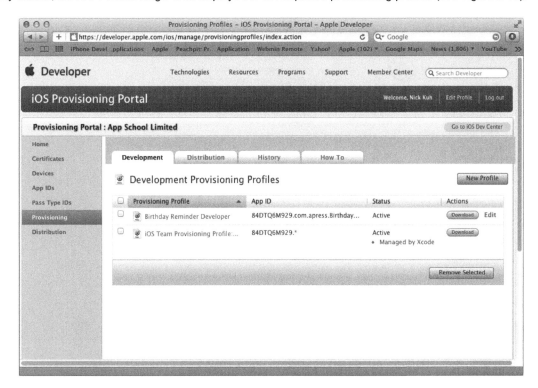

Figure 2-15. The resulting provisioning profile

If the new provisioning profile initially displays as Pending, simply refresh the page a couple of times until it displays as ready for download.

You'll note from Figure 2-15 that in my Provisioning Portal, I have a second developer provisioning profile named iOS Team Provisioning Profile. This is a generic profile that Xcode created automatically for me. Once you start using Xcode and Xcode's Organizer, you'll be prompted to log in to your Apple Developer account. From there, Xcode will ask you if you'd like it to create a team provisioning profile. I recommend you do this. The team provisioning profile is managed by Xcode. Each time you connect a new development device to your Mac, Xcode's Organizer automatically adds the device UDID to your Provisioning Portal and to the team provisioning profile. This means you'll be able to quickly build and run test iOS projects from Xcode on your development devices without having to create a separate development profile for every app. It's a handy feature in Xcode 4.

The resulting provisioning profile is a file that you download to your Mac and double-click to autoinstall. The installation process opens Xcode. Switching to Xcode's Organizer window (Window ⏵ Organizer or ⌘⇧2) and selecting Provisioning Profiles under Library in the left column should display your newly installed development provisioning profile (see Figure 2-16).

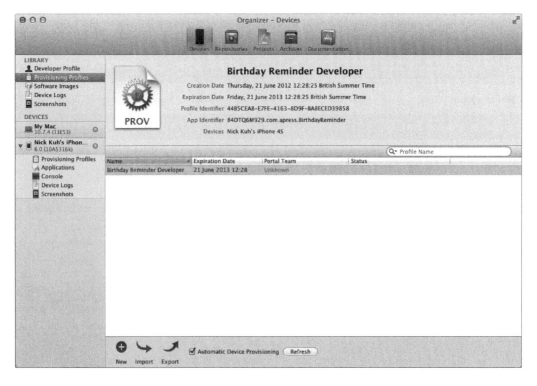

Figure 2-16. Installed *Birthday Reminder* provisioning profile in Xcode's Organizer window

Now that you've created your development provisioning profile, you'll be able to run *Birthday Reminder* on your iPhone in the next chapter. The provisioning profile will only permit *Birthday Reminder* to run on devices that you added and connected with the profile via the iOS Provisioning Portal.

If you buy another iPhone, it's important to note that this generated profile will not permit *Birthday Reminder* to run on the new device. Likewise, *Birthday Reminder* will not run on your friend's iPhone unless you've added his UDID to the iOS Provisioning Portal.

Adding new devices to a provisioning profile that you've already installed requires you to:

1. Edit and modify the provisioning profile via the iOS Provisioning Portal.

2. Download the updated profile to your Mac.

3. Delete the out-of-date profile in Xcode's Organizer *before* double-click installing.

4. Double-click the newly downloaded provisioning profile to autoinstall.

At this point, if you're creating an app that you plan to distribute via the App Store or to beta testers, you will save yourself time in the future by repeating the provisioning profile generation process for two additional profiles for your app:

- the Ad Hoc provisioning profile

- the App Store provisioning profile (see Chapter 14 for the app submission process)

Ad Hoc distribution

The purpose of Ad Hoc distribution is to build internal release versions of your app during development. For example, if you distribute your app to beta testers, you'll generate these beta builds against an Ad Hoc provisioning profile.

You will still need to add the UDID's of all the devices that you wish to include in beta testing. You have up to 100 device slots within the iOS Provisioning Portal.

Summary

If you've kept up with the complex process of provisioning throughout this chapter, then pat yourself on the back! This process is a bit of a pain when you're starting out.

I assure you it's worth it. We're now ready to roll with Xcode. So let's start by setting up our project.

Chapter 3

Setting Up Our Xcode Project

Welcome to Xcode! It's time to get our hands dirty.

At this point, there's nothing we could have done wrong to mess up our app. Let's try to keep it that way!

Throughout this chapter, you'll become familiar with working with Xcode. You'll jump right in and create a new iOS project for your *Birthday Reminder* app. I'll teach you how to embed and assign icons, and launch screens for your app. By the end of the morning, we'll look at how to deploy and debug your project as a working app on your iPhone or iPod Touch.

Getting started

Firing up Xcode for the first time presents you with a few initial options in a Welcome to Xcode window (see Figure 3-1).

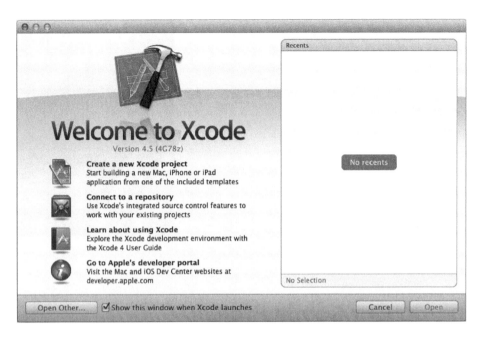

Figure 3-1. The Welcome to Xcode window

You can reopen Xcode's welcome window at any point via Window ➤ Welcome to Xcode or with the ⇧⌘1 shortcut. The options available to you from the welcome window include:

- *Create a new Xcode project*: This will be our starting point.

- *Connect to a repository*: Xcode has built-in version control compatibility with Git and Subversion. If, like me, you prefer your coding IDE (integrated development environment) to mind its own business and stick to what it does best (coding), then that's fine too. I don't use this feature of Xcode. I prefer running Git via the command line. If you want to use Git or Subversion directly in Xcode, then go right ahead—although it's beyond the scope of this book to delve further into it.

- *Learn about Xcode*: This option opens the documentation section of the Organizer window. It's worth taking an initial look at the About Xcode documentation. The first screen includes a diagram that highlights the section areas and panels of the Xcode workspace that we'll be making use of throughout this book (see Figure 3-2).

- *Go to Apple's developer portal*: A springboard hyperlink to the Apple Developer web site.

Begin by selecting the third option, Learn about Xcode. You'll enter Xcode's documentation section within the Organizer. Figure 3-2 is a screenshot taken from the first page of documentation. It's worth taking an initial look at the various IDE panels for each section of Xcode's user interface. I'll make references to them throughout the remainder of the book.

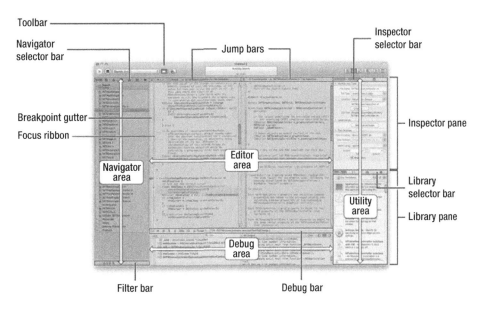

Toolbar

Navigator
selector bar

Jump bars

Inspector
selector bar

Breakpoint gutter

Focus ribbon

Navigator
area

Editor
area

Inspector pane

Library
selector bar

Utility
area

Library pane

Debug
area

Filter bar

Debug bar

Figure 3-2.: A breakdown of the IDE from Xcode's documentation

Note the Navigation area on the left; this is where you'll typically access any file in your project's hierarchy via the Project Navigator pane. The Editor area in the center is where you'll work on writing class code files or creating user interfaces with a Storyboard file. The right side of the IDE is known as the Utility area; it consists of the Inspector and Library panes. Here's where you'll use the attributes inspector to modify selected object attributes when working with storyboards or defining the UML (Unified Modeling Language) of your Core Data entities, for example. The pane at the bottom of the IDE is the Debug area, where logs and errors are printed to the console during the debug sessions for your apps.

Let's create a new project! From the menu, select File ➤ New ➤ Project or use the ⇧⌘N shortcut. Xcode will now present you with a range of project templates to choose from as a starting point (see Figure 3-3).

For some projects, certain templates will save you development time. The Master-Detail template, for example, generates a project with a navigation controller and an embedded root view controller—and you're good to go.

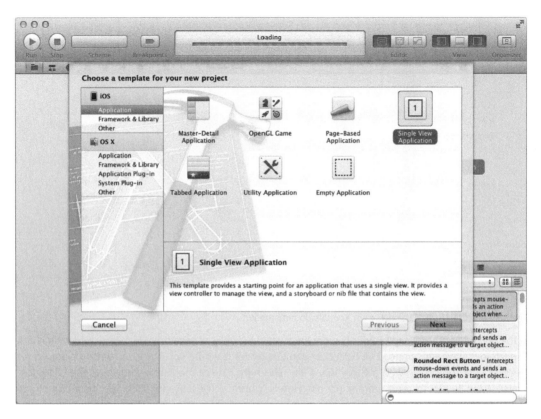

Figure 3-3. Choosing a starting project template

Call me anal-retentive (well, go on then!), but I like to keep as much control of the code in my apps as I can. Some of these Xcode templates—especially the ones that include a Core Data model—inject a lot of initial code into your project. You can clean this up after your project generates. For our project, however, I'd like you to choose one of the simplest templates: the Single View Application.

Xcode will now ask you to fill in a few additional options for our new project (see Figure 3-4).

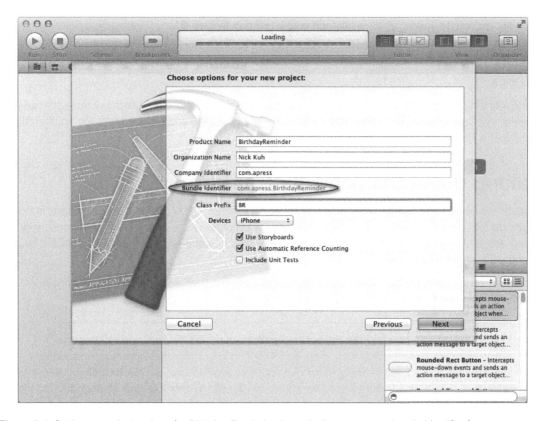

Figure 3-4. Setting up project options for *Birthday Reminder* dynamically generates a bundle identifier for our app.

- *Product Name*: Enter **BirthdayReminder** (case sensitive with no spaces). We need this to match the last section of our app bundle identifier embedded in our development provisioning profile (this was set up in Chapter 2).

- *Organization Name*: Xcode prepopulates any new class file with details about the author/company, set here in the comments above the code. If I put "Nick Kuh" in this field, then each new class I create in my project will include Copyright (c) Nick Kuh in its header comments. For your project, enter either your name or company name.

- *Company Identifier*: You'll need to enter the same reverse domain path you used for your provisioning profile in Chapter 2: [com/co.uk/etc].[your_domainname].

- *Class Prefix*: Enter **BR**, short for *Birthday Reminder*. You'll discover that most third-party Objective-C code libraries prefix their classes with two or three initials. With my own reusable class libraries, I use NK (Nick Kuh). For project-specific classes that you don't intend to reuse outside of your project, use a suitable prefix. Class prefixing is not compulsory, but it's worth implementing now as a good practice.

You'll also be able to specify whether the app you're building targets iPhone, iPad, or is a universal app: a single app with two user interfaces—one for iPhone and one for iPad. For our project, we're iPhone only.

Finally, ensure that Storyboarding and ARC (Automatic Reference Counting) are selected. Then we're good to go.

On the following screen, choose a location on your hard drive to save the new *Birthday Reminder* project. Deselect the Create Local Git Repository option unless you want Xcode to initiate a Git source control repository for you.

Breaking down the project structure

Because we chose the Single View Application project template, Xcode has automatically added a storyboard to our project containing a single view. As I mentioned in Chapter 1, each of the main views in an app should always be controlled by a view controller class. Xcode has generated `BRViewController` to control the single view in the current project.

By default, the left navigator panel of Xcode displays the Project Navigator. The Project Navigator lists all the files, groups, and frameworks included in our project (see Figure 3-5).

> *Note: Selecting files within the Project Navigator displays the file in Xcode's Editor area.*

When iOS attempts to load our *Birthday Reminder* app, it expects to find an Objective-C file titled `main.m` as its entry point. There should be no need for you to modify `main.m` for this app or any other, so please don't touch this file further!

What you will notice is that `main.m` references the `BRAppDelegate` class. `main.m` includes a single function that generates a single instance of our Application Delegate class when iOS launches our app.

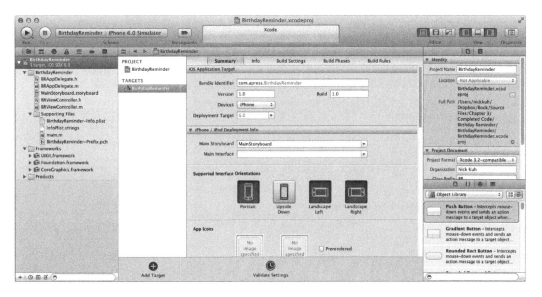

Figure 3-5. The initial generated project structure

Application delegate

The Application Delegate is a class that you can modify. BRAppDelegate subclasses UIResponder and implements the protocol methods of UIApplicationDelegate.

You'll see that Xcode has automatically stubbed out some of the main UIApplicationDelegate methods. The main methods in the UIApplicationDelegate protocol respond to key application events, such as the following:

- application:didFinishLaunchingWithOptions: Executes once, as soon as your app first launches.

- applicationDidEnterBackground: Executes every time the user exits our app—by tapping the iPhone home button, for example. Our app remains alive—but in a frozen, inactive state. Other app code will not execute after this point. We can execute code here when the delegation method is called, but primarily for any data saving or freeing up of memory.

- applicationDidBecomeActive: Our app has become active because the user relaunched via the home screen or multitasking bar.

> Note: To learning more about any method (or class), highlight the method and use the
> ⌃⌘? keyboard shortcut to display quick help for the selected item (see Figure 3-6).

Figure 3-6. Quick Help. Click the links to access the full documentation.

Info.plist

Select and view `BirthdayReminder-Info.plist`. You'll find this important file within the Supporting Files group. This is the configuration file that Xcode bunsdles into our app. The settings within the `Info.plist` file determine how iOS instantiates our app.

Because we selected Use Storyboard earlier when selecting our project setup options, the project template has created a storyboard and assigned the Main Storyboard File Base Name configuration property (see Figure 3-7).

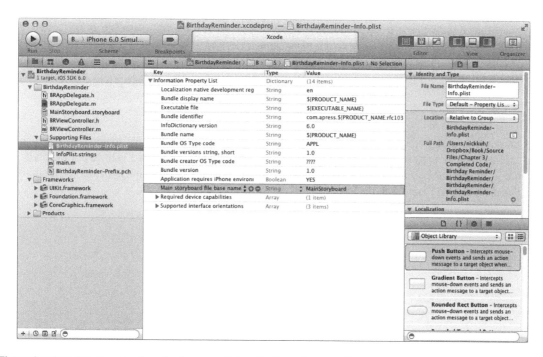

Figure 3-7. MainStoryboard automatically generated by Xcode project template and defined in the Info.plist

There are many configuration settings that you assign within the `Info.plist`, including embedded font lists; whether the status bar is on or off; and URL types (local URL schemes that iOS associates and links to your app from other apps).

Prefix header

Xcode has also added a `BirthdayReminder-Prefix.pch` file to our project. This is a global file header that the Xcode compiler precompiles into every one of the Objective-C source classes in our project. You can define global functions or import declarations of common classes in the prefix header to avoid repetitive import declarations throughout your classes.

Storyboards

Storyboards are a key tool in the iOS developer's workflow. Apple added storyboards to Xcode in iOS 5, and they've gotten even better in iOS 6. The definition of a storyboard from Apple's documentation reads "a storyboard is a visual representation of the user interface of an iOS application, showing screens of content and the connections between those screens."

Our *Birthday Reminder* project will include a single storyboard that defines every screen in our app, as well as the connections and transitions between those screens. Using Xcode's editor, we'll lay out buttons, labels, and other subviews within each screen of our storyboard and create the connections between screens.

Storyboards in Xcode make it much quicker to build iOS apps than was possible prior to iOS 5. In Chapters 5 and 6, we'll storyboard every view in our app.

In keeping with code learning traditions, I think it's about time for a Hello World example.

Hello World

Let's take a look at the storyboard that Xcode has autogenerated. Select MainStoryboard.storyboard from the files in the Project Navigator. The Editor area will become populated with two subpanels: the Document Outline panel and the Storyboard panel. If the Document Outline panel is hidden, you can open it, as I've illustrated in Figure 3-8.

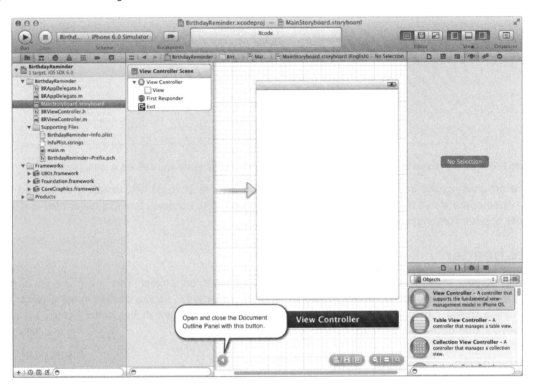

Figure 3-8. When viewing storyboard files, you can hide/show the Document Outline panel.

Our main and only view should be visible on the storyboard. Click and select the view. The Document Outline panel should update to highlight the current selection. Notice the dark bar beneath the view? This represents the view controller assigned to this view. Click and select the dark bar. The Document Outline selection should update to indicate that you have selected the view controller.

Keeping the view controller selected, switch the top Utilities pane to the third tab, which should present the identity inspector (see Figure 3-9).

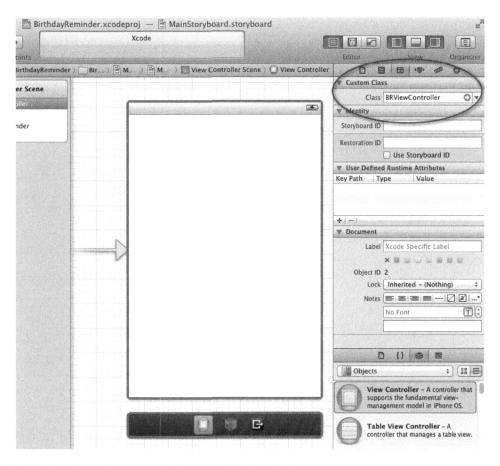

Figure 3-9. Viewing the owning view controller class via the identity inspector

The identity inspector reveals the custom class of the current selection in our storyboard: BRViewController. In Chapter 5, we'll learn how to use the identity inspector to assign custom classes to view controllers and views.

If it's not already selected, then switch the bottom utility pane to the third tab, the Object Library, as shown in Figure 3-9.

> *Tip: Set up Xcode's panel layout to your preferences. You'll find three toggle buttons in the right side of the toolbar for hiding/showing the Navigator, Debug, and Utilities areas.*

With the view rather than the view controller in our storyboard selected, scroll down through the Object Library. You'll find all the user interface components of the iOS SDK listed. Find the label object. Drag a label instance out of the library and drop it in the center of the main view. Double-click the label and change the text to **Hello World** (see Figure 3-10).

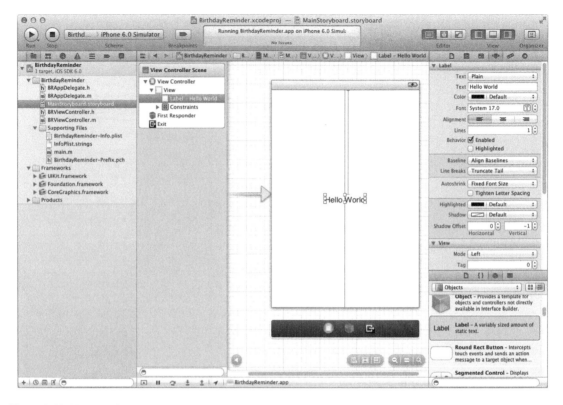

Figure 3-10. Hello World

Note in Figure 3-10 that I've toggled the top-right utility pane to the attributes inspector that displays the text, font name and size, text color, alignment, and so on.

Now that you've added the label to the view, you've successfully created a subview within your main view. If you select the main view again, you'll be able to modify the view properties, such as the background color.

If you haven't discovered this already, the Build and Run button on the left side of Xcode's toolbar compiles and launches our project in the iOS simulator (see Figure 3-11). You can toggle the destination in the Active Scheme drop-down bar between the iPhone and iPad simulators.

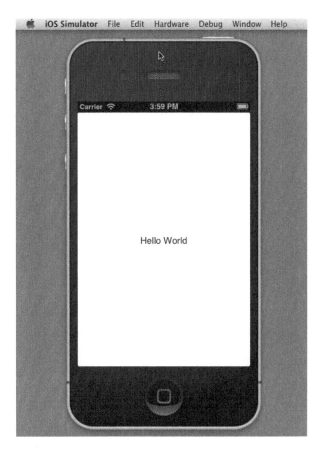

Figure 3-11. An app running in the iOS simulator

You should see your project launch and display the Hello World label you added to the view.

You can emulate device rotation in the simulator with the ⌘← and ⌘→ keyboard shortcuts, or Hardware ➤ Rotate Left / Hardware ➤ Rotate Right.

Birthday Reminder isn't going to support multi-orientation for this project, however, so let's now set the supported interface orientations of our app to just *Portrait*. In the project navigator select the BirthdayReminder project and then select the BirthdayReminder target. You will be presented with a summary screen that includes a *Supported Interface Orientations* section. Uncheck the *Landscape Left* and *Landscape Right* options as shown in Figure 3-12. That's it, our app will no longer rotate to landscape orientations. Build and run to test it out.

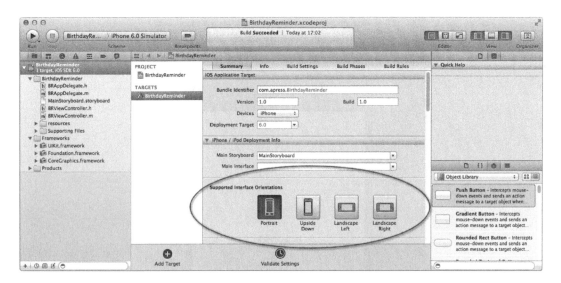

Figure 3-12. Configuring supported interface orientations for our app

I'd also like you to switch off a new piece of technology that Apple introduced in iOS 6 called Auto Layout. Auto Layout is a powerful kit that will take care of all of your app's view position and size changes. It's also an advanced topic for experienced iOS developers, and as we're not supporting multiorientation, I promise you, it will cause us more grief than it's worth!

Select your storyboard in the Project Navigator, and then select the File Inspector first tab in the Utility pane and deselect Use Autolayout, as highlighted in Figure 3-13.

> *Note: If you'd like to learn more about Auto Layout, I recommend checking out Matthijs Hollemans' tutorial at www.raywenderlich.com/20881/beginning-auto-layout-part-1-of-2.*

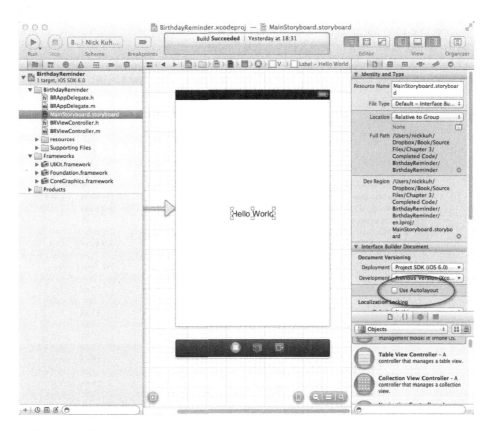

Figure 3-13. Switching off Auto Layout for our app

Adding an icon and launch screen

Xcode created three, default, plain black launch screen images when we created our new project. We'll learn about each of these default images shortly, but for now, I'd like you to delete these files from Xcode. Open the Supporting Files group and multiselect `Default.png`, `Default@2x.png`, and `Default-568h@2x.png`. Click the Delete key and then select the Move to Trash button.

Xcode's Project Navigator lists a hierarchy of files and groups. Groups are not the same thing as folders in the Finder. You can create groups and subgroups in Xcode, and drag and drop your class files within the group hierarchy. However, your modified structure will not be mirrored in the Finder; that is, you could have a complex group and file hierarchy in Xcode, but in the Finder, all your class files could be on the root project level.

I found this group concept quite confusing initially. One solution is to first create new folders in the Finder and then add those folders as groups to your Xcode project. A little weird, but it works.

We're now going to add to our project the icon and launch screen images included in the source code for this chapter. To do so, open your project folder in the Finder, and create a new folder named resources. Within resources, create a subfolder named images. Now copy across all the images from the assets folder of the supplied source code into your new images directory (see Figure 3-14).

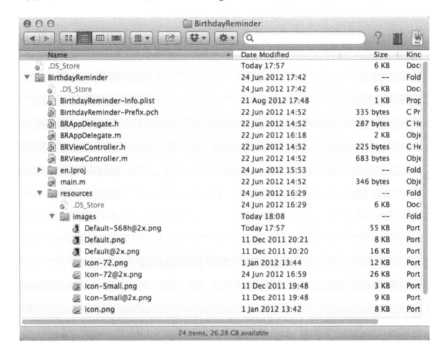

Figure 3-14. Adding all the image resources for the project via the Finder

Now switch back to Xcode. Notice how nothing has changed here? We've added directories and files to our BirthdayReminder directory in the Finder, but until we add these files to our Xcode project through the IDE, they will remain ignored.

Select the main BirthdayReminder group in the Project Navigator. Then, using the keyboard shortcut ⌘⌘A or File ➤ Add Files to BirthdayReminder, navigate to our resources directory.

Ensure that Create Groups for Any Added Folders is selected (see Figure 3-15) and click the Add button.

Figure 3-15. Adding all of the image resources to the Xcode project

Another way to add Finder folders and files to an Xcode project is to drag the new folder from the Finder directly into the Xcode IDE, and then drop the folder straight into the Project Navigator. Xcode will then present you with a dialog box. Unless you prefer to reference the new files outside of your main project directory, then select the Copy Items into Destination Group's Folder check box and the Create Groups for Any Added Folders option before clicking the Add button.

Run and debug. Did you spot any new changes to your app? If you're quick, you'll have seen the new launch image that appears on the screen for a few milliseconds before our Hello World view. Tap the home button on the simulator to view the *Birthday Reminder* icon on the home screen. If it's still a white rounded rectangle, then remove *Birthday Reminder* from the simulator by pressing and holding the icon and tapping the Delete button. Now build and run again. You should now see that our white home screen icon has become the *Birthday Reminder* icon (see Figure 3-16). Magic, huh?

Tip: If Xcode ever fails to display expected changes in your app, such as a replacement icon, always attempt a Product ➤ Clean to clear the debug cache.

Figure 3-16. The *Birthday Reminder* icon displayed in the iOS Simulator

The reason the icon and launch screen are automatically detected is due to some of the file names that I set for certain images you just added to your project. iOS draws the retina and non-retina icon and launch image for your app, automatically utilizing the most suitably sized version depending on the device it's running on.

There are other ways to specify the icons for retina and non-retina iPhones and iPads, but this is the simplest approach. Create icons and splash screens that adhere to the following size and naming rules, and you'll discover that they work for any iOS project:

- `Default.png` and `Default@2x.png`: This is your launch image. If your app is a full-screen app, then the dimensions of `Default.png` should be 320×480 pixels and `Default@2x.png` should be 640×960 pixels. *Birthday Reminder* allows the iOS status bar to display, so we need to remove 20 points off the height of our launch image. Thus, `Default.png` should be 320×460 pixels and `Default@2x.png` should be 640×920 pixels.

- `Default-568h@2x.png`: This is your launch image for the iPhone 5 display. It should be 640×1136 pixels since all iPhone 5s support a retina display. If you don't include this file, then iOS will assume that your app doesn't support the taller native iPhone 5 screen and will display your app letterboxed (black bars across the top and bottom of the screen).

- `Icon.png` and `Icon@2x.png`: This is your app's icon PNG that is displayed on the iPhone home screen. `Icon.png` should be 57×57 pixels and `Icon@2x.png` should be 114×114 pixels.

- `Icon-72.png` and `Icon-72@2x.png`: This is the icon that displays for iPad users who install your iPhone app (even though the targeted device is iPhone only). If you don't include this version of the icon, then the default 57×57 iPhone icon will be used; it will look pixilated and ugly when resized on an iPad. `Icon-72.png` should be 72×72 pixels; it displays on non-retina iPads. `Icon-72@2x.png` should be 114×114 pixels; it displays on retina iPads.

- `Icon-Small.png` and `Icon-Small@2x.png`: This is the icon displayed in the iOS Settings, notifications screens, and in Spotlight searches. Again, if you don't supply this, then iOS will use your main 57×57 icon and resize it to 29×29 points.

Take a closer look at our icon graphic in Photoshop or Preview. The rounded corners and the shine are added dynamically by iOS. Our icon design bleeds to the edge of every corner and side.

The *Birthday Reminder* icon looks better without the iOS shine. No problem—we can easily fix this via our project's `Info.plist` configuration file (see Figure 3-17).

Although it's not listed by default, there's a setting titled Icon Already Includes Gloss Effect that we can add as a new row to the `.plist` file. With `BirthdayReminder-Info.plist` selected in the Project Navigator, control-click the Editor area and select Add Row from the contextual menu. A new row is added to the `.plist` and you'll be able to locate the icon gloss setting. You'll also need to change the value to Yes. Save your changes, then build and run. Your icon should lose the shine and look cleaner on the simulator's home screen.

> *Tip: Changes to icons sometimes require a couple of build and runs or product cleans to take effect.*

We have one additional aesthetic change to make to our app icon. By default, the `Info.plist` assigns the name of your project as the title displayed on the iPhone home screen beneath the icon. `BirthdayReminder` is more than the 12-character display title limit and will therefore be truncated by iOS. This is easy to fix by changing the Bundle Display Name property in the `Info.plist` to `Birthdays` (see Figure 3-17). Build and run. No more truncation—hooray!

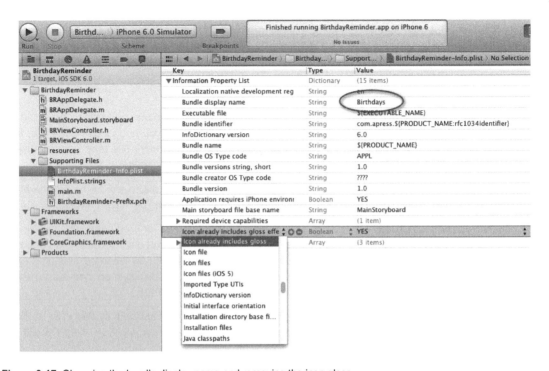

Figure 3-17. Changing the bundle display name and removing the icon gloss

Running the app on your iPhone

To enable your project to run and debug on your iPhone, you'll need to have successfully created a development provisioning profile in Chapter 2.

The app bundle ID that you set for your provisioning profile needs to match the bundle identifier listed in your Xcode project.

In my project, the bundle identifier is com.apress.BirthdayReminder. For your profile and project, this should be [com/co.uk/etc].[domainname].BirthdayReminder.

> *Tip: If required, you can modify the bundle identifier in the target summary pane or Info.plist file for your project.*

Plug your iPhone into your Mac via a USB cable.

After a few seconds, Xcode should recognize the device and add your iPhone as an optional destination in the Active Scheme drop-down menu, top left, next to the Run button.

Toggling the destination setting from the simulator to your iPhone will then set you up to run your project directly on your device. Try it!

If this fails, then it could be because of one or more of the following reasons:

- There's a problem with your signing certificate.

- There's a problem with your provisioning profile, such as the embedded app bundle ID doesn't match your project bundle ID; your certificate wasn't added to the provisioning profile; or your iPhone UDID wasn't added to the provisioning profile.

- Your project should be named `BirthdayReminder` (case sensitive). You might want to restart this chapter if you've chosen something different. Renaming a project in Xcode is no easy task, unfortunately!

Select your `BirthdayReminder` project in Xcode's Project Navigator. Then select the `BirthdayReminder` target. Next, select Build Settings ➤ All ➤ Code Signing ➤ Debug ➤ iPhone Developer. If everything is set up correctly, then you should find that Xcode has recognized and associated the Debug build of your project with your development provisioning profile (see Figure 3-18). This is the connection that successfully allows you to run your version of *Birthday Reminder* on your iPhone.

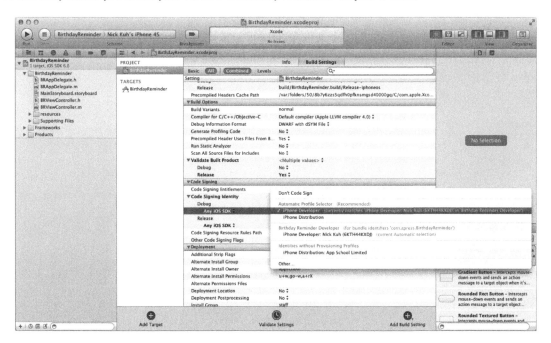

Figure 3-18. Changing the destination of the Active Scheme to your iPhone and checking the connection between project and provisioning profile

Summary

You should now be familiar with the structure of iOS projects in Xcode.

- You've generated your `BirthdayReminder` project using Xcode's Single View Application project template.

- You've modified the `Info.plist`, your app's configuration settings, and seen the results in the iOS simulator.

- We've taken a first look at Storyboarding and the Object Library. We now know how to add the iOS SDK UI component views to our storyboard via drag-and-drop.

- We've learned how to add external resource folders to our Xcode project. The same process works for adding other file types like third-party code libraries.

- We've learned how to add multiple optimized icons and launch images to our app.

- You've (hopefully) managed to run and debug your app on your iPhone.

One thing we haven't yet embarked on is writing code. Well, I think we've put it off long enough. Let's get tough with Objective-C!

Chapter 4

Objective-C and Xcode: Developing a Blackjack Game

You're going to learn Objective-C in this chapter! As per the hands-on nature of this book, you'll be learning on the job, building an object-oriented blackjack game that implements the MVC (Model-View-Controller) paradigm.

The aim here is to get familiar with the structure and syntax of Objective-C: how to create classes; the syntax of methods; pointers and primitives—and a whole lot more.

The Game

We're going to build a simplified version of blackjack, so there are a few caveats:

- Players will have just two options during gameplay: Stand or Hit.

- There'll be no betting (sorry!).

- We're going to implement a maximum card limit per player of five cards.

How to play

For those of you not familiar with the game, blackjack is a card game in which the players compete against the dealer.

The objective of the game is to make 21 points with your hand.

You have to beat the dealer to win the game. At the end of the game, if you have the same number as or fewer points than the dealer, you lose (this is the version we'll make).

If your hand goes over 21, then you've bust—and you lose.

At the start of the game, two cards are dealt to each player and the dealer: the hole cards. You get to see both of your hole cards. In some versions of the game, you get to see one of the dealer's cards but not the other, so you have some indication of the strength of his hand. That's the version we're going to build.

In blackjack, each card has a points value, as follows:

- *Ace*: Either 11 points or 1 point, whichever gives you a better score without going bust

- *Face cards (jack, queen, king)*: 10 points

- *Everything else*: The value of the card

You have to make all of your decisions before the dealer. You repeatedly decide whether to *hit*—and have another card added to your hand from the pack. When you're happy with your hand (it's as close to 21 as you're prepared to risk), you *stand*—and it's the dealers turn. He plays out his hand and only has to match or beat your cards to win.

There are other rules to the game, but I think we've got plenty here for a good demo app.

Ready to start? First, make a duplicate of the Starting Code project folder from the Source Files for Chapter 4 to work from.

You'll find that I've already embedded the image and icon assets for our project. As per Chapter 3, I selected the Single View Application template as a starting point for this project.

There's just one view and view controller in our blackjack game, so select the main storyboard file and let's build our view.

Creating the view

In this first stage of our blackjack game development, we'll begin by learning how to create basic user interfaces in Xcode: how to add and configure buttons, labels, and images in a view, and how to create connections to those subviews to control them with code at runtime.

Setting the background color of a view

Open the blackjack project's storyboard file and ensure that the document outline pane is visible; this makes view selection simpler and more accurate when working with user interfaces.

Using the outline inspector, select the main view in the storyboard and then change the background color to a suitable blackjack green using the attributes inspector, as shown in Figure 4-1.

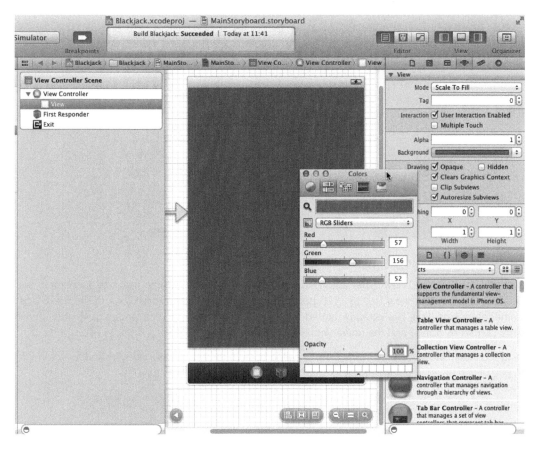

Figure 4-1. Setting the background color of a view

Adding labels, images, and buttons

Next, drag and drop two label views (UILabel) from the Object Library onto the view: one to display above the dealer's cards and one to display above the player's cards (see Figure 4-2).

Using the attributes inspector again, change the font face and size of the labels to System Bold/17 points, and type in the text **Dealer** and **Player**, respectively.

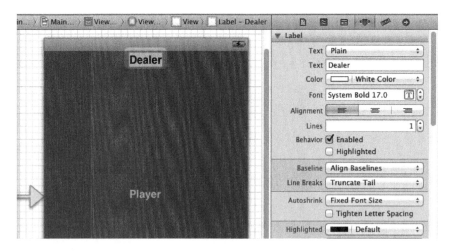

Figure 4-2. Adding Label Views (UILabel)

Now drag a new image view (UIImageView) onto the main view. Using the size inspector, set the dimensions of the image view to 118×176 points. These are the fixed dimensions of the card face and back images assets that I've already added to the blackjack project (I've added both the non-retina versions (118×176 pixels) and the retina versions (236×352 pixels)).

Keeping the image view selected in the Editor, switch back to the attributes inspector and select the `card-back.png` image asset to set the image property of the image view (see Figure 4-3).

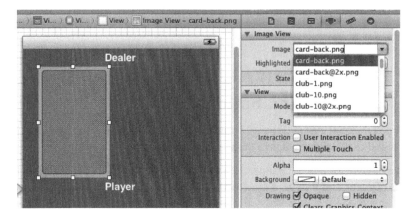

Figure 4-3. Adding an image view (UIImageView) and setting its image property

---

Tip: By selecting `card-back.png` and not `card-back@2x.png`, iOS SDK will automatically use `card-back@2x.png` on retina devices and `card-back.png` on non-retina devices like the iPhone 3GS.

With the card image view selected in the Editor, create nine additional duplicate cards: ⌘D or Edit ➤ Duplicate. Layer the cards into two hands of five, layering up from left to right for each hand (see Figure 4-4). To arrange the layering of cards, use Editor ➤ Arrange ➤ Send to Front.

Drag and drop two round rect buttons (UIButton) from the Object Library onto the main view.

> *Tip:* UIButton *is confusingly named Round Rect button in the Object Library. This* is *the main iOS button component, however, and it can also be used for custom buttons with graphic skin images.*

Resize, position, and enter the titles for each button, as per Figure 4-4.

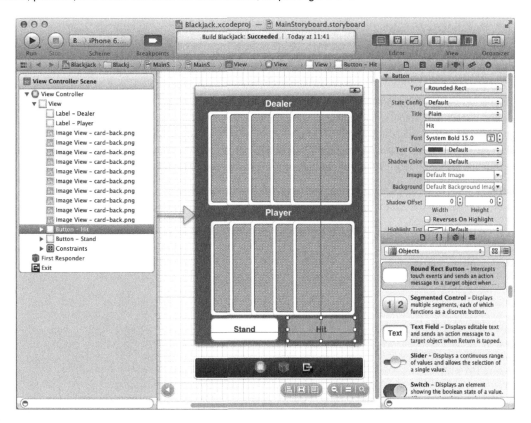

Figure 4-4. The final view layout

You should now have a final view layout that resembles Figure 4-4.

We've added labels, image views, and buttons to the main view of our storyboard. In iOS, each view or screen is controlled by a view controller class instance. Our main blackjack view's view controller is an instance of the BJViewController class in our project. At this point, we haven't made any modifications to the view controller itself: the view controller doesn't know anything about these newly added subviews.

Outlets: connecting the view

To clear up any confusion at this point, views and view controllers are not the same thing. The view controller owns the view. In MVC terms, the view controller is the controller and the view is, as you'd expect, the view!

The view should have no knowledge of the view controller that owns it whereas, the view controller can have as much, or as little, knowledge of the view it owns as you deem necessary.

In our blackjack app, we need to keep references to all the cards and buttons. We're going to hide and show cards, and change the image associated with each card to simulate dealt hands. Keeping references to the Hit and Stand buttons enables us to switch user interactivity on and off. For example, we don't want the player to be able to tap the Hit or Stand buttons when it's the dealer's turn.

So, how do we connect up the view to its view controller?

Well, first it will be helpful to see both the storyboard and BJViewController class simultaneously. Xcode makes this possible in a split editor pane. On the right-hand side of the Xcode toolbar, toggle the selected Editor option to select Assistant Editor. This should change the Editor layout to a split pane. If the right jump bar isn't already set to Automatic, then select this option. Xcode should now automatically select the header file that defines the public interface of the BJViewController class (see Figure 4-5).

You can also modify Xcode's view layout and hide the Navigator, Inspector, and Debug areas via the View toggle buttons next to the Editor buttons.

You should be left with a better workspace layout for connecting your view and view controller, as shown in Figure 4-5.

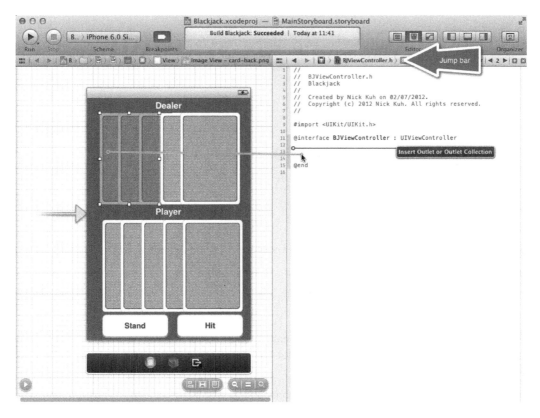

Figure 4-5. Ctrl+drag between view and view controller to create outlets and action connections

Back to business: we want to create references in BJViewController to each of the card image views and Hit and Stand buttons in our view. To do this, we're going to Ctrl+drag from each image view and button to the view controller interface, as shown in Figure 4-5. It seems a little odd at first, but it's pretty cool once you get used to the process. When you release the mouse, Xcode presents you with options to create an outlet in BJViewController. Assuming you've dragged from the first dealer card, name the outlet dealerCard1 (see Figure 4-6). Ensure the Storage setting is set to Weak and click Connect.

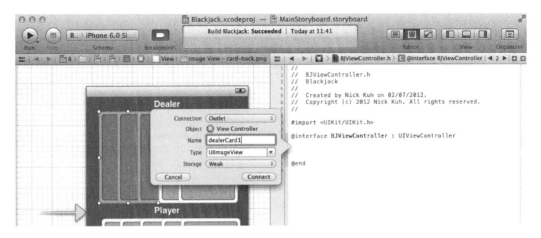

Figure 4-6. Ctrl+drag between view and view controller to create outlets and action connections

Xcode automatically generates the following Objective-C code for our new outlet in the BJViewController header file:

```
@property (weak, nonatomic) IBOutlet UIImageView *dealerCard1;
```

Repeat this process for the remaining dealer card image views, naming the outlets dealerCard1, dealerCard2, and so forth. Then do the same for the player cards, again naming them playerCard1, playerCard2, and so on.

Now create outlets to the Stand and Hit buttons, naming them standButton and hitButton, respectively. The generated code in BJViewController.h interface should end up as follows:

```
#import <UIKit/UIKit.h>

@interface BJViewController : UIViewController

@property (weak, nonatomic) IBOutlet UIImageView *dealerCard1;
@property (weak, nonatomic) IBOutlet UIImageView *dealerCard2;
@property (weak, nonatomic) IBOutlet UIImageView *dealerCard3;
@property (weak, nonatomic) IBOutlet UIImageView *dealerCard4;
@property (weak, nonatomic) IBOutlet UIImageView *dealerCard5;

@property (weak, nonatomic) IBOutlet UIImageView *playerCard1;
@property (weak, nonatomic) IBOutlet UIImageView *playerCard2;
@property (weak, nonatomic) IBOutlet UIImageView *playerCard3;
@property (weak, nonatomic) IBOutlet UIImageView *playerCard4;
@property (weak, nonatomic) IBOutlet UIImageView *playerCard5;

@property (weak, nonatomic) IBOutlet UIButton *standButton;
@property (weak, nonatomic) IBOutlet UIButton *hitButton;

@end
```

Actions: Responding to controls

We've created references to all the card image views and buttons, so we'll now be able to access and control their attributes at runtime, in the code of our `BJViewController` implementation file: setting the image property and visibility of the image views, and enabling and disabling the buttons.

Notice anything else we've missed? How will our view controller class capture button tap events?

We only specify outlets in one direction between view controller and view. So the view has no knowledge of its owner view controller. Our view controller class needs to know when the user taps the Stand or Hit buttons.

Buttons are controls. `UIButton` not only inherits from `UIView` but, like all other user interface controls in the iOS SDK, `UIButton` inherits directly from `UIControl`. Because Xcode recognizes instances of `UIButton` as subclasses of `UIControl`, it automatically offers us an additional connection type: `Action`.

The Objective-C mechanism for handling user interaction events and passing them from user interface controls to methods of any Objective-C class type is called target-action. When a button is tapped, the tap event can be passed to a method. We're going to create two new methods in our view controller that will be triggered in response to a Touch Up Inside event for either the Hit or Stand buttons. A Touch Up Inside event is triggered when the user touches a control and lifts up her finger on top of it. It's the equivalent action of a mouseup event on a computer.

Xcode can automatically generate target-action code using a similar Ctrl+drag process we implemented when creating outlets. Ctrl+drag from each button to the `BJViewController.h` interface but change the connection type to `Action`, ensure that Touch Up Inside is the selected event type, and repeat the process to create the following two action method handlers in your view controller interface header file (see Figure 4-7):

```
- (IBAction)didTapStandButton:(id)sender;
- (IBAction)didTapHitButton:(id)sender;
```

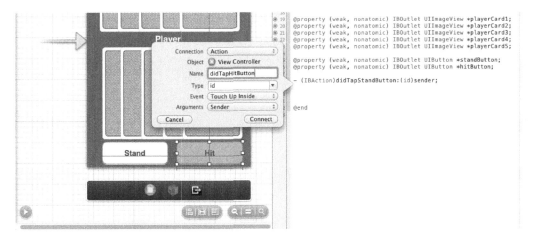

Figure 4-7. Connecting actions from the button controls to BJViewController

> *Note: Xcode can also create outlets and actions by control-clicking views and then dragging outlets and actions from the contextual menu.*

We're done with the view for our basic blackjack game. We've learned the basics of adding and arranging labels, buttons, and image views to create a view using Xcode's built-in UI layout tool. With storyboards, Xcode enables us to layout our app's views and create connections between them. We'll learn more about storyboarding tomorrow in Chapters 5 and 6, but for now we're going to move on to studying the basics of Objective-C classes, properties, methods, and object types.

Objective-C basics

Not only has Xcode autogenerated the outlet declarations in BJViewController.h header files, it's also added code to the BJViewController.m source file.

Sticking with the Assistant Editor layout, select BJViewController.h in the main left split pane so that we can examine both the header and implementation files for the view controller simultaneously (see Figure 4-8). There are a few ways to do this:

- Using the left-side jump bar, navigate to BJViewController.h.

- Revealing the navigator pane temporarily, select BJViewController.h, and then hide the navigator pane once more.

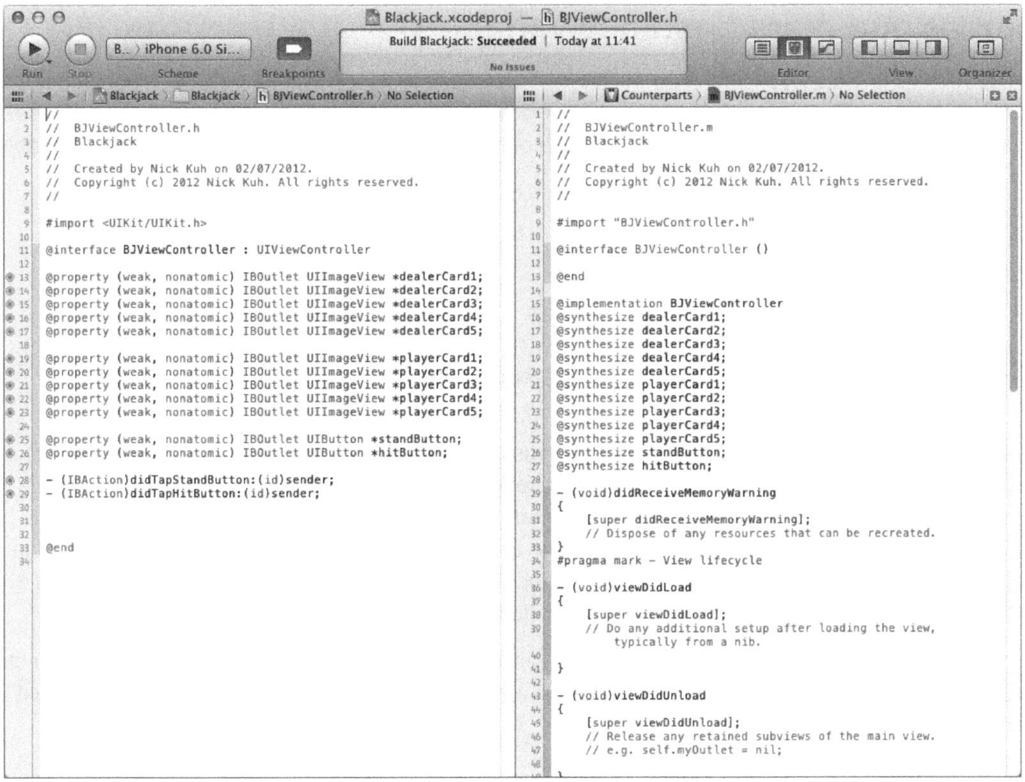

Figure 4-8. Xcode has autogenerated Objective-C code for our outlet and action connections

So what's a header and source file? I'm glad you asked!

Understanding the header and source files

An Objective-C class typically consists of two files: the header file and the source file. The header uses the file extension .h and the source uses the extension .m. The header is the public interface for your class: its API (application programming interface). The source is where you'll define the implementation of your class properties and methods.

Other classes wishing to reference or create instances of your class need to import YourClass.h file. You'll notice in Figure 4-8 that BJViewController.m also imports BJViewController.h. Any Objective-C implementation file imports its counterpart header file before presenting the implementation of the class properties and methods.

Properties and iVars (instance variables)

Class properties in Objective-C must be declared in the interface of a class. By default, properties are read and writable. A read/write property consists of two accessor methods: one to retrieve the value of the property and one to set the value. The actual value of the property is stored in an *iVar* (instance variable).

As an example, the header interface file of a class might look like this:

```
#import <Foundation/Foundation.h>

@interface Person : NSObject
{
        NSString *personName;
}
@property (strong, nonatomic) NSString *personName;
@end
```

In the header file example, we're declaring a new custom class: Person. Person inherits from parent class NSObject. Person contains a property named personName, which sets or returns an NSString value. The example header file also declares an iVar named personName. Although the two declarations have identical names, one is the property name and one is the iVar name. The iVar is the private variable that the Person class uses to store the string pointer. When the personName property is accessed, the property getter is invoked and it returns a reference to the personName iVar.

Now that we've declared that Person has a string property of personName, the Xcode compiler expects us to create the property's getter and setter accessor methods. In the source file Person.m, this would look like the following:

```
#import "Person.h"
@implementation Person
//personName property setter
-(void) setPersonName:(NSString *)personNameNew
{
    personName = personNameNew;
}

//personName property getter
-(NSString *)personName
{
    return personName;
}
@end
```

Wow, that's a lot of code just to get and set a string! Luckily, Xcode can automate the process of creating getters and setters using the synthesize directive in the class implementation file as follows:

```
#import "Person.h"

@implementation Person

@synthesize personName;
```

@end

The `synthesize` directive automatically generates getter/setter code just like in the first, more verbose implementation example. Xcode's compiler also recognizes the identically named iVar we've declared, and assigns it as the private storage variable for the property `personName`.

What's *not* ideal is to use an identical name for our property and our iVar: like in the example we've just seen! Luckily, the compiler allows us to declare a private iVar for property storage directly in the synthesize directive. Here's how:

```
@synthesize personName = _personName;
```

We don't have to use an underscore, but it's a commonly used convention by Cocoa developers to differentiate between properties and iVar names.

At WWDC 2012, Apple announced improvements to property and iVar declaration in modern Objective-C. With Xcode 4.5+, there's *no longer any need to add synthesize declarations to your class implementation*. The compiler now does it for you automatically. However, it is important to understand the code that the compiler automates.

If you don't synthesize, then your implementation code will look like this:

```
Person.m:
#import "Person.h"
@implementation Person
@end
```

Nice and clean. Xcode automatically adds the following synthesis code:

```
@synthesize personName = _personName;
```

So if you don't synthesize, then Xcode now *automatically creates an underscore* iVar for you.

If you synthesize like this:

```
Person.m:
#import "Person.h"
@implementation Person
@synthesize personName;
@end
```

Then your iVar is named `personName` and not `_personName`. So in the case of the blackjack outlets we added earlier in the chapter, Xcode added synthesize code to `BJViewController.m` automatically:

```
@synthesize dealerCard1;
```

The resulting iVar is named `dealerCard1` and not `_dealerCard1`. The main reason for this difference in iVar naming behavior is to ensure backward compatibility with older code, before Apple's 2012 modifications to Objective-C.

Creating a private class interface: class extensions

In `BJViewController.m`, notice the code that Xcode has added before the implementation code:

```
@interface BJViewController ()

@end
```

This is known in Objective-C as a *class extension*. A class extension enables us to define private properties. So with our blackjack app, we can declare properties within the BJViewController.m class extension that are only accessible internally by the BJViewController.m source file. Other classes only import the BJViewController.h header file, so the interface remains hidden from external access but is available within our source implementation for this class. Let's add a couple of private properties to BJViewController.m:

```
@interface BJViewController ()

@property (nonatomic,strong) NSArray *dealerCardViews;
@property (nonatomic,strong) NSArray *playerCardViews;

@end
```

Did you spot the brackets after the class name, indicating to the compiler that we're declaring a class extension?

We don't need to synthesize the two new array properties; Xcode's compiler does this for us.

Arrays

Note that the syntax for declaring the class extension is similar to the public interface but not identical:

```
@interface BJViewController ()
@property (nonatomic,strong) NSArray *dealerCardViews;
@property (nonatomic,strong) NSArray *playerCardViews;
@end
```

We're creating two arrays, one to retain references to the dealer's card views and one to retain references to the player's card views. The arrays will be used to index the displayed cards; that is, the first element of the dealerCardViews array will be a reference to dealerCard1.

By default, Objective-C synthesizes all pointers to nil. So when would be a good time for us to instantiate the two arrays? At what point in the view life cycle will we have access to the card image view outlets we've configured?

Anyone? Anyone? Bueller?... Bueller?... Bueller?...

Did you spot the viewDidLoad method in BJViewController.m? That's the first point at which our view controller has access to its view. Any outlets will have been connected for us at that point by the compiler. So viewDidLoad is the perfect place to instantiate the new dealerCardViews and playerCardViews arrays. Here's the code to add:

```
- (void)viewDidLoad
{
    [super viewDidLoad];
```

```
    self.dealerCardViews =
@[self.dealerCard1,self.dealerCard2,self.dealerCard3,self.dealerCard4,self.dealerCard5];
    self.playerCardViews =
@[self.playerCard1,self.playerCard2,self.playerCard3,self.playerCard4,self.playerCard5];
}
```

Prior to Xcode 4.5, we'd have defined our arrays with the more verbose [NSArray arrayWithObjects:] syntax as follows:

```
- (void)viewDidLoad
{
    [super viewDidLoad];

    self.dealerCardViews = [NSArray
arrayWithObjects:self.dealerCard1,self.dealerCard2,self.dealerCard3,self.dealerCard4,self.deal
erCard5, nil];
    self.playerCardViews = [NSArray
arrayWithObjects:self.playerCard1,self.playerCard2,self.playerCard3,self.playerCard4,self.play
erCard5, nil];

}
```

Both of these implementations work identically, but the first requires less code—and less is more in my book! In the first example, we're using the new Objective-C literals syntax. We'll be using literals a lot throughout the book because it's cleaner, more concise, and easier to read.

There are two types of arrays in Objective-C: NSArray and NSMutableArray. As the class names imply, one is mutable and the other is not. Once an NSArray has been instantiated, it cannot be modified, that is, you cannot add and remove elements to/from the array. For the purpose of indexing card views, a non-mutable NSArray works just fine for these properties: we're not going to be removing and adding card views, just showing and hiding them.

Init, Initializers, and designated initializers (constructors)

The closest thing Objective-C has to a constructor in its class structure is a method referred to as an *initializer*. This initializer is a method of a class that is called just once, at the moment the class is instantiated. Returning to our Person example, if we made no further changes to the class, then we would instantiate new instances of Person, like this:

```
Person *p = [[Person alloc] init];
```

alloc is a low-level class method that you should never need to override. When alloc is called, memory is allocated to the class and, as in the case of our example, an instance of Person is instantiated and init is then called on that instance.

At the moment, we haven't created an initializer for Person. But Person inherits from NSObject, which has an initializer called init. So we still need to call the initializer of the superclass.

Within the source file Person.m, we can override init as follows:

```
-(id)init
{
    self = [super init];
    if (self) {
        //set up some default property values?
    }
    return self;
}
```

Initializer methods should always return a reference to themselves. We use the generic object type id to enable the initializer to be subclassed. id simply implies that the return value will be an object.

There are other ways to create initializers without subclassing; for example, we may want to pass in a custom parameter to the initializer of our Person class:

```
-(id)initWithName:(NSString *)name
{
    self = [super init];
    if (self) {
        self.personName = name;
    }
    return self;
}
```

Notice how our custom initializer calls init on the superclass NSObject? init is also the designated initializer of NSObject—the initializer that all subclasses must call in their own initialization methods. It's a little confusing, so I'll reinforce that: the *designated initializer* is the initialization method that must be called first when instantiating instances of a class directly or via its subclasses.

In our example, initWithName could be the designated initializer of Person if we decided to enforce every instance of Person to have its personName property set on instantiation.

> Tip: Top-level classes like NSObject have an initializer method called init. As almost all classes in Cocoa inherit from NSObject it is customary for your class initializer to call [super init] within its own initializer(s).

Some classes have multiple initializers: arrays, for example:

- initWithArray:
- initWithArray:copyItems:
- initWithContentsOfFile:
- initWithContentsOfURL:
- initWithObjects:
- initWithObjects:count:

So it's up to you to pick the most suitable initializer.

Factory/convenience methods

Some Objective-C classes include *factory* or *convenience methods*. These are class methods that take care of the alloc init instantiation process and return new class instances. The following are the factory methods of an array:

```
+ array
+ arrayWithArray:
+ arrayWithContentsOfFile:
+ arrayWithContentsOfURL:
+ arrayWithObject:
+ arrayWithObjects:
+ arrayWithObjects:count:
```

I typically use factory methods to create arrays and dictionaries (hash tables).

```
NSMutableArray *arr = [NSMutableArray arrayWithObjects:@"one",@"two",@"three", nil];

NSMutableArray *arrWithOneObject = [NSMutableArray arrayWithObject:@"one"];

NSMutableDictionary *dictionary = [NSMutableDictionary
dictionaryWithObjectsAndKeys:@"value1",@"key1","value2",@"key2", nil];

NSMutableDictionary *dictionaryWithOneObject = [NSMutableDictionary
dictionaryWithObject:@"myValue" forKey:@"myKey"];
```

> *Note: We could also use literals to simplify the creation of arrays and dictionaries in these examples. However, literals create non-mutable objects, so we'd additionally need to call* mutableCopy *to generate mutable copies of our dictionaries and arrays.*

Let's get back to our blackjack game.

Do you remember earlier when I said that views and view controllers are not the same? In some circumstances, your view may get discarded by iOS but your view controller remain. Consider a complex navigation controller. The user has drilled deep into the navigation of the app, and so the view controlled by the first view controller in the navigation stack is no longer visible. If your app is running low on memory, then all of your view controllers may receive intermittent memory warnings via the didReceiveMemoryWarning method of UIViewController. By default, didReceiveMemoryWarning releases its main view if the view no longer has a parent view to free up unrequired memory. The UIViewController itself will not be released from memory because it remains one of the view controllers of the navigation controller.

We'll explore more of the details of the view life cycle in Chapter 5, but at this stage, it's just worth noting that the view property of a view controller may be released and reloaded by iOS. .

In viewDidUnload of BJViewController our outlets to the image views will be nullified, so it's important that we clear the two arrays we created earlier to reference all the dealer and player cards. If we do nothing, then the cards remain in memory because arrays retain references to their elements—and we'll leak memory.

Add the following code to the viewDidUnload method, after the call to [super viewDidUnload]:

```
- (void)viewDidUnload
{
    [super viewDidUnload];
    self.dealerCardViews = nil;
    self.playerCardViews = nil;
}
```

Please note that the following code produces identical results:

```
- (void)viewDidUnload
{
    [super viewDidUnload];
    [self setDealerCardViews:nil];
    [self setPlayerCardViews:nil];

}
```

In Objective-C, you can use either dot syntax to reference the setter through the property, or directly call the synthesized setter method as shown in the second example.

The code calls the synthesized setters for the dealerCardViews and playerCardViews properties, and releases the iVar storage references _dealerCardViews and _playerCardViews, which, in turn, release the array element references to each card view, and avoids potential memory leaks.

> Note: Arrays and dictionaries retain references to pointers. To avoid memory leaks, it's up to you to manage your arrays and dictionary properties.

Switching off/on multiorientation support

At this point, let's also switch off multiorientation for our app. Our blackjack game is intended only to be viewed in portrait orientation.

Scroll further down BJViewController.m and override the following view controller method:

```
- (NSUInteger)supportedInterfaceOrientations
{
    // We're not going to support multiple device orientation for this game
    return UIInterfaceOrientationMaskPortrait;
}
```

In addition to defining supported orientations in the target summary panel as we learned in Chapter 3, we can optionally define supported orientations directly within our view controller sub classes. We have to following orientation options to return:

```
UIInterfaceOrientationMaskPortrait
UIInterfaceOrientationMaskLandscapeLeft
UIInterfaceOrientationMaskLandscapeRight
UIInterfaceOrientationMaskPortraitUpsideDown
```

```
UIInterfaceOrientationMaskLandscape
UIInterfaceOrientationMaskAll
UIInterfaceOrientationMaskAllButUpsideDown
```

On iPhone, by default, view controllers return UIInterfaceOrientationMaskAllButUpsideDown so all orientations are supported except upside-down orientation. Now you should find that the app will no longer rotate.

As we learned in Chapter 3, we can switch off multiorientation support globally in our app in Xcode by selecting the Blackjack project in the Project Navigator and then the Blackjack target. Then, from the target's Summary tab, toggle off Landscape Left and Landscape Right in the Supported Interface Orientations section of the summary screen, as shown in Figure 4-9.

Figure 4-9. Switching off device orientation

I've introduced you to the structure of Objective-C classes, properties, iVars, initializers, class, and instance methods. It's been a brief introduction, but should form the foundation understanding you'll require for the hands-on learning you'll experience by building blackjack and *Birthday Reminder* apps.

The Model

In this next section of the chapter, we'll learn about object-oriented Objective-C. We'll learn about NSObject, the core foundation object class, and how to subclass and extend it. We'll further develop our blackjack game and learn how to implement basic MVC patterns in Objective-C.

We haven't quite finished with the controller yet, but for now we're going to switch to our model. The model for our app is going to comprise two custom classes: a card value object class and the game model. We could break the model down further and add a model class for the player and dealer, but for illustration purposes, two classes will suffice.

The card model

We're going to create a class that will represent the data of each card in a pack. This is a single-pack game of blackjack, so there will be 52 instances of our card class instantiated at the beginning of each hand. Don't worry. We'll make sure the cards get shuffled. It's good practice when creating model classes to subclass Apple's NSObject class because we inherit a few basic methods for free. Let's get started.

Subclassing NSObject

We've already seen a basic example of how to subclass NSObject with my earlier Person example. What I haven't shown you is the Xcode process to create new custom classes.

Open the Project Navigator pane, again via the toggle buttons top-right in the Xcode toolbar. Then select the data group within the project hierarchy.

> Tip: When creating new classes or adding files to an Xcode project, always first select the destination for the new files within the Project Navigator.

Use the ⌘N keyboard shortcut or File ➤ New ➤ File to be presented with a selection of new file templates. If it's not already selected, then choose the Objective-C Class option from the Cocoa Touch collection (see Figure 4-10).

Figure 4-10. Creating a new Objective-C class

On the next screen, ensure that the subclass option is set to NSObject and name your class BJDCard. I'm introducing another common naming convention. By adding a D to our BJ class prefix, we're indicating that this is a data class and we'll use this convention for other data or value object model classes.

Xcode will ask you where to save the new class file(s). As the data group is mapped to a folder within the Xcode project also called data, you should, by default, be automatically presented with the correct location to save the file. If not, then navigate to the data folder within the Xcode project you're working from and click the Create button (see Figure 4-11).

Figure 4-11. Saving the new BJDCard class to the data folder

If it's not already selected, then select the newly generated BJDCard header file in the Project Navigator and close the navigator again. You should now be viewing both the header and the source files for the new BJDCard class in Xcode's Assistant Editor layout.

We'll start by adding a couple of properties to BJDCard.

Header:

```
#import <Foundation/Foundation.h>

@interface BJDCard : NSObject

@property (nonatomic) int digit;
@property (nonatomic) BOOL isFaceUp;

@end
```

You won't need to make any changes to the source file for now because Xcode's compiler automates the synthesis of our two new properties. The result should look like Figure 4-12.

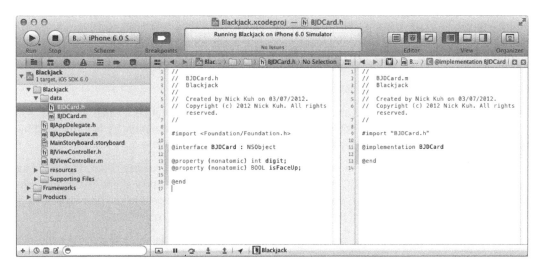

Figure 4-12. Adding properties and synthesized iVars to BJDCard

Declaring pointers and primitives

The property declaration syntax should look pretty familiar from our work on BJViewController. However, the syntax of our previous property declarations looked slightly different than this. Our dealerCardViews array in BJViewController, for example, was declared like this:

@property (nonatomic,strong) NSArray *dealerCardViews;

Whereas digit in BJDCard is declared like this:

@property (nonatomic) int digit;

The difference between the two properties is that arrays are pointers (references) to objects and integers are primitive data types where the actual value of the primitive is the property. In object-oriented languages like ActionScript, pointers and primitives are declared identically. In Objective-C, you'll need to get used to the differences in syntax.

Pointer declarations in all scopes use an * before the property or variable name. Primitive declarations like integers, floats, and Booleans do not. Arrays, dictionaries, and every reference to an instance of any Objective-C class are pointers.

Retain and release, and ARC (Automatic Reference Counting)

In iOS, references to pointers are either weak or strong. The memory management in iOS tracks the number of strong pointer references to an object and, as soon as the strong reference count hits zero, the system determines that the object is no longer needed by your application, deallocates any memory to the object, and disposes of the object.

In the past (pre–iOS 5) developers were responsible for all their strong reference counts. The old syntax for this was:

```
[myObject retain];//increments the strong reference count to the object by 1
//do something
[myObject release];//deducts  the strong reference count by 1
```

Developers had to be very careful to ensure that strong reference count hit zero when an object was no longer needed to ensure apps were not leaking memory. An app that leaks memory is terminated by the system when it consumes more memory than the system deems acceptable.

Apple introduced a very well-received new piece of technology in the 2011 release of Xcode 4.2. It's called Automatic Reference Counting or ARC for short. At compile time, ARC adds all the retain and release references to your code automatically, so it's now much easier for developers to get on with writing great code, and not spending a great deal of time keeping track of strong object references.

However, it's still really important that you have some idea about what's going on under the hood of your application.

Let's re-examine two pointer references we created in BJViewController:

```
@property (nonatomic ,weak) IBOutlet UIImageView *dealerCard1;
@property (nonatomic,strong) NSArray *dealerCardViews;
```

The main differences between the two property pointer declarations that I want to alert you to are the keywords *weak* and *strong*. These keywords instruct the compiler how to treat these property pointer references. By default, a pointer property reference will be *strong*. That makes sense for properties like our array of dealerCardViews. This array is created in our view controller class and not referenced anywhere else in the app. If we hint to the compiler that the property is *weak*, then as soon as the app has executed viewDidLoad, the dealerCardViews property is set to nil by the compiler. There are no other strong references to the array, so once we're out of the viewDidLoad scope, the compiler assumes that the object is no longer needed and can be released.

With Interface Builder outlets like dealerCard1, however, the reference should be weak. By simply adding the dealerCard1 image view to its parent view, we've created a strong reference between the parent and child view. We don't want the reference to dealerCard1 in our view controller to be strong, because in the event of the main view being unloaded, its child views will no longer be available, and we want the system to be able to dispose of the memory these removed views are consuming. Hence. we use weak references for outlets to subviews.

There are exceptions to this rule. It's possible to add views and other objects to the top level of a storyboard scene; that is, objects that are not subviews of the view. In this case, you would require a strong outlet reference from your view controller class to ensure the object isn't trashed by the system for having zero strong references.

Enumerators

Apple uses a lot of enumerators in Cocoa Touch and iOS SDK. We've already encountered the device orientation enumerator `UIInterfaceOrientation`, where we're only supporting the orientation enumerator value `UIInterfaceOrientationPortrait` in our app.

It's easy enough to create our own custom enumerators. We're going to do that now in `BJDCard.h`.

```
typedef enum : int
{
    BJCardSuitClub = 0,
    BJCardSuitSpade,
    BJCardSuitDiamond,
    BJCardSuitHeart
}BJCardSuit;
```

Type this code into the header file of your `BJDCard` class, *before* the interface declaration. Our custom enumerator is a new Objective-C type we're defining as `BJCardSuit`. By defining the suit in the header file outside of the interface declaration, we're making this enumerator available for other classes to use. `BJDCard` is really just a value object, so we should enable external classes to change the suit of our card. We're stating that each element of the enumerator should be an integer and that the first enum value listed (`BJCardSuitClub`) is equal to zero. `BJCardSuitSpade` is equal to 1, `BJCardSuitDiamond` is equal to 2, and so on.

Now that we've defined the custom suit enumerator, we can create a new property of `BJDCard` called `suit`, as follows:

```
@property (nonatomic) BJCardSuit suit;
```

You should end up with the changes to `BJDCard`, as illustrated in Figure 4-13.

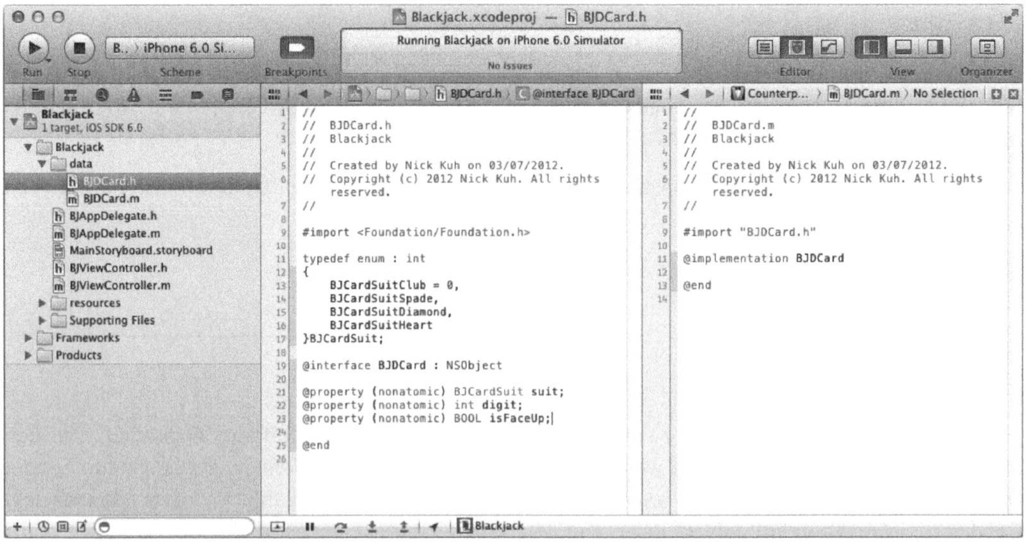

Figure 4-13. BJDCard with the new suit enumerator property

Methods

Let's add a few public methods to BJDCard. Similar to public properties, if we wish to add public methods to a class, then we first declare the method signature in the public interface of the class in the header file. So, within the interface declaration of BJDCard.h, add the following three method signatures:

```
-(BOOL) isAnAce;
-(BOOL) isAFaceOrTenCard;
-(UIImage *)getCardImage;
```

We have added three instance method signatures to our class. Within our application, whenever an instance of BJDCard exists, the app assumes that it is possible for any of these three methods to be called on the instance. We haven't actually defined the implementation of any of these methods, but the compiler now allows us to attempt to call these methods. In reality, this would crash our app at runtime. The compiler also warns us that we haven't actually implemented the methods for which we've declared signatures.

It's time to implement the first two of these methods. In the implementation source file, add the following code:

```
-(BOOL) isAnAce
{
    if (self.digit == 1) return YES;
    return NO;
}

-(BOOL) isAFaceOrTenCard
{
    if (self.digit > 9) return YES;
```

```
    return NO;
}
```

As I explained at the start of this chapter, in blackjack, aces and face cards have a different points value, so we're creating a couple of useful methods that will be used by the game model logic to determine whether instances of BJDCard are aces or face cards. The digit property of BJDCard instances is a value between 1 and 13: 1 being an ace, 11 a jack, 12 a queen, and 13 a king.

These methods check the value of the digit property and then return a Boolean value, which in Objective-C is defined as YES (true) or NO (false).

The methods of BJDCard don't implement any parameters, but now is a good time for us to familiarize ourselves with the syntax of a method declaration in Objective-C. Here's a diagram from Apple's own documentation:

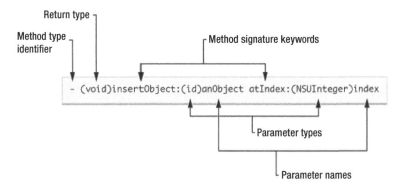

Figure 4-14. Objective-C method declaration syntax

Method declarations in Objective-C are fairly verbose to say the least! Each parameter has a *method signature keyword* and a *parameter name* (see Figure 4-14). Note that the actual reference to each parameter is defined after the parameter type. So if you were implementing Apple's method in the preceding example, the anObject and index keywords would be the names of the incoming parameters.

We'll be revisiting method syntax throughout this book, so don't worry too much if this example has totally thrown you!

Let's implement our third BJDCard method, getCardImage. This method is called by our view controller every time it wants to render a card face-up on the screen. Internally, the method checks the suit of the card (thanks to our custom enumerator BJCardSuit) and dynamically creates a string that matches the file name of the correct image from the bank of retina and non-retina PNG files that I've already linked into this project for you. Here's the code:

```
-(UIImage *)getCardImage
{
    NSString *suit;

    switch (self.suit) {
        case BJCardSuitClub:
```

```
        suit = @"club";
        break;
    case BJCardSuitSpade:
        suit = @"spade";
        break;
    case BJCardSuitDiamond:
        suit = @"diamond";
        break;
    case BJCardSuitHeart:
        suit = @"heart";
        break;

    default:
        break;
}


NSString *filename = [NSString stringWithFormat:@"%@-%d.png",suit,self.digit];

return [UIImage imageNamed:filename];

}
```

We've used a switch statement on the suit property of our BJDCard instance and translated that value to populate a local string variable called suit. Notice how we must use the syntax self.suit to refer to the property. Calling suit without self results in a compiler error because the compiler assumes you're trying to call an instance variable. Remember how the compiler synthesizes our suit property and creates an iVar named _suit for us? So we could run a switch statement on _suit instead, and we'd get the same results.

The getCardImage method finally generates a string with the full file name of the corresponding face-up image for the card. We're using a factory method of NSString to achieve this. In NSString's stringWithFormat initializer, it automatically replaces placeholder variables in the declared format with the variables we pass in as additional parameters. To declare a string variable in the format, use the %@ syntax. To declare an integer variable, use the %d syntax. Use %@ when replacing any object like NSString, NSNumber, NSArray, and so on. This is useful for debugging purposes. If you need to print the contents of an array to the debugger, for example, you can use the following code:

```
NSLog(@"My arr contents: %@",myAppVariable);
```

Finally, we generate a new image instance using UIImage's factory method imageNamed and pass the file name of the image in our application bundle:

```
[UIImage imageNamed:filename];
```

We return the image instance.

We've learned how to create a new class in Xcode that extends NSObject. We've also learned the syntax for adding properties and methods to our class, as well as how to reference properties and their underlying iVars. Things are heating up. If I'm moving too fast for you, don't panic, I'm rapidly introducing you to code and syntax that you will get plenty of chances to revisit in our main *Birthday Reminder* app after this chapter.

The game model

Let's leave BJDCard for the time being, but before you do, be sure that the app compiles OK. Build and run the app. You should just see the view layout we created at the beginning of the chapter. As long as your version of the app doesn't crash, you're doing just fine!

I'm afraid I cheated a little in the preparation for this app. I have written some of the code for you. The aim of this chapter is to introduce you to Objective-C, and if I stepped you through every line of code for a blackjack app, this chapter might start to resemble a book itself!

Let's add a new class to our app. I've already written the majority of the new BJDGameModel class, so you need to add the actual class files to your project rather than creating the file from scratch.

First select the data group in the Project Navigator, and using the ⌘A keyboard shortcut or File ➤ Add Files to "Blackjack", navigate to the BJDGameModel header and source files, multiselect them both, and add them to your project (see Figure 4-15).

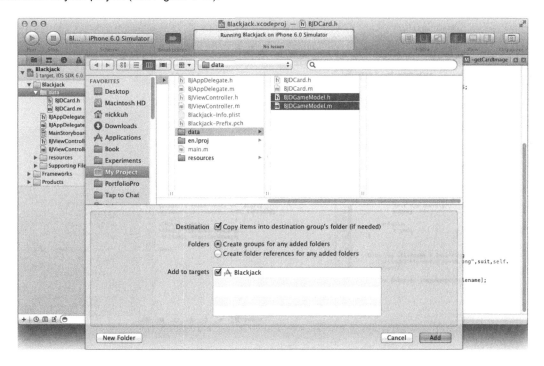

Figure 4-15. Adding BJDGameModel header and source files to the Xcode project

BJDGameModel references BJDCard, so just to check you haven't missed anything during the development of BJDCard, it would be worthwhile building and running again to ensure that your project still compiles without error.

Let's take a look at the code I've provided for you in BJDGameModel. Remaining in Assistant Editor layout, we can quickly scan the public interface properties and methods in the header file (see Figure 4-16). BJDGameModel is a class that manages a pack of cards and dealer and player hands; each array contains multiple instances of BJDCard. BJDGameModel also manages the game stages. In each game of blackjack, the player goes first, followed by the dealer, and then the game is over. So you'll see that I've created another custom enumerator to track these three game stages:

```
typedef enum : int
{
    BJGameStagePlayer,
    BJGameStageDealer,
    BJGameStageGameOver
}BJGameStage;
```

Our game model exposes a public gameStage property. Our view controller, BJViewController, has access to the model and is therefore able to check the game stage at any point and determine how to render the view based on the model.

Figure 4-16. Dissecting BJDGameModel

> *Note: You can use the jumpbar to quickly find method and property declarations and implementations in the header and source files (see Figure 4-16).*

There's one other property in our model: `maxPlayerCards`. As I mentioned earlier in the chapter, this is one of the caveats of our implementation of blackjack: we're permitting a maximum of five cards per dealer or player hand. If the player's hand reaches five cards and he hasn't yet gone bust, then his turn is over and the game stage progresses to the dealer's turn.

Did you spot this code in the header:

```
@class BJDCard;
```

This is what's known as a forward class declaration. Some of the public methods in `BJDGameModel` return instances of `BJDCard`. The compiler will complain if we don't either import `BJDCard` in the header like this:

```
#import "BJDCard.h"
```

Or add a forward class declaration like the one I've implemented. The forward class declaration lets the compiler know that although we haven't yet declared the `BJDCard` class, it will be declared—trust us, compiler! You'll see that I've actually imported `BJDCard.h` in the source implementation of `BJDGameModel.m`. In general, this is the best way to include references to other classes in your header files, via forward class declarations. Then be sure to import the header(s) in the source file.

Although importing `BJDCard.h` in the `BJDGameModel.h` header file works fine on this occasion, you will run into horrible compiler errors at some point if you continue to work this way. An error will occur if you have two classes that both reference each other in the header file. They are both relying on the other file to be imported by the compiler first, so the compiler gets its knickers in a twist! The solution: use forward class declarations in your header files rather than import declarations.

Our MVC blackjack implementation

The way our game will work is that `BJViewController` is the controller in our MVC implementation. The controller has access to the model, but the model has no knowledge whatsoever of the controller. It's a similar one-way relationship with the controller and the view.

`BJViewController` will control the show: when the app first loads, `BJViewController` calls `resetGame` on the model and then renders the view to represent the model. During the player's turn, `BJViewController` listens for the Touch Up Inside action on the Stand and Hit buttons, and tells the model to deal a new card. Again, `BJViewController` renders the view. `BJViewController` also calls the `updateGameStage` method of the model, which checks whether the player has gone bust or reached his maximum five-card hand, and progresses the game stage accordingly.

Once it's the dealer's turn, `BJViewController` renders the second card face-up and asks the model to check whether the dealer should stand, again via the `updateGameStage` method. If the dealer needs to hit, then `BJViewController` implements a delay timer to simulate the dealing of a third card. `BJViewController` calls `updateGameStage` again, and then deals another delayed card until the dealer goes bust or wins.

Class methods

Within the BJDGameModel source file, you'll find a private property named cards, which is a mutable array where we store our pack of 52 BJDCard instances. We've declared the array as mutable because we'll be popping cards off the array as they are dealt into the playerCards and dealerCards mutable arrays. However, I haven't provided you with prewritten code for generating a pack of cards. So let's do that now!

The controller calls the resetGame method of BJDGameModel. This is where we need to generate a pack of cards. At the moment, cards is set to an empty array:

```
self.cards = [NSMutableArray array];
```

We could run a loop here in the BJDGameModel class directly, but generating a pack of 52 cards might be something we want to do in other card games. Seems to me this would make a suitable convenience method for the actual BJDCard class. We've already seen how some classes, like NSArray and NSDictionary, expose factory/convenience methods for generating instances of themselves. In this case, we'll create a class method on BJDCard that generates a mutable array of 52 instances of BJDCard!

Switch back to work on the BJDCard class in the Assistant Editor. Have you discovered that in Xcode, you can have multiple Objective-C files open simultaneously? You can even set your multiple files to all use the Assistant Editor layout. Double-clicking a file in the Project Navigator opens a new window by default in Xcode. I prefer viewing multiple tabs than windows. To set Xcode to open a new tab rather than a new window, go into the Xcode General Preferences, and under Double-Click Navigation, change the selected option to Uses Separate Tab.

Now viewing BJDCard.h, let's declare our new class method in the header:

```
+(NSMutableArray *) generateAPackOfCards;
```

Do you notice the subtle difference between the syntax of class methods and instance methods (the other three in this class)? The syntax for declaring a class method uses a "+" rather than a "–" at the beginning of the declaration. Now switch to working on BJDCard.m in the source file, and add the following code:

```
+(NSMutableArray *) generateAPackOfCards
{
    NSMutableArray *arr = [NSMutableArray array];

    BJDCard *card;

    int suit,digit;

    for (suit=0;suit<4;suit++) {
        for (digit=1;digit<=13;digit++)
        {
            card = [[BJDCard alloc] init];
            card.suit = suit;
            card.digit = digit;
            [arr addObject:card];
        }
    }
```

```
    return arr;
}
```

Looking through the code, you'll see that we've set up one loop inside another. The first outer loop iterates four times: once for each card suit. So, a quarter of the generated cards have their suit set to 0, a quarter have their suit set to 1, and so on. Do you remember our custom suit enumerator BJCardSuit? Here's the code to jog your memory:

```
typedef enum : int
{
    BJCardSuitClub = 0,
    BJCardSuitSpade,
    BJCardSuitDiamond,
    BJCardSuitHeart
}BJCardSuit;
```

With this declaration syntax, the compiler assigns integer 0 as a BJCardSuitClub, integer 1 as a BJCardSuitSpade, and so on. So in our generateAPackOfCards method, those suit values will match the enumerator values in the original enumerator declaration.

Getting back to generateAPackOfCards analysis, you'll see that we start by declaring an empty local scope mutable array:

```
NSMutableArray *arr = [NSMutableArray array];
```

And then in the heart of our loop(s), we alloc/init new instances of BJDCard, set the suit and digit, and then add them to the local array with the mutable array instance method addObject:.

Once complete, we return our array.

Build and run your app to check there are still no errors!

We're done with the BJDCard class for our blackjack game. So we're now going to make some changes to BJDGameModel to take advantage of the new generateAPackOfCards method we just wrote.

In BJDGameModel, replace this line of code from the resetGame method implementation:

```
self.cards = [NSMutableArray array];
```

with this:

```
self.cards = [BJDCard generateAPackOfCards];
```

Great, we have 52 cards in our array! Only thing is that the cards aren't shuffled. Hmm... this will be a pretty boring game of blackjack. What's the solution?

Shuffling the cards: Objective-C categories

Objective-C's NSMutableArray class doesn't have a shuffle method, unfortunately. So we're going to have to write one ourselves. But isn't a shuffle quite a useful additional method for a mutable array? Wouldn't it be cool if we could add our method to the NSMutableArray class? Well, guess what? We can with Objective-C categories!

Adding a category to an existing class is typically achieved by creating a new Objective-C header and source file. We'll add the file to the data group, so open the Project Navigator and ensure that data is selected. Now, again with the ⌘N shortcut or File ➤ New ➤ New File, select the Objective-C category option from the Cocoa Touch file templates. On the next screen type **Shuffle** into the Category text field and **NSMutableArray** into the Category On text field (see Figure 4-17).

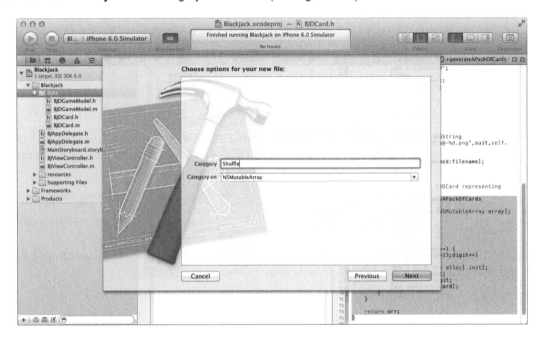

Figure 4-17. Adding an Objective-C category to NSMutableArray

Create the new file in the data folder of the Finder. Ensure that you're viewing the newly created NSMutableArray+Shuffle header and source files in the Assistant Editor layout.

> *Tip: Occasionally Xcode doesn't automatically display the counter part header/source file in the Assistant Layout. To resolve this, click the jumpbar and change the selected option to Counterparts.*

You'll see that a category file has a similar layout to a class file, but note the category name added within parenthesis after the interface keyword. Modify the category header as follows:

```
#import <Foundation/Foundation.h>
@interface NSMutableArray (Shuffle)

-(void) shuffle;

@end
```

Now modify the source implementation to include the new shuffle method:

```objc
#import "NSMutableArray+Shuffle.h"

@implementation NSMutableArray (Shuffle)

- (void)shuffle
{
    int count = [self count];

    NSMutableArray *dupeArr = [self mutableCopy];
    count = [dupeArr count];
    [self removeAllObjects];

    for (int i = 0; i < count; ++i) {
        // Select a random element between i and the end of the array to swap with.
        int nElements = count - i;
        int n = (arc4random() % nElements);
        [self addObject:dupeArr[n]];
        [dupeArr removeObjectAtIndex:n];
    }

}

@end
```

Our custom shuffle method performs the following process:

- Creates a duplicate copy of the mutable array.

- Empties the array.

- Loops through the duplicate array randomly extracting elements (in our app's case these are the instances of BJDCard), re-adds them to the mutable array, and removes them from the duplicate.

We're done creating the shuffle category: so back to BJDGameModel.

In order for the compiler to allow us to call our new shuffle category method on NSMutableArray, we'll need to import the file we just created. So, at the top of BJDGameModel.m add the import declaration:

```objc
#import "NSMutableArray+Shuffle.h"
```

Now you should be able to call the shuffle method directly on self.cards after generating the pack. So the resetGame method should end up looking like this:

```objc
-(void) resetGame
{
    self.cards = [BJDCard generateAPackOfCards];

    [self.cards shuffle];

    self.playerCards = [NSMutableArray array];
    self.dealerCards = [NSMutableArray array];
    self.gameStage = BJGameStagePlayer;
}
```

Cool, huh?

In our blackjack game, it's the model that determines when the game has ended. The game could end for a few reasons: the player goes bust, the dealer goes bust, the dealer hits a fifth maximum card, or the dealer stands. The controller, BJViewController, needs to update the view when the game is over, let the user know who won, and permit him to play again. However, as per the rules of the MVC pattern, the model must remain ignorant of the view and the controller. So how can we alert BJViewController to the game over event?

The answer is Apple's NSNotificationCenter.

Dispatching notifications between classes

Apple has kindly provided Cocoa developers with the NSNotificationCenter, which negates most reasons to use any kind of third-party architectural framework. I remember when being a good Flash and Flex developer wasn't just about knowing how to write good ActionScript, it was also about which of the numerous third-party frameworks to use when building complex web applications and games—PureMVC, Cairngorm, Swiz, and Robotlegs to name but a few.

Well, forget third-party architectural frameworks for iOS SDK app development; the notification center adds a native broadcast and observer mechanism to all Objective-C objects. Our model will be able to fire off a notification into the abyss of our program. As long as our view controller (or any other object) has registered as an observer of our custom notification, we can rest assured that the view controller will catch the event, and respond and update the view accordingly.

So let's add a notification dispatch to from the model.

Each dispatched notification must be an instance of NSNotification, which has a name property that is used by observing classes when registering for notifications. So we'll define the name of our game over notification in a constant string.

Right at the top of the BJDGameModel.h header file, define the notification name:

```
#define BJNotificationGameDidEnd     @"BJNotificationGameDidEnd"
```

Some developers keep a single file just for constant declarations. In the case of declaring notification names, another common convention is to add the notification name declarations to the header file of the dispatching class like we've just done.

Now, switch to the source file for BJGameModel and locate the notifyGameDidEnd method. The method is currently empty. However, BJDGameModel is already calling this method at all the points when the game has ended. We need to achieve two things when we send our notification: alerting any observing objects that the game has ended and letting them know who won. Update notifyGameDidEnd as follows:

```
-(void) notifyGameDidEnd
{
    NSNotificationCenter *notificationCenter = [NSNotificationCenter defaultCenter];

    //wrapping a Boolean into an NSNumber object using literals syntax
    NSNumber *didDealerWin = @(self.didDealerWin);
```

```
    //creating a dictionary using literals syntax
    NSDictionary *dict = @{@"didDealerWin": didDealerWin};

    [notificationCenter postNotificationName:BJNotificationGameDidEnd object:self
userInfo:dict];
}
```

I realize that's a lot of new code to digest, so let's step through it. The notification broadcasts are sent through an instance of NSNotificationCenter. We don't even need to worry about instantiating that class because Cocoa has created a default, single instance behind the scenes that we can access through the NSNotificationCenter convenience method defaultCenter.

Next, we need to include the details of whether the dealer or player won in our notification. The notification object we're going to send permits us to include an NSDictionary instance in its userInfo property. This is the reason we're creating an NSDictionary on the following line of code.

The problem is that the self.didDealerWin property is a Boolean primitive. Primitive data types cannot be set as values in dictionaries or arrays. The solution is to wrap the Boolean primitive in an object and pass the pointer into the dictionary. We do this by creating an instance of the NSNumber class.

> Note: Primitive data types cannot be set as values in dictionaries or arrays. Wrap the primitive in an instance of the NSNumber class. You can wrap float, integers, and Booleans in NSNumber instances.

Finally, we post our notification via the single, default NSNotificationCenter:

```
[notificationCenter postNotificationName:BJNotificationGameDidEnd object:self userInfo:dict];
```

This method creates a notification with the given name (BJNotificationGameDidEnd constant string), sender (our BJDGameModel class instance), and information (our dictionary instance and winner data) and posts it to the registered notification observers.

Build and run, and then check that your code compiles OK. We're done with our model: back to BJViewController to hook everything up!

Hooking it all together

The rest of our work is in the source implementation file for BJViewController. We're finally going to see the results of our hard work building the model represented in our view!

Close all the model classes and open only BJViewController.m in the standard editor. Begin by importing both BJDGameModel.h and BJDCard.h:

```
#import "BJViewController.h"
#import "BJDGameModel.h"
#import "BJDCard.h"
```

Now to add a new private model property to the private class extension of BJViewController.m source:

```
@interface BJViewController ()

@property (nonatomic,strong) NSArray *dealerCardViews;
@property (nonatomic,strong) NSArray *playerCardViews;
@property (nonatomic,strong) BJDGameModel *gameModel;
@end
```

Within the implementation of BJViewController.m, add place holders for two new private methods:

```
- (void)renderCards
{

}

- (void)restartGame
{

}
```

> Note: To avoid compiler warnings prior to Xcode 4.5, it was necessary to either declare private method signatures in your class extension or place the method implementations high in the implementation file and before any callers. This is now a thing of the past and you can order your private methods however you like and without declaring method signatures.

In addition, we're going to override the designated initializer of UIViewController in our subclass as follows:

```
-(id) initWithCoder:(NSCoder *)aDecoder
{
    self = [super initWithCoder:aDecoder];
    if (self) {
        self.gameModel = [[BJDGameModel alloc] init];
        [[NSNotificationCenter defaultCenter] addObserver:self
selector:@selector(handleNotificationGameDidEnd:) name:BJNotificationGameDidEnd
object:self.gameModel];
    }
    return self;
}
```

UIViewController has multiple designated initializers: initWithCoder: and initWithNibName:bundle:. However, when instantiated from a storyboard initWithCoder: it is the initializer that gets automatically invoked.

In our BJViewController designated initializer, we're doing two things here: instantiating an instance of BJDGameModel and registering to receive notifications from the model when the game ends. We've registered for the game end notification to fire a method in our view controller that we've yet to write: handleNotificationGameDidEnd:.

Using the @selector directive in the addObserver method of the NSNotificationCenter is similar to the target-action mechanism we covered in Interface Builder UIControl target-actions at the beginning of the chapter. When the game ends, BJDGameModel sends a new notification via the notification center that, in turn, invokes the handleNotificationGameDidEnd method in the BJViewController observing class.

We'll implement the handleNotificationGameDidEnd method at the end of this chapter. Next, I'd like you to add the full code for the new restartGame method:

```
- (void)restartGame
{
    [self.gameModel resetGame];
    BJDCard *card;

    card = [self.gameModel nextPlayerCard];
    card.isFaceUp = YES;
    card = [self.gameModel nextDealerCard];
    card.isFaceUp = YES;

    card = [self.gameModel nextPlayerCard];
    card.isFaceUp = YES;

    [self.gameModel nextDealerCard];

    [self renderCards];

    self.standButton.enabled = self.hitButton.enabled = YES;
}
```

The restartGame method initially calls resetGame on the model. We recently worked on resetGame method in BJDGameModel—we generate a new shuffled pack of cards and empty the arrays for tracking dealer and player cards.

Next, we instruct the model to deal two cards to the dealer and to the player. Note how we set the first dealer card face-up and not the second. This instruction is rendered into our view in the renderCards method we've not yet written.

We also enable the player's Stand and Hit buttons because the player goes first in blackjack. When it's the dealer's turn, we'll disable these buttons.

There are two places in our view controller where we'll call restartGame: 1) when a game ends and the player wishes to play again, and 2) the first time the view appears on screen. In order to cater for the second scenario, which method of BJViewController do we need to add a call to restartGame? Do you remember the view life cycle I introduced at the beginning of this chapter? We initiated our dealerCardViews and playerCardViews array properties in the viewDidLoad method. For our app, this method is a perfectly reasonable place to call [self restartGame]. An equally suitable candidate is the viewWillAppear: method. viewWillAppear: is invoked the moment before it is displayed on screen. We will restart our game and render our view just before the app displays it:

```
- (void)viewWillAppear:(BOOL)animated
{
    [super viewWillAppear:animated];
    [self restartGame];
}
```

All set? Let's now implement the `renderCards` method:

```
- (void)renderCards
{
    int maxCard = self.gameModel.maxPlayerCards;

    BJDCard *dealerCard;
    BJDCard *playerCard;
    UIImageView *dealerCardView;
    UIImageView *playerCardView;

    for (int i=0; i<maxCard; i++) {
        dealerCardView = self.dealerCardViews[i];
        playerCardView = self.playerCardViews[i];

        dealerCard = [self.gameModel dealerCardAtIndex:i];
        playerCard = [self.gameModel playerCardAtIndex:i];

        dealerCardView.hidden = (dealerCard == nil);
        if (dealerCard && dealerCard.isFaceUp) {
            dealerCardView.image = [dealerCard getCardImage];
        }
        else {
            dealerCardView.image = [UIImage imageNamed:@"card-back.png"];
        }

        playerCardView.hidden = (playerCard == nil);
        if (playerCard && playerCard.isFaceUp) {
            playerCardView.image = [playerCard getCardImage];
        }
        else {
            playerCardView.image = [UIImage imageNamed:@"card-back.png"];
        }
    }
}
```

OK, here's where things get exciting. First, we declare some variables in the local method scope: `maxCard` (five cards per player); `dealerCard` and `playerCard` (instances of `BJDCard`); and `dealerCardView` and `playerCardView` (instances of `UIImageView` that we added to our storyboard right at the beginning of the chapter).

We loop through the main code block five times, and for each iteration, we assign the values of our card model and view variables. Note that we populate the card model for `dealerCard` and `playerCard` directly from the public methods `dealerCardAtIndex` and `playerCardAtIndex` of the `BJDGameModel` class. If you investigate these methods, you'll see at they either return a `BJDCard` instance or `nil` if the index is greater than the highest index of the array of player cards, that is `[self.gameModel dealerCardAtIndex:2]` will return `nil` if the dealer only has two cards (indexes 0 and 1).

If the returned card is `nil`, then we simply hide the corresponding card view because it means that card has not yet been dealt:

```
dealerCardView.hidden = (dealerCard == nil);
```

and

```
playerCardView.hidden = (playerCard == nil);
```

If the corresponding card is not nil, we also check whether the BJDCard instance is face-up or not. If it's face-up, then we use the getCardImage method we wrote to retrieve an image to set on the UIImageView. If the card is face-down, then we default the image displayed in the UIImageView to our card back image:

```
dealerCardView.image = [UIImage imageNamed:@"card-back.png"];
```

Once you've added all this code to the renderCards method, you should find that when you build and run your app, the cards dealt to the dealer and player will render (see Figure 4-18).

Figure 4-18. Hmm… Should I stand or hit?

Things are starting to take shape! I want to play the game, but the Stand and Hit buttons are currently doing nothing. Let's change that.

Look, I cheated again, OK? I prewrote some of the code for automating the dealer's turn, so first off, scroll down BJViewController and uncomment the following three private dealer methods:

```
#pragma mark - Automated Dealer Play

-(void) showSecondDealerCard
{
    BJDCard *card = [self.gameModel lastDealerCard];
    card.isFaceUp = YES;
    [self renderCards];
    [self.gameModel updateGameStage];
    if (self.gameModel.gameStage != BJGameStageGameOver) {
        [self performSelector:@selector(showNextDealerCard) withObject:nil afterDelay:0.8];
    }

}

-(void) showNextDealerCard
{
    //next card
    BJDCard *card = [self.gameModel nextDealerCard];
    card.isFaceUp = YES;
    [self renderCards];
    [self.gameModel updateGameStage];
    if (self.gameModel.gameStage != BJGameStageGameOver) {
        [self performSelector:@selector(showNextDealerCard) withObject:nil afterDelay:0.8];
    }
}

- (void)playDealerTurn {
    self.standButton.enabled = self.hitButton.enabled = NO;
    [self performSelector:@selector(showSecondDealerCard) withObject:nil afterDelay:0.8];
}
```

showSecondDealerCard, showNextDealerCard, and playDealerTurn are all methods I wrote to automate the dealer's turn. So, once the player's turn finishes, the idea is that playDealerTurn should be called first. The first thing this method does is prevent any button interaction by disabling the Stand and Hit buttons.

Next, we make use of the super-handy performSelector:withObject:afterDelay method of NSObject that enables delayed method calls. The delay is defined in seconds, so we're setting a 0.8-second delay between each card rendered and dealt to the dealer.

The showNextDealerCard and playDealerTurn are virtually identical. The only difference is that when the second dealer card is turned face-up, it's already been dealt so we call

```
BJDCard *card = [self.gameModel lastDealerCard];
```

rather than

```
BJDCard *card = [self.gameModel nextDealerCard];
```

After each card is dealt and rendered, the controller also asks the model to update the game stage; that is, the game ends if the dealer hits the five-card limit or goes bust.

Responding to user interaction

Before the dealer can go, we need to write the code for the Hit and Stand button action methods. Stand is pretty straightforward:

```
- (IBAction)didTapStandButton:(id)sender {
    self.gameModel.gameStage = BJGameStageDealer;
    [self playDealerTurn];
}
```

The controller tells the model that the game stage has progressed to the dealer's turn and we'll then call playDealerTurn.

There's a bit more to the Hit method:

```
- (IBAction)didTapHitButton:(id)sender {
    BJDCard *card = [self.gameModel nextPlayerCard];
    card.isFaceUp = YES;
    [self renderCards];

    [self.gameModel updateGameStage];
    if (self.gameModel.gameStage == BJGameStageDealer) {
        [self playDealerTurn];
    }
}
```

First, the controller asks the model to deal another player card. The controller renders the card face-up in the view. Now the controller tells the model to update the game stage; that is, the game may now be over because the player has gone bust or reached the maximum five-card limit. BJViewController checks to see if the player's turn is over and if so, plays the automated dealer methods:

```
if (self.gameModel.gameStage == BJGameStageDealer) {
    [self playDealerTurn];
}
```

Awesome. You can now play an entire game of blackjack! Build and run to give it a go.

Oops, did your app crash at the end of the game? What did we miss?

Ah yes, we never got round to implementing the handleNotificationGameDidEnd: method in BJViewController. Do you remember the notification we subscribed to in the designated initializer of this class? We need to add that method! Here's the code:

```
-(void) handleNotificationGameDidEnd:(NSNotification *)notification
{
    NSDictionary *userInfo = notification.userInfo;

    NSNumber *num = userInfo[@"didDealerWin"];

    NSString *message = [num boolValue] ? @"Dealer won!" : @"You won!";
```

```
    UIAlertView *alert = [[UIAlertView alloc] initWithTitle:@"Game Over" message:message
delegate:nil cancelButtonTitle:nil otherButtonTitles:@"Play Again", nil];
    [alert show];
}
```

In our notification handler, we're able to extract the winner via the `userInfo` property. We're expecting a dictionary with an `NSNumber` property that's wrapping a Boolean primitive. So we also have to extract the primitive Boolean to check if the dealer won or not:

```
NSString *message = [num boolValue] ? @"Dealer won!" : @"You won!";
```

We end up with a winning message that we then display in an alert view (see Figure 4-19).

Figure 4-19. Yay! It only took me five build and run attempts to get a winning screenshot!

Protocols and the delegate pattern

But we're not quite done yet. Our app is no longer crashing, but as soon as we dismiss the alert, our game is over. The buttons are disabled and we have no way to play again. That's no good! What we'll do is change our OK button to read Play Again, and then restart the game as soon as the button is pressed.

How do we know when the button is pressed? The UIAlertView class does not expose its button properties, so we can't tap into the target-action mechanism in this instance. Instead, like many of Apple's iOS SDK components, UIAlertView subscribes to the delegate pattern.

UIAlertView has a weak reference property called a *delegate*. UIAlertView doesn't care which object wishes to be its delegate as long as the object implements the UIAlertViewDelegate protocol. A *protocol* is similar to a class interface: it defines a set of method signatures that the protocol will implement. However, a protocol can also define *optional* method signatures. In order for BJViewController to set itself as the delegate of the alert view, it first needs to declare that it implements the UIAlertViewDelegate protocol. To do this, we switch momentarily to the header file of BJViewController.

Change the first line of the interface declaration from

```
@interface BJViewController : UIViewController
```

to

```
@interface BJViewController : UIViewController <UIAlertViewDelegate>
```

If you check out the header file of UIAlertViewDelegate, you'll discover that all the methods of the UIAlertViewDelegate are optional. So the compiler won't generate any warnings about our code, even though we haven't added any UIAlertViewDelegate protocol methods yet.

> Note: When a class declares that it implements a protocol that includes mandatory methods, the compiler will display a warning if your class doesn't actually implement those methods.

Now back to the source file for BJViewController. We need to make a small change to the code that displays the alert in the handleNotificationGameDidEnd: method:

```
UIAlertView *alert = [[UIAlertView alloc] initWithTitle:@"Game Over" message:message
delegate:self cancelButtonTitle:nil otherButtonTitles:@"Play Again", nil];
[alert show];
```

Notice how we've now set ourselves as the delegate of the alert view?

Finally, we're going to add one of the UIAlertViewDelegate methods to our implementation of BJViewController:

```
- (void)alertView:(UIAlertView *)alertView clickedButtonAtIndex:(NSInteger)buttonIndex
{
    [self restartGame];
}
```

> Tip: When adding delegate methods, a quick way to implement the method code is to copy it directly from the Organizer's documentation and paste it into your class.

That's it, we're done! You should find that you can now build and run the game—and play blackjack again and again and again.

Summary

That was an epic journey! We touched on many parts of Objective-C in this chapter. I'm sure that some of them are still quite confusing. However, that's the reason you'll read the rest of this book: the syntax declaration and implementation for Objective-C methods, properties, instance variables, protocols, selectors, Interface Builder outlets, actions, and so on, will become more and more familiar as we progress with the *Birthday Reminder* app.

You've reached the end of Day 1! Tomorrow we'll return to our main project, *Birthday Reminder*. If you feel that we've covered a lot of code and you're a little lost, do not worry, we're going to spend the whole day tomorrow on Chapters 5 and 6, storyboarding the user interface of our app. There will be coding, but without the level of information overload you've experienced in this chapter.

Day 2

Storyboarding the User Interface

Chapter 5

iPhone App Navigation, Views, and View Controllers

It's Day 2 and the sun is shining (well, it is here in Brighton anyway!). We're back with our main *Birthday Reminder* project. Throughout today, we'll spend 100 percent of our time working on the user interface of our app.

This morning (this chapter), we'll explore the relationship between views and view controllers, as well as how to storyboard our app's navigation: pushing, popping, presenting, and dismissing view controllers on and off the navigation stack.

This afternoon (Chapter 6), we'll have fun with views and user interface controls, implementing and handling interactivity in some of the main screens of the *Birthday Reminder* app. We'll complete the day by spending some time integrating the iPhone's Photo Library and camera directly into our project.

Multiple view apps

Up until now, we've only included a single view and view controller in both the *Birthday Reminder* and blackjack apps. For some apps, like simple games, a single view is sufficient. However, multiple view apps enable large amounts of content to be presented to users through a small screen device in a clear and structured form.

Birthday Reminder is a multiview application. Each birthday object in our model includes a name, birth date, profile photo, gift notes, and a link to Facebook user details, or phone and e-mail details imported from the native Address Book. That would be a lot of data to display clearly in a single view for potentially hundreds of birthdays! By creating a multiview application on the home view, our user will see just summary information about each stored birthday, such as a small-profile photo, name, and the number of days until each birthday. When the user taps on a particular birthday, it drills down a level in the navigation, presenting the Birthday Detail view that includes a larger-profile photo display and full details about our friend and his or her birthday (see Figure 5-1).

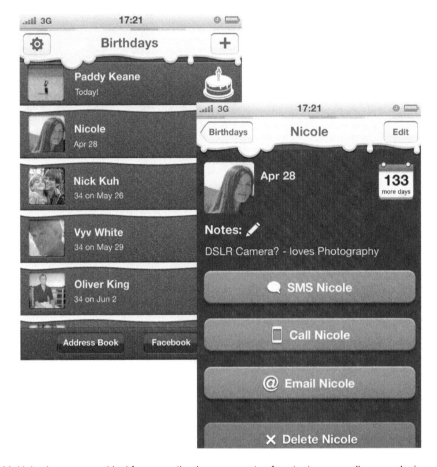

Figure 5-1. Multiple view apps are ideal for presenting large amounts of content on a small screen device.

We'll continue working on our main *Birthday Reminder* app throughout the remainder of this book. Open the *Birthday Reminder* Xcode project you built in Chapter 3. Alternatively, open the starting source code for this chapter.

> Note: If you decide to start working from the source code at any point during the book, be sure to update the bundle identifier in the Info.plist from com.apress.BirthdayReminder to com.yourdomain.BirthdayReminder.

Mastering views and view controllers

In the first half of this chapter, I walk you through the basics of views and view controllers. By working with storyboards, you'll learn how easy it is to build up a navigation hierarchy between screens in your app. You'll also gain understanding of the view life cycle and when and where to add code to view controllers in response to users navigating your app.

With your *Birthday Reminder* project open, begin by deleting any label or other subview you previously added to the main view in the Hello World example.

Adding a navigation controller

In order to add a Birthday Detail scene, we'll first add a navigation controller instance to our storyboard. Navigation controllers manage drilldown stacks of multiple view controllers. As a new view controller is pushed onto the navigation controller stack, the navigation controller animates the current view off screen left and slides in the new view from the right.

Currently, we have a single view controller and a single view in our storyboard. I'd like you to select the view controller and not the view. To do this, click the circular orange icon below and to the left of the view (see Figure 5-2).

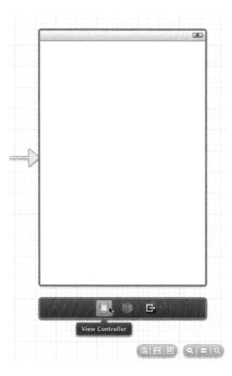

Figure 5-2. Selecting the view controller

With the view controller selected in the storyboard, adding a new parent navigation controller is simple work from Xcode's menu bar: Editor ➤ Embed In ➤ Navigation Controller. The result should look like Figure 5-3.

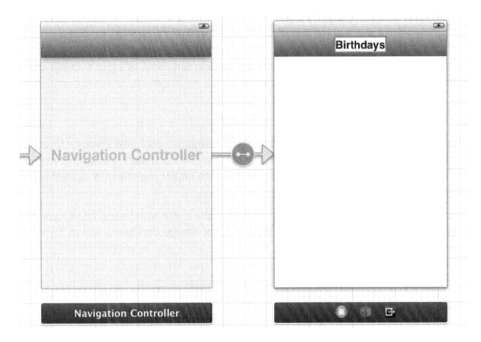

Figure 5-3. A view controller embedded in a navigation controller

Once embedded in a navigation controller, the view controller inherits a navigation bar from its new parent container view controller. Double-click the simulated navigation bar of the view controller to enter the navigation title **Birthdays** (see Figure 5-3).

Storyboard scenes and the root view controller

Every main view or screen in iOS Apps is typically owned and managed by an instance of Apple's `UIViewController` class. In order to create our multiple-view app, we'll add additional view controllers to the storyboard, each of which will control its own view. The combination of a view and view controller is referred to as a *scene* in storyboard terminology.

The very first view controller that is presented by your app is known as the *root view controller*. Did you notice that the new navigation controller in our storyboard has an arrow pointing to it from its left side? That is Xcode's way of indicating that this is the root view controller. Be sure not to delete the root view controller from your storyboard, or else Xcode's compiler won't be able to interpret your storyboard anymore. ☹

Although our home view controller is now embedded in a navigation controller, we still only have a single scene in our app, albeit with a navigation bar. We're now going to add a second scene to our storyboard, which will eventually become the Birthday Detail view. We add new scenes by dragging new view controller instances from the Object Library onto the storyboard. I find it easier to do this with the storyboard zoomed out a little. To achieve this, tap the minus magnifying glass button on the storyboard once (bottom-right corner of the editor pane). Then drag and drop a new view controller (UIViewController) instance from the Object Library onto the storyboard (see Figure 5-4).

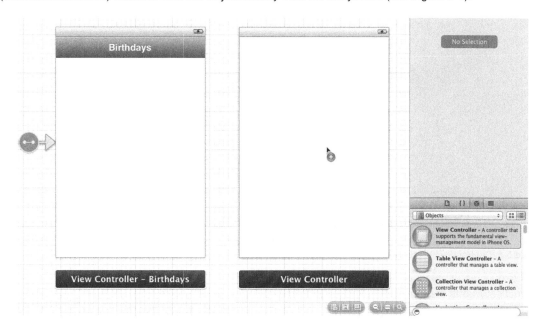

Figure 5-4. Adding a new view controller scene

Did you notice that the new view controller doesn't have a navigation bar added to it like our first view controller? That's because we haven't connected it to our navigation controller yet. Apart from when it's transitioning views, a navigation controller only shows one view controller from its stack at a time: the top one. To push our new view controller onto the navigation controller, we need to create a *segue* connection.

Pushing a view controller with a segue

A segue or UIStoryboardSegue is an object that defines a visual transition from one view controller to another. Add a button to your first view controller, name it Push Birthday Detail View Controller (hmmm, catchy!), and then create a segue from the button to the second view controller by control-dragging from the button to the second view controller (see Figure 5-5).

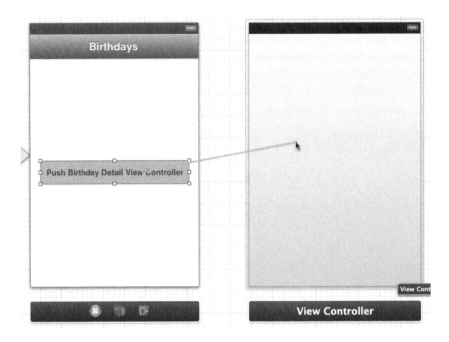

Figure 5-5. Control-drag to create a segue

A contextual menu presents you with three types of segue: Push, Modal, and Custom. Select Push. Xcode automatically adds the inherited navigation bar from our navigation controller to the new view controller, and displays an arrow between the first and second view controllers to indicate the new segue connection (see Figure 5-6).

Figure 5-6. The new segue connection

Add a title to the second view controller, Birthday Detail. Build and run your app. You should be able to navigate between the first and second view controllers using the button on the first controller and the dynamically generated Back button on the second. Pretty easy, huh?

Creating view controller classes

At this point, we could happily continue to add new view controller scenes to our storyboard, and connect them with segues to our hearts' content. Our storyboard would grow, but no new Objective-C classes would be added to our project. Storyboarding has its limitations, and our app will be kind of boring if we can't add view controller–specific code at some point. The solution is to create subclasses of UIViewController and assign them to each view controller in our storyboard via the identity inspector.

Before we create the new subclasses of UIViewController, let's organize our Xcode project to keep our user interface classes separate from our data classes. In the Finder, create a new folder within your project titled user-interface, and within that folder create a subfolder titled view-controllers. Then select the top-level BirthdayReminder group in Xcode, and add the folders to your project as new groups: File ➤ Add Files to "BirthdayReminder" (see Figure 5-7).

Figure 5-7. Keeping our project organized

In the project navigator, select the newly added view-controllers group and with the ⌘N shortcut or File ➤ New ➤ File, choose the Objective-C class option from the Cocoa Touch file templates. Name the new class BRHomeViewController and change the subclass to UIViewController. As shown in Figure 5-8, leave Targeted for iPad and With XIB for User Interface unchecked.

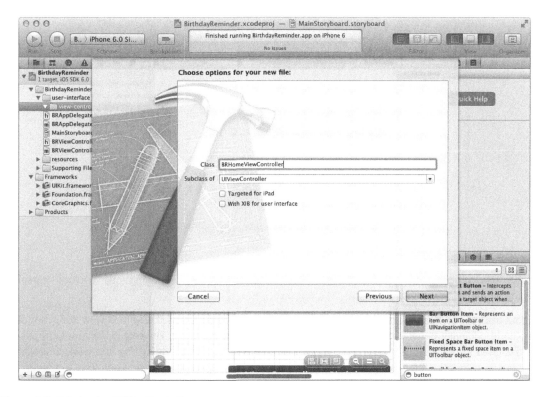

Figure 5-8. Subclassing UIViewController

Once you've created `BRHomeViewController` header and source files, repeat the process to create another `UIViewController` subclass named `BRBirthdayDetailViewController`.

We now need to connect our new view controller subclasses to our two storyboard view controllers. To do so, select the first view controller and change its custom class via the identity inspector to `BRHomeViewController` (see Figure 5-9).

Figure 5-9. Setting the custom class of the first home view controller

Repeat this process for the Birthday Detail view controller, changing its custom class to BRBirthdayDetailViewController.

BRViewController header and source files are now redundant. This was the default view controller class that Xcode originally generated for us when we first created our project. By default, BRViewController was assigned to our first view controller; we've just changed that, reassigning the first view controller so that it is now owned by the new BRHomeViewController class. Let's clean up and get rid of the redundant BRViewController header and source files. Multiselect BRViewController.h and BRViewController.m files in the project navigator, and then hit the Delete key. Next, click the Move to Trash button in the dialog window (see Figure 5-10).

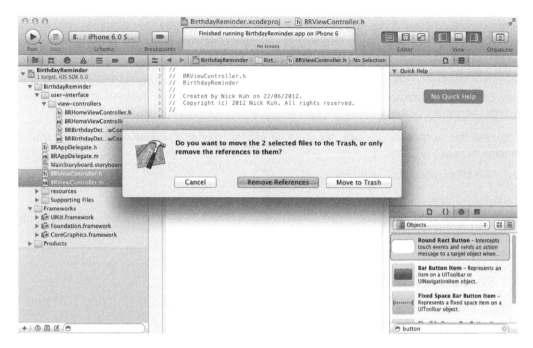

Figure 5-10. Deleting redundant BRViewController files

View and view controller life cycle

To become a good iOS programmer, it's essential to understand the life cycle of views and view controllers. In our app, we currently have one navigation controller that manages the flow of child view controllers and their views. When the navigation controller transitions from the home to the detail view controller, it moves the home view off the screen and slides the detail view onto the screen. During this process, the navigation controller invokes the following important view controller methods in our two view controller subclasses:

- (void)viewWillAppear:(BOOL)animated;

- (void)viewDidAppear:(BOOL)animated;

- (void)viewWillDisappear:(BOOL)animated;

- (void)viewDidDisappear:(BOOL)animated;

If the Birthday Detail view controller is pushed onto the navigation controller, then viewWillDisappear: is invoked on the home view controller just before its view begins to animate off screen. As soon as the animation completes, the view is automatically removed from the view hierarchy and viewDidDisappear: is invoked on the home view controller.

Likewise, just before the Birthday Detail view controller is animated onto the navigation controller stack, viewWillAppear: is invoked on the Birthday Detail view controller. Once the slide in push animation completes, viewDidAppear: is then triggered.

The Birthday Detail view controller is popped off the navigation stack when the Back button is tapped. The Birthday Detail view controller receives a viewWillDisappear: callback, followed shortly afterward by viewDidDisappear:.

Let's try this for ourselves. Replace the current BRBirthdayDetailViewController.m source file implementation with the following:

```
#import "BRBirthdayDetailViewController.h"

@implementation BRBirthdayDetailViewController

-(id) initWithCoder:(NSCoder *)aDecoder
{
    self = [super initWithCoder:aDecoder];
    if (self) {
        NSLog(@"initWithCoder");
    }
    return self;
}

-(void) dealloc
{
    NSLog(@"dealloc");
}

-(void) viewDidLoad
{
    [super viewDidLoad];
    NSLog(@"viewDidLoad");
}

-(void) viewWillAppear:(BOOL)animated
{
    [super viewWillAppear:animated];
    NSLog(@"viewWillAppear");
}

-(void) viewDidAppear:(BOOL)animated
{
    [super viewDidAppear:animated];
    NSLog(@"viewDidAppear");
}

-(void)viewWillDisappear:(BOOL)animated
{
    [super viewWillDisappear:animated];
    NSLog(@"viewWillDisappear");
}
```

```
-(void)viewDidDisappear:(BOOL)animated
{
    [super viewDidDisappear:animated];
    NSLog(@"viewDidDisappear");
}
```

@end

> Note: When overriding UIViewController methods, be sure to call the super method implementation to avoid any problems at runtime.

Build and run the project and check out the debug log as you push and pop BRBirthdayDetailViewController.

Familiarize yourself with the order that these methods are invoked. There are also a few additional view controller methods in the new code that you should also be aware of.

viewDidLoad

viewDidLoad is a method triggered in all subclasses of UIViewController as soon as its main view first loads; any storyboard outlets are available at this point in your view controller code. But be careful of viewDidLoad. It is not a view controller initializer. Indeed, viewDidLoad can be called multiple times during the life of a view controller. If the system gets short of memory, the default behavior for UIViewController instances is to release their view if it's not on screen. It's perfectly reasonable that BRHomeViewController's view might be removed if a memory warning is triggered by the system and the Birthday Detail view is the current on-screen view. Note, however, that a memory warning will not remove the BRHomeViewController instance from the navigation stack, just its view. If the user then navigates back to the Home view controller, iOS rebuilds the home view from the storyboard and viewDidLoad is invoked a second time on the Home view controller.

> Tip: viewDidLoad is the first point of access to your Interface Builder outlets. So when viewDidLoad is invoked, you should execute any view customization code.

View controller initializers

The best place to create model data retained by your view controller throughout its life cycle is at the point of instantiation and not when viewDidLoad is invoked. A common mistake by new iOS programmers is to initialize *everything* during the viewDidLoad method.

Hooking into the initializer of a UIViewController is not as obvious as it could be. There are two important initializers to be aware of: initWithNibName:bundle: and initWithCoder:. Typically, a view controller is either initialized with an NIB/XIB file or a storyboard file. We're sticking with Storyboards for all the initialization in *Birthday Reminder*, so it's the initWithCoder: initializer that we should hook into when instantiating models or mapping dictionaries.

dealloc

Dealloc is the last method that is invoked in any NSObject subclass instance just before being released from memory. So you can see that when you pop the Birthday Detail view controller off the navigation stack, it is discarded by iOS and not retained, keeping our app's memory footprint to a minimum.

Thanks to ARC, any strong references to property iVars are released automatically, so there's no need to directly nil out iVars in dealloc anymore. This used to be a major cause of memory leaks prior to ARC and iOS 5.

> Note: The compiler will not permit direct calls to [super dealloc]. You can guarantee that dealloc will be invoked for all subclasses of NSObject in the inheritance tree, however.

Navigating view controllers

For the remainder of the morning, we'll pick up speed implementing our app navigation. You'll learn how to populate navigation bars and toolbars with bar button items, and how and when to present and dismiss modal view controllers in your app.

We'll continue to storyboard this morning and discover just how easy it is to build out our *Birthday Reminder* navigation hierarchy via Xcode's storyboard WYSIWYG drag-and-drop UI.

Bars and bar button items

Navigation and toolbars feature in thousands of iPhone and iPad apps. As we'll learn in Chapter 9, they are easy to customize and instantly recognizable by iOS users.

As you'll discover in the remainder of this chapter, in iOS it's very easy to populate both navigation bars and toolbars with buttons—not the standard buttons we've used previously, but a component in iOS known as a *bar button item* (UIBarButtonItem).

Navigation bars

Navigation bars reside at the top of the screen and typically comprise of a title and bar button items: one or more buttons to the left and to the right of the centered title. By default, a navigation bar controlled by a navigation controller automatically displays a Back button item to the left of the title, enabling users to easily back up through a series of screens they've delved through in the hierarchy of our app.

Our navigation controller includes a navigation bar (UINavigationBar) as standard. We already know how to modify the title of each view controller in our navigation through storyboarding. Now let's add a couple of bar button items to the home view navigation bar. It's as simple as dragging them from the Object Library onto the left and right side of the navigation bar (see Figure 5-11).

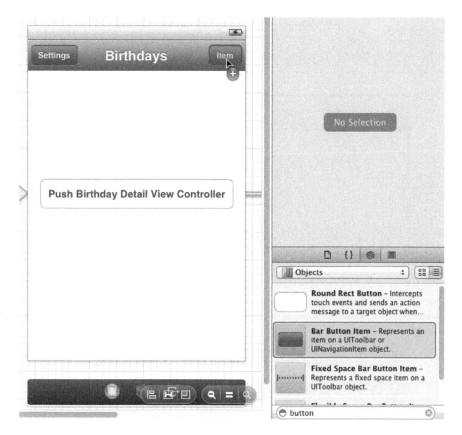

Figure 5-11. Adding bar button items to a navigation bar

Bar button items (UIBarButtonItem) are not the same as regular buttons (UIButton); they can reside only in navigation bars and toolbars. A bar button item can display a text title, an image icon, or a custom view. We'll explore these options when we move onto appearance skinning in Chapter 9. For now, we're going stick to text, so type in **Settings** for the left button and **Add Birthday** for the right button.

> Note: In earlier versions of iOS, navigation bars were limited to three items: a title and single left and right bar button items. In iOS 5 and 6, we have more flexibility. We can add multiple left and right bar button items, but due to space constraints, I'd not recommend more than one item per side on iPhone.

Toolbars

We've already learned that a navigation bar is automatically generated when we embed a view controller within a navigation controller. Navigation controllers also include a toolbar free of charge. By default, it's hidden, but we can change that. Select the navigation controller and toggle on the Shows Toolbar option (see Figure 5-12). Voilà! A toolbar appears for all of our view controllers!

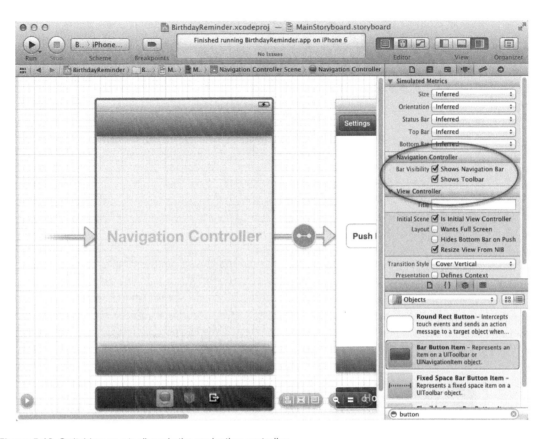

Figure 5-12. Switching on a toolbar via the navigation controller

Now all of the view controllers in the navigation stack will inherit the parent navigation controller's toolbar. That's what we want for the home view, but not the detail view. That's easy enough to solve. Select the detail view controller in the storyboard and toggle on the Hides Bottom Bar on Push attribute. Build and run, and you should see a toolbar for the first view, but not the second.

Now to add some bar button items to the toolbar for our Home view controller. Select the Home view controller in the storyboard and drag two bar button item instances onto it from the Object Library. Name them Address Book and Facebook respectively. Notice the way toolbars are different from navigation bars: the new bar button items align to the left rather than one on either side of a title. We can center our two buttons by adding three instances of the Flexible Space bar button item (see Figure 5-13).

Figure 5-13. Centering Toolbar bar button items

Presenting a modal view controller

Earlier in the chapter, we learned how to *push* a view controller onto a navigation controller stack using view controllers and segue transitions. Another common method of changing the front visible view controller is by *presenting* a modal view controller.

Modal view controllers are not added to the navigation stack, but rather placed in front of the topmost view controller: in front of the actual navigation controller in the case of *Birthday Reminder*.

We're now going to present a new Edit Birthday view controller that is displayed in our app whenever the user is either adding or editing a birthday. The process to set up and present a modal view controller is very similar to setting up a new view controller to push. First, drag a new view controller instance from the Object Library onto the storyboard. You can place new storyboard scenes wherever you like, but to keep things organized for our project, place the new Edit Birthday view controller above the Birthday Detail view controller.

Now to create a new segue transition and connect the new view controller into our hierarchy. Control-drag from the Add Birthday button in the Birthday Detail view to the new Edit Birthday view controller. From the choice of storyboard segues, this time select Modal. The results should look like Figure 5-14.

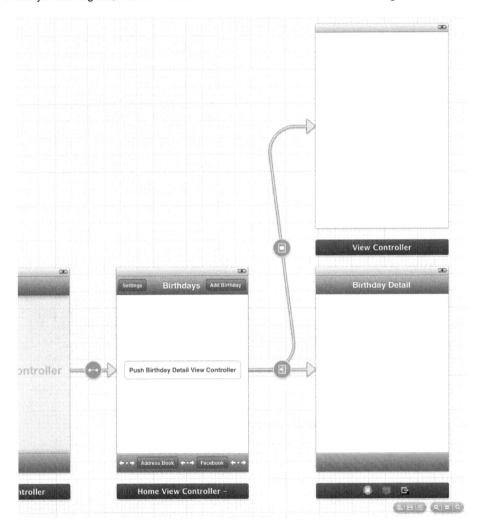

Figure 5-14. Creating a modal segue

Try a build and run. You should be presented with the new view controller when tapping the Add Birthday button, which animates in from the bottom of the screen. Why do you think the new view doesn't have a navigation bar like all the other views in our app? Because the new modal view controller has no navigation controller as its parent container: it's simply presented in front of the existing navigation. To remedy this, we actually need to place our Edit Birthday view controller within its own navigation controller. We've done this before. Simply select the new Edit Birthday view controller and from Xcode's menu: Editor

➤ Embed In ➤ Navigation Controller. The Edit Birthday view controller slides right in the storyboard to make way for the newly added navigation controller (see Figure 5-15).

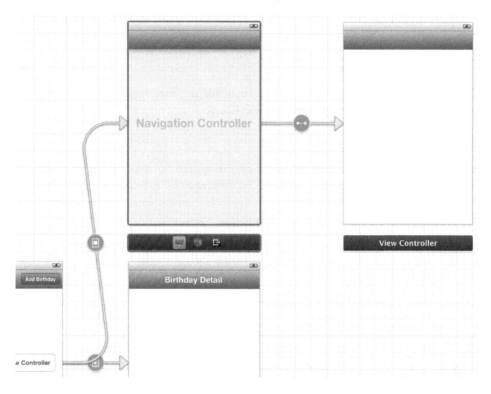

Figure 5-15. A navigation controller presented modally

Xcode is intelligent enough to replace the Edit Birthday view controller with its new navigation controller. The navigation controller becomes the actual view controller that is presented when Add Birthday is tapped. In the storyboard, select the Edit Birthday view controller again and enter the title **Edit Birthday**, and add Cancel and Save bar button items either side of the title (see Figure 5-16).

Figure 5-16. Edit Birthday bar button items and title

Dismissing a modal view controller

Now we reach a minor roadblock: how do we dismiss the modal navigation controller when the Cancel button is tapped? The answer is not to drag a new segue from the Cancel button to the root navigation controller. You can do this to create a new segue, but the result is that a duplicate of the root view controller is created by the storyboard, and pushed or presented on top of the existing modal view controller. That's not what we're after.

There are two ways we can dismiss our modal view controller, and both require us to write code. Let's step through option 1, by creating an *unwind segue* (new in iOS 6).

Unwind segues

Unwind segues can be created in storyboards as long as you've created an *unwind action* in the view controller you wish to unwind to (navigate back to). An unwind action is recognized by the compiler based on the following method signature format:

```
-(IBAction)unwindActionMethodName:(UIStoryboardSegue *)segue;
```

The method name can be whatever we like, as long as it matches this signature format. In our app, we want to unwind back to the Home view controller when the Cancel button is tapped, so that's where we'll declare and implement an unwind action.

Add the following method declaration to BRHomeViewController.h:

```
-(IBAction)unwindBackToHomeViewController:(UIStoryboardSegue *)segue;
```

Switch to the BRHomeViewController.m source file and implement the unwind action:

```
-(IBAction)unwindBackToHomeViewController:(UIStoryboardSegue *)segue
{
    NSLog(@"unwindBackToHomeViewController!");
}
```

Back with the focus on the Edit Birthday view controller in your storyboard, Control-drag from the Cancel button to the Exit icon below and to the right of the Exit view controller. A contextual menu should appear and enable you to select your unwindBackToHomeViewController: unwind action, as shown in Figure 5-17. You've just created an unwind segue!

Figure 5-17. Creating an unwind segue

Build and run. You should now be able to dismiss the modally presented Edit Birthday view controller when you tap the Cancel bar button item.

When performing an unwind segue, iOS automatically unwinds the exiting view controller to the view controller that owns the unwind action. That's why we don't have to write any execution code to deal with dismissing the modal view controller. But hold on, what if we do want to dismiss a modal view controller with code? I'm glad you asked that!

Dismissing a modal view controller with code

In your storyboard, remove the exit segue you just created. To do this, Control-click the Cancel button and tap the X button next to the unwindBackToHomeViewController: action.

Now create a new view controller subclass for your Edit Birthday scene, naming it BRBirthdayEditViewController, and assign it to your Edit Birthday view on the storyboard using the identity inspector. If you need help with this, flip back to the "Creating View Controller Classes" section of this chapter for step-by-step instructions.

Using the Assistant Editor layout, control-drag to create a new action from the Cancel button to the BRBirthdayEditViewController.h header named cancelAndDismiss (see Figure 5-18).

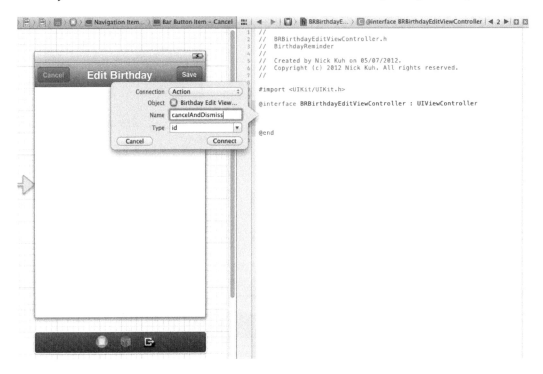

Figure 5-18. Adding a cancelAndDismiss: action

Switching to implement the new cancelAndDismiss: action in BRBirthdayEditViewController.m source file, we dismiss the modal view controller by calling UIViewController's dismissModalViewControllerAnimated:completion: method.

```
- (IBAction)cancelAndDismiss:(id)sender {
    NSLog(@"Cancel!");
    [self dismissViewControllerAnimated:YES completion:^{
        //any code we place inside this block will
        //run once the view controller has been dismissed
        NSLog(@"Dismiss complete!");
    }];
}
```

In Objective-C, a block is a segment of code that is passed around like a variable. The second parameter in UIViewController's dismissModalViewControllerAnimated:completion: method is a block. When the dismiss animation completes, our block of code executes.

Build and run. You should be able to dismiss the Birthday Edit view controller and see a delay between the Cancel! and Dismiss Complete! debug logs.

But what if we want to present other modal view controllers in our app? We'll end up having to copy and paste the `cancelAndDismiss:` method into other view controller subclasses. Duplicate code is never a good thing for a good programmer! Luckily for us, Objective-C is an object-oriented language, so we can solve this thanks to inheritance and subclassing.

Subclassing: creating a core view controller

We now have three custom view controllers in our project. Each of those view controllers is a subclass of Apple's `UIViewController` class. Now here's a very handy technique I'd like to introduce: we can create a core sub class of `UIViewController` and then tweak all of our individual view controller classes to subclass the core view controller rather than `UIViewController` directly. The benefit of doing this is that we can then add common/shared methods and properties to the core view controller class, and all individual view controllers will inherit those methods and properties automatically.

Confused? Or does that make perfect sense?! It should become clearer once we get into the code.

First, let's create our new core view controller class. Select the `view-controllers` group in the project navigator and then File ➤ New ➤ File to choose the Objective-C class option from the Cocoa Touch file templates. Name the new class `BRCoreViewController` and ensure the subclass is set to `UIViewController`.

Type in the following two Interface Builder action method signatures directly into the `BRCoreViewController.h` header:

```
#import <UIKit/UIKit.h>

@interface BRCoreViewController : UIViewController

- (IBAction)cancelAndDismiss:(id)sender;
- (IBAction)saveAndDismiss:(id)sender;

@end
```

Switch to `BRCoreViewController.m` and begin deleting all the default method code that Xcode has added from the file template. Replace it with the following implementation:

```
#import "BRCoreViewController.h"

@interface BRCoreViewController ()

@end

@implementation BRCoreViewController

-(void) viewDidLoad
{
    [super viewDidLoad];
    self.view.backgroundColor = [UIColor grayColor];
}

-(IBAction)cancelAndDismiss:(id)sender
```

```
{
    NSLog(@"Cancel");
    [self dismissViewControllerAnimated:YES completion:^{
        //view controller dismiss animation completed
    }];
}

- (IBAction)saveAndDismiss:(id)sender
{
    NSLog(@"Save");
    [self dismissViewControllerAnimated:YES completion:^{
        //view controller dismiss animation completed
    }];
}

@end
```

In addition to the cancelAndDismiss: and saveAndDismiss: action methods, we're setting our view's background color to gray via the viewDidLoad method; this results in any subclass of BRCoreViewController automatically inheriting this code and coloring their own view gray. Clever!

Open the header files of the view controllers we've created so far: BRHomeViewController.h, BRBirthdayDetailViewController.h, and BRBirthdayEditViewController.h. All three classes currently inherit from UIViewController directly. Change this so that they each inherit from BRCoreViewController instead:

For BRHomeViewController.h:

```
#import <UIKit/UIKit.h>
#import "BRCoreViewController.h"

@interface BRHomeViewController : BRCoreViewController

@end
```

For BRBirthdayDetailViewController.h:

```
#import <UIKit/UIKit.h>
#import "BRCoreViewController.h"

@interface BRHomeViewController : BRCoreViewController

@end
```

For BRBirthdayEditViewController.h:

```
#import <UIKit/UIKit.h>
#import "BRCoreViewController.h"

@interface BRBirthdayEditViewController : BRCoreViewController
    - (IBAction)cancelAndDismiss:(id)sender;

@end
```

Note how we should also delete the cancelAndDismiss: action method from BRBirthdayEditViewController.h because this action is now handled by the BRCoreViewController superclass. Switch to BRBirthdayEditViewController.m and remove the entire implementation of cancelAndDismiss:.

We have yet to connect our Save button in the birthday edit view to our newly added saveAndDismiss: action. Control-drag from the Save button to its view controller owner, as shown in Figure 5-19. You'll be prompted with all of the Interface Builder outlets and action connections. Select the saveAndDismiss action. Do you see how it was inherited from our core view controller?

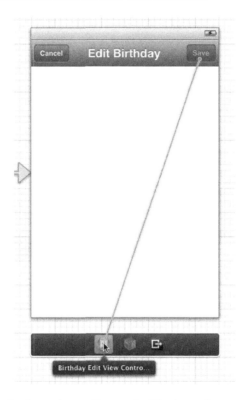

Figure 5-19. Connecting the Save bar button item to the saveAndDismiss: action

Build and run (see Figure 5-20). Hey, has every view turned gray?! Here's where the penny should (hopefully) drop. By taking advantage of adding a core view controller subclass, we're able to change every single instance of any view controller that subclasses our core view controller in just one place: the core view controller class code. At the moment, every view controller inherits the gray background view color setting code. Can you see how we might extend this technique further for *Birthday Reminder*? All of our views have a custom background image in the designs, a checkered background like our launch image. In one convenient place, we'll be able to add this image to the background of every view in our app that subclasses core view controller. We'll do this when we get to the chapter on skinning, but for now, we've got a bunch of scenes to add to our storyboard.

Figure 5-20. The benefits of subclassing view controllers—if you like gray, that is

Our Edit Birthday view controller is used for both adding and editing birthdays. So we'll create a second segue connection to the Edit Birthday navigation controller. Add an Edit bar button item to the right side of the Birthday Detail navigation bar, and then Control-drag from the new button to the Edit Birthday navigation controller. Select Modal from the Storyboard Segue transition options (see Figure 5-21).

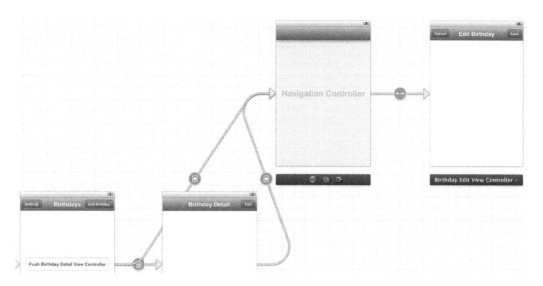

Figure 5-21. Multiple segue connections to the Edit Birthday navigation controller

Adding a note-taking view controller

When users view one of their friend's birthdays in the Birthday Detail view, they'll be able to edit notes on their friends, such as gift ideas. As a general rule, I recommend presenting modal view controllers whenever your app is enabling your user to edit or add data. This technique creates a distinction between viewing saved data and editing saved data.

Add a new view controller scene to your storyboard to the right of the Birthday Detail scene. As we're going to present the new note editing view controller modally, we'll embed it in its own navigation controller like we did with the Edit Birthday view controller. Select the new view controller. From the menu bar, select Editor ➤ Embed In ➤ Navigation Controller. Now title the new notes view controller **Edit Notes** and add Cancel and Save buttons like we did for the Edit Birthday view controller (see Figure 5-22).

Drag and drop a new Round Rect button (not to be confused with the bar button item) from the Object Library onto the Birthday Detail view, and title it **Edit Notes**.

Your new view controller and navigation controller should resemble Figure 5-22.

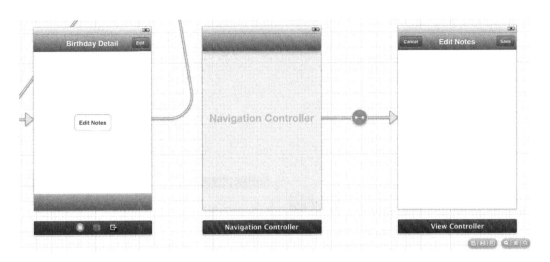

Figure 5-22. Adding a note-taking view

Now connect the new view controller with a modal segue by control-dragging from the Edit Notes button to the new navigation controller. Select the Modal option.

Now to create a view controller class for the Edit Notes scene. Create and add a new class to the view-controllers group and name it BRNotesEditViewController. This time, instead of subclassing UIViewController, simply subclass BRCoreViewController (see Figure 5-23).

Figure 5-23. BRNotesEditViewController subclasses BRCoreViewController

Back in your storyboard, select the new Edit Notes view controller, and using the identity inspector, change the custom class to BRNotesEditViewController. Now Control-drag from the Cancel and Save bar button items to create Interface Builder connections to the cancelAndDismiss: and saveAndDismiss: action methods of the owning view controller respectively.

Build and run to confirm that you can now open and dismiss the new Edit Notes view controller.

Flip to a settings view

Let's continue to build our web of view controller navigation. Add a new view controller to your storyboard just below the Birthday Detail view controller. Embed it in a navigation controller. Add a title, Settings, and a Done bar button item to the right of the title (see Figure 5-24).

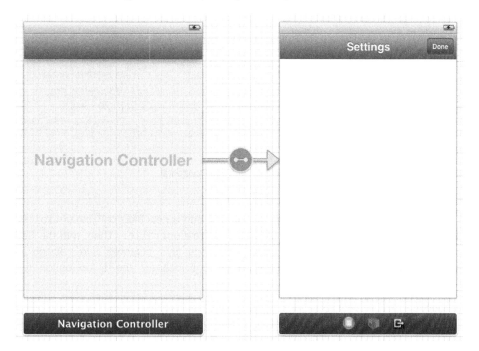

Figure 5-24. A new Settings view controller embedded in a navigation controller

Control-drag from the Settings bar button item on the home view to the Settings navigation controller and create a new modal segue connection.

The iOS SDK includes multiple built-in transition animation options when pushing and presenting view controllers. Rather than sticking with the default slide in from the bottom of the screen animation, we'll set our new segue to flip in the Settings navigation controller. As highlighted in Figure 5-25, you can click and select the new segue, and then using the attributes inspector, change the Transition setting to Flip Horizontal.

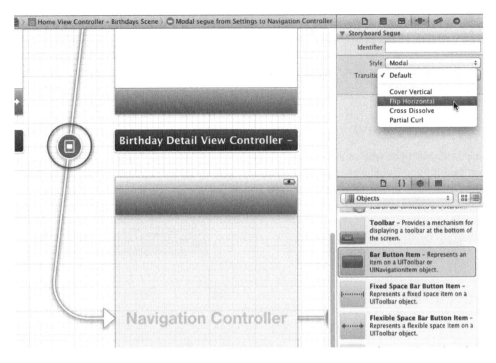

Figure 5-25. Changing the transition style of a modal segue to Flip Horizontal

Build and run—and take it for a spin (pun intended!).

In order to dismiss the Settings view controller, we need to add a new BRCoreViewController subclass to our view-controller group and name it BRSettingsViewController. Then, with the Settings view controller selected in the storyboard, use the identity inspector to assign the new BRSettingsViewController class. Now Control-drag and connect the Done button to the view controller's saveAndDismiss: action method.

While we're working on the Settings view controller, let's add one last view controller, linked from the Settings scene. The new notification time view controller is the view controller that enables our users to change the default notification time of their birthday reminders.

First, add a new Round Rect button to the Settings view and title it **Set Alert Time**. Then add a new view controller scene to the right of the Settings scene. Give it a title, Alert Time, and then Control-drag from the Set Alert Time button to the newly added view controller, and create a push segue. This should add a simulated navigation bar to the new view controller. Enter a title, **Alert Time**, as shown in Figure 5-26.

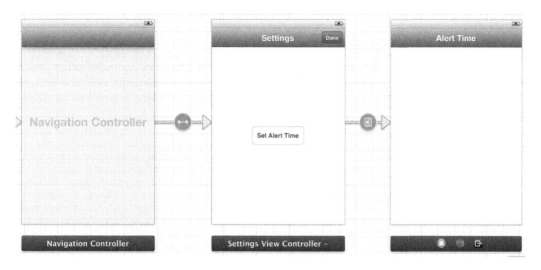

Figure 5-26. Pushing a view controller onto the modally presented Settings view controller

In keeping with all of our view controllers so far, let's create another subclass of BRCoreViewController, name it BRNotificationTimeViewController, and with the notification time view controller selected in the storyboard, use the identity inspector to assign the newly created BRNotificationTimeViewController class.

Build and run. If all of your views are gray, then the view controller class association should have worked as expected.

Summary

We came a long way in this chapter.

We explored how to build a complex navigation hierarchy using Xcode's drag-and-drop storyboarding technology. You should now be familiar with the limitations of storyboarding: we need to subclass UIViewController and assign our subclasses to storyboard view controllers in order to do anything fun with our user interface.

We touched on the benefits of adding a shared core view controller. As your app grows, so does the number of views and view controllers in your project. By using the core view controller approach, you can centralize many of your reusable methods and properties. Apart from the benefit of writing less code, this means bugs should be resolvable in one place and not require fixes in every one of your view controller classes. Skinning views also becomes a centralized procedure: much cleaner and more manageable, as we shall see in Chapter 9.

A challenge

Here's a challenge to test your newfound storyboarding knowledge. Build a new app from scratch using the Single View Application Xcode project template. Embed the default view controller into a navigation controller. Add a button or bar button item that pushes on another view controller to the first view controller. Finally, see if you can also create a modally presented view controller that can be dismissed. Let me know how it works out.

Chapter 6

Views, Controls, Camera, Action!

It's time for us to start working with user interface controls and learn how to handle view interaction. We'll spend the rest of the day developing the user interface of the edit birthday, edit notes, and notification time views. These three candidates utilize a number of controls from the iOS SDK (such as date pickers, switches, and text fields), which we'll add to our views along with code to handle control interaction.

By the end of the day (and chapter), we'll have progressed to the use of gesture recognizers to catch finger interaction events. We'll even get as far as learning how to utilize the iPhone's camera and Photo Library directly from our app. There's plenty to learn here, so we'd better get started!

User interface controls and components

As developers, we have two choices when adding user interface instance components to our views: create and add them in code, or add them via drag-and-drop to nibs and storyboard files. Throughout the development of the *Birthday Reminder* app, we primarily use the simpler drag-and-drop approach of developing our UIs directly in our storyboard files.

As you become a more advanced iOS developer, you may find that occasionally creating a component in code is the better or only option you have. Storyboarding is always going to have its limitations. For *Birthday Reminder*, however, the vast majority of our user interface design and layout is achieved perfectly well with storyboarding.

Edit birthday view: date pickers, switches, and text fields

With your *Birthday Reminder* project open in Xcode, select the edit birthday view and begin by adding an instance of each of the following from the Object Library to the view (see Figure 6-1). Use the size inspector to set the position and size values listed.

- A *text field* (UITextField): x=89, y=22, width=221.

- A *label* (UILabel): Change the text to **Include Year**, and then position and size (x=125, y=165, width=99, height=27).

- A *switch* (UISwitch): x=231, y=165.

- A *date picker* (UIDatePicker): x=0, y=200, width=320.

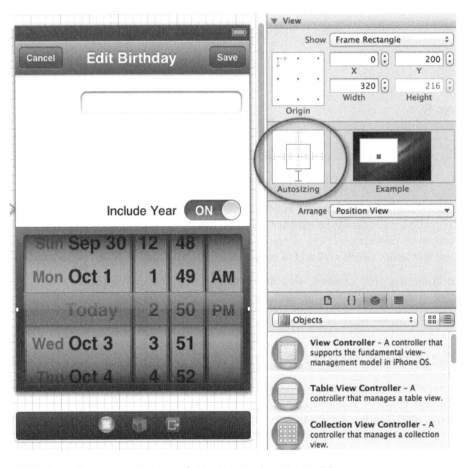

Figure 6-1. Edit birthday view populated with text field, label, switch, and date picker

With our current implementation of this view, the date picker, Include Year label, and switch are going to float above an 88-point high empty space on the taller iPhone 5 display. By using autosizing, however, we can change this and force these components to remain pinned to the bottom of the UI. On each of these three components, set the bottom margin to remain fixed by modifying the autosize mask values as shown in Figure 6-1. Select each of the components in turn to apply the new autosizing values.

Next, we're going to create Interface Builder outlets in `BRBirthdayEditViewController` for our four new user interface components as well as an outlet for the Save bar button item.

Ensure the Edit Birthday view controller scene is selected in your storyboard, hide the right-side Inspector pane, and switch Xcode to the Assistant Editor mode (see Figure 6-2).

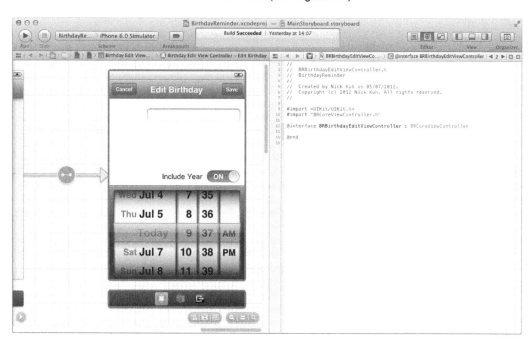

Figure 6-2. Xcode's Assistant Editor layout: perfect for creating Interface Builder connections

Control-drag from the Save bar button item, name text field, year label, switch, and date picker to create five weak outlets in the `BRBirthdayEditViewController.h` header with the following names: `saveButton`, `nameTextField`, `includeYearLabel`, `includeYearSwitch`, and `datePicker`, respectively. The end result should add the following code to your header file:

```
#import <UIKit/UIKit.h>
#import "BRCoreViewController.h"

@interface BRBirthdayEditViewController : BRCoreViewController

@property (weak, nonatomic) IBOutlet UIBarButtonItem *saveButton;
@property (weak, nonatomic) IBOutlet UITextField *nameTextField;
@property (weak, nonatomic) IBOutlet UILabel *includeYearLabel;
```

```
@property (weak, nonatomic) IBOutlet UISwitch *includeYearSwitch;
@property (weak, nonatomic) IBOutlet UIDatePicker *datePicker;
```

@end

Configuring text fields and responding to text changes

Back in the storyboard, let's set a couple of attributes for the name text field. Select the text field, and using the attributes inspector, begin by entering **Name**, the placeholder text. Placeholder text displays in a light-gray color when a text field is empty. It's a great way to prompt a user to enter text without having to add another label above or next to the text entry field.

Change the Clear button attribute to Appears While Editing. This instructs iOS to display a handy X button to the inside right of the text field so that the user can easily clear the name text with one tap and enter a new name.

Hiding the keyboard

The final attribute we're going to modify is the Return key. Change the default value to Done. When the user taps the name text field and begins to enter text, the keyboard automatically appears, covering the date picker. We need to consider this and ensure we provide the user with the means to dismiss the keyboard and modify the birthday date. By changing the Return key value to Done, we indicate to the user that tapping the Return key will clear the keyboard. To dismiss the keyboard when a text field's Return button is tapped requires our view controller to subscribe as the text field's delegate.

In the BRBirthdayEditViewController.h header, we must declare that this class implements the UITextFieldDelegate protocol:

@interface BRBirthdayEditViewController : BRCoreViewController**<UITextFieldDelegate>**

Now Control-drag from the text field to the view controller in the storyboard to assign the Edit Birthday view controller as the delegate of the text field (see Figure 6-3). Select Delegate from the Outlets list that pops up.

Figure 6-3. Control-drag from the text field to the view controller to connect the delegate outlet

There are no mandatory methods in the UITextFieldDelegate protocol, so we should get no errors or warnings from the compiler at this point. However, if we want to catch the user tapping the Done button, we need to add the textFieldShouldReturn: UITextFieldDelegate method to our view controller class. In the BRBirthdayEditViewController.m source file, add the following code:

```
#pragma mark UITextFieldDelegate

- (BOOL)textFieldShouldReturn:(UITextField *)textField
{
    [self.nameTextField resignFirstResponder];
    return NO;
}
```

You don't need to add the pragma mark, but it's a handy way to divvy up sections of code and keep things tidy: I like to keep a tidy ship! Pragma marks are recognized by the Jump bar in Xcode and highlighted to help you navigate groups of class methods and properties: clever comments.

Setting and removing the focus on editable text components in iOS is achieved via the becomeFirstResponder and resignFirstResponder methods, respectively. Build and run your app. You should now find that tapping the name text field automatically presents a keyboard with the Done button, and that tapping Done dismisses the keyboard.

Tracking and responding to text changes

Now to track when the user enters or clears text from the name text field. Just like all the other buttons and control components, UITextField is a subclass of UIControl. Any subclass of UIControl implements the target-action design pattern. We set our view controller as a target of the text field, specify which action event we wish to respond to, and the selector method of our class to call when that event occurs.

Create an Interface Builder action connection by dragging from the text field to the BRBirthdayEditViewController.h header interface. Change the connection type to Action, enter the name didChangeNameText, and change the event type to Editing Changed (see Figure 6-4). Click Connect!

Figure 6-4. Creating an action to detect text editing changes

Xcode should generate our didChangeNameText: action method signature:

```
- (IBAction)didChangeNameText:(id)sender;
```

Switch to BRBirthdayEditViewController.m and enter the following implementation for this method:

```
- (IBAction)didChangeNameText:(id)sender {
    NSLog(@"The text was changed: %@",self.nameTextField.text);
}
```

Build and run. As you enter and modify text in the name field, you should see your changes printed out in the Debug panel. Awesome!

Enabling and disabling the Save button

Better user experience often means fewer choices, keeping things simple. We don't want our user to attempt to save new and edited birthdays without providing a name. Displaying an alert message error when not all the conditions of a save are met is an unnecessary, aggressive user experience (see Figure 6-5).

Figure 6-5. Alert views are not always the best solution.

Another (and in my opinion, better) solution is to disable the Save bar button item and automatically enable it as soon as the user has entered one or more characters into the Name text field. We'll first add a private method to BRBirthdayEditViewController.m to check whether text has been entered, and enable or disable the Save button accordingly. Add a new method to BRBirthdayEditViewController.m named updateSaveButton. We won't declare the method signature for updateSaveButton in the header file because it's private and only for use within the BRBirthdayEditViewController class code:

```
-(void) updateSaveButton
{
    self.saveButton.enabled = self.nameTextField.text.length > 0;
}
```

Now, when to call our new `updateSaveButton` method? There are two places we should update our Save button: when our view is about to appear and when the name text field is edited. We know exactly when these events occur: in `viewWillAppear:` and when our new custom action method `didChangeNameText:` fires. Here's the code to add to `BRBirthdayEditViewController.m`:

```
-(void) viewWillAppear:(BOOL)animated
{
    [super viewWillAppear:animated];
    [self updateSaveButton];
}

- (IBAction)didChangeNameText:(id)sender {
    NSLog(@"The text was changed: %@",self.nameTextField.text);
    [self updateSaveButton];
}
```

Build and run. You should find that the Save button autoenables when you start typing into the name text field. Cool, huh?

Capturing toggling switches

Some people don't really want to share their actual age, just their birthday. We're going to respect their wishes and make the year of birth optional with a flick of a switch. But how do you think we hook into a switch as soon as it's toggled? Does "target-action" ring any bells? A `UISwitch` is also a subclass of `UIControl`, so we just need to know which event gets dispatched when the switch is toggled.

In the same way that we connected the Editing Changed action of the text field to `BRBirthdayEditViewController.h`, we perform the same Control-drag procedure from the switch to the `BRBirthdayEditViewController.h` interface. Change the new connection to an Action. Xcode should automatically pick the most typical event type based on the currently selected `UIControl`. For switches, the Value Changed event is the one we're after. Name the new action `didToggleSwitch` and click Connect (see Figure 6-6).

Figure 6-6. Creating a new switch Value Changed action callback

Now to implement the new action method:

```
- (IBAction)didToggleSwitch:(id)sender {
    if (self.includeYearSwitch.on) {
        NSLog(@"Sure, I'll share my age with you!");
    }
```

```
    else {
        NSLog(@"I'd prefer to keep my birthday year to myself thank you very much!");
    }
}
```

Build and run, and give it a go.

Monitoring date picker updates

The date picker (UIDatePicker) control has a number of different modes: Time, Date, Date and Time, and Countdown Timer. Feel free to experiment with the four different options, but for the purposes of *Birthday Reminder*, select the date picker in the storyboard, and via the attributes inspector, change the mode to Date.

Just like the switch control, the date picker also supports the Value Changed event, so in the same way as you did with the switch, Control-drag to create a new Value Changed *action* from the date picker and name it didChangeDatePicker. Now implement the new action method in BRBirthdayEditViewController.m:

```
- (IBAction)didChangeDatePicker:(id)sender {
    NSLog(@"New Birthdate Selected: %@",self.datePicker.date);
}
```

Build and run. Piece of cake, right?

Multilined text view in the edit notes view

We've explored how to handle text field interactions, but text fields only permit a single line of text to be entered. For our notes editor, one line of text for jotting down gift ideas is unlikely to be adequate!

If you need a text entry field for multiple lines, then you'll need to add an editable text view (UITextView) component to your app.

In your storyboard, move your attention to the Edit Notes view controller. Drag a text view instance onto the view and position it: x=0, y=10, width=320, and height=190 (see Figure 6-7).

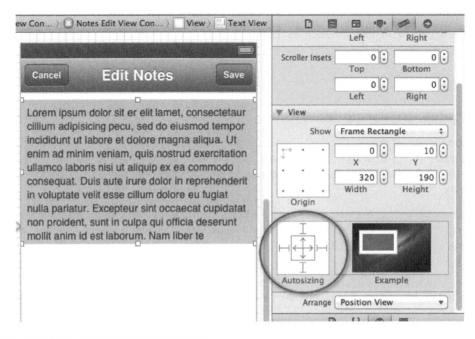

Figure 6-7. Adding a text view to the edit notes view

There's a good reason for setting our text view at this position and size. It leaves precisely 216 points of screen space below the text view. In portrait orientation, the keyboard is 216 points high, so we're ensuring that the keyboard will not cover any important elements in our view when the user is typing in birthday present notes.

Although our 190-point high text view will look great on an iPhone 4S, on the iPhone 5 screen, there's going to be an 88-point space between the bottom of the text view and the keyboard. We can fix this by setting the autosize mask of the text view to a flexible width and height, but fixed top, bottom, left, and right values. Change the autosizing properties to match those highlighted in Figure 6-7.

Keeping the text view selected, toggle to the attributes inspector. You'll note (no pun intended!) that text views can contain editable and noneditable multilined text. We can toggle the editable attribute as required. Delete the *lorem ipsum* text using the attributes inspector.

Working with the Assistant Editor layout, use the Control-drag technique to create outlets from the Save bar button item and text view in BRNotesEditViewController.h. Name the new outlets saveButton and textView, respectively. You should end up with the following code in your header file:

```
#import "BRCoreViewController.h"

@interface BRNotesEditViewController : BRCoreViewController

@property (weak, nonatomic) IBOutlet UIBarButtonItem *saveButton;
@property (weak, nonatomic) IBOutlet UITextView *textView;

@end
```

Text views enable users to write an unlimited amount of text. If the text is greater in height than its bounds, the text automatically becomes scrollable. For this reason, UITextView is a subclass of UIScrollView. UITextView is therefore not a subclass of UIControl, so we don't have any target-action events to work with like when we added a UITextField. To capture text changes in an instance of UITextView, we'll need to subscribe as the text view's delegate and implement the UITextViewDelegate protocol. Modify the interface declaration of BRNotesEditViewController.h to include the UITextViewDelegate protocol reference in angled brackets:

@interface BRNotesEditViewController : BRCoreViewController **<UITextViewDelegate>**

Control-drag from the text view to the Edit Notes view controller to assign the delegate outlet property of the text view to the Edit Notes view controller (see Figure 6-8).

Figure 6-8. Assigning the text view delegate outlet

The method from the UITextViewDelegate protocol that we're interested in is the textViewDidChange: callback. This method fires every time there's a change to the text in the text view. Here's the implementation to add to BRNotesEditViewController.m:

#pragma mark UITextViewDelegate

```
- (void)textViewDidChange:(UITextView *)textView
{
    NSLog(@"User changed the notes text: %@",self.textView.text);
}
```

Build and run. Check that your changes to the notes text field are printed to Xcode's debugger.

Displaying the keyboard for text controls and views

What would be great is if we didn't have to wait until the user taps the text view to show the keyboard. Ideally, we just want the keyboard onscreen as soon as our edit notes view appears. One line of code achieves this if we add a viewWillAppear: callback:

```
-(void) viewWillAppear:(BOOL)animated
{
    [super viewWillAppear:animated];
    [self.textView becomeFirstResponder];
}
```

Similar to the way we called resignFirstResponder to dismiss the keyboard when the Return key was tapped for the text field in the Edit Birthday view controller, we can also focus on text fields and editable text views by invoking the becomeFirstResponder method.

Preparing the notification time view controller

The Notification Time view controller displays a subsetting view in which users can select the time of day they'd like their birthday reminders to fire.

Multiline centered labels

First, add a label and a date picker component to the notification time view in your storyboard. Enter the following text into the label:

What time of day do you want your Birthday Reminders?

Position and size the label (x=20, y=20, width=280, height=87). By default, label components only display a single line of vertically centered text. You may find that your text is also shrunk to fit the new size you've just imposed. Using the attributes inspector, you can increment the Lines value to 3 and change the Alignment value to center the label text (see Figure 6-9).

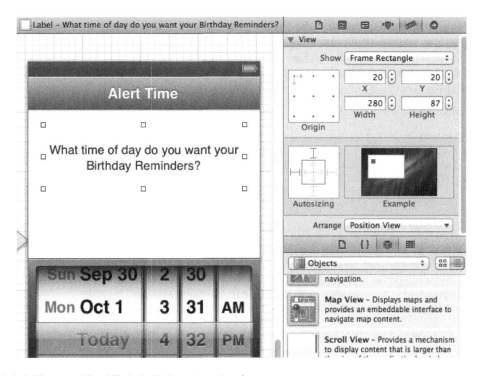

Figure 6-9. Adding a multiline UILabel with the text centered

Using the date picker as a time setting control

Ensure the date picker is pinned to the bottom of the view (just as you did for the Edit Birthday view) and then change its Mode attribute to Time. Set the Interval attribute of the date picker to five minutes (see Figure 6-10).

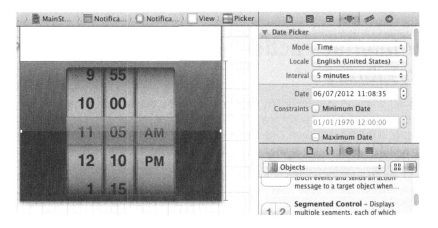

Figure 6-10. Configuring the date picker as a time setting control

Control-drag to create outlets for both the label and the date picker in the BRNotificationTimeViewController.h header: whatTimeLabel and timePicker, respectively. Control-drag again from the date picker to BRNotificationTimeViewController.h to create an Interface Builder action for the Value Changed event, and name the action didChangeTime:. BRNotificationTimeViewController.h should end up as follows:

```
#import "BRCoreViewController.h"

@interface BRNotificationTimeViewController : BRCoreViewController
@property (weak, nonatomic) IBOutlet UILabel *whatTimeLabel;
@property (weak, nonatomic) IBOutlet UIDatePicker *timePicker;
- (IBAction)didChangeTime:(id)sender;

@end
```

Now, when the user changes the time displayed on our date picker, our new didChangeTime: action is invoked. This enables us to grab the date value of UIDatePicker, but how can we extract just the hour and minutes that the user has set? Here's the code to add to the implementation of didChangeTime::

```
- (IBAction)didChangeTime:(id)sender {
    NSDateComponents *components = [[NSCalendar currentCalendar]
components:NSHourCalendarUnit|NSMinuteCalendarUnit fromDate:self.timePicker.date];

    NSLog(@"Changed time to: %d:%d",components.hour,components.minute);
}
```

We're going to become best friends with the NSDateComponents over the next few days. It's a very powerful class for manipulating a date and dividing it into individual year, month, day, minute, and second components. We instantiate an instance of NSDateComponents from the current calendar of the user's device, and we pass in unit flags, specifying which components we're interested in— just hour and minutes for this example. We also pass in the date from our date picker. We can then directly access the hour and minute properties of our NSDateComponents instance. We'll explore more uses of NSDateComponents in latter chapters when we have to figure our the number of days remaining until each saved birthday, the age users will be on their next birthday, and many other date-related values.

More user interface action with the camera and Photo Library

Any birthday added or imported into our *Birthday Reminder* app will be able to have an associated photo. The photo, however, is optional. If a birthday has an associated photo, then we'll display it on the home screen birthday list. It will display even larger on the birthday detail and edit screens. If there's no photo associated with a birthday, then we'll display a birthday cake instead. ☺

Let's start this photo feature by adding some new subviews to the edit birthday view in our storyboard. Drag a new view (UIView) instance onto the edit birthday view from the Object Library. Use the size inspector to position the subview (x=10 and y=20). Resize the view to width=71 and height=71 (see Figure 6-11).

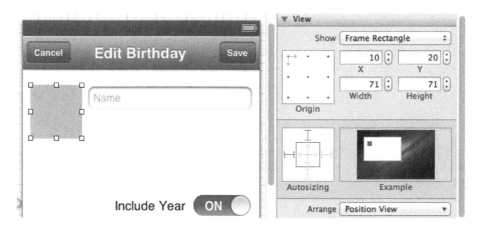

Figure 6-11. Adding an image view holder

The newly added view is a container view for a thumbnail background image, the birthday photo, and a Pic Photo label. By default, Xcode sets an opaque white background color on any new view added to a storyboard. Our holder needs to be transparent, but not invisible because it will eventually have round rectangle corners. Keeping the container view selected, use the attributes inspector to change the background color of the view to Apple's built-in clear color (see Figure 6-12).

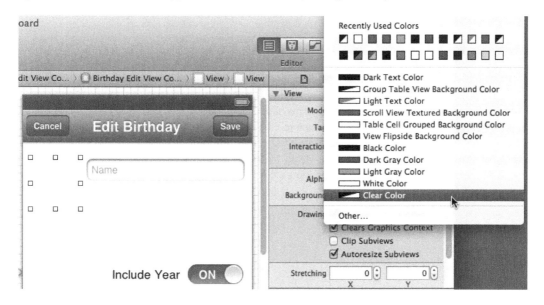

Figure 6-12. Making a view's background transparent with a clear color

Within the source code for this chapter, you'll find four new retina and non-retina image assets to add to your project. Drag, drop, and add the images to the `resources/images` group in your Xcode project (see Figure 6-13).

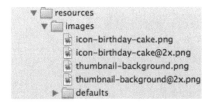

Figure 6-13. Birthday cake and thumbnail background image assets added to the project

Back in our edit birthday view, drag a new image view (UIImageView) from the Object Library into the container view. Then position it (x=0, y=0, width=71, height=71) to match its parent view. With your new image view selected, use the attributes inspector to change its image property to thumbnail-background.png, one of the image assets we just added to our project. The image displayed should be a round cornered thumbnail background PNG.

Repeat the process of adding, positioning, and sizing a new image view again; but this time, select the icon-birthday-cake.png image to sit in front of the thumbnail background (see Figure 6-14).

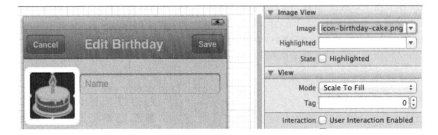

Figure 6-14. A container view with two subviews: thumbnail background and birthday cake image views

Add a third subview to the container view. This time it's a new label (UILabel) instance. Using the attributes inspector, change the label's alignment to Center, its font size to system 12, its text color to Light Text Color, and its text to Pic Photo. Scrolling through the attributes inspector to the View attributes of the label, tap the Background color swatch. Using the Gray Scale Slider, create and apply a new Black color with 50 percent opacity to the label (see Figure 6-15).

Figure 6-15. Creating a new translucent color with 50 percent opacity

Finally, position the new label (x=0, y=56, width=71, height=15). The results should look like Figure 6-16.

Figure 6-16. Our holder complete with images and label

Using the Assistant Editor layout, create new outlets in BRBirthdayEditViewController.h for the container view, image view with the cake, and label view, naming them photoContainerView, photoView, and picPhotoLabel, respectively. When views are layered on top of one another, the most accurate way to ensure you're Control-dragging from the right view is to open the document outline pane and drag directly from the view hierarchy in the document outline to the header file (see Figure 6-17).

Figure 6-17. Control-drag new outlets from the document outline pane

The resulting outlet code in `BRBirthdayEditViewController.h` header:

```
@property (weak, nonatomic) IBOutlet UIView *photoContainerView;
@property (weak, nonatomic) IBOutlet UILabel *picPhotoLabel;
@property (weak, nonatomic) IBOutlet UIImageView *photoView;
```

Gesture recognizers

We're going to prompt the user to take a new photo with the camera or select a photo from their iPhone Photo Library to assign to the birthday they are adding or editing. Our Pic Photo label already indicates that the user needs to tap the image icon to replace the default cake image.

Our app needs to respond to the user tapping the photo container view. We can't use target-action because `UIView` is not a subclass of `UIControl`. Instead, we need to add a *tap gesture recognizer* to capture the user tapping with their finger on the view.

Scroll down through the Object Library until you find the tap gesture recognizer (`UITapGestureRecognizer`) object. Drag a new instance onto the photo container view in the document outline (see Figure 6-18).

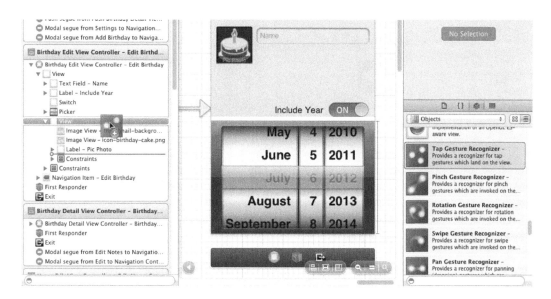

Figure 6-18. Drag and drop the new tap gesture recognizer onto the container view in the document outline pane

Xcode displays the newly added tap gesture recognizer instance in the document outline pane (at the bottom of the list of objects). Control-click the added tap gesture recognizer to open its contextual menu. You'll see the new gestureRecognizers outlet collection that connects the recognizer to the photo container view.

We've already done enough to detect a tap on the photo container view, but we need to also create an action connection from the tap gesture recognizer to BRBirthdayEditViewController.h.

Using the Assistant Editor with BRBirthdayEditViewController.h displaying in the right pane and the storyboard in the left pane, Control-drag from the tap gesture recognizer to BRBirthdayEditViewController.h to create a new action called didTapPhoto, as shown in Figure 6-19.

Figure 6-19. Creating an action from the tap gesture recognizer named didTapPhoto:

Jump into BRBirthdayEditViewController.m and add a call to NSLog to check the photo tapping is working:

```
- (IBAction)didTapPhoto:(id)sender {
    NSLog(@"Did Tap Photo!");
}
```

Build and run. Does the debug print our Did Tap Photo! each time you tap on the cake? Excellent. ☺

Implementing an action sheet

We want to give the user the option to pick a photo from their library *or* take a photo with the camera. We're going to present these two options via an *action sheet*. Before we extend the didTapPhoto: method, we need to declare in our header file that BRBirthdayEditViewController implements the UIActionSheetDelegate protocol:

```
@interface BRBirthdayEditViewController : BRCoreViewController<UITextFieldDelegate,
UIActionSheetDelegate>
```

Now to finish the didTapPhoto: method:

```
- (IBAction)didTapPhoto:(id)sender {
    NSLog(@"Did Tap Photo!");
    if (![UIImagePickerController
isSourceTypeAvailable:UIImagePickerControllerSourceTypeCamera]) {
        NSLog(@"No camera detected!");
        return;
    }

    UIActionSheet *actionSheet = [[UIActionSheet alloc] initWithTitle:nil delegate:self
cancelButtonTitle:@"Cancel" destructiveButtonTitle:nil otherButtonTitles:@"Take a
Photo",@"Pick from Photo Library", nil];
```

```
        [actionSheet showInView:self.view];
}
```

Build and run. Do you get the resulting action menu displayed in Figure 6-20? No? Are you running it on the iOS simulator? You are? Well, that's the reason then. The iOS simulator doesn't have a camera, so it gets caught by our conditional statement; that is, no camera source type is available, so don't give the user the option to take a photo with the camera:

```
if (![UIImagePickerController isSourceTypeAvailable:UIImagePickerControllerSourceTypeCamera])
{
        NSLog(@"No camera detected!");
        return;
}
```

Figure 6-20. Displaying an action sheet

You'll need to run the app on a device with a camera to have the option to take a photo with the camera.

UIImagePickerController: taking photos and browsing the Photo Library

There are a number of ways that iOS apps can take photos with the iPhone camera and access the user's Photo Library. The easiest by far is to use a component from the iOS SDK called UIImagePickerController. It does all the hard work for us. We're going to lazy load an instance of

Apple's `UIImagePickerController` class and create two new private methods in `BRBirthdayEditViewController`: one for taking photos and one for selecting photos from the Photo Library.

`BRBirthdayEditViewController` assigns itself as a delegate of `UIImagePickerController`. So first, let's update our interface header:

```
@interface BRBirthdayEditViewController : BRCoreViewController<UITextFieldDelegate,
UIActionSheetDelegate, UIImagePickerControllerDelegate, UINavigationControllerDelegate>
```

The delegate property of `UIImagePickerController` is defined as an object that implements both `UIImagePickerControllerDelegate` and `UINavigationControllerDelegate` protocols; so even though we're not going to implement any `UINavigationControllerDelegate` method signatures, we'll still include this protocol in the `BRBirthdayEditViewController` header to avoid compiler warnings.

Switch back to the `BRBirthdayEditViewController.m` source file and add the following private property declaration:

```
@interface BRBirthdayEditViewController()

@property (nonatomic, strong) UIImagePickerController *imagePicker;

@end;
```

We can override the getter for our new image picker property and only instantiate an instance of the imager picker controller when it's first referenced. This is known as *lazy loading*. Add the accessor method to the `BRBirthdayEditViewController.m` implementation:

```
-(UIImagePickerController *) imagePicker
{
    if (_imagePicker == nil) {
        _imagePicker = [[UIImagePickerController alloc] init];
        _imagePicker.delegate = self;
    }
    return _imagePicker;
}
```

Now let's implement our two new methods for taking and browsing photos:

```
-(void) takePhoto
{
    self.imagePicker.sourceType = UIImagePickerControllerSourceTypeCamera;
    [self.navigationController presentViewController:self.imagePicker animated:YES
completion:nil];
}

-(void) pickPhoto
{
    self.imagePicker.sourceType = UIImagePickerControllerSourceTypePhotoLibrary;
    [self.navigationController presentViewController:self.imagePicker animated:YES
completion:nil];
}
```

Just like dismissing a modal view controller, we can pass in a block as the third parameter of the presentViewController:animated:completion: view controller method. However, as we don't have any code to run once the presentation animation completes, we can simply pass in nil instead.

To invoke our takePhoto and pickPhoto methods, we need to add a delegate method from the UIActionSheetDelegate protocol to our class so that we respond to the user selecting one of the two action options from action sheet:

```
#pragma mark UIActionSheetDelegate

- (void)actionSheet:(UIActionSheet *)actionSheet
didDismissWithButtonIndex:(NSInteger)buttonIndex
{
    if (buttonIndex == actionSheet.cancelButtonIndex) return;

    switch (buttonIndex) {
        case 0:
            [self takePhoto];
            break;
        case 1:
            [self pickPhoto];
            break;
    }
}
```

Build and run. You should now be able to browse, select, and take photos with UIImagePickerController, as per Figure 6-21.

Figure 6-21. Not quite looking my best!

If you're running the app on the simulator, then you still won't see the `UIImagePickerController`. However, the simulator does have a Photo Library, so rather than displaying an action sheet with options, we'll just present the user with the Photo Library if no camera is detected:

Modify the `didTapPhoto:` method to the following:

```
- (IBAction)didTapPhoto:(id)sender {

    NSLog(@"Did Tap Photo!");

    if                                             (![UIImagePickerController
isSourceTypeAvailable:UIImagePickerControllerSourceTypeCamera]) {

        NSLog(@"No camera detected!");

        [self pickPhoto];

        return;

    }

    UIActionSheet *actionSheet = [[UIActionSheet alloc] initWithTitle:nil delegate:self
cancelButtonTitle:@"Cancel"       destructiveButtonTitle:nil       otherButtonTitles:@"Take       a
Photo",@"Pick from Photo Library", nil];
```

```
    [actionSheet showInView:self.view];

}
```

We've just added a direct call to the new pickPhoto method if no camera is detected for the device.

We're not quite done yet. UIImagePickerController appears to be taking photos, but how do we get hold of the photo data when it completes? Via a delegate callback method, of course! We've already declared that BRBirthdayEditViewController implements UIImagePickerControllerDelegate protocol, so add the following code to grab the image data from our UIImagePickerController instance:

```
#pragma mark UIImagePickerControllerDelegate

- (void)imagePickerController:(UIImagePickerController *)picker
didFinishPickingMediaWithInfo:(NSDictionary *)info {

    [picker dismissViewControllerAnimated:YES completion:nil];

    UIImage *image = info[UIImagePickerControllerOriginalImage];

    self.photoView.image = image;
}
```

By defining the UIImagePickerControllerDelegate protocol method, imagePickerController: didFinishPickingMediaWithInfo:, we are returned the image data from UIImagePickerController as one of the properties of an info NSDictionary passed into the callback method as a parameter. We set the image property of our photoView image view and swap the birthday cake image for the newly taken or selected photo.

Tweaking image view rendering

Depending on the dimensions of the photo you're taking or selecting with the image picker, you may have noticed that the resulting image doesn't retain its aspect ratio. Instead, it's squashed or stretched to fit the image view bounds. When I first started learning iOS and came across this problem, my initial thoughts were to either resize and center the image view or to generate a new cropped image to fit the dimensions of the image view. It turns out that the solution is a great deal simpler than either of these approaches. UIView has a property called contentMode that determines how the content of the view is rendered. contentMode defaults to UIViewContentModeScaleToFill, that is, it simply stretches or squashes its drawn contents to the dimensions of its bounds. If we change the contentMode property value to UIViewContentModeScaleAspectFill, the aspect ratio of our image will be respected and the image will fill the bounds of the image view it's being rendered into.

Back in the storyboard, select the photoView image view. Using the attributes inspector change the Mode setting to Aspect Fill. Build and run. This time, you should find that your selected photo is now sized to fill the bounds of the image view without distorting the image. The only problem is that the overlapping sides or the top and bottom of the image are not getting cropped. Again, that's an easy one to solve. Keeping the image view selected, in the attributes inspector you'll find an attribute called Clip Subviews (UIView.clipsToBounds). Switch Clip Subviews on. Build and run. How about that? Nicely cropped and centered square thumbnails that match the bounds of our image view (see Figure 6-22)! How easy was that?!

> Note: At the moment, we're filling a small thumbnail image view with a potentially very large photograph. At a later stage of development, we generate thumbnails from large images; otherwise, our app very quickly consumes a lot of memory from rendering, unnecessarily large images.

Figure 6-22. Bad, Better, Best!

Summary

You've reached the end of Day 2! Today has been all about building basic iOS user interfaces and navigation. You learned

- How to build a navigation hierarchy of view controllers as scenes in a storyboard.

- How to create view controller subclasses and assign them to view controllers in our storyboard.

- How to connect our views and subviews with custom view controllers through Interface Builder outlets and actions.

- How to understand the delegate pattern, to implement protocols in our view controllers, and respond to protocol method callbacks.

- How to implement the native iPhone camera and Photo Library into our app.

We've made a great start on the navigation and user interface, but we've not tackled data handling in iOS. Guess what we're up to tomorrow? That's right, *working with data*. Sleep well. ☺

Day 3

Working With Data

Chapter 7

Table Views, Arrays, and Dictionaries—Oh My!

Day 3 is data day! Up until now, we've focused on the user interface and navigation of our *Birthday Reminder* app. Today, we're going to learn how to integrate data into our app.

In this chapter, we'll learn how to create and manipulate an array of dictionaries, and populate our app from the data. In Chapter 8, we'll modify our data implementation to use a persistent storage solution using Apple's Core Data framework.

Table views

Table views are a central component for many iPhone apps—and *Birthday Reminder* is no exception. Table views enable iPhone apps to display large amounts of content on a small screen device in a long scrollable list.

Figure 7-1 displays the final table view we'll present on the home screen of our app—listing as many birthdays as the user has friends and relations! The user will also be able to pick any birthday in the list, and the app will navigate to display the details of the chosen birthday, sliding the table view off to the left and replacing it with the Birthday Detail view sliding in from the right.

Figure 7-1. UITableView: a core component of the *Birthday Reminder* app

The initial challenge we're going to master is to load an array of celebrity birthdays from a local property list file in our project into a native array of birthday dictionaries. We'll display the celebrity names, birthdays, and locally stored photos in a table view.

From the assets folder included in the source code for this chapter, begin by importing the birthdays.plist file and the Celebrity Pics folder into the resources group of your Xcode project, as shown in Figure 7-2.

Figure 7-2. Celebrity pics and birthdays.plist resources added to our project

Focus your storyboard on the Home view controller. Begin by deleting the Push Birthday Detail View Controller button. This automatically deletes the temporary segue from the Home view controller to the Birthday Detail view controller. Now drag a new table view instance (not to be confused with a table view controller instance) from the Object Library onto the home view (see Figure 7-3). The table view becomes a subview of our main home view (don't replace your home view!).

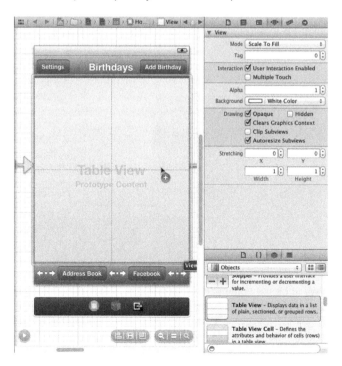

Figure 7-3. Adding a table view to our home view

Select the new table view and use the attributes inspector to increment the Prototype Cells setting to 1, which adds a new prototype cell to the table view for us to work with (see Figure 7-4).

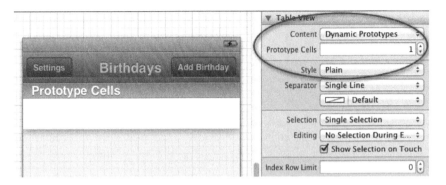

Figure 7-4. Adding a prototype cell to the table view

We can style our prototype cell from a list of table cell styles designed by Apple, or we can customize the prototype table view cell directly and add subviews, setting background colors, and so forth. We'll learn about creating custom table view cells in Chapter 9; but for now, select the prototype cell and use the attributes inspector to change its style to Subtitle (see Figure 7-5). The subtitle-style table cell provides a bold title and subtitle labels that we can set text for at runtime.

Now enter a reuse identifier value into the Identifier text field of the attributes inspector. Enter **Cell** as the text (see Figure 7-5).

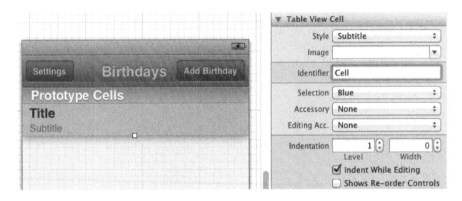

Figure 7-5. Setting up a reusable prototype table cell

Apple designed table views to be very optimized. The purpose of the reuse identifier is to enable instances of UITableViewCell to be reused for multiple table rows; for example, if your table is 416 points high and the height of each table cell is 100 pixels, then the table view only needs to generate five instances of UITableViewCell to display hundreds and hundreds of rows! If you don't supply a reuse identifier, then each instance of a UITableViewCell generated for our table view will only be used once, and that could result in a very memory hungry app, not to mention the performance implications.

You should be able to build and run your app at this point, although the table view will just show empty rows for the time being.

With the Home view controller scene selected in your storyboard, create a new Interface Builder outlet from the BRHomeViewController.h header file to the table view and name it tableView.

BRHomeViewController.h should now look like the following:

```
#import <UIKit/UIKit.h>
#import "BRCoreViewController.h"

@interface BRHomeViewController : BRCoreViewController

-(IBAction)unwindBackToHomeViewController:(UIStoryboardSegue *)segue;
@property (weak, nonatomic) IBOutlet UITableView *tableView;

@end
```

Table data source and delegate protocols

In Chapter 4, we first looked at the alert view component (UIAlertView) and learned that we need our view controller to subscribe as its delegate in order to catch Alert button click events. The same delegate pattern applies when working with table views, only a table view has two types of delegates: one for the controller and one for the data model.

We're going to set the view controller of the table view to be both the data source and the delegate. To do this, we have to indicate in the BRHomeViewController.h header that this class will adhere to both the UITableViewDataSource and UITableViewDelegate protocols. Modify your header by adding the delegate and data source implementation declaration:

```
@interface BRHomeViewController : BRCoreViewController <UITableViewDelegate,
UITableViewDataSource>
```

Next, we need to assign the delegate and the dataSource outlets of the table view to BRBirthdayTableViewController. We'll do this via the storyboard: Control-drag from the table view to the view controller object in the bar beneath the view, and you'll be prompted to select the dataSource or delegate properties. Assign both to the Home view controller (see Figure 7-6).

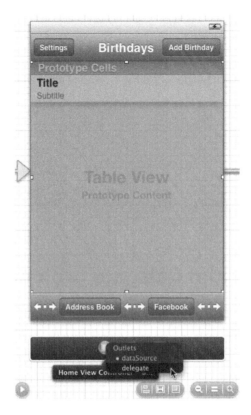

Figure 7-6. Setting the dataSource and delegate of the table view to BRHomeViewController

The assigned dataSource object of a table view must implement the UITableViewDataSource protocol. When the table view loads, it requests from its dataSource the number of table sections and number of rows in each section. The designated dataSource object also generates instances of UITableViewCell in response to requests from the table view. The UITableViewDataSource protocol has two required method signatures that the compiler should warn you about if you don't implement them:

```
- (NSInteger)tableView:(UITableView *)tableView numberOfRowsInSection:(NSInteger)section;
```

```
- (UITableViewCell *)tableView:(UITableView *)tableView cellForRowAtIndexPath:(NSIndexPath *)indexPath;
```

So we'd better add these methods to the source implementation of BRHomeViewController:

```
#pragma mark UITableViewDataSource
```

```
- (UITableViewCell *)tableView:(UITableView *)tableView cellForRowAtIndexPath:(NSIndexPath *)indexPath
{
    UITableViewCell *cell = [self.tableView dequeueReusableCellWithIdentifier:@"Cell"];
```

```
    return cell;
}

- (NSInteger)tableView:(UITableView *)tableView numberOfRowsInSection:(NSInteger)section
{
    return 100;
}
```

Did you notice how we're referencing the `Cell` reuse identifier to grab reusable instances of the table cell prototype from our storyboard? Table views manage the reuse process directly: as soon as a table cell is scrolled out of the visible view, it is added to a reuse stack of cells and returned by the table view when we call `dequeueReusableCellWithIdentifier:`.

Our implementation of `tableView:numberOfRowsInSection:` returns an integer of 100. We're letting our table view know that there should be 100 rows in the table.

Build and run your app. You should see lots of table rows of the subtitle style we set earlier (see Figure 7-7).

Figure 7-7. One hundred table rows!

If you select any of the table rows in the simulator or on your device, you'll find that the selected row turns blue and remains selected. We're going to modify the selection handling by implementing one of the UITableViewDelegate methods in our Home view controller:

```
#pragma mark UITableViewDelegate

- (void)tableView:(UITableView *)tableView didSelectRowAtIndexPath:(NSIndexPath *)indexPath
{
    [self.tableView deselectRowAtIndexPath:indexPath animated:YES];
}
```

You should now find that when you run the app, the rows fade out elegantly on touch to indicate that the user interaction was recognized.

The rows of our *Birthday Reminder* cells are 72 points high. The default height of a table cell is only 44 points. With our table view selected, we can modify the cell height in our storyboard using the size inspector by incrementing the Row Height to 72 (see Figure 7-8).

Figure 7-8. Modifying the default row height of our table view

> *Note: Table views also support variable row height. You can determine individual row heights by implementing the tableView:heightForRowAtIndexPath method of the UITableViewDelegate protocol.*

I think we need to load in some real data from our birthdays.plist. Let's get to work loading dynamic data into our table.

Populating the table view with an array and a plist

The birthdays.plist file we added to our project at the beginning of this chapter contains an array of ten celebrity birthday dictionaries. Plists or *property lists* are XML files that adhere to a scheme that

Objective-C understands and can convert into native objects: arrays, dictionaries, numbers, strings, and so forth.

Tip: You can create your own plists *via File   New   File. Chose the Property List option from the Resource templates.*

When our Home view controller instantiates, we're going to create an array of birthday dictionaries loaded from birthdays.plist. Declare a new birthdays array property in the private interface of BRHomeViewController.m:

```
@interface BRHomeViewController()
@property (nonatomic,strong) NSMutableArray *birthdays;
@end
```

Now to instantiate our birthdays array. As we learned in Chapter 5, view controllers instantiated from storyboards have a designated initializer, initWithCoder:. So we'll generate our new array by overriding the designated initializer:

```
- (id) initWithCoder:(NSCoder *)aDecoder
{
    self = [super initWithCoder:aDecoder];

    if (self) {
        NSString* plistPath = [[NSBundle mainBundle] pathForResource:@"birthdays"
ofType:@"plist"];
        NSArray *nonMutableBirthdays = [NSArray arrayWithContentsOfFile:plistPath];

        self.birthdays = [NSMutableArray array];

        NSMutableDictionary *birthday;
        NSDictionary *dictionary;
        NSString *name;
        NSString *pic;
        UIImage *image;
        NSDate *birthdate;

        for (int i=0;i<[nonMutableBirthdays count];i++) {
            dictionary = [nonMutableBirthdays objectAtIndex:i];
            name = dictionary[@"name"];
            pic = dictionary[@"pic"];
            image = [UIImage imageNamed:pic];
            birthdate = dictionary[@"birthdate"];
            birthday = [NSMutableDictionary dictionary];
            birthday[@"name"] = name;
            birthday[@"image"] = image;
            birthday[@"birthdate"] = birthdate;

            [self.birthdays addObject:birthday];
        }
    }
}
```

```
    return self;
}
```

The root node of the `birthdays.plist` file is an array: an array of dictionary objects. NSArray has a convenience method `arrayWithContentsOfFile:` that creates and populates a non-mutable array with non-mutable objects from a `plist` file. However, we want the dictionaries in our `birthdays` array to be mutable because we'll be enabling the user of our app to change the celebrity names and photos via the edit birthday view. The only option we have to make these non-mutable dictionaries mutable is to create new mutable versions from the non-mutable versions. So we loop through all the non-mutable dictionaries and create new mutable birthday dictionaries:

```
birthday = [NSMutableDictionary dictionary];
birthday[@"name"] = name;
birthday[@"image"] = image;
birthday[@"birthdate"] = birthdate;
[self.birthdays addObject:birthday];
```

Note how we also initialize new UIImage instances based on the `pic` string value of each birthday dictionary loaded from the `plist`:

```
pic = dictionary[@"pic"];
image = [UIImage imageNamed:pic];
```

The resulting `self.birthdays` array is mutable and contains mutable birthday dictionaries with the `name`, `birthdate`, and `image` properties that we'll use to populate each cell of our table view.

Check that your app still compiles and runs OK. You shouldn't have any errors or warnings if the `plist` data is loading and parsing OK.

> Note: Your storyboard may include a warning about the Birthday Detail scene being unreachable, but we'll fix that later. It shouldn't prevent your project from compiling.

Currently, we're telling the table view that it contains 100 rows. Instead, modify the returned value to the count of birthdays in our array:

```
- (NSInteger)tableView:(UITableView *)tableView numberOfRowsInSection:(NSInteger)section
{
    return 100;
    return [self.birthdays count];
}
```

Now to populate the table view cells. Whenever the table view requests a table view cell instance from its data source (our Home view controller), it passes in a reference to itself and a reference to the index path of the cell. An index path contains two values: *section* and *row*. In this example, the row value is equivalent to the index of the birthday object in our `birthdays` array. The section value is always 0 in our app because we're only going to implement a single section table view.

Here's the new implementation of `tableView:cellForRowAtIndexPath:` in your Home view controller.

```
- (UITableViewCell *)tableView:(UITableView *)tableView cellForRowAtIndexPath:(NSIndexPath *)indexPath
```

```
{
    UITableViewCell *cell = [self.tableView dequeueReusableCellWithIdentifier:@"Cell"];

    NSMutableDictionary *birthday = self.birthdays[indexPath.row];

    NSString *name = birthday[@"name"];
    NSDate *birthdate = birthday[@"birthdate"];
    UIImage *image = birthday[@"image"];

    cell.textLabel.text = name;
    cell.detailTextLabel.text = birthdate.description;
    cell.imageView.image = image;

    return cell;
}
```

Using the `indexPath.row` value, we can obtain the mutable birthday dictionary associated with the requested table cell row. Table view cells (`UITableViewCell`) have two default label properties: `textLabel` and `detailTextLabel`, which we then populate with the `name` and `birthdate` string values, respectively. Table view cells also contain an image view property (`imageView`) that we set to the value of the image (`UIImage`) property stored in our birthday dictionary.

Build and run. You should see the populated celebrity table view, as shown in Figure 7-9.

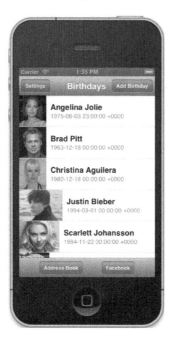

Figure 7-9. Our first table view with dynamically generated data!

Passing data with segues

Our next challenge is to push the Birthday Detail view controller onto the main navigation controller when a celebrity birthday cell is tapped. There are two typical ways to achieve this. One way is to expand our `tableView:didSelectRowAtIndexPath` method to create a new view controller instance in code and then pushing the view controller onto the navigation controller containing our Home view controller:

```
[self.navigationController pushViewController:myViewControllerInstance animated:YES];
```

However, we're going to stick with the more visual approach we learned in Chapter 5: by pushing a view controller with a storyboard segue. Control-drag from the prototype table cell in your Home view controller to the Birthday Detail view controller, and then release and select the *push* segue option (see Figure 7-10).

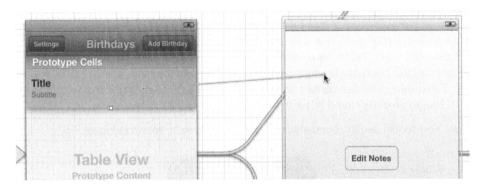

Figure 7-10. Creating a push segue from a prototype table cell

Xcode creates the new push segue and reapplies the inferred navigation bar to the Birthday Detail view controller that we set up in Chapter 5. Now, when any instance of our prototyped table cell is selected, it pushes our Birthday Detail view controller onto the navigation stack.

Add a new image view (`UIImageView`) instance to the Birthday Detail view controller, position it x=10, y=20, and size it to 71×71 points. Keeping the new image view selected and using the attributes inspector, change the view mode to Aspect Fill and toggle on Clip Subviews, as shown in Figure 7-11. This results in a nicely clipped, square thumbnail when an image is assigned to this image view, just like we implemented into our edit birthday view in Chapter 6.

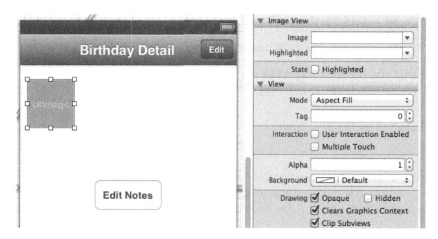

Figure 7-11. Adding and configuring an image view for square thumbnail display within the Birthday Detail view

Continuing work with storyboards and using the Assistant Editor layout, control-drag from the new image view to create a new outlet in the BRBirthdayDetailViewController.h header file named photoView:

```
#import <UIKit/UIKit.h>
#import "BRCoreViewController.h"


@interface BRBirthdayDetailViewController : BRCoreViewController

@property (weak, nonatomic) IBOutlet UIImageView *photoView;

@end
```

We're also going to add a new mutable birthday dictionary property to our Birthday Detail view controller. The new property is set from the Home view controller when a birthday in the table view is tapped by the user. Update BRBirthdayDetailViewController.h and add the new mutable dictionary property:

```
#import <UIKit/UIKit.h>
#import "BRCoreViewController.h"


@interface BRBirthdayDetailViewController : BRCoreViewController

@property(nonatomic,strong) NSMutableDictionary *birthday;
@property (weak, nonatomic) IBOutlet UIImageView *photoView;

@end
```

Now toggle to the BRBirthdayDetailViewController.m source and extend the current viewWillAppear: method of BRBirthdayDetailViewController.m to read and render the details of the new birthday dictionary property each time our detail view appears:

```
-(void) viewWillAppear:(BOOL)animated
{
    [super viewWillAppear:animated];
    NSLog(@"viewWillAppear");
```

```
    NSString *name = self.birthday[@"name"];
    self.title = name;
    UIImage *image = self.birthday[@"image"];
    if (image == nil) {
        //default to the birthday cake pic if there's no birthday image
        self.photoView.image = [UIImage imageNamed:@"icon-birthday-cake.png"];
    }
    else {
        self.photoView.image = image;
    }
}
```

Setting the `title` property of a view controller updates the centered text on the navigation bar when a view controller is displayed within a navigation controller. We'll also set the image value of our new image view to the image contained in the birthday dictionary, or fallback onto our cake image if none exists.

We've finished preparing our Birthday Detail view for data. We'll now switch our attention back to the Home view controller and write code to pass the selected birthday dictionary to the Birthday Detail view controller when it's pushed onto the navigation stack via the segue transition.

Understanding segue identifiers

In addition to view lifecycle methods (viewDidLoad, viewWillAppear:, etc.), subclasses of Apple's UIViewController class can override callback methods that relate to segue transitions. That's exactly what we're going to do now by overriding the prepareForSegue:sender: method in our Home view controller class. Add the following new code to BRHomeViewController.m implementation:

```
#pragma mark Segues

-(void) prepareForSegue:(UIStoryboardSegue *)segue sender:(id)sender
{
    NSLog(@"prepareForSegue!");
}
```

If you build and run the app, you should see the newly added log statement, prepareForSegue!, appear each time you select a celebrity birthday from the home screen; that is, just at the point that the segue transition is invoked.

In the prepareForSegue:sender: method, we are provided with a reference to the segue we added to our storyboard. However, any code we add to prepareForSegue:sender: will be invoked for *any* segue transition from our home screen to any other screen—our add birthday segue, for example! We need to be able to identify which segue transition is currently executing, and from that, we can determine the view controller that is transitioning onto the screen and how to handle the event.

In your storyboard, select the segue linking the Home view controller to the Birthday Detail view controller, and using the attributes inspector, add a string identifier to the segue itself. Name the segue identifier BirthdayDetail (see Figure 7-12).

Figure 7-12. Adding a segue identifier

Now that we have a method for identifying which view controller is being pushed or presented, we can extend prepareForSegue:sender: in our BRHomeViewController.m implementation:

```
-(void) prepareForSegue:(UIStoryboardSegue *)segue sender:(id)sender
{
    NSLog(@"prepareForSegue!");
    NSString *identifier = segue.identifier;

    if ([identifier isEqualToString:@"BirthdayDetail"]) {
        //First get the data
        NSIndexPath *selectedIndexPath = self.tableView.indexPathForSelectedRow;
        NSMutableDictionary *birthday = self.birthdays[selectedIndexPath.row];

        BRBirthdayDetailViewController *birthdayDetailViewController =
segue.destinationViewController;
        birthdayDetailViewController.birthday = birthday;

    }
}
```

Before I get into the details of this code, you'll need to first import BRBirthdayDetailViewController.h into BRHomeViewController.m. Scroll up to the top of the BRHomeViewController.m source file and add the import statement:

```
#import "BRBirthdayDetailViewController.h"
```

Exploring the prepareForSegue:sender: code, our home to birthday detail segue has a BirthdayDetail identifier. We can check and access this string via the segue.identifier property. If the identifier matches the BirthdayDetail string, then we know that the current segue transition is between the Home and Birthday Detail view controllers, and so the new view controller must be an instance of BRBirthdayDetailViewController.

We can grab the selected birthday dictionary by obtaining the index path of the currently selected table row:

```
NSIndexPath *selectedIndexPath = self.tableView.indexPathForSelectedRow;
```

From the selected index path, we can extract the row property that matches the index of the related birthday dictionary in our self.birthdays array.

The segue also exposes a reference to the Birthday Detail view controller via its `destinationViewController` property.

Finally, we set the `birthday` dictionary property of our detail view controller:

```
BRBirthdayDetailViewController *birthdayDetailViewController =
segue.destinationViewController;
birthdayDetailViewController.birthday = birthday;
```

This code runs before the Birthday Detail view controller is added to the navigation stack, and so when `viewWillAppear:` is invoked in the detail view controller, it already has access to the `birthday` dictionary and can update its title and `photoView` image properties, respectively.

Build and run. The Birthday Detail view updates to display the selected celebrity name in its navigation bar title and the image in the photo view (see Figure 7-13).

Figure 7-13. Passing data to an updating Birthday Detail view

Adding new birthdays

Open the `BRBirthdayEditViewController.h` header file in Xcode and then add a new birthday dictionary property, just like we did for the Birthday Detail view controller:

```
@property (nonatomic, strong) NSMutableDictionary *birthday;
```

In the BRBirthdayEditViewController.m source file, modify the viewWillAppear: implementation to update its subviews based on the key values in the birthday dictionary:

```
-(void) viewWillAppear:(BOOL)animated
{
    [super viewWillAppear:animated];

    NSString *name = self.birthday [@"name"];
    NSDate *birthdate = self.birthday[@"birthdate"];
    UIImage *image = self.birthday[@"image"];

    self.nameTextField.text = name;
    self.datePicker.date = birthdate;
    if (image == nil) {
        //default to the birthday cake pic if there's no birthday image
        self.photoView.image = [UIImage imageNamed:@"icon-birthday-cake.png"];
    }
    else {
        self.photoView.image = image;
    }

    [self updateSaveButton];
}
```

Back in the storyboard, select the segue between the home view and Edit Birthday navigation controllers, and then give it an AddBirthday identifier.

In the BRHomeViewController.m source file, begin by importing BRBirthdayEditViewController.h:

```
#import "BRBirthdayEditViewController.h"
```

We'll now complete the prepareForSegue:sender: implementation and handle the segue that's invoked when the Add Birthday bar button item is tapped by the user:

```
-(void) prepareForSegue:(UIStoryboardSegue *)segue sender:(id)sender
{
    NSString *identifier = segue.identifier;

    if ([identifier isEqualToString:@"BirthdayDetail"]) {
        //First get the data
        NSIndexPath *selectedIndexPath = self.tableView.indexPathForSelectedRow;
        NSMutableDictionary *birthday = self.birthdays[selectedIndexPath.row];

        BRBirthdayDetailViewController *birthdayDetailViewController =
segue.destinationViewController;
        birthdayDetailViewController.birthday = birthday;
    }
    else if ([identifier isEqualToString:@"AddBirthday"]) {
        //Add a new birthday dictionary to the array of birthdays

        NSMutableDictionary *birthday = [NSMutableDictionary dictionary];

        birthday[@"name"] = @"My Friend";
        birthday[@"birthdate"] = [NSDate date];
```

```
        [self.birthdays addObject:birthday];

        UINavigationController *navigationController = segue.destinationViewController;

        BRBirthdayEditViewController *birthdayEditViewController =
(BRBirthdayEditViewController *) navigationController.topViewController;
        birthdayEditViewController.birthday = birthday;
    }
}
```

When the user taps Add Birthday from the Home view controller and our prepareForSegue:sender: method is invoked, we immediately create a new mutable birthday dictionary, assign it a default name and birth date values, and add it to the self.birthdays array:

```
NSMutableDictionary *birthday = [NSMutableDictionary dictionary];

birthday[@"name"] = @"My Friend";
birthday[@"birthdate"] = [NSDate date];
[self.birthdays addObject:birthday];
```

Because our Edit Birthday view controller is a child of a navigation view controller that is presented modally, the segue's destinationViewController property is that navigation controller. From that navigation controller reference, we can also obtain a reference to the edit birthday view controller and finally set the new birthday property on the edit view controller:

```
BRBirthdayEditViewController *birthdayEditViewController = (BRBirthdayEditViewController *)
navigationController.topViewController;
birthdayEditViewController.birthday = birthday;
```

Although we've modified the model (the array of birthdays), the table view in our Home view controller will not automatically refresh. That's easy to fix since we have an outlet reference to the table view from the Home view controller. In the BRHomeViewController.m source file, override viewWillAppear: to ensure that our table view is reloaded every time the Home view controller is about to appear:

```
-(void) viewWillAppear:(BOOL)animated
{
    [super viewWillAppear:animated];
    [self.tableView reloadData];
}
```

Build and run. You can now add birthdays (see Figure 7-14)!

Figure 7-14. Adding friends and birthdays!

OK, well you can add someone called My Friend as many times as you like, but not much more! We'll improve on this shortly.

Note that in our current implementation, Save and Cancel do exactly the same thing: nothing! A new birthday dictionary is created by the Home view controller and is added to the `birthdays` array.

In order to implement Cancel functionality, we could consider two options:

- Passing the birthdays array to the edit view controller, as well as the selected `birthday` dictionary, and setting up the `cancelAndDismiss:` method to delete the birthday object from the array: `[self.birthdays removeObject:self.birthday]`.

- Creating your own delegate protocol for birthday editing, subscribing the Home view controller as the delegate of the Edit Birthday view controller, and removing the birthday dictionary from the `birthdays` array in the Home view controller code in response to a delegate callback method.

We won't, however, be implementing the Cancel and Save buttons in this chapter because we'll work in these features using Core Data in the next chapter.

Editing existing birthdays

In your storyboard, locate the segue between the Birthday Detail and the Edit Birthday view controllers, and give it an `EditBirthday` identifier. Just as we've done for the Home view controller, we'll now implement a `prepareForSegue:sender:` method in the `BRBirthdayDetailViewController.m` source. First, import `BRBirthdayEditViewController.h`:

```
#import "BRBirthdayEditViewController.h"
```

And then add our custom `prepareForSegue:sender:` method:

```
-(void) prepareForSegue:(UIStoryboardSegue *)segue sender:(id)sender
{
    NSString *identifier = segue.identifier;

    if ([identifier isEqualToString:@"EditBirthday"]) {
        //Edit this birthday
        UINavigationController *navigationController = segue.destinationViewController;

        BRBirthdayEditViewController *birthdayEditViewController =
(BRBirthdayEditViewController *) navigationController.topViewController;
        birthdayEditViewController.birthday = self.birthday;
    }
}
```

We pass our reference to the `birthday` dictionary in the Birthday Detail view controller along to the Edit Birthday view controller. The rest of the code should look very familiar!

Build and run. You can now select celebrity birthdays, display them in the Birthday Detail view controller, and then tap the Edit button to pass and display the selected birthday in the Edit Birthday view controller.

Our final challenge is to update the mutable birthday dictionaries that we're passing around the application via the Edit Birthday view controller.

Reopen the `BRBirthdayEditViewController.m` source file. Let's first update our target-action handlers for the name text field and date picker interaction:

```
- (IBAction)didChangeNameText:(id)sender {
    NSLog(@"The text was changed: %@",self.nameTextField.text);
    self.birthday[@"name"] = self.nameTextField.text;
    [self updateSaveButton];
}
```

and...

```
- (IBAction)didChangeDatePicker:(id)sender {
    NSLog(@"New Birthdate Selected: %@",self.datePicker.date);
    self.birthday[@"birthdate"] = self.datePicker.date;
}
```

We're updating the `name` key value of the referenced birthday dictionary whenever the user edits the birthday name text field. Likewise, we update the `birthdate` if the user changed the selected date in the date picker.

Finally, we're also going to enable the user to change the photo image stored in the birthday dictionary:

```
- (void)imagePickerController:(UIImagePickerController *)picker
didFinishPickingMediaWithInfo:(NSDictionary *)info {

    [picker dismissViewControllerAnimated:YES completion:nil];

    UIImage *image = info[UIImagePickerControllerOriginalImage];

    self.photoView.image = image;

    self.birthday[@"image"] = image;
}
```

Build and run.

You can now add new birthdays and set the name, birth date, and photo. You can even edit existing celebrity birthdays (see Figure 7-15)!

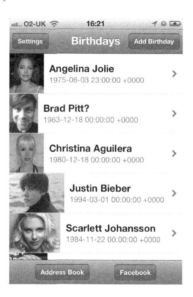

Figure 7-15. What's wrong with this picture?!

Summary

In this chapter, we learned how to work with basic table views and table view cells. We discovered how easy it is to dynamically populate table views with an array of custom dictionary objects.

We also learned how to allow one view controller to modify data also referenced by another view controller and refresh the display whenever `viewWillAppear:` is invoked (just before a view controller is presented by your app).

We learned how to hook into the `prepareForSegue:sender:` method of view controller subclasses and pass data objects between view controllers.

You may have noticed a significant flaw in our application: none of the data is persistent between sessions. As soon as you re-run the app, it reloads the `birthdays.plist` and clears any data modifications. Fear not, young Daniel-san. Next up, we shall be unlocking the mysteries of Core Data persistence. ☺

Chapter 8

Data Persistence with Core Data

Continuing our data discovery day, you're going to learn how to build a data storage solution using Core Data: Apple's powerful framework for persisting data to the file system. When you reach the end of this chapter, your app will be reading and writing birthday objects to disk using Core Data. Birthday objects will remain available even if your app gets shut down for any reason.

Core Data powers the data management of many of your favorite apps, from Twitter and Instagram to Apple's Mail and Calendar apps. These apps enable you to view data even when your iPhone is offline: diary entries in your Calendar, recently received e-mails, previously downloaded tweets. Enabling your apps to store data for offline usage dramatically improves user experience, enables fast access to data, and negates the need to keep a persistent Internet connection.

Birthday Reminder will provide users with three ways to add new birthdays: by importing from Facebook, by importing from the iPhone Address Book, or by adding them manually via the edit birthday view controller. Once a birthday is imported, it no longer needs to access its original source; in other words, a birthday imported from Facebook will not require our app to keep connecting to Facebook, it will remain independently persistent in our app, even if our user is offline.

Although the initial learning curve of Core Data is quite steep, I wanted to introduce you to it in this book because once you get a handle on the basics, it presents all kinds of possibilities for persistent data management in your apps. The code we'll write for *Birthday Reminder* only scratches the surface of Core Data, enabling our app to read, write, and update birthday model objects containing text, number, date, and binary (image thumbnails) attributes. However, should your future apps require a more complex data model, rest assured that Core Data will become your best friend and you'll have the foundation knowledge to build upon.

An introduction to Core Data

Core Data is Apple's object-relational mapping (ORM) solution for local data storage. This means that as Cocoa developers, we get to generate and work with data objects in our native programming language, Objective-C. Core Data then takes care of translating those data objects and relationships into another form that can be saved to disk. By default, the underlying storage for Core Data is an SQLite database. However, our apps should never need to connect directly to the underlying database. Core Data acts as the gateway to the file storage system and includes the management and model classes that our application code needs access to in order to create, edit, and delete model class instances and save persistent changes.

To introduce you to Core Data, let's begin by creating an example project from Apple's project templates.

Creating a Core Data application

Apple includes Core Data as an option for many of their Xcode templates, so let's check one out now. Fire up Xcode and create a new iPhone project based on the Master-Detail template, as shown in Figure 8-1.

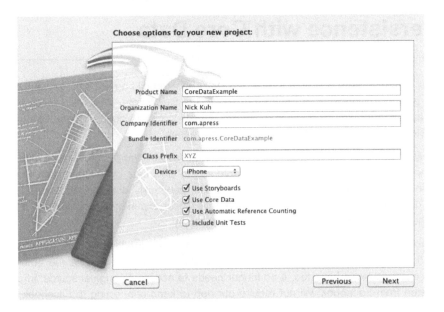

Figure 8-1. New Master-Detail Core Data example project options

Name your project CoreDataExample and ensure that the Use Core Data option is selected. Build and run the new project in the simulator. Tap the Add button a few times, and then the Edit button; you should see similar results to Figure 8-2.

Figure 8-2. Master-Detail Core Data project running

As you can see in Figure 8-2, the iPhone application generated from the Master-Detail template using Core Data enables the user to create, view, and delete data model objects containing a time stamp property. Rebuild and run the app. You'll discover the data model objects are still displayed; they are persistent and have been saved to disk by a little Core Data magic. However, it's important that we understand a little more about how Core Data works and what's behind that magic.

The persistent store

Under the hood, Core Data translates and stores any saved data changes to the *persistent store*. The persistent store can be set to any of the follow three storage types:

- *In memory* (NSInMemoryStoreType): This type of storage isn't actually persistent if an app is forced to quit. It's often used for runtime caching of data objects.

- *Flat binary file* (NSBinaryStoreType): In some cases, using a flat binary file might improve performance of data retrieval; but the downside is that as stored data grows, so too will the size of the binary file and initial loading time.

- *SQLite database* (NSSQLiteStoreType): This is the most common storage type by Core Data driven applications and the default used by the Apple project templates.

We'll be opting for the SQLite database storage type. It should ensure that our app remains scalable for large data sets. I'd generally recommend sticking with this default choice for the majority of Core Data powered apps.

At runtime, initializing a Core Data driven app involves creating an instance of a persistent store coordinator (NSPersistentStoreCoordinator) to create Core Data's connection to the persistent store.

Let's take a quick look at this code in our CoreDataExample project in the AppDelegate.m file:

```
- (NSPersistentStoreCoordinator *)persistentStoreCoordinator
{
    if (_persistentStoreCoordinator != nil) {
        return _persistentStoreCoordinator;
    }

    NSURL *storeURL = [[self applicationDocumentsDirectory]
URLByAppendingPathComponent:@"CoreDataExample.sqlite"];

    NSError *error = nil;
    _persistentStoreCoordinator = [[NSPersistentStoreCoordinator alloc]
initWithManagedObjectModel:[self managedObjectModel]];
    if (![_persistentStoreCoordinator addPersistentStoreWithType:NSSQLiteStoreType
configuration:nil URL:storeURL options:nil error:&error]) {
        NSLog(@"Unresolved error %@, %@", error, [error userInfo]);
        abort();
    }

    return _persistentStoreCoordinator;
}
```

In the highlighted code, you can see that we're defining a local URL to an SQLite database file. We're also connecting the instantiated persistent store coordinator to the persistent store, passing in NSSQLiteStoreType as the storage type. These are the only references to the underlying database we'll make: Core Data will take care of the rest. Core Data will create the SQLite database at the location specified (if it hasn't already created it in a previous session) and will manage the database for us. In the future, if our data model changes and requires migration, in most cases Core Data can update and modify the database for us automatically.

> Note: I recommend researching Core Data's migration options for initializing a persistent store coordinator. By switching on lightweight migration for most projects, you'll ensure that future changes you make to your data model are automatically migrated by Core Data.

You may also have noticed in the preceding code that the persistent store coordinator is instantiated with a reference to a *managed object model*, which is your custom model object graph: a definition of each data object in your model, the attributes of each object, and the relationships between objects. But what exactly are those objects?

Entities and managed objects

In Core Data, the native Objective-C data objects that are created, edited, and modified are defined by class descriptions known as *entities*. From these entity descriptions, Core Data generates object instances called *managed objects*, which can have attribute types such as strings, numbers, and dates. Managed objects can also have relationships to other managed objects in the model. All managed objects are either instances or subclasses of the NSManagedObject class.

We access the attributes of a managed object using key-value methods. Delving into the MasterViewController.m source file, we can see how to set a managed object attribute:

```
[newManagedObject setValue:[NSDate date] forKey:@"timeStamp"];
```

And how to retrieve the value of a managed object attribute:

```
[object valueForKey:@"timeStamp"];
```

As we'll discover later in the chapter, we can also subclass NSManagedObject, a step up from key-value coding because it enables us to strongly type attributes.

But how do we define entities and create managed objects? Xcode includes a UML modeling tool for developers that we'll look at next.

The Core Data model file

Let's take a closer look at the Core Data model from the Master-Detail project template. The model file will have the same name as your project, so select CoreDataExample.xcdatamodeld in the Project Navigator (see Figure 8-3).

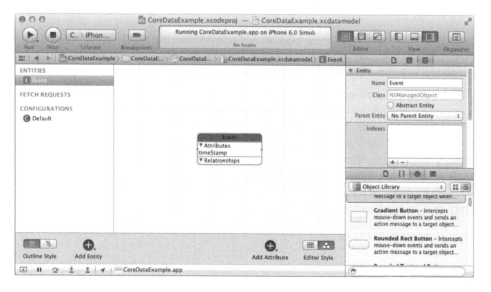

Figure 8-3. A basic Core Data model

In Figure 8-3, you can see that I've kept the utility pane open because it includes the data model inspector when working with a Core Data model file, so we can view entity and attribute details depending on the selection in the main editor pane. You can toggle between a UML graph-style display of your data model and a table-style display of your data model, as shown in Figure 8-4.

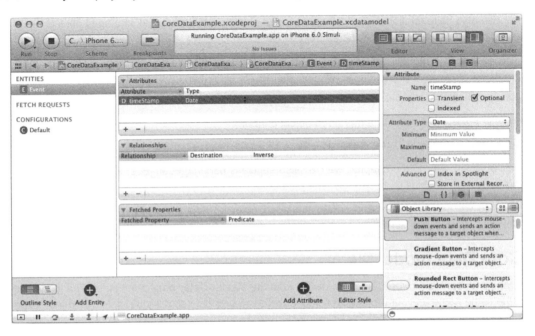

Figure 8-4. Viewing the data model with the table-style editor

As you can see in Figures 8-3 and 8-4, our model has just one entity, named Event. The Event entity has one attribute, named timeStamp. In Figure 8-3, with the Event entity selected, we can see that managed objects based on this entity will automatically be assigned to the default NSManagedObject class.

In Figure 8-4, viewing the data model with the table-style editor option, I've selected the Event entity and the editor lists the attributes (similar to properties) of the Event entity. In the case of Apple's example project, Event has just one attribute: timeStamp. Selecting timeStamp in the editor will also reveal the details for this entity attribute: it's an optional property with a data type of NSDate. So each time the Add button is tapped, the master view controller creates a new Event instance and sets its timeStamp value to the current date. It then saves the Core Data context.

Initializing a Core Data model

In summary, the anatomy of a Core Data stack can be presented as shown in Figure 8-5.

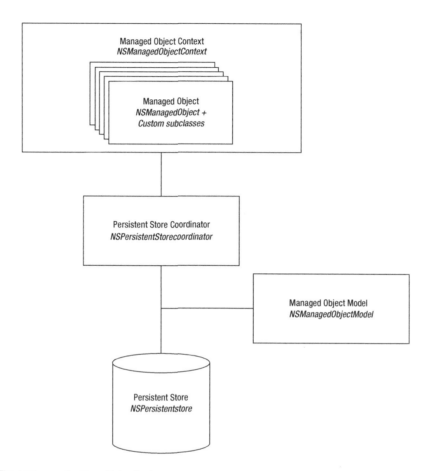

Figure 8-5. The anatomy of a Core Data stack

At the bottom of the stack, the persistent store (SQLite database by default). We add the persistent store to the persistent store coordinator, which we initiate with a managed object model. The managed object model is based on the xcdatamodeld file we just looked at in Xcode. Finally, we create a managed object context (NSManagedObjectContext) instance with which we can both create and access managed object instances to use in our application. But what's a managed object context?

The NSManagedObjectContext is the only class we'll really care about once our Core Data model has initialized when our program first runs. Adding, editing, and deleting entities will be achieved directly via the managed object context.

A little confused? Don't worry, for fairly simple applications like *Birthday Reminder*, the code to initialize a Core Data store and model can be virtually identical for every app you build. All better now? Good stuff!

What is a managed object context?

A *managed object context* is the representation of all the Core Data objects in our application, and their relationships to one another. Although we'll only use a single managed object context in our *Birthday Reminder* app, it's not uncommon to create multiple managed object contexts in an iOS App. Multiple managed object contexts can share a persistent store. However, if we make changes to the entities in one managed object context, they will not be reflected in another unless we save and merge the contexts.

With a single managed object context of our Core Data model, we'll be able to add new entities, change attributes, and when required, delete entities. When we want to write our managed object context changes to disk, we'll need to save the managed object context.

Adding, editing, deleting, and saving entities

In the Master-Detail example app, once the AppDelegate has initialized the model, store, and managed object context, it passes a reference to the managed object context onto the master view controller:

```
controller.managedObjectContext = self.managedObjectContext;
```

The master view controller can now add, edit, delete, and save Core Data entities all via its reference to the managed object context.

To understand the code required to add, edit, delete, and save Core Data entities, we can simplify a great deal of the code in Apple's master view controller to the following examples:

Adding

```
NSManagedObject *newManagedObject = [NSEntityDescription
insertNewObjectForEntityForName:@"Event" inManagedObjectContext:self.managedObjectContext];
```

All Core Data entities are instances or subclass instances of the NSManagedObject class. However, unlike most other Objective-C classes, we don't create instances of NSManagedObject via alloc init. Instead, we invoke the class method of NSEntityDescription and pass in our entity name and a reference to the managed object context.

Editing

By default, entities defined in our Core Data model are instances of Apple's NSManagedObject class. In order to set a property, we call the setValue:forKey: method of NSManagedObject:

```
[aManagedObject setValue:[NSDate date] forKey:@"timeStamp"];
```

With the data model inspector, however, we can also specify custom value object classes for entities that Xcode can build for use in our apps. The advantage of this is strict data-typing; so the preceding code would change to:

```
aManagedObject.timeStamp = [NSDate date];
```

We'll learn more about custom entity classes when we integrate a new Core Data model into our *Birthday Reminder* app later in the chapter.

Deleting

Deleting Core Data entities is a simple as:

```
[self.managedObjectContext deleteObject:aManagedObject];
```

Saving

When we're ready for Core Data to write our changes to disk (the persistent store), we call save: on the managed object context:

```
NSError *error = nil;
    if ([self.managedObjectContext hasChanges]) {
        if (![self.managedObjectContext save:&error]) {//save failed
            NSLog(@"Save failed: %@",[error localizedDescription]);
        }
        else {
            NSLog(@"Save succeeded");
        }
    }
```

Examples of when we'd call save are at the point a user taps the Save button in the edit birthday view controller or after we've finished importing a batch of birthdays.

Implementing Core Data into Birthday Reminder

Before we can start implementing Core Data into our *Birthday Reminder* app, we need to add the Core Data framework to our project's target. The target is the resulting iPhone app that Xcode compiles for us whenever we build our project.

Adding the Core Data framework

To add an Apple framework to our project, first select the BirthdayReminder project in the Project Navigator, then select the BirthdayReminder target and finally select Build Phases tab, as shown in Figure 8-6.

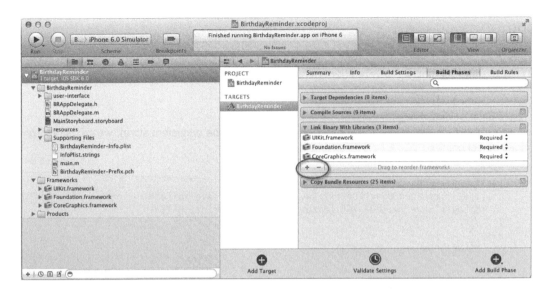

Figure 8-6. Preparing to add a new framework

Expand the Link Binary With Libraries pane and you'll see the frameworks already linked into our project: UIKit, Foundation, and CoreGraphics. To add Core Data, tap the highlighted + button and double-click CoreData.framework, listed in the modal window. Great, Core Data framework has been added! We can now reference Core Data classes in our app. Before we do, though, there's an easy way to import the Core Data framework header for all classes in our app: by defining the import declaration in our project's prefix file. Locate and select BirthdayReminder-Prefix.pch in the Project Navigator . Now add the Core Data import declaration alongside the Foundation and UIKit import declarations:

```
#ifdef __OBJC__
    #import <UIKit/UIKit.h>
    #import <Foundation/Foundation.h>
    #import <CoreData/CoreData.h>
#endif
```

We will now be able to make references to Core Data framework classes without having to repeatedly import the main Core Data framework header.

Let's move on to creating a Core Data model for our app.

Creating a Core Data model

Up until this point, we've focused primarily on the user interface of our app. Now that we're moving our attention to the dark data side, let's create a new folder to store all Core Data and Model classes. Add a new folder named data to the root directory of your *Birthday Reminder* project, and then add the new data folder as a new group to your Xcode project (see Figure 8-7).

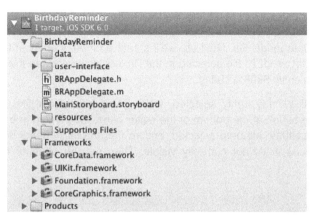

Figure 8-7. New data group added to project directory

In the Project Navigator, select the newly added data group, and with the ⌘N keyboard shortcut or File ➤ New ➤ File, choose the Data Model option from the Core Data file templates. Name the new data model BirthdayReminder.xcdatamodeld and tap the Create button, as shown in Figure 8-8.

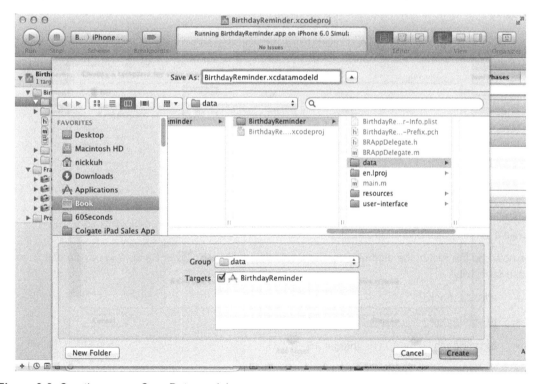

Figure 8-8. Creating a new Core Data model

Defining Core Data entities

We've created a Core Data model file. Next up, we'll create a birthday entity in the model. With the new BirthdayReminder.xcdatamodeld file selected in the Project Navigator, tap the Add Entity button in the editor and name the new entity BRDBirthday.

Now with the new BRDBirthday entity selected, we're going to add our first attribute, birthDay, by tapping the Add Attribute button at the bottom of the editor pane, then typing in birthDay as the attribute name. With the new birthDay attribute selected, ensure that the utility panel is open and toggle to the data model inspector pane if it's not currently visible. Then set the attribute type to Integer 16 (see Figure 8-9).

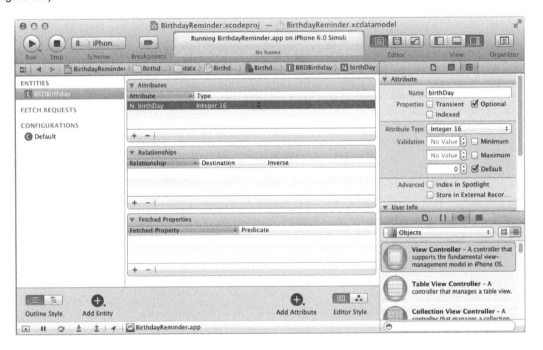

Figure 8-9. Defining Core Data entity attributes

Let's now add the rest of the attributes for our Birthday entity as follows. Be sure to pay careful attention to case sensitivity:

- addressBookID   Integer 16
- birthDay   Integer 16
- birthMonth   Integer 16
- birthYear   Integer 16
- facebookID   String
- imageData   Binary Data

- name   String

- nextBirthday   Date

- nextBirthdayAge   Integer 16

- notes   String

- picURL   String

- uid   String

Notice how we can also store binary data in Core Data entity attributes? This is perfect for storing image icon data. picURL will solely be used for the Facebook birthdays profile photo URLs. Facebook users regularly change their profile photo, so rather than caching their pics, we'll ensure that we regularly download the latest Facebook profile photos.

I've purposefully avoided including a birth date attribute. As we'll discover tomorrow, both Facebook and Address Book birthdays often don't include the birth year, so we won't actually always know the full birth date for our birthdays, just the month and day in some cases.

Now select the BRDBirthday entity rather than its attributes. The data model inspector should update and permit you to modify the default NSManagedObject class that the BRDBirthday entity is currently assigned to. Change this to BRDBirthday (see Figure 8-10).

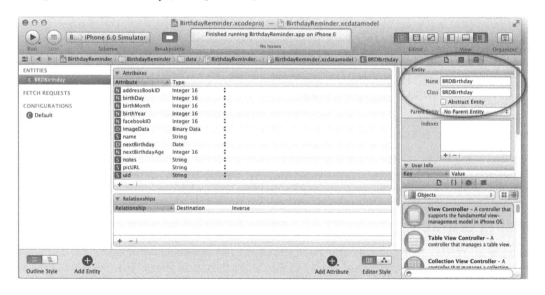

Figure 8-10. Assigning BRDBirthday entity to BRDBirthday class

Xcode is going to generate an NSManagedObject subclass named BRDBirthday for us with all of the birthday attributes we've specified.

With the data group selected in the Project Navigator, begin the process of creating a new NSManagedObject subclass for birthdays using the ⌘N keyboard shortcut or File ➤ New ➤ File, and selecting the NSManagedObject subclass from the Core Data collection (see Figure 8-11).

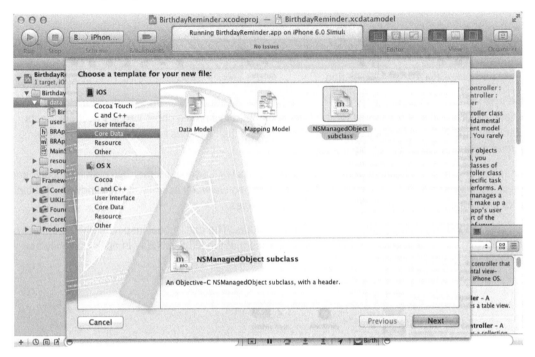

Figure 8-11. Creating an NSManagedObject subclass

On the next dialog screen, select the data folder in the Finder as the designation for the new class. Leave Use Scalar Properties for Primitive Data Types deselected and click Create.

Take a look at the BRDBirthday class that Xcode has generated for us. Notice how all of our integers are now NSNumber objects rather than primitives? As with dictionaries and arrays, Core Data can't use primitives as attributes; this is why they are wrapped in NSNumber instances.

Extending entities

Creating BRDBirthday as a subclass of NSManagedObject has additional advantages. We can add new methods and non-persistent properties directly to the BRDBirthday subclass. The birthdays in our store will be listed in order of the next pending birthday in the Home view controller. We've already created attributes on BRDBirthday to store the next birthday date and the next birthday age, but we have yet to set their values.

> Note: The one caveat to adding code to NSManagedObject subclasses is that you will
> need to ensure that you don't overwrite the Xcode-generated entity classes if you ever
> make changes to your Core Data model. You will just need to manually add/remove
> your changes to your entity subclasses.

Open the BRDBirthday.h header and add the following new public methods and property declarations:

```
@property (nonatomic,readonly) int remainingDaysUntilNextBirthday;
@property (nonatomic,readonly) NSString *birthdayTextToDisplay;
@property (nonatomic,readonly) BOOL isBirthdayToday;

-(void)updateNextBirthdayAndAge;
-(void)updateWithDefaults;
```

The following is a rundown on how these new properties and methods will be used in *Birthday Reminder*:

- remainingDaysUntilNextBirthday: Provides our users with a day count until each friend's next birthday.

- birthdayTextToDisplay: Human-readable text string such as "44 Tomorrow" or "34 on May 26".

- isBirthdayToday: If it's the user's birthday today, then we'll display a birthday cake image instead of their birthday countdown (see Chapter 9).

- updateNextBirthdayAndAge: We'll use this method to update the nextBirthday and nextBirthdayAge.

- updateWithDefaults: We'll call this method when the **Add Birthday** button is tapped to set the basic attributes required by BRDBirthday entities, namely birthdayDay and birthMonth.

Switch to BRDBirthday.m source file, and let's add the implementations of these new instance methods and properties:

```
-(void)updateNextBirthdayAndAge
{
    NSDate *now = [NSDate date];

    NSCalendar *calendar = [NSCalendar currentCalendar];

    NSDateComponents *dateComponents = [[NSCalendar currentCalendar]
components:NSYearCalendarUnit|NSMonthCalendarUnit|NSDayCalendarUnit fromDate:now];
    NSDate *today = [calendar dateFromComponents:dateComponents];

    dateComponents.day = [self.birthDay intValue];
    dateComponents.month = [self.birthMonth intValue];

    NSDate *birthdayThisYear = [calendar dateFromComponents:dateComponents];

    if ([today compare:birthdayThisYear] == NSOrderedDescending) {
        //birthday this year has passed so next birthday will be next year
```

```
        dateComponents.year++;
        self.nextBirthday = [calendar dateFromComponents:dateComponents];
    }
    else {
        self.nextBirthday = [birthdayThisYear copy];
    }

    if ([self.birthYear intValue] > 0) {
        self.nextBirthdayAge = [NSNumber numberWithInt:dateComponents.year - [self.birthYear
intValue]];
    }
    else {
        self.nextBirthdayAge = [NSNumber numberWithInt:0];
    }

}
```

Our code assumes that the birthDay and birthMonth properties will always be set for instances of BRDBirthday. This gives us enough to calculate our friend's birthday this year. We create an instance of NSDateComponents with the date right now. This ensures that the year property of our NSDateComponents instance is automatically set to the current year. Then, we override the day and month properties of NSDateComponents with the day and month of this friend's birthday. Now our instance of NSDateComponents has enough data to calculate the date of our friend's birthday this year. From our birthdayThisYear value, we can ascertain whether the date has passed or not, and set BRDBirthday's nextBirthday value to the friend's birthday this year or next year.

> Note: By extracting the nextBirthday from an instance of NSDateComponents, which we've initiated with the unit flags NSYearCalendarUnit, NSMonthCalendarUnit, and NSDayCalendarUnit, we will retrieve a date that corresponds to 00:00 on the morning of the birthday day. This is important to understand when making date comparisons between days of the year rather than hours, minutes, and seconds.

If a birth year has been set for the birthday entity, then we set the nextBirthdayAge to the difference between the friend's birth year and the year of their next birthday (this year or next). Alternatively, if the friend has kept his/her birth year private, then we default the nextBirthdayAge to 0.

Let's implement the updateWithDefaults method:

```
-(void) updateWithDefaults
{
    NSDateComponents *dateComponents = [[NSCalendar currentCalendar]
components:NSYearCalendarUnit|NSMonthCalendarUnit|NSDayCalendarUnit fromDate:[NSDate date]];

    self.birthDay = @(dateComponents.day);
    self.birthMonth = @(dateComponents.month);
    self.birthYear = @0;

    [self updateNextBirthdayAndAge];
```

```
}
```

Now to add our three readonly getter methods: remainingDaysUntilNextBirthday, birthdayTextToDisplay, and isBirthdayToday:

```objc
-(int) remainingDaysUntilNextBirthday
{
    NSDate *now = [NSDate date];
    NSCalendar *calendar = [NSCalendar currentCalendar];
    NSDateComponents *componentsToday = [calendar
components:NSYearCalendarUnit|NSMonthCalendarUnit|NSDayCalendarUnit fromDate:now];
    NSDate *today = [calendar dateFromComponents:componentsToday];

    NSTimeInterval timeDiffSecs = [self.nextBirthday timeIntervalSinceDate:today];

    int days = floor(timeDiffSecs/(60.f*60.f*24.f));

    return days;
}

-(BOOL) isBirthdayToday
{
    return [self remainingDaysUntilNextBirthday] == 0;
}

-(NSString *) birthdayTextToDisplay {

    NSDate *now = [NSDate date];
    NSCalendar *calendar = [NSCalendar currentCalendar];
    NSDateComponents *componentsToday = [calendar
components:NSYearCalendarUnit|NSMonthCalendarUnit|NSDayCalendarUnit fromDate:now];
    NSDate *today = [calendar dateFromComponents:componentsToday];

    NSDateComponents *components = [calendar components:NSMonthCalendarUnit|NSDayCalendarUnit
fromDate:today toDate:self.nextBirthday options:0];

    if (components.month == 0) {
        if (components.day == 0) {
            //today!

            if ([self.nextBirthdayAge intValue] > 0) {
                return [NSString stringWithFormat:@"%@ Today!",self.nextBirthdayAge];
            }
            else {
                return @"Today!";
            }
        }
        if (components.day == 1) {
            //tomorrow!
            if ([self.nextBirthdayAge intValue] > 0) {
                return [NSString stringWithFormat:@"%@ Tomorrow!",self.nextBirthdayAge];
            }
            else {
```

```
                    return @"Tomorrow!";
                }
            }
        }

    NSString *text = @"";

    if ([self.nextBirthdayAge intValue] > 0) {
        text = [NSString stringWithFormat:@"%@ on ",self.nextBirthdayAge];
    }

    static NSDateFormatter *dateFormatterPartial;

    if (dateFormatterPartial == nil) {
        dateFormatterPartial = [[NSDateFormatter alloc] init];
        [dateFormatterPartial setDateFormat:@"MMM d"];
    }

    return [text stringByAppendingFormat:@"%@",[dateFormatterPartial
stringFromDate:self.nextBirthday]];
}
```

You should be able to read through and make sense of the code for the remainingDaysUntilNextBirthday and isBirthdayToday methods, but birthdayTextToDisplay needs some additional explanation. The most important line of code is the following one:

```
NSDateComponents *components = [calendar components:NSMonthCalendarUnit|NSDayCalendarUnit
fromDate:today toDate:self.nextBirthday options:0];
```

NSDateComponents class can also be used to calculate the difference between two dates. By initializing the NSDateComponents instance with the NSMonthCalendarUnit and NSDayCalendarUnit unit flags, we can obtain the number of months and days between today and the friend's next birthday. If both of these values are equal to 0, then the friend's birthday must be today! Or if the month difference value is 0 and the day value is 1, then the friend's next birthday is one day away— tomorrow!

Be sure that your version of the app still compiles OK. You won't see any differences in the app for the time being because we've yet to convert our birthdays array data model to the new Core Data storage model. We're not even initializing our Core Data model yet in code. That's our next task.

Initializing our Core Data model

When we looked at Apple's example Core Data code, we found all of the initialization code in the application delegate class. However, it's common practice to create a singleton model class and initialize the Core Data model once in the singleton instance. That way any class in our project can access the managed object context directly though the model singleton.

Let's begin by creating a singleton model class. Create a new subclass of NSObject in the data group and name the class BRDModel. To set up our singleton class, we'll provide access to our model only via a class method called sharedInstance. The BRDModel sharedInstance method will create the single instance of BRDModel or simply return it if it already exists. First, define the class method in BRDModel.h:
```
#import <Foundation/Foundation.h>
```

```
@interface BRDModel : NSObject
```

+ (BRDModel*)sharedInstance;

```
@end
```

Now switch to the implementation of the new class method in BRDModel.m:
```
#import "BRDModel.h"
```

```
@implementation BRDModel
```

```
static BRDModel *_sharedInstance = nil;
+ (BRDModel*)sharedInstance
{
    if( !_sharedInstance ) {
            _sharedInstance = [[BRDModel alloc] init];
    }
        return _sharedInstance;
}
```

```
@end
```

The sharedInstance method initializes an instance of its own class. This is a fairly common technique for implementing singletons in Objective-C. Whenever we wish to access the model in our application, we'll just reference [BRDModel sharedInstance]. Next, let's grab the Core Data initialization code from Apple's own Master-Detail app we created earlier in the chapter. Locate the AppDelegate.h header file and copy the declarations of the persistent store coordinator, the managed object model, and the managed object context and paste them straight into the BRDModel.h header as highlighted in the following:

```
#import <Foundation/Foundation.h>
```

```
@interface BRDModel : NSObject
```

```
+ (BRDModel*)sharedInstance;
```

@property (readonly, strong, nonatomic) NSManagedObjectContext *managedObjectContext;
@property (readonly, strong, nonatomic) NSManagedObjectModel *managedObjectModel;
@property (readonly, strong, nonatomic) NSPersistentStoreCoordinator
***persistentStoreCoordinator;**

```
@end
```

Switch to the BRDModel.m source file and synthesize the three new Core Data properties, just like in the AppDelegate.m source file:

```
@implementation BRDModel
```

@synthesize managedObjectContext = _managedObjectContext;
@synthesize managedObjectModel = _managedObjectModel;
@synthesize persistentStoreCoordinator = _persistentStoreCoordinator;

> *Note: We manually add synthesize code on this occasion to ensure that each property points to an underbar instance variable. Xcode's compiler doesn't automatically do this with* readonly *properties.*

Then copy over the implementations of the three Core Data accessor methods and the applicationDocumentsDirectory helper private method from Apple's own code in AppDelegate.m from the Master-Detail project. Remove the comments if you like, but more importantly replace the two string occurrences of CoreDataExample with the name of our *Birthday Reminder* Core Data model, BirthdayReminder, as highlighted in the following code:

```
- (NSManagedObjectContext *)managedObjectContext
{
    if (_managedObjectContext != nil) {
        return _managedObjectContext;
    }

    NSPersistentStoreCoordinator *coordinator = [self persistentStoreCoordinator];
    if (coordinator != nil) {
        _managedObjectContext = [[NSManagedObjectContext alloc] init];
        [_managedObjectContext setPersistentStoreCoordinator:coordinator];
    }
    return _managedObjectContext;
}

// Returns the managed object model for the application.
// If the model doesn't already exist, it is created from the application's model.
- (NSManagedObjectModel *)managedObjectModel
{
    if (_managedObjectModel != nil) {
        return _managedObjectModel;
    }
    NSURL *modelURL = [[NSBundle mainBundle] URLForResource:@"BirthdayReminder"
withExtension:@"momd"];
    _managedObjectModel = [[NSManagedObjectModel alloc] initWithContentsOfURL:modelURL];
    return _managedObjectModel;
}

// Returns the persistent store coordinator for the application.
// If the coordinator doesn't already exist, it is created and the application's store added
to it.
- (NSPersistentStoreCoordinator *)persistentStoreCoordinator
{
    if (_persistentStoreCoordinator != nil) {
        return _persistentStoreCoordinator;
    }

    NSURL *storeURL = [[self applicationDocumentsDirectory]
URLByAppendingPathComponent:@"BirthdayReminder.sqlite"];

    NSError *error = nil;
```

```
    _persistentStoreCoordinator = [[NSPersistentStoreCoordinator alloc]
initWithManagedObjectModel:[self managedObjectModel]];
    if (![_persistentStoreCoordinator addPersistentStoreWithType:NSSQLiteStoreType
configuration:nil URL:storeURL options:nil error:&error]) {
        NSLog(@"Unresolved error %@, %@", error, [error userInfo]);
        abort();
    }

    return _persistentStoreCoordinator;
}

#pragma mark - Application's Documents directory

// Returns the URL to the application's Documents directory.
- (NSURL *)applicationDocumentsDirectory
{
    return [[[NSFileManager defaultManager] URLsForDirectory:NSDocumentDirectory
inDomains:NSUserDomainMask] lastObject];
}
```

Now would be a good time to check that your app still compiles OK, although you won't see any changes yet because we're still in the preparation stage of the Core Data implementation.

Connecting table views to result sets with NSFetchedResultsController

In order to retrieve stored result sets of Core Data entities, Apple provides a handy fetching class named NSFetchedResultsController. Not only will a fetched results controller perform an initial ordered fetch of Core Data entities based on a query, it also provides delegate callback methods to alert its delegate of changes to the results set. Changes like newly added, modified or removed managed objects. It's a very powerful class and we'll be using it to keep track of the list of BRDBirthday entities in our Core Data store and display them in our Home view controller.

Open the header file for BRHomeViewController.h and declare that our Home view controller implements the NSFetchedResultsControllerDelegate protocol:

```
@interface BRHomeViewController :
BRCoreViewController<UITableViewDelegate,UITableViewDataSource,
NSFetchedResultsControllerDelegate>
```

Open the BRHomeViewController.m source file, import our new BRDBirthday.h and BRDModel.h headers, and declare a new fetched results controller private property in the Home view controller:

```
#import "BRHomeViewController.h"
#import "BRBirthdayDetailViewController.h"
#import "BRBirthdayEditViewController.h"
#import "BRDBirthday.h"
#import "BRDModel.h"

@interface BRHomeViewController()
@property (nonatomic, strong) NSFetchedResultsController *fetchedResultsController;
@property (nonatomic,strong) NSMutableArray *birthdays;
```

@end

We'll lazy-load our fetched results controller; that is, we'll only instantiate it at the first moment it's required in code. To do this, we override the getter accessor method for self.fetchedResultsController. We check to see if the instance variable _fetchedResultsController has not yet been instantiated before we create the stored fetched results controller instance. Add the new accessor method for fetchedResultsController to BRHomeViewController.m:

```
#pragma mark Fetched Results Controller to keep track of the Core Data BRDBirthday managed
objects

- (NSFetchedResultsController *)fetchedResultsController {
    if (_fetchedResultsController == nil) {

        NSFetchRequest *fetchRequest = [[NSFetchRequest alloc] init];

        //access the single managed object context through model singleton
        NSManagedObjectContext *context = [BRDModel sharedInstance].managedObjectContext;

        //fetch request requires an entity description - we're only interested in BRDBirthday
managed objects
        NSEntityDescription *entity = [NSEntityDescription entityForName:@"BRDBirthday"
inManagedObjectContext:context];
        fetchRequest.entity = entity;

        //we'll order the BRDBirthday objects in name sort order for now
        NSSortDescriptor *sortDescriptor = [[NSSortDescriptor alloc]
initWithKey:@"nextBirthday" ascending:YES];
        NSArray *sortDescriptors = [[NSArray alloc] initWithObjects:sortDescriptor, nil];
        fetchRequest.sortDescriptors = sortDescriptors;

        self.fetchedResultsController = [[NSFetchedResultsController alloc]
initWithFetchRequest:fetchRequest managedObjectContext:context sectionNameKeyPath:nil
cacheName:nil];
        self.fetchedResultsController.delegate = self;
        NSError *error = nil;
        if (![self.fetchedResultsController performFetch:&error]) {

            NSLog(@"Unresolved error %@, %@", error, [error userInfo]);
            abort();
        }

    }

        return _fetchedResultsController;
}
```

A fetched results controller needs a fetch request: it needs to know the type of managed objects it should be fetching and the order of the results it should return. So we first create an NSFetchRequest instance and then pass it to our new NSFetchedResultsController. We set the entity of the fetch request to be our only entity, BRDBirthday, and we specify that the results should be returned in order of the nextBirthday string attribute of BRDBirthday.

Finally, we invoke the results controller to run the fetch request via the performFetch: method to populate our fetched results controller with all the BRDBirthday managed objects in the store (none for now!).

There's a good reason that we set the Home view controller as a delegate of the fetched results controller: we want any changes to the results set as newly added or edited birthday managed objects to be caught by our retained fetched results controller. Apple's developer documentation states: *A delegate must implement at least one of the change tracking delegate methods in order for change tracking to be enabled. Providing an empty implementation of* controllerDidChangeContent: *is sufficient.*[1]

So, in order to ensure our fetched results controller is kept up-to-date, we'll implement an empty NSFetchedResultsControllerDelegate protocol method into the BRHomeViewController.m class:

```
#pragma mark NSFetchedResultsControllerDelegate

- (void)controllerDidChangeContent:(NSFetchedResultsController *)controller {
    //The fetched results changed
}
```

Locate the two UITableViewDataSource protocol methods for populating our table view (tableView:cellForRowAtIndexPath: and tableView:numberOfRowsInSection:) and replace them with the following:

```
- (UITableViewCell *)tableView:(UITableView *)tableView cellForRowAtIndexPath:(NSIndexPath
*)indexPath
{
    UITableViewCell *cell = [self.tableView dequeueReusableCellWithIdentifier:@"Cell"];

    BRDBirthday *birthday = [self.fetchedResultsController objectAtIndexPath:indexPath];

    cell.textLabel.text = birthday.name;
    cell.detailTextLabel.text = birthday.birthdayTextToDisplay;
    cell.imageView.image = [UIImage imageWithData:birthday.imageData];
    return cell;
}

- (NSInteger)tableView:(UITableView *)tableView numberOfRowsInSection:(NSInteger)section
{
    id <NSFetchedResultsSectionInfo> sectionInfo = [[self.fetchedResultsController sections]
objectAtIndex:section];
    return [sectionInfo numberOfObjects];
}
```

---

[1] iOS Developer Library, "NSFetchedResultsController Class Reference,"
http://developer.apple.com/library/ios/#DOCUMENTATION/CoreData/Reference/NSFetchedResultsController_Class/
Reference/Reference.html.

We access entities in the results set of our fetched results controller via the objectAtIndexPath: method. Like tables, fetched results controllers can have multiple sections. In our case, there will be just one section containing all the BRDBirthday entities in our Core Data store.

Your app will now be attempting to initialize the new empty Core Data model. With a bit of luck, you should now be able to build and run your app without error. However, if it compiles but crashes, then ensure that you replaced any reference to CoreDataExample to BirthdayReminder in the code copied from Apple's example Master-Detail template project. Additionally, the new Core Data model may not have been copied into the target bundle; this can be easily resolved by trying one or both of the following:

- Run a product clean with the ⇧⌘K shortcut or Product ➤ Clean.

- If that fails, then delete Birthday Reminder from the simulator or device, and build and run afresh.

Assuming you can now build and run, our app is now empty of birthdays (see Figure 8-12).

Figure 8-12. Connected to the Core Data model, but without any birthdays

Populating the Core Data store

Before we start creating new BRDBirthday instances from our Core Data model, we'll add a new saveChanges method to BRDModel. It's a public instance method, so add the declaration to BRDModel.h:

```
- (void)saveChanges;
```

And then the implementation into BRDModel.m source file:

```
- (void)saveChanges
{
    NSError *error = nil;
    if ([self.managedObjectContext hasChanges]) {
        if (![self.managedObjectContext save:&error]) {//save failed
            NSLog(@"Save failed: %@",[error localizedDescription]);
        }
        else {
            NSLog(@"Save succeeded");
        }
    }
}
```

Let's populate our database and birthdays table view in the Home view controller by importing the celebrity birthdays into our Core Data model. Delete and replace your current version of initWithCoder: in BRHomeViewController.m with the following:

```
- (id) initWithCoder:(NSCoder *)aDecoder
{
    self = [super initWithCoder:aDecoder];

    if (self) {
        NSString* plistPath = [[NSBundle mainBundle] pathForResource:@"birthdays"
ofType:@"plist"];
        NSArray *nonMutableBirthdays = [NSArray arrayWithContentsOfFile:plistPath];

        BRDBirthday *birthday;
        NSDictionary *dictionary;
        NSString *name;
        NSString *pic;
        NSString *pathForPic;
        NSData *imageData;
        NSDate *birthdate;
        NSCalendar *calendar = [NSCalendar currentCalendar];

        NSManagedObjectContext *context = [BRDModel sharedInstance].managedObjectContext;

        for (int i=0;i<[nonMutableBirthdays count];i++) {
            dictionary = nonMutableBirthdays[i];

            birthday = [NSEntityDescription insertNewObjectForEntityForName:@"BRDBirthday"
inManagedObjectContext:context];

            name = dictionary[@"name"];
            pic = dictionary[@"pic"];
            birthdate = dictionary[@"birthdate"];
            pathForPic = [[NSBundle mainBundle] pathForResource:pic ofType:nil];
            imageData = [NSData dataWithContentsOfFile:pathForPic];
            birthday.name = name;
```

```
            birthday.imageData = imageData;
            NSDateComponents *components = [calendar
components:NSYearCalendarUnit|NSMonthCalendarUnit|NSDayCalendarUnit fromDate:birthdate];
            //New literals syntax, same as
            //birthday.birthDay = [NSNumber numberWithInt:components.day];
            birthday.birthDay = @(components.day);
            birthday.birthMonth = @(components.month);
            birthday.birthYear = @(components.year);
            [birthday updateNextBirthdayAndAge];
        }
        [[BRDModel sharedInstance] saveChanges];
    }

    return self;
}
```

For now, we're just creating new Core Data BRDBirthday entities and setting the attributes name, imageData, birthDay, birthMonth, and birthYear for each of the celebrity birthdays. We also invoke our extended updateNextBirthdayAndAge method for each newly created birthday managed object, which will populate the nextBirthday and nextBirthdayAge attributes. Once we've looped through the plist of birthday dictionaries and inserted a new birthday entity for each, we call our new saveChanges method on the model.

Now build and run. You should see the celebrities. Build and run a couple more times. Are you noticing anything odd, like what's shown in Figure 8-13?

Figure 8-13. Too many Biebers?

Every time we rebuild and run the app, we create and save a batch of new BRDBirthday managed objects in the Home view controller's initWithCoder: initializer. As long as we've saved once to Core Data on a previous app session, we're also able to pre-populate the fetched results controller's results set even before importing from the celebrity plist birthdays. So the data is indeed persisting as expected. The problem is we just keep creating new duplicate birthday instances and adding them to the data store each time we run our app. We need to add a way to avoid importing duplicates.

Duplicate entities and synchronization

An effective way to avoid adding duplicate birthday managed objects is by referencing a unique identifier on the BRDBirthday instances to check whether we've already created a matching birthday in our store. That's the reason we created a uid string attribute when we defined BRDBirthday entity in our Core Data model.

We'll use the celebrity names as the unique identifier (when we move on to importing from Facebook or the Address Book, we'll use unique profile identifiers). Before creating new birthday managed objects, we'll loop through the birthday dictionaries from the plist and concatenate all the names into an array of unique ids. We'll then use the array of ids to create a Core Data fetch request that returns any existing BRDBirthday entities with matching uids. We'll create the fetch request for existing birthdays within a new method of our BRDModel singleton class, as this duplicate-checking functionality will also come in handy when we start importing from other sources, like Facebook and the Address Book.

Switch to BRDModel.

Add a new public method declaration to BRDModel.h:

```
-(NSMutableDictionary *) getExistingBirthdaysWithUIDs:(NSArray *)uids;
```

Switch to the BRDModel.m source file and import BRDBirthday:

```
#import "BRDBirthday.h"
```

And then the implementation:

```
-(NSMutableDictionary *) getExistingBirthdaysWithUIDs:(NSArray *)uids
{
    NSFetchRequest *fetchRequest = [[NSFetchRequest alloc] init];

    NSManagedObjectContext *context = self.managedObjectContext;

    //NSPredicates are used to filter results sets.
    //This predicate specifies that the uid attribute from any results must match one or more
of the values in the uids array
    NSPredicate *predicate = [NSPredicate predicateWithFormat:@"uid IN %@", uids];
    fetchRequest.predicate = predicate;

    NSEntityDescription *entity = [NSEntityDescription entityForName:@"BRDBirthday"
inManagedObjectContext:context];
    fetchRequest.entity = entity;
```

```
    NSSortDescriptor *sortDescriptor = [[NSSortDescriptor alloc] initWithKey:@"uid"
ascending:YES];
    NSArray *sortDescriptors = [[NSArray alloc] initWithObjects:sortDescriptor, nil];
    fetchRequest.sortDescriptors = sortDescriptors;

    NSFetchedResultsController *fetchedResultsController = [[NSFetchedResultsController alloc]
initWithFetchRequest:fetchRequest managedObjectContext:context sectionNameKeyPath:nil
cacheName:nil];

    NSError *error = nil;
    if (![fetchedResultsController performFetch:&error]) {

        NSLog(@"Unresolved error %@, %@", error, [error userInfo]);
        abort();
    }

    NSArray *fetchedObjects = fetchedResultsController.fetchedObjects;

    NSInteger resultCount = [fetchedObjects count];

        if (resultCount == 0) return [NSMutableDictionary dictionary];//nothing in the Core
Data store

    BRDBirthday *birthday;

        NSMutableDictionary *tmpDict = [NSMutableDictionary dictionary];

    int i;

    for (i = 0; i < resultCount; i++) {
        birthday =  fetchedObjects[i];
        tmpDict[birthday.uid] = birthday;
    }

    return tmpDict;
}
```

We're creating another fetched results controller, but only in the temporary scope of our new `getExistingBirthdaysWithUIDs:` method. Once the results have been retrieved from the managed object context, they are packaged into a dictionary using the `uid` attribute as the keys and the `BRDBirthday` managed objects as the values.

Notice that we now create an `NSPredicate` instance so that the fetched request is restricted only to `BRDBirthday` entities that match the predicate query:

```
NSPredicate *predicate = [NSPredicate predicateWithFormat:@"uid IN %@", uids];
fetchRequest.predicate = predicate;
```

The `NSPredicate` class is used for filtering a results set. This code should optimize the results set for scalability because we only request `BRDBirthday` managed objects in the results set that have the `uid` attribute matching one or more of the values in the `uids` array parameter.

Back in our Home view controller, we'll now add to the `initWithCoder:` method to take advantage of our model's `getExistingBirthdaysWithUIDs:` method:

```objc
- (id) initWithCoder:(NSCoder *)aDecoder
{
    self = [super initWithCoder:aDecoder];

    if (self) {
        NSString* plistPath = [[NSBundle mainBundle] pathForResource:@"birthdays"
ofType:@"plist"];
        NSArray *nonMutableBirthdays = [NSArray arrayWithContentsOfFile:plistPath];

        BRDBirthday *birthday;
        NSDictionary *dictionary;
        NSString *name;
        NSString *pic;
        NSString *pathForPic;
        NSData *imageData;
        NSDate *birthdate;
        NSCalendar *calendar = [NSCalendar currentCalendar];

        NSString *uid;
        NSMutableArray *uids = [NSMutableArray array];
        for (int i=0;i<[nonMutableBirthdays count];i++) {
            dictionary = [nonMutableBirthdays objectAtIndex:i];
            uid = dictionary[@"name"];
            [uids addObject:uid];
        }
        NSMutableDictionary *existingEntities = [[BRDModel sharedInstance]
getExistingBirthdaysWithUIDs:uids];


        NSManagedObjectContext *context = [BRDModel sharedInstance].managedObjectContext;

        for (int i=0;i<[nonMutableBirthdays count];i++) {
            dictionary = nonMutableBirthdays[i];

            uid = dictionary[@"name"];

            birthday = existingEntities[uid];

            if (birthday) {//birthday already exists

            }
            else {//birthday doesn't exist so create it
                birthday = [NSEntityDescription
insertNewObjectForEntityForName:@"BRDBirthday" inManagedObjectContext:context];
                existingEntities[uid] = birthday;
                birthday.uid = uid;

            }
```

```
        birthday = [NSEntityDescription insertNewObjectForEntityForName:@"BRDBirthday"
inManagedObjectContext:context];

        name = dictionary[@"name"];
        pic = dictionary[@"pic"];
        birthdate = dictionary[@"birthdate"];
        pathForPic = [[NSBundle mainBundle] pathForResource:pic ofType:nil];
        imageData = [NSData dataWithContentsOfFile:pathForPic];
        birthday.name = name;
        birthday.imageData = imageData;
        NSDateComponents *components = [calendar
components:NSYearCalendarUnit|NSMonthCalendarUnit|NSDayCalendarUnit fromDate:birthdate];
        //New literals syntax, same as
        //birthday.birthDay = [NSNumber numberWithInt:components.day];
        birthday.birthDay = @(components.day);
        birthday.birthMonth = @(components.month);
        birthday.birthYear = @(components.year);
        [birthday updateNextBirthdayAndAge];
    }
    [[BRDModel sharedInstance] saveChanges];
    }

    return self;
}
```

Before testing out the new code, you'll need to delete the old version of *Birthday Reminder* from the simulator or your device, because we haven't written any code to clear out existing duplicates. This is just to ensure they don't occur when importing new birthdays. Now build and run a few times. You should no longer see duplicate celebrities listed in the table view.

The getExistingBirthdaysWithUIDs: method of our model returns a mutable dictionary of existing birthday entities with their unique ids as the keys. We can reference this mutable dictionary for each birthday dictionary we want to import:

```
birthday = existingEntities[uid];
if (birthday) {
    //birthday already exists
}
else {
    //birthday doesn't exist
}
```

If the birthday entity doesn't exist, we create it. If it does already exist, then we don't create a new one, we'll just update its attributes.

Transitioning from dictionaries to entities

We're now going to replace the current references in our project to birthday dictionaries with references to our new BRDBirthday managed object. We're going to work through the Birthday Detail and Edit view controllers and then resolve the prepareForSegue:sender: method in our Home view controller to get it parsing managed birthday objects instead of dictionaries. Let's get to work!

Birthday detail view controller

Modify the BRBirthdayDetailViewController.h interface:

```
#import <UIKit/UIKit.h>
#import "BRCoreViewController.h"
@class BRDBirthday;

@interface BRBirthdayDetailViewController : BRCoreViewController

@property(nonatomic,strong) NSMutableDictionary *birthday;
@property(nonatomic,strong) BRDBirthday *birthday;
@property (weak, nonatomic) IBOutlet UIImageView *photoView;

@end
```

Switch to the BRBirthdayDetailViewController.m source file and import BRDBirthday:

```
#import "BRDBirthday.h"
```

Then modify the viewWillAppear: method so that the title and the image will be directly updated from the BRDBirthday entity attributes:

```
-(void) viewWillAppear:(BOOL)animated
{
    [super viewWillAppear:animated];
    NSLog(@"viewWillAppear");
    NSString *name = self.birthday[@"name"];
    self.title = name;
    self.title = self.birthday.name;
    UIImage *image = self.birthday[@"image"];
    UIImage *image = [UIImage imageWithData:self.birthday.imageData];
    if (image == nil) {
        //default to the birthday cake pic if there's no birthday image
        self.photoView.image = [UIImage imageNamed:@"icon-birthday-cake.png"];
    }
    else {
        self.photoView.image = image;
    }
}
```

You should be able to build and run fine with these changes, but the compiler will generate a couple of warnings in the Home view controller and Birthday Detail view controller relating to the prepareForSegue: sender: implementations. Ignore these warning for now. As long as you can build the app, you're doing fine.

Birthday edit view controller

Modify the BRBirthdayEditViewController.h interface (as you just did for the BRBirthdayDetailViewController.h interface) by adding a forward class declaration for our BRDBirthday entity:

```
#import <UIKit/UIKit.h>
#import "BRCoreViewController.h"
@class BRDBirthday;
```

And replacing the birthday class type with BRDBirthday:

```
@property (nonatomic, strong) NSMutableDictionary *birthday;
```

```
@property(nonatomic,strong) BRDBirthday *birthday;
```

Don't worry about the new compiler errors in BRBirthdayEditViewController.m. We're going to work our way through resolving them next.

Switch to the BRBirthdayEditViewController.m source file and import the BRDBirthday.h and BRDModel.h headers:

```
#import "BRDBirthday.h"
#import "BRDModel.h"
```

Begin by adding a new private method to break apart the date selected by the date picker:

```
- (void)updateBirthdayDetails {
    NSCalendar *calendar = [NSCalendar currentCalendar];
    NSDateComponents *components = [calendar components:NSYearCalendarUnit |
NSMonthCalendarUnit | NSDayCalendarUnit fromDate:self.datePicker.date];
    self.birthday.birthMonth = @(components.month);
    self.birthday.birthDay = @(components.day);
    if (self.includeYearSwitch.on) {
        self.birthday.birthYear = @(components.year);
    }
    else {
        self.birthday.birthYear = @0;
    }
    [self.birthday updateNextBirthdayAndAge];
}
```

When manipulating the date selected, we're utilizing an Objective-C class called NSDateComponents. Apple's NSDateComponents class is a utility class that enables us to break NSDate instances into their individual components—years, months, days, and so forth.

We need our new updateBirthdayDetails method to be invoked whenever the user changes the date picker value or the Include Year switch, so let's modify those methods accordingly:

```
- (IBAction)didChangeDatePicker:(id)sender {
    NSLog(@"New Birthdate Selected: %@",self.datePicker.date);
    self.birthday[@"birthdate"] = self.datePicker.date;
    [self updateBirthdayDetails];
}

- (IBAction)didToggleSwitch:(id)sender {
    if (self.includeYearSwitch.on) {
        NSLog(@"Sure, I'll share my age with you!");
    }
    else {
```

```
        NSLog(@"I'd prefer to keep my birthday year to myself thank you very much!");
    }
    [self updateBirthdayDetails];
}
```

Next, let's get rid of the error when the name text field is modified by the user:

```
- (IBAction)didChangeNameText:(id)sender {
    NSLog(@"The text was changed: %@",self.nameTextField.text);
    self.birthday[@"name"] = self.nameTextField.text;
    self.birthday.name = self.nameTextField.text;
    [self updateSaveButton];
}
```

We also need to amend our viewWillAppear:animated: method to account for the changes to the way BRDBirthday stores birthdays into their day, month, and year components rather than date. Delete and replace the current implementation of viewWillAppear: with the following:

```
-(void) viewWillAppear:(BOOL)animated
{
    [super viewWillAppear:animated];

    self.nameTextField.text = self.birthday.name;

    NSCalendar *calendar = [NSCalendar currentCalendar];
    NSDateComponents *components = [calendar components:NSYearCalendarUnit |
NSMonthCalendarUnit | NSDayCalendarUnit fromDate:[NSDate date]];

    if ([self.birthday.birthDay intValue] > 0) components.day = [self.birthday.birthDay
intValue];
    if ([self.birthday.birthMonth intValue] > 0) components.month = [self.birthday.birthMonth
intValue];
    if ([self.birthday.birthYear intValue] > 0) {
        components.year = [self.birthday.birthYear intValue];
        self.includeYearSwitch.on = YES;
    }
    else {
        self.includeYearSwitch.on = NO;
    }
    [self.birthday updateNextBirthdayAndAge];
    self.datePicker.date = [calendar dateFromComponents:components];

    if (self.birthday.imageData == nil)
    {
        self.photoView.image = [UIImage imageNamed:@"icon-birthday-cake.png"];
    }
    else {
        self.photoView.image = [UIImage imageWithData:self.birthday.imageData];
    }

    [self updateSaveButton];

}
```

Creating image thumbnails

Our birthday edit view controller still has one last compiler error in our implementation of imagePickerController: didFinishPickingMediaWithInfo. Let's fix that with the following change:

```
- (void)imagePickerController:(UIImagePickerController *)picker
didFinishPickingMediaWithInfo:(NSDictionary *)info {

    [picker dismissModalViewControllerAnimated:YES];

    UIImage *image = info[UIImagePickerControllerOriginalImage];

    self.photoView.image = image;

    [self.birthday setObject:image forKey:@"image"];
    self.birthday.imageData = UIImageJPEGRepresentation (image,1.f);

}
```

Core Data allows us to store binary data attributes for entities. This doesn't mean we can pass an instance of UIImage to the BRDBirthday.imageData attribute. Instead, we pass an instance of NSData. UIKit includes a utility method to convert a UIImage instance into a JPG NSData representation—UIImageJPGRepresentation and set a JPG compression quality from 0 to 1 (1 meaning one hundred percent quality).

We have a bit of a problem here. We're currently saving potentially very large images taken by the iPhone camera into our Core Data model. These images will only ever be displayed in our app in small thumbnail image views. It's bad practice to display a very large image in a small image view. iOS will still need to iterate over every pixel in our very large image before it can draw the small thumbnail. Our app will suffer a significant performance hit if our users start adding and editing birthdays, picking large photo files. We need to generate optimized smaller versions of any photo added to a birthday. We'll achieve this by creating a new Objective-C category file and adding our own custom createThumbnailToFillSize: method on UIImage.

Add a categories folder to your user-interface folder and then add the categories folder as a new group in your Xcode project. In the Project Navigator, select the newly added categories group; and with the ⌘N keyboard shortcut or File ➤ New ➤ File, choose the Objective-C category option from the Cocoa Touch file templates. Input Thumbnail into the Category text field and UIImage into the Category on text field (see Figure 8-14).

Figure 8-14. Creating an Objective-C category on UIImage

Now for the code. In UIImage+Thumbnail.h, we add our declaration of the new custom createThumbnailToFillSize: method:

```
@interface UIImage (Thumbnail)

-(UIImage *) createThumbnailToFillSize:(CGSize)size;

@end
```

Switching to UIImage+Thumbnail.m, add the implementation:

```
#import "UIImage+Thumbnail.h"

@implementation UIImage (Thumbnail)

-(UIImage *) createThumbnailToFillSize:(CGSize)size
{
    CGSize mainImageSize = self.size;

    UIImage *thumb;

    CGFloat widthScaler = size.width / mainImageSize.width;
    CGFloat heightScaler = size.height / mainImageSize.height;

    CGSize repositionedMainImageSize = mainImageSize;

    CGFloat scaleFactor;
    // Determine if we should shrink based on width or hight
```

```
    if(widthScaler > heightScaler)
    {
        // calculate based on width scaler
        scaleFactor = widthScaler;
        repositionedMainImageSize.height = ceil(size.height / scaleFactor);
    }
    else {
        // calculate based on height scaler
        scaleFactor = heightScaler;
        repositionedMainImageSize.width = ceil(size.width / heightScaler);
    }

    UIGraphicsBeginImageContext(size);

    CGFloat xInc = ((repositionedMainImageSize.width-mainImageSize.width) / 2.f) *scaleFactor;
    CGFloat yInc = ((repositionedMainImageSize.height-mainImageSize.height) / 2.f)
*scaleFactor;

    [self drawInRect:CGRectMake(xInc, yInc, mainImageSize.width * scaleFactor,
mainImageSize.height * scaleFactor)];
    thumb = UIGraphicsGetImageFromCurrentImageContext();
    UIGraphicsEndImageContext();

    return thumb;
}

@end
```

Our new UIImage category will create a cropped and resized image that fills the size passed into the createThumbnailToFillSize: method. By implementing this functionality into a category, we simply need to import our category file into any file that needs to create optimized images. Then we'll be able to call createThumbnailToFillSize: on any instance of UIImage to create thumbnails to fit the dimensions that we specify. How cool is that?!

Let's try it now. First, import the new category into BRBirthdayEditViewController.m:

```
#import "UIImage+Thumbnail.h"
```

Now modify the imagePickerController:didFinishPickingMediaWithInfo: implementation to the following:

```
- (void)imagePickerController:(UIImagePickerController *)picker
didFinishPickingMediaWithInfo:(NSDictionary *)info {

    [picker dismissViewControllerAnimated:YES completion:nil];

    UIImage *image = info[UIImagePickerControllerOriginalImage];

    CGFloat side = 71.f;
    side *= [[UIScreen mainScreen] scale];

    UIImage *thumbnail = [image createThumbnailToFillSize:CGSizeMake(side, side)];
    self.photoView.image = thumbnail;
```

```
    self.birthday.imageData = UIImageJPEGRepresentation (thumbnail,1.f);

    self.photoView.image = image;
    self.birthday.imageData = UIImageJPEGRepresentation (image,1.f);
}
```

Seventy-one points is the maximum length side of the square thumbnail images in our app. However, we also want to cater for retina displays. To do this we multiply the 71 points by the screen scale value; the screen scale is 2 on retina displays; the screen scale is 1 on non-retina displays.

Cancelling Core Data changes

In the last chapter, we implemented cancelAndDismiss: and saveAndDismiss: methods into our core view controller, enabling any subclassed view controller to easily dismiss itself when presented modally. In the case of our birthday edit view controller, we need to add further functionality when the Save and Cancel buttons are tapped. We need to cancel or save the changes to our Core Data store. We've already added a saveChanges public method to our model that will do just that, so first let's invoke saveChanges from BRBirthdayEditViewController.m:

```
- (IBAction)saveAndDismiss:(id)sender
{
    [[BRDModel sharedInstance] saveChanges];
    [super saveAndDismiss:sender];
}
```

You'll be pleased to discover that cancelling changes to CoreData is even simpler than saving changes. Here's the new public method to add to BRDModel:

BRDModel.h:

```
- (void)cancelChanges;
```

BRDModel.m:

```
- (void)cancelChanges
{
    [self.managedObjectContext rollback];
}
```

Calling the managed object context's rollback method will remove any changes from the Core Data model since the last save. That includes newly inserted BRDBirthday entities that have never been saved/written to the persistent store. This is incredibly handy because it means we can create a new BRDBirthday entity in our Home view controller when the user taps the Add Birthday button; and by the miracle of Core Data, this temporary entity is thrown away simply by rolling back the managed object context when the Cancel button is tapped via the birthday edit view controller.

Back in BRBirthdayEditViewController.m, let's override the cancelAndDismiss: implementation:

```
- (IBAction)cancelAndDismiss:(id)sender {
    [[BRDModel sharedInstance] cancelChanges];
    [super cancelAndDismiss:sender];
}
```

Back to the home view controller

Back working on our BRHomeViewController.m source file, we're now going to modify the prepareForSegue:sender: method to work with the birthday managed objects rather than the dictionaries from the previous chapter. The following are the code changes:

```
-(void) prepareForSegue:(UIStoryboardSegue *)segue sender:(id)sender
{
    NSString *identifier = segue.identifier;

    if ([identifier isEqualToString:@"BirthdayDetail"]) {
        //First get the data
        NSIndexPath *selectedIndexPath = self.tableView.indexPathForSelectedRow;
        BRDBirthday *birthday = [self.fetchedResultsController
objectAtIndexPath:selectedIndexPath];
        NSMutableDictionary *birthday = [self.birthdays objectAtIndex:selectedIndexPath.row];

        BRBirthdayDetailViewController *birthdayDetailViewController =
segue.destinationViewController;
        birthdayDetailViewController.birthday = birthday;

    }
    else if ([identifier isEqualToString:@"AddBirthday"]) {
        //Add a new birthday

        NSManagedObjectContext *context = [BRDModel sharedInstance].managedObjectContext;
        BRDBirthday *birthday = [NSEntityDescription
insertNewObjectForEntityForName:@"BRDBirthday" inManagedObjectContext:context];
        [birthday updateWithDefaults];
        NSMutableDictionary *birthday = [NSMutableDictionary dictionary];

        [birthday setObject:@"My Friend" forKey:@"name"];
        [birthday setObject:[NSDate date] forKey:@"birthdate"];
        [self.birthdays addObject:birthday];

        UINavigationController *navigationController = segue.destinationViewController;

        BRBirthdayEditViewController *birthdayEditViewController =
(BRBirthdayEditViewController *) navigationController.topViewController;
        birthdayEditViewController.birthday = birthday;
    }
}
```

When the user taps the Add Birthday button, we create a new BRDBirthday entity in the Core Data managed object context, but we don't save the context. That way, if the user cancels her action to create a new birthday, the managed object context will rollback and our new birthday entity will be erased.

Build and run! You should be able to add and edit birthdays, and your changes should remain persistent between sessions.

Saving notes

Now that we've got our Core Data saving model up and running, let's save the birthday notes that we're enabling our users to write. Open the BRNotesEditViewController.h header, and begin by adding a forward class declaration for our BRDBirthday entity, and add a new birthday property:

```objectivec
#import <UIKit/UIKit.h>
#import "BRCoreViewController.h"
@class BRDBirthday;

@interface BRNotesEditViewController : BRCoreViewController <UITextViewDelegate>

@property(nonatomic,strong) BRDBirthday *birthday;
@property (weak, nonatomic) IBOutlet UIBarButtonItem *saveButton;
@property (weak, nonatomic) IBOutlet UITextView *textView;

@end
```

Import BRDBirthday and BRDModel and synthesize the new birthday property in BRNotesEditViewController.m:

```objectivec
#import "BRNotesEditViewController.h"
#import "BRDModel.h"
#import "BRDBirthday.h"
```

Just like the birthday edit and detail view controllers, we'll update the view with content from the birthday entity when the view is about to be displayed:

```objectivec
-(void) viewWillAppear:(BOOL)animated
{
    [super viewWillAppear:animated];
    self.textView.text = self.birthday.notes;
    [self.textView becomeFirstResponder];
}
```

As the user makes changes to birthday notes, we'll update the birthday entity:

```objectivec
- (void)textViewDidChange:(UITextView *)textView
{
    NSLog(@"User changed the notes text: %@",textView.text);
    self.birthday.notes = self.textView.text;
}
```

Finally, just like the edit birthday view controller, we'll ask the model singleton to save or cancel the user's changes when he taps the Cancel or Save buttons:

```objectivec
- (IBAction)cancelAndDismiss:(id)sender {
    [[BRDModel sharedInstance] cancelChanges];
    [super cancelAndDismiss:sender];
}

- (IBAction)saveAndDismiss:(id)sender
```

```
{
    [[BRDModel sharedInstance] saveChanges];
    [super saveAndDismiss:sender];
}
```

In order to see our hard work pay off, we still need to pass in a reference to the birthday entity being viewed in the Birthday Detail view controller when the notes editor is presented by the segue transition. Open your storyboard and locate the segue between the Birthday Detail view controller and the edit birthday navigation view controller. Select the segue, and then enter the identifier EditNotes (see Figure 8-15).

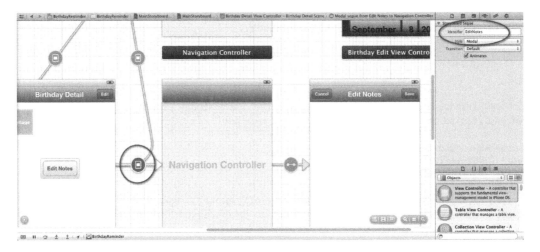

Figure 8-15. Adding a segue identifier for the note editor navigation controller

Now open BRBirthdayDetailViewController.m and import the notes editor view controller:

```
#import "BRNotesEditViewController.h"
```

And update the prepareForSegue:sender method so that it passes a reference to its birthday entity when it presents the notes editor:

```
-(void) prepareForSegue:(UIStoryboardSegue *)segue sender:(id)sender
{
    NSString *identifier = segue.identifier;

    if ([identifier isEqualToString:@"EditBirthday"]) {
        //Edit this birthday
        UINavigationController *navigationController = segue.destinationViewController;

        BRBirthdayEditViewController *birthdayEditViewController =
(BRBirthdayEditViewController *) navigationController.topViewController;
        birthdayEditViewController.birthday = self.birthday;
    }
    else if ([identifier isEqualToString:@"EditNotes"]) {
        //Edit this birthday
        UINavigationController *navigationController = segue.destinationViewController;
```

```
        BRNotesEditViewController *birthdayNotesEditViewController =
(BRNotesEditViewController *) navigationController.topViewController;
        birthdayNotesEditViewController.birthday = self.birthday;
    }
}
```

Build and run. Pick a celebrity or one of your own added birthdays. Edit the notes associated with that birthday and save them. Repeat this process a few times. You'll see the notes persisting between sessions.

Cleaning up

Now that we're done implementing Core Data storage, we can dispose of the redundant birthdays array property in BRHomeViewController.m:

```
@interface BRHomeViewController ()

@property (nonatomic,strong) NSMutableArray *birthdays;
@property (nonatomic, strong) NSFetchedResultsController *fetchedResultsController;

@end
```

That's it. We're done with Core Data! Build and run. You should be able to add and edit birthdays, photos, and notes. Your changes should reflect immediately in all view controllers, and even after shutting down *Birthday Reminder*. This is the beauty of Core Data.

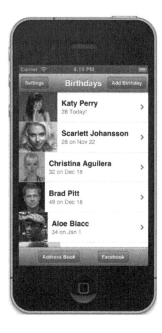

Figure 8-16. Happy Birthday Katy!

Summary

Well done getting through the Core Data chapter! This is as hard as it gets in this book. You've had to digest a lot of new information this morning because Core Data is quite an advanced iOS framework. We've only really skimmed the surface of its capabilities, but for storing birthdays persistently—or any other data type for that matter—Core Data really is the way to go.

Up next this afternoon, we're going to look at iOS skinning approaches and how to make *Birthday Reminder* look pretty. So grab a quick lunch—and I'll see you back here in an hour!

Chapter 9

iOS Skinning: Make Your Apps Lickable

By the end of today, our *Birthday Reminder* app is going to look very much like the final product. We're not going to add a load of new features this afternoon; instead, our work will focus on improving the look and feel of our user interface and making it stand out from the hundreds of other birthday reminder apps in the App Store.

But before we dive into code, let's take a moment out of our busy iPhone developer day to let me tell you a short story. One beautiful spring day last year, I was at the park with my nine-year-old son, eating ice cream in the sun. We had a bit of an accident with the ice cream and big blob of it landed on my iPhone. As is the way in the modern world, soon my Twitter followers were treated to the breaking news that I had just licked my iPhone (see Figure 9-1).

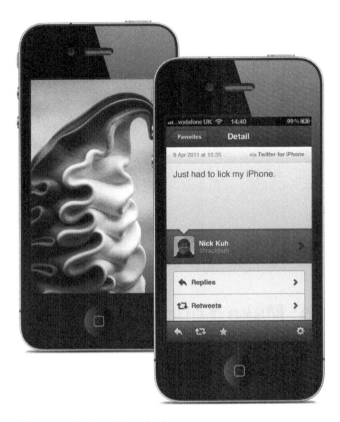

Figure 9-1. Ice cream and iPhones don't mix well together!

No context. I just had to lick my iPhone. Ice cream aside, these days we iOS users are treated to more and more beautiful user interface design. I put it to you that some iPhone apps are just so darn beautiful and the user-experience so utterly polished that you do want to grab these apps and lick 'em! Or is that just me? So we're going to call these *lickable* apps from now on! ☺

I want my apps to have that lickable quality. What is it that makes these apps stand out? What makes an app lickable?

What makes an app lickable?

Great design is influenced by personal choice, so here are a few of my favorite iPhone app user interface designs (see Figure 9-2). I've selected AirBnB, Jamie's Recipes, Momento, and Path. These apps all have beautiful user interface designs and icons. They stand out from the hundreds of thousands of apps that iPhone users get to pick and choose from. It's not enough anymore just to have a great idea for an app. Your app needs the level of polish and quality that these kind of chart-leading apps bring to the table.

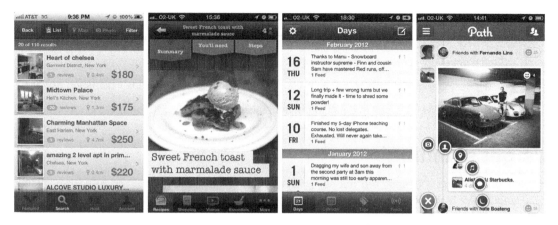

Figure 9-2. A selection of lickable apps: AirBnB, Jamie's Recipes, Momento, Path

So let's look a little more closely at these example apps. What makes them lickable? Design-wise, what do these four apps have in common? Here's what I've noticed. All of them have made extensive use of common user interface components that Apple has included in the iOS SDK. Navigation bars, toolbars, table views, image views, and so on. Even though these apps each have a unique, exquisite design, iPhone users instantly recognize the common user controls that we use every day in most other iPhone apps. We know to flick and scroll a table view—it comes instinctively because it's deeply integrated into the Apple iOS user experience. We know that the navigation bar for all of these apps will keep us updated on our location in the app hierarchy. We know what the tab bar at the bottom of the first three apps is for— we'll happily jump between the top section levels and won't get lost or confused by the app navigation.

These apps all have beautiful and distinctive designs, and at the same time, they are immediately user-friendly for regular iOS users. As a user, I don't want to have to learn how to use your app. I don't want to have to trawl through any help pages to get up and running, I just want the experience to be intuitive. How many of Apple's own apps include a Help section? Zero, that's how many!

The lesson to learn here is that you can make beautiful apps without breaking the rules of the HIG (Apple's Human Interface Guidelines) by attempting to create a new kind of user experience simply to be original. It's not worth it! One of the main reasons that the iPhone has been so phenomenally successful comes down to the software and user experience conventions that Apple invented and then opened to third-party developers. We already have the tools to make wonderful user interfaces, and now with iOS 5 and 6, we have so many new ways to reskin the existing UIKit components that we can make beautiful, lickable apps very efficiently.

> *Tip: I recommend that you read and learn the HIG, Apple's iOS Human Interface Guidelines document. You'll find it on Apple's web site at* `http://developer.apple.com/library/ios/#DOCUMENTATION/UserExperience/C onceptual/MobileHIG/Introduction/Introduction.html.`

If you're not a designer, then I suggest you flick back to Chapter 1 at some point and have a reread through my description of the design process I work through for each app I build.

1. Sketch out every screen on paper.

2. Find a designer on dribbble.com to turn your sketches into beautiful, retina Photoshop designs.

3. Get skinning. We'll cover it in detail throughout this chapter.

Let's get skinning!

The rules for skinning iOS apps are not set in stone. There's no CSS. There's no XML user interface layout language or equivalent. The code for skinning iOS components is just that: code. Objective-C code.

Create a core view controller

Remember how we created a core view controller back in Chapter 5? Every view controller in our app subclasses `BRCoreViewController`, which in turn subclasses Apple's `UIViewController`. We did this to take advantage of object-oriented programming, whereby we can centralize common code and logic into the core view controller. That's how we made the background of every view in our app a gray color. This existing code in `BRCoreViewController` makes every main screen view a gray color.

```
-(void) viewDidLoad
{
    [super viewDidLoad];

    self.view.backgroundColor = [UIColor grayColor];
}
```

The *Birthday Reminder* user interface design makes extensive use of a dark, checkered background image. So let's add this background image to every view controlled by a `BRCoreViewController` subclass.

Add `app-background.png` and `app-background@2x.png` image files to your project. You'll find them in the assets folder within the source code for this chapter. Now add two more lines of code to `BRCoreViewController`'s `viewDidLoad` method:

```
-(void) viewDidLoad
{
    [super viewDidLoad];
    self.view.backgroundColor = [UIColor grayColor];
    UIImageView *backgroundView = [[UIImageView alloc] initWithImage:[UIImage
imageNamed:@"app-background.png"]];
    [self.view insertSubview:backgroundView atIndex:0];
}
```

Build and run. Our background image is now set on every screen (see Figure 9-3). How cool was that?!

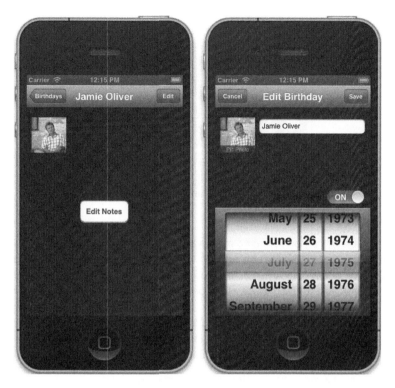

Figure 9-3. By adding just two lines of code, the checkered background image now appears in the view of every view controller subclass of BRCoreViewController in our app.

> *Note: Apple's* UIImageView *class caches images generated via the* imageNamed: *class method, so even though this method will be called by every view controller in our app, the image is only loaded into memory by iOS once.*

On retina devices, UIImageView automatically loads the app-background@2x.png version of our background image simply because of the @2x naming convention. You do need to ensure that your @2x images are exactly double the width and height of your non-retina images. So for this image, the non-retina app-background.png image file is 320×460 pixels and the retina version is 640×920 pixels to fill the iPhone screen (minus the status bar).

Custom table view cells

Let's take a closer look at the Photoshop design for our table of home screen birthdays (see Figure 9-4).

Figure 9-4. Close-up of the custom table cell design

The standard Apple table cell styles support a maximum of two labels: an image and an accessory view on the right side of the table cell. This won't be enough to meet the requirements of our custom design (see Figure 9-5). Take a look at the birthday reminder cells for Nicole and Nick Kuh. Each cell has four labels: one for the friend's name, one for the birthday text, one for the number of days until the next birthday, and one for the *more days* or *more day* text. In addition, the thumbnail image view for each friend has round corners, and it nicely centers and crops portrait and landscape images. This isn't the default behavior for the `imageView` property of the `UITableViewCell` class. We'll have to subclass `UITableViewCell` and create a custom table cell for reuse when displaying birthdays.

Open the storyboard file in Xcode, then center and focus in on the home view controller scene. Select the prototype table cell. Using the attributes inspector, change the style of the cell to Custom. Change the Selection parameter to None. Get rid of the disclosure indicator (right arrow) by changing the accessory setting to None.

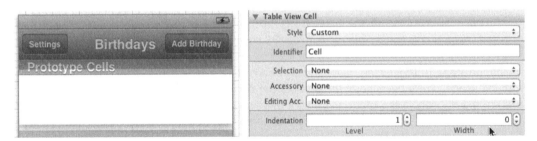

Figure 9-5. Creating a custom table view cell

Add two image views to the custom table cell by dragging them in from the Object Library. Using the size inspector, position one image view (x=11 points and y=13 points) and set both its width and height to 52 points. This will be the icon view that displays photos of our friends. Keeping the icon image view selected, use the attributes inspector to change the view's Mode value to Aspect Fill, and switch on the Clip Subviews option (see Figure 9-6).

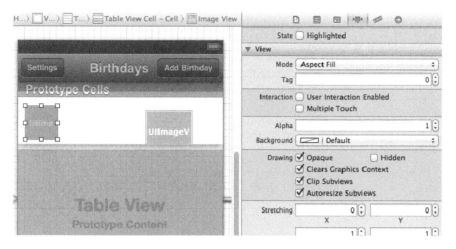

Figure 9-6. Configuring the icon image view

Now select the second image view you added. We'll use this image view to display either a calendar icon background behind the remaining days' labels or a birthday cake image if it's our friend's birthday today. Position the second image view (x=261 points, y=14 points) and set its width to 48 points and height to 50 points. We're going to set the default background of this image right in our storyboard. From the assets folder in the source code, locate and add the `icon-days-remaining.png` and `icon-days-remaining@2x.png` image files to your project. Now set the `Image` property of the right-side image view to the newly added `icon-days-remaining.png` file using the attributes inspector, as shown in Figure 9-7.

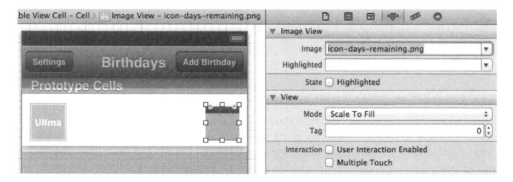

Figure 9-7. Configuring the days remaining background image view

Drag and drop four label view instances onto your custom table view cell. Using a combination of the attributes inspector to set the font attributes and the size inspector to set the position and size, configure the four labels as shown in Table 9-1.

Table 9-1. Labels

Label	Font System	Position	Size	
Name label	bold 17	x=76, y=22	w=177, h=21	
Birthday label	13	x=76, y=43	w=177, h=21	
Remaining days count label	bold 17	x=266, y=29	w=37, h=20	Set Autoshrink to Minimum Font Size 10 points and center align the text
Remaining days sublabel	9	x=260, y=45	w=51, h=20	Centered text alignment

The end result should look like Figure 9-8.

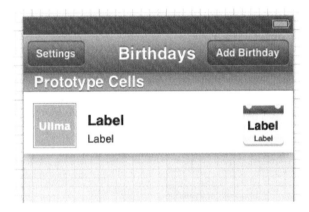

Figure 9-8. Configuring our prototype cell's labels and image views

We've added and configured all the custom subviews required for our birthday table view cell, but until we hook up some outlets to the subviews, we don't have any way to target and style the labels or image views. The question is where do we define these outlets? Not in our home view controller. The custom prototype cell that we've been working on is going to be the view layout that iOS will use when generating reusable instances of Apple's UITableViewCell class. So the logical way to create a custom table view cell with custom subviews is by subclassing UITableViewCell.

Add a components folder to your user-interface folder in the Finder, and then add the components folder as a new group in your Xcode project. In the project navigator, select the newly added components group and create a new Objective-C class file within it. Name your subclass BRBirthdayTableViewCell and select UITableViewCell from the drop-down menu of the Subclass of text field (see Figure 9-9).

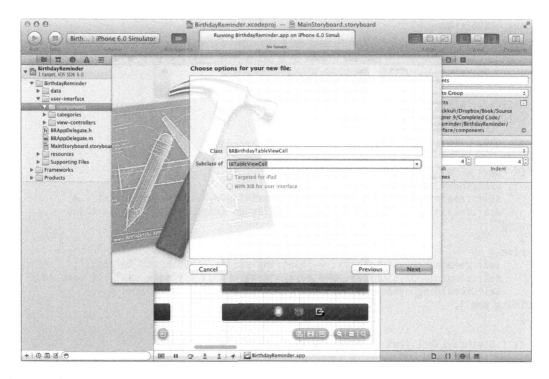

Figure 9-9. Subclassing UITableViewCell

Once you've created the new BRBirthdayTableViewCell class, open the header and source files in the Assistant Editor layout, and add the following code for each:

BRBirthdayTableViewCell.h:

```
#import <UIKit/UIKit.h>

@class BRDBirthday;

@interface BRBirthdayTableViewCell : UITableViewCell

@property(nonatomic,strong) BRDBirthday *birthday;
@property (nonatomic, weak) IBOutlet UIImageView* iconView;
@property (nonatomic, weak) IBOutlet UIImageView* remainingDaysImageView;
@property (nonatomic, weak) IBOutlet UILabel* nameLabel;
@property (nonatomic, weak) IBOutlet UILabel* birthdayLabel;
@property (nonatomic, weak) IBOutlet UILabel* remainingDaysLabel;
@property (nonatomic, weak) IBOutlet UILabel* remainingDaysSubTextLabel;

@end
```

Source:

```
#import "BRBirthdayTableViewCell.h"
```

```objc
#import "BRDBirthday.h"

@implementation BRBirthdayTableViewCell

-(void) setBirthday:(BRDBirthday *)birthday
{
    _birthday = birthday;
    self.nameLabel.text = _birthday.name;

    int days = _birthday.remainingDaysUntilNextBirthday;

    if (days == 0) {
        //Birthday is today!
        self.remainingDaysLabel.text = self.remainingDaysSubTextLabel.text = @"";
        self.remainingDaysImageView.image = [UIImage imageNamed:@"icon-birthday-
cake.png"];
    }
    else {
        self.remainingDaysLabel.text = [NSString stringWithFormat:@"%d",days];
        self.remainingDaysSubTextLabel.text = (days == 1) ? @"more day" : @"more days";
        self.remainingDaysImageView.image = [UIImage imageNamed:@"icon-days-
remaining.png"];
    }

    self.birthdayLabel.text = _birthday.birthdayTextToDisplay;

}

@end
```

Table view cells get reused. This makes scrolling a long table very efficient because the table view reuses just a few table cells to give the impression of a very long table of rows. We've created a birthday property on our custom table view cell. When the home view controller configures each table view cell, it will pass the birthday entity to the table view cell via cell.birthday = aBirthday. By overriding the birthday setter of our table view cell, we can update the labels and images of our table cell whenever the birthday property is set.

Let's leave the BRBirthdayTableViewCell class files for the time being and return to the storyboard. With the custom table view cell selected, we can change the class of the prototype cell using the Identity Inspector. BRBirthdayTableViewCell will be recognized automatically by Xcode because it's a UITableViewCell subclass (see Figure 9-10).

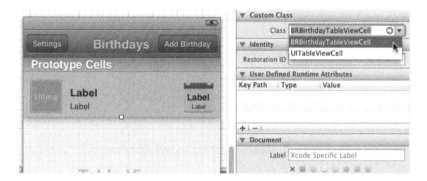

Figure 9-10. Assigning our custom class to the table view cell prototype with the identity inspector

Now to hook up the table cell outlets. Control-drag directly from the background of the prototype table cell to each of the added subviews. You'll discover that Xcode has recognized the outlets from the BRBirthdayTableViewCell code and will enable you to connect them to the subviews (see Figure 9-11). Awesome!

Figure 9-11. Hooking up the label and image view outlets from BRBirthdayTableViewCell.

Connect the outlets as follows:

- iconView: the image view on the left of the table cell
- remainingDaysImageView: the image view on the right of the table cell
- nameLabel: the top-left label
- birthdayLabel: the bottom-left label
- remainingDaysLabel: the top-right label
- remainingDaysSubTextLabel: the bottom-right label

Leave the view for now and make a few modifications to the BRHomeViewController.m source file.

Import BRBirthdayTableViewCell.h into BRHomeViewController.m. Then scan through the implementation file and modify tableView:cellForRowAtIndexPath: as follows:

```
- (UITableViewCell *)tableView:(UITableView *)tableView cellForRowAtIndexPath:(NSIndexPath *)indexPath
{
    UITableViewCell *cell = [tableView dequeueReusableCellWithIdentifier:@"Cell"];

    BRDBirthday *birthday = [self.fetchedResultsController objectAtIndexPath:indexPath];

    BRBirthdayTableViewCell *brTableCell = (BRBirthdayTableViewCell *)cell;
    brTableCell.birthday = birthday;
    if (birthday.imageData == nil)
    {
        brTableCell.iconView.image = [UIImage imageNamed:@"icon-birthday-cake.png"];
    }
    else {
        brTableCell.iconView.image = [UIImage imageWithData:birthday.imageData];
    }
    cell.textLabel.text = birthday.name;
    cell.detailTextLabel.text = birthday.birthdayTextToDisplay;
    cell.imageView.image = [UIImage imageWithData:birthday.imageData];

    return cell;
}
```

Build and run. You should see something like Figure 9-12.

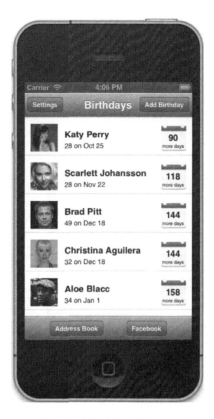

Figure 9-12. Nicely cropped square thumbnails and custom labels displaying birthday data

Table view cell background images

Time to add the custom chocolate sponge and icing to our table view. This should be a piece of cake (pun intended)! Add `table-row-icing-background.png`, `table-row-icing-background@2x.png`, `table-row-background.png`, and `table-row-background@2x.png` image files to your project. Instances of `UITableViewCell` have a `backgroundView` property that we can set to any `UIView` instance. So we'll create an image and an image view to display the image, and then set the image view as the background view of the cell. Unless this is the top layer of the cake, we'll use our newly added table row background image that includes a layer of icing. If it's the top layer of the cake (the first row), then we will use the table row background image without icing.

We'll add the code directly to the `tableView:cellForRowAtIndexPath:` in `BRHomeViewController.m` source, because that's the point when we'll know which row of the table we're skinning. Add the following code at the end of this method, but before the last `return cell;` line:

```
    UIImage *backgroundImage = (indexPath.row == 0) ? [UIImage imageNamed:@"table-row-
background.png"] : [UIImage imageNamed:@"table-row-icing-background.png"];
    brTableCell.backgroundView = [[UIImageView alloc] initWithImage:backgroundImage];
```

Build and run. Nice cake layers are added (see Figure 9-13).

Figure 9-13. Table cell cake layers with added icing!

Creating a "style sheet"

As I pointed out earlier, iOS skinning doesn't work like CSS, so we're not going to create a traditional style sheet file. We're going to create a single Objective-C class that will take care of all our app's styling needs in one, centralized place. Our style sheet class will work like a utility class, whereby we'll call styling methods, passing in a reference to labels and views, and let our utility class take care of adding rounded corners, setting fonts and colors, and so forth.

Select the user-interface Xcode group and create a new Objective-C class file within it. Name your subclass BRStyleSheet and enter NSObject into the Subclass of text field.

Work the following code into the new BRStyleSheet.h header:

```
#import <Foundation/Foundation.h>

typedef enum : int {
    BRLabelTypeName = 0,
    BRLabelTypeBirthdayDate,
    BRLabelTypeDaysUntilBirthday,
    BRLabelTypeDaysUntilBirthdaySubText,
    BRLabelTypeLarge
}BRLabelType;

@interface BRStyleSheet : NSObject

+(void)styleLabel:(UILabel *)label withType:(BRLabelType)labelType;
+(void)styleRoundCorneredView:(UIView *)view;

@end
```

Notice how the two public methods of our new style sheet class are both class methods? We're not going to instantiate an instance of BRStyleSheet, we'll just use it like a utility class from anywhere in our app where we want to style a label or view.

We created custom enumerators back in Chapter 4 when we pieced together the blackjack app. We had an enumerator to keep track of the game state. Here we're creating a label type enumerator so that whenever we pass a reference to a label view into the styleLabel:withType: method, we also pass a type that determines the font, text color, and so forth, that the style sheet method will apply. We create a different enumerator label type for each different style. So if we want the same styling to be applied to two different labels, we'll pass in the same BRLabelType value for them both.

Our styling code is going to utilize properties of Core Animation layers to add shadows and round corners. We won't cover Core Animation in any detail in this book, but it's worth noting that in iOS, every UIView is actually rendered in a Core Animation Layer and CALayers have shadow and corner radius properties. In order to set shadow and corner radius values on our labels and views, we'll first need to import Apple's QuartzCore framework, otherwise Xcode will not recognize the CALayer properties we'll access with our styling code.

We'll import the QuartzCore framework just as we imported the Core Data framework. Select your BirthdayReminder project in the Project Navigator and then select the BirthdayReminder target. Now select the Build Phases tab in the Editor. Expand the Link Binary With Libraries collection. Click the + button and then locate the QuartzCore.framework from the iOS folder to add it to your project.

Back in the BRStyleSheet.m source file, we'll define some fonts and colors for our style sheet. These are fonts and colors that we'll use for our styling methods so if we ever need to change a font or color in the future, the process will be quick and painless in our single styling class. We're going to define these style value constants as follows:

```
#import "BRStyleSheet.h"
#import <QuartzCore/QuartzCore.h>

#define kFontLightOnDarkTextColour [UIColor colorWithRed:255.0/255 green:251.0/255
blue:218.0/255 alpha:1.0]
```

```
#define kFontDarkOnLightTextColour [UIColor colorWithRed:1.0/255 green:1.0/255
blue:1.0/255 alpha:1.0]

#define kFontNavigationTextColour [UIColor colorWithRed:106.f/255.f green:62.f/255.f
blue:39.f/255.f alpha:1.f]
#define kFontNavigationDisabledTextColour [UIColor colorWithRed:106.f/255.f
green:62.f/255.f blue:39.f/255.f alpha:0.6f]
#define kNavigationButtonBackgroundColour [UIColor colorWithRed:255.f/255.f
green:245.f/255.f blue:225.f/255.f alpha:1.f]
#define kToolbarButtonBackgroundColour [UIColor colorWithRed:39.f/255.f green:17.f/255.f
blue:5.f/255.f alpha:1.f]
#define kLargeButtonTextColour [UIColor whiteColor]

#define kFontNavigation [UIFont fontWithName:@"HelveticaNeue-Bold" size:18.f]
#define kFontName [UIFont fontWithName:@"HelveticaNeue-Bold" size:15.f]
#define kFontBirthdayDate [UIFont fontWithName:@"HelveticaNeue" size:13.f]
#define kFontDaysUntilBirthday [UIFont fontWithName:@"HelveticaNeue-Bold" size:25.f]
#define kFontDaysUntillBirthdaySubText [UIFont fontWithName:@"HelveticaNeue" size:9.f]
#define kFontLarge [UIFont fontWithName:@"HelveticaNeue-Bold" size:17.f]
#define kFontButton [UIFont fontWithName:@"HelveticaNeue-Bold" size:30.f]
#define kFontNotes [UIFont fontWithName:@"HelveticaNeue" size:16.f]
#define kFontPicPhoto [UIFont fontWithName:@"HelveticaNeue-Bold" size:12.f]
#define kFontDropShadowColour [UIColor colorWithRed:1.0/255 green:1.0/255 blue:1.0/255
alpha:0.75]

@implementation BRStyleSheet

@end
```

Now to add our two styling class methods within the BRStyleSheet implementation:

```
@implementation BRStyleSheet

+(void)styleLabel:(UILabel *)label withType:(BRLabelType)labelType
{
    switch (labelType) {
        case BRLabelTypeName:
            label.font = kFontName;
            label.layer.shadowColor = kFontDropShadowColour.CGColor;
            label.layer.shadowOffset = CGSizeMake(1.0f, 1.0f);
            label.layer.shadowRadius = 0.0f;
            label.layer.masksToBounds = NO;
            label.textColor = kFontLightOnDarkTextColour;
            break;
        case BRLabelTypeBirthdayDate:
            label.font = kFontBirthdayDate;
            label.textColor = kFontLightOnDarkTextColour;
            break;
        case BRLabelTypeDaysUntilBirthday:
            label.font = kFontDaysUntilBirthday;
            label.textColor = kFontDarkOnLightTextColour;
            break;
        case BRLabelTypeDaysUntilBirthdaySubText:
```

```
            label.font = kFontDaysUntillBirthdaySubText;
            label.textColor = kFontDarkOnLightTextColour;
            break;
        case BRLabelTypeLarge:
            label.textColor = kFontLightOnDarkTextColour;
            label.layer.shadowColor = kFontDropShadowColour.CGColor;
            label.layer.shadowOffset = CGSizeMake(1.0f, 1.0f);
            label.layer.shadowRadius = 0.0f;
            label.layer.masksToBounds = NO;
            break;
        default:
            label.textColor = kFontLightOnDarkTextColour;
            break;
    }

}

+(void)styleRoundCorneredView:(UIView *)view
{
    view.layer.cornerRadius = 4.f;
    view.layer.masksToBounds = YES;
    view.clipsToBounds = YES;
}

@end
```

When styling labels, we're directly accessing the layer (CALayer) property of the label views to define shadow settings on the layer. Likewise, for styling views, we're setting the cornerRadius property of the view's underlying core animation layer.

Time to test out our style sheet class! Open the BRBirthdayTableViewCell.m source file. Begin by importing BRStyleSheet.h at the top of the file. BRBirthdayTableViewCell is the subclass of UITableViewCell. So this class is a view class and not a view controller class. Unlike our previous view controller outlets, we can't just hook into a viewDidLoad method to make changes to our Interface Builder outlets properties. When it comes to styling the image views and labels in our custom table view cell, we only need this code to run once when the outlets are first generated by iOS. So an ideal place to add the styling code is to override the outlet accessor setters and add our styling there. Here's the code to add to BRBirthdayTableViewCell.m:

```
-(void) setIconView:(UIImageView *)iconView
{
    _iconView = iconView;
    if (_iconView) {
        [BRStyleSheet styleRoundCorneredView:_iconView];
    }
}
-(void) setNameLabel:(UILabel *)nameLabel
{
    _nameLabel = nameLabel;
    if (_nameLabel) {
        [BRStyleSheet styleLabel:_nameLabel withType:BRLabelTypeName];
```

```
    }
}

-(void) setBirthdayLabel:(UILabel *)birthdayLabel
{
    _birthdayLabel = birthdayLabel;
    if (_birthdayLabel) {
        [BRStyleSheet styleLabel:_birthdayLabel withType:BRLabelTypeBirthdayDate];
    }
}


-(void) setRemainingDaysLabel:(UILabel *)remainingDaysLabel
{
    _remainingDaysLabel = remainingDaysLabel;
    if (_remainingDaysLabel) {
        [BRStyleSheet styleLabel:_remainingDaysLabel withType:BRLabelTypeDaysUntilBirthday];
    }
}

-(void) setRemainingDaysSubTextLabel:(UILabel *)remainingDaysSubTextLabel
{
    _remainingDaysSubTextLabel = remainingDaysSubTextLabel;
    if (_remainingDaysSubTextLabel) {
        [BRStyleSheet styleLabel:_remainingDaysSubTextLabel
withType:BRLabelTypeDaysUntilBirthdaySubText];
    }
}
```

Build and run. You should see the label styles and image round corners applied, just like in Figure 9-14. As iOS hooks up each label outlet, we pass the reference to the label into the styleLabel:withType: class method of BRStyleSheet, which in turn sets the font, text color, shadows, and so forth.

Figure 9-14. Styled text and round corner image views

Customizing navigation and toolbar appearance

The first change we'll make to our home screen navigation bar is to modify the left and right bar button items to display icons rather than text. From the assets in the source folder for this chapter, add the icon-add-new.png, icon-add-new@2x.png, icon-settings.png, and icon-settings@2x.png image files to your project. With your home view controller scene selected in the storyboard, delete the title of the left bar button item and select the icon-settings.png file from the Image attribute drop-down menu. Repeat this process for the right bar button item, this time selecting the icon-add-new.png image file (see Figure 9-15).

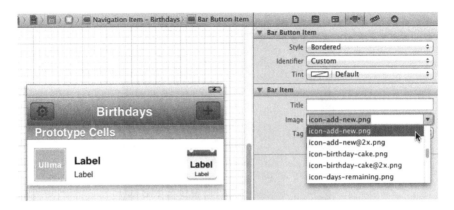

Figure 9-15. Assigning image icons to UIBarButtonItems

Before we progress further, if you haven't added the remaining images from the assets folder in the source code for this chapter to your project then do so now: button-blue.png, button-blue@2x.png, button-red.png, button-red@2x.png, icon-call.png, icon-call@2x.png, icon-delete.png, icon-delete@2x.png, icon-email.png, icon-email@2x.png, icon-facebook.png, icon-facebook@2x.png, icon-notes.png, icon-notes@2x.png, navigation-bar-background.png, navigation-bar-background@2x.png, icon-sms.png, icon-sms@2x.png, tool-bar-background.png and tool-bar-background@2x.png.

Appearance APIs: simple yet powerful

Apple introduced the Appearance APIs into the iOS SDK in version 5.0. Prior to iOS 5, it was a fairly complex process to change the design of common user interface components like navigation bars, toolbars, and bar button items further than a little tinting.

When iOS 5 launched, Apple added a number of new public methods to many of the iOS UI components that are solely for the purpose of modifying the component appearances: changing background images and tinting individual parts of complex UI components like UISlider or UIProgressBar.

Before iOS 5, if we desired the title of our navigation bar to use a custom font or wanted to add a shadow, we didn't have direct access to the label in the navigation bar. Instead, we'd have to implement a workaround involving creating a new label, dynamically sizing it, and assigning the custom label as the titleView property of each navigation bar. What a hassle! Thankfully, Apple made a gigantic leap forward with iOS 5's appearance APIs. Not only do we now have many additional customization options for the majority of the UI components, we can even define our appearance settings on a global level. For example, we can state in code that every single instance of a navigation bar should use a particular custom background image, or that every bar button item should be tinted with a certain color and styled with a certain font. This means that we can actually define all of our appearance APIs in one place. Where do you think would be a suitable place? How about our global style sheet class?

Let's now switch to the BRStyleSheet.h header file. We're going to declare one more public class method:

```
+(void)initStyles;
```

In the BRStyleSheet.m source file, add an empty implementation of our new initStyles method for now:

```
+(void) initStyles
{

}
```

We'll invoke initStyles just once when our app first launches. Open your app delegate class BRAppDelegate.m source file. Import BRStyleSheet.h and then add one line of code to the application:didFinishLaunchingWithOptions: method:

```
- (BOOL)application:(UIApplication *)application didFinishLaunchingWithOptions:(NSDictionary *)launchOptions
{
    [BRStyleSheet initStyles];
    return YES;
}
```

The application:didFinishLaunchingWithOptions: method is the first code in our program to execute and it will run only once. This is the place to initialize all of our global custom appearance styles. So let's now switch back to BRStyleSheet.m and see exactly what's possible with appearance APIs. Here's the first few lines of styling code to add to initStyles:

```
//NAVIGATION BAR
    NSDictionary *titleTextAttributes = [NSDictionary dictionaryWithObjectsAndKeys:
                                    kFontNavigationTextColour, UITextAttributeTextColor,
                                    [UIColor whiteColor], UITextAttributeTextShadowColor,
                                    [NSValue valueWithUIOffset:UIOffsetMake(0, 2)],
UITextAttributeTextShadowOffset,
                                    kFontNavigation, UITextAttributeFont,nil];
    [[UINavigationBar appearance] setTitleTextAttributes:titleTextAttributes];

    //Setting a background image with the birthday cake icing
    [[UINavigationBar appearance] setBackgroundImage:[UIImage imageNamed:@"navigation-bar-
background.png"] forBarMetrics:UIBarMetricsDefault];
```

In iOS 5, Apple added a new titleTextAttributes property to UINavigationBar, enabling us to pass in a dictionary of optional style attributes for the navigation bar title: text color, shadow color, shadow offset, and the font. Note that titleTextAttributes is a property of UINavigationBar. Rather than style each of the navigation bars in our app individually, however, we can optionally set the titleTextAttributes property on a global level via the appearance proxy of the UINavigationBar class (i.e., [UINavigationBar appearance]). Likewise, UINavigationBar has another instance method, setBackgroundImage:forBarMetrics:, which we can access globally through the appearance proxy of the UINavigationBar class. Build and run your project (see Figure 9-16).

Figure 9-16. Stylized navigation bar title and background icing image

Our `navigation-bar-background.png` image is higher than the default navigation bar height of 44 points. Our custom dripping-icing image is 60 points in height and includes alpha transparency. This will work just fine in iOS. Your icing should now be dripping nicely over the table view!

Appearance styles for containers

Excellent. Let's continue with the `initStyles` method of `BRStyleSheet.m`. Add the next block of appearance API styling code:

```
NSDictionary *barButtonItemTextAttributes;

//NAVIGATION BUTTONS

    //Tint of the navigation button backgrounds
    [[UIBarButtonItem appearanceWhenContainedIn:[UINavigationBar class],nil]
setTintColor:kNavigationButtonBackgroundColour];

    barButtonItemTextAttributes = [NSDictionary dictionaryWithObjectsAndKeys:
```

```
                    kFontNavigationTextColour, UITextAttributeTextColor,
                    [UIColor whiteColor], UITextAttributeTextShadowColor,
                    [NSValue valueWithUIOffset:UIOffsetMake(0, 1)],
UITextAttributeTextShadowOffset,nil];
    [[UIBarButtonItem appearanceWhenContainedIn:[UINavigationBar class], nil]
setTitleTextAttributes:barButtonItemTextAttributes forState:UIControlStateNormal];

    NSDictionary *disabledBarButtonItemTextAttributes = [NSDictionary
dictionaryWithObjectsAndKeys:
                        kFontNavigationDisabledTextColour,
UITextAttributeTextColor,
                    [UIColor whiteColor], UITextAttributeTextShadowColor,
                    [NSValue valueWithUIOffset:UIOffsetMake(0, 1)],
UITextAttributeTextShadowOffset,nil];
    [[UIBarButtonItem appearanceWhenContainedIn:[UINavigationBar class], nil]
setTitleTextAttributes:disabledBarButtonItemTextAttributes forState:UIControlStateDisabled];
```

Build and run. The result should be tinted bar button items, as shown in Figure 9-17.

Figure 9-17. Tinted bar button items

In the latest code, I've introduced the appearanceWhenContainedIn: styling method. The significance of this second appearance API is that we can specify that iOS only apply the cream-color style to instances of UIBarButtonItem that appear within the UINavigationBar container class. If we stick to setting a global style on all instances of the UIBarButtonItem class, then our style is also applied to the Address Book and Facebook bar button item instances in the toolbar. Our app design has a very different skin for the toolbar and its bar button items, so that wouldn't be ideal. Let's now add toolbar styling to our initStyles method:

```
//TOOLBAR

    //Toolbar cake background image
    [[UIToolbar appearance] setBackgroundImage:[UIImage imageNamed:@"tool-bar-background.png"]
forToolbarPosition:UIToolbarPositionAny barMetrics:UIBarMetricsDefault];

    //TOOLBAR BUTTONS
    //Dark background of Toolbar Buttons
    //Tint of the toolbar button backgrounds
    [[UIBarButtonItem appearanceWhenContainedIn:[UIToolbar class],nil]
setTintColor:kToolbarButtonBackgroundColour];

    //White text on UIBarButtonItems
    barButtonItemTextAttributes = [NSDictionary dictionaryWithObjectsAndKeys:[UIColor
whiteColor], UITextAttributeTextColor,nil];
    [[UIBarButtonItem appearanceWhenContainedIn:[UIToolbar class], nil]
     setTitleTextAttributes:barButtonItemTextAttributes forState:UIControlStateNormal];
```

Build and run. Your home screen should be looking almost identical to our home screen design by now (see Figure 9-18).

Figure 9-18. Stylized toolbar and bar button items in the toolbar

Applying our style sheet to the rest of the app

We're almost done with our style sheet class, but we need to apply the label and image styling to the other screens in our app, so let's get that done now.

Styling the alert time view

The navigation bar and custom view background styling are automatically applied to all screens in our app, but the instruction text in BRNotificationTimeViewController is too dark against the checkered background, so open BRNotificationTimeViewController.m, import BRStyleSheet.h, and add a viewDidLoad implementation:

```
-(void) viewDidLoad
{
    [super viewDidLoad];
    [BRStyleSheet styleLabel:self.whatTimeLabel withType:BRLabelTypeLarge];
}
```

Build and run. The instruction text should now be styled, as shown in Figure 9-19.

Figure 9-19. Styled Alert Time setting view

Styling the birthday edit view

We'll apply the same styling process to the Birthday Edit view controller. Open BRBirthdayEditViewController.m, import BRStyleSheet.h, and then style the Include Year text label and photo container by adding a viewDidLoad implementation:

```
-(void)viewDidLoad
{
    [super viewDidLoad];
    [BRStyleSheet styleLabel:self.includeYearLabel withType:BRLabelTypeLarge];
    [BRStyleSheet styleRoundCorneredView:self.photoContainerView];
}
```

Build and run (see Figure 9-20).

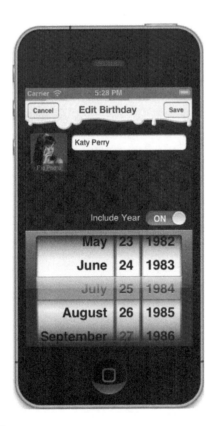

Figure 9-20. Stylized Birthday Edit view

Styling the notes edit view

The Notes Edit view controller displays a text view rather than a label, so we'll need to add a new text view styling method to our style sheet. In the BRStyleSheet.h header, declare the new method:

```
+(void)styleTextView:(UITextView *)textView;
```

Then implement the new styleTextView: class method into the BRStyleSheet.m source file:

```
+(void)styleTextView:(UITextView *)textView
{
    textView.backgroundColor = [UIColor clearColor];
    textView.font = kFontNotes;
    textView.textColor = kFontLightOnDarkTextColour;
    textView.layer.shadowColor = kFontDropShadowColour.CGColor;
    textView.layer.shadowOffset = CGSizeMake(1.0f, 1.0f);
    textView.layer.shadowRadius = 0.0f;
    textView.layer.masksToBounds = NO;
}
```

Open BRNotesEditViewController.m, import BRStyleSheet.h, and then style the text view in the viewDidLoad implementation:

```
-(void) viewDidLoad
{
    [super viewDidLoad];
    [BRStyleSheet styleTextView:self.textView];
}
```

Build and run (see Figure 9-21).

Figure 9-21. Stylized edit notes view

Creating and styling the birthday detail view

Our Birthday Detail view is looking pretty empty of content at the moment, but we'll soon fix that (see Figure 9-22).

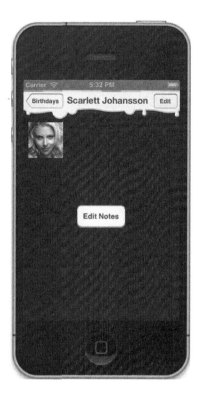

Figure 9-22. Birthday detail view: before

Scroll views and scrollable content

We're going to set up our Birthday Detail view to be scrollable if its content height is greater than the available view height. The height of the content on this screen will vary because we'll display the user-generated birthday notes and buttons to allow the user to post on their friend's Facebook wall, or to e-mail, SMS, or call their friend on his/her birthday. The content height will vary depending on the user-generated note text length, so we'll need to calculate the content height in our view controller at runtime.

In your storyboard, drag a scroll view onto the Birthday Detail view from the Object Library. Resize the scroll view to fit the bounds of the Birthday Detail view. Using the document outline pane, multiselect the button and image view, and drag them onto the scroll view. Xcode will move the button and image view to become children of the scroll view rather than the main view, as shown in Figure 9-23.

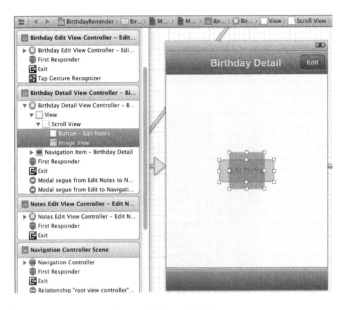

Figure 9-23. Button and image view, now subviews of the scroll view

We want the scroll view to always fill the available space of its parent view. Although this won't change because our app doesn't support portrait orientation, it's worth setting up the scroll view autosizing settings to a flexible width, a flexible height, and a fixed top, bottom, and sides, as shown in Figure 9-24.

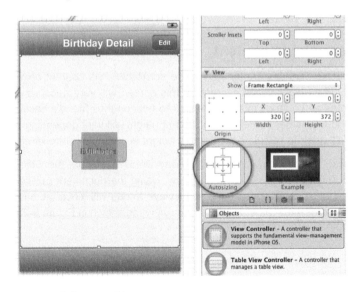

Figure 9-24. Configuring our scroll view autosizing

Before we fix the positioning of our subviews, let's add two more image views to the scroll view. Position, size, and configure the image views as shown in Table 9-2.

Table 9-2. Image Views

Image View	Position	Size	
Thumbnail background image view	x=10, y=19	w=71, h=71	Ensure that the background image view is behind the photo view. Set the image view's Image property to thumbnail-background.png.
Remaining days image view	x=260, y=20	w=48, h=50	Set the image view's Image property to icon-days-remaining.png.
Reposition the original photo image view	x=10, y=19	w=71, h=71	

The layout of your view should resemble Figure 9-25.

Figure 9-25. Image views configured and positioned

Now to add five new label views. Position, size, and configure the label views as shown in Table 9-3.

Table 9-3. New Label Views

Label	Font System	Position	Size	
Birthday label	bold 17	x=89, y=28,	w=164, h=21	
Remaining day count label	bold 17	x=265, y=35	w=37, h=19	Set Autoshrink to Minimum Font Size 10 points and center align the text
Remaining day count sublabel	9	x=259, y=51	w=51, h=20	Centered text alignment
Notes title label	17	x=10, y=102	w=69, h=22	Text notes
Notes text label	15	x=10, y=133	w=300, h=17	In the attributes inspector, set the Lines property to 100 to enable multiple lines of notes

The layout of your view should now resemble Figure 9-26.

Figure 9-26. Labels configured and positioned

We're going to modify the Edit Notes button and turn it into a pencil icon. Delete the Edit Notes text. Using the attributes inspector, set the Image property to icon-notes.png. Change the button type to Custom to remove the round rectangle border. Now position the button (x=51, y=91) and size it (w=44 and h=44).

Next up, buttons. Add five buttons to the scroll view and position, size, and configure them as shown in Table 9-4.

Table 9-4. Buttons

Button	Position	Size	Image	Text
Facebook button	x=6, y=156	w=307, h=60	icon-facebook.png	Post on Friend's Wall
Call button	x=6, y=221	w=307, h=60	icon-call.png	Call Friend
SMS button	x=6, y=286	w=307, h=60	icon-sms.png	SMS Friend
Email button	x=6, y=351	w=307, h=60	icon-email.png	Email Friend
Delete button	x=6, y=416	w=307, h=60	icon-delete.png	Delete Friend

Even though the Email and Delete buttons move out of sight, you can use the document outline pane to select them and then configure with the attributes and size inspectors. You should end up with a layout that looks like Figure 9-27.

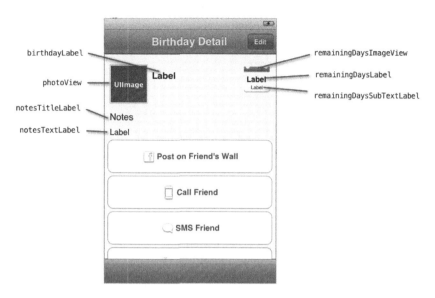

Figure 9-27. Buttons configured and positioned

Using the Assistant Editor layout, I'd now like you to Control-drag to create new outlets and actions in BRBirthdayDetailViewController.h for the new views and buttons we've just added to the Birthday Edit view. If you can't access a view because it's hidden behind another, then you can optionally drag from the document outline pane to BRBirthdayDetailViewController.h. Here's the resulting BRBirthdayDetailViewController.h file with the new outlets and actions. Make sure yours matches when you're done:

```objc
#import <UIKit/UIKit.h>
#import "BRCoreViewController.h"
@class BRDBirthday;

@interface BRBirthdayDetailViewController : BRCoreViewController

@property(nonatomic,strong) BRDBirthday *birthday;
@property (weak, nonatomic) IBOutlet UIImageView *photoView;

@property (weak, nonatomic) IBOutlet UIScrollView *scrollView;
@property (weak, nonatomic) IBOutlet UILabel *birthdayLabel;
@property (weak, nonatomic) IBOutlet UILabel *remainingDaysLabel;
@property (weak, nonatomic) IBOutlet UILabel *remainingDaysSubTextLabel;
@property (weak, nonatomic) IBOutlet UILabel *notesTitleLabel;
@property (weak, nonatomic) IBOutlet UILabel *notesTextLabel;
@property (weak, nonatomic) IBOutlet UIImageView *remainingDaysImageView;
@property (weak, nonatomic) IBOutlet UIButton *facebookButton;
@property (weak, nonatomic) IBOutlet UIButton *callButton;
@property (weak, nonatomic) IBOutlet UIButton *smsButton;
@property (weak, nonatomic) IBOutlet UIButton *emailButton;
@property (weak, nonatomic) IBOutlet UIButton *deleteButton;
```

```
- (IBAction)facebookButtonTapped:(id)sender;
- (IBAction)callButtonTapped:(id)sender;
- (IBAction)smsButtonTapped:(id)sender;
- (IBAction)emailButtonTapped:(id)sender;
- (IBAction)deleteButtonTapped:(id)sender;

@end
```

Using the regular editor, switch to BRBirthdayDetailViewController.m and begin by importing BRStyleSheet.h. Just like earlier, we'll add the label and round-corner styling in the viewDidLoad implementation:

```
-(void) viewDidLoad
{
    [super viewDidLoad];

    [BRStyleSheet styleRoundCorneredView:self.photoView];

    [BRStyleSheet styleLabel:self.birthdayLabel withType:BRLabelTypeLarge];
    [BRStyleSheet styleLabel:self.notesTitleLabel withType:BRLabelTypeLarge];
    [BRStyleSheet styleLabel:self.notesTextLabel withType:BRLabelTypeLarge];
    [BRStyleSheet styleLabel:self.remainingDaysLabel withType:BRLabelTypeDaysUntilBirthday];
    [BRStyleSheet styleLabel:self.remainingDaysSubTextLabel
withType:BRLabelTypeDaysUntilBirthdaySubText];
}
```

Build and run. The labels and photo view should be nicely styled, as shown in Figure 9-28.

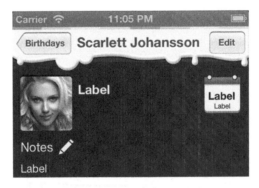

Figure 9-28. Labels and photo view styled in the Birthday Detail view

To add the birthday content to the detail view, we'll first add the highlighted code to *BRBirthdayDetailViewController.m*'s viewWillAppear: method:

```
-(void) viewWillAppear:(BOOL)animated
{
    [super viewWillAppear:animated];

    self.title = self.birthday.name;
    UIImage *image = [UIImage imageWithData:self.birthday.imageData];
```

```
if (image == nil) {
    //default to the birthday cake pic if there's no birthday image
    self.photoView.image = [UIImage imageNamed:@"icon-birthday-cake.png"];
}
else {
    self.photoView.image = image;
}

int days = self.birthday.remainingDaysUntilNextBirthday;

if (days == 0) {
    //Birthday is today!
    self.remainingDaysLabel.text = self.remainingDaysSubTextLabel.text = @"";
    self.remainingDaysImageView.image = [UIImage imageNamed:@"icon-birthday-
cake.png"];
}
else {
    self.remainingDaysLabel.text = [NSString stringWithFormat:@"%d",days];
    self.remainingDaysSubTextLabel.text = (days == 1) ? @"more day" : @"more days";
    self.remainingDaysImageView.image = [UIImage imageNamed:@"icon-days-
remaining.png"];
}

self.birthdayLabel.text = self.birthday.birthdayTextToDisplay;
}
```

The code is virtually the same as the code we used in BRBrithdayTableViewCell.m. The results should look like Figure 9-29.

Figure 9-29. (a) A day countdown is displayed (b) or a cake if it's the friend's birthday

Calculating text size

Our Birthday Detail view controller should also display any user-generated notes. We want the notes to display immediately below the Notes title label and then the row of buttons to appear after the notes. So we need to make the contents of our scroll view layout dynamically based on the height of the notes text. We're enabling our users to write multiple lines of notes, so we need to dynamically measure the height that the note text label requires. NSString has a method, sizeWithFont:constrainedToSize:lineBreakMode:, which is perfect for calculating the height required. We'll now incorporate this by adding the following code to the end of our viewWillAppear: implementation of BRBirthdayDetailViewController.m:

```
    NSString *notes = (self.birthday.notes && self.birthday.notes.length > 0) ?
self.birthday.notes : @"";

    CGFloat cY = self.notesTextLabel.frame.origin.y;

    CGSize notesLabelSize = [notes sizeWithFont:self.notesTextLabel.font
constrainedToSize:CGSizeMake(300.f, 300.f) lineBreakMode:NSLineBreakByWordWrapping];

    CGRect frame = self.notesTextLabel.frame;
    frame.size.height = notesLabelSize.height;
    self.notesTextLabel.frame = frame;

    self.notesTextLabel.text = notes;

    cY += frame.size.height;
    cY += 10.f;

    CGFloat buttonGap = 6.f;

    cY += buttonGap * 2;

    NSMutableArray *buttonsToShow = [NSMutableArray
arrayWithObjects:self.facebookButton,self.callButton, self.smsButton, self.emailButton,
self.deleteButton, nil];

    UIButton *button;

    int i;

    for (i=0;i<[buttonsToShow count];i++) {
        button = [buttonsToShow objectAtIndex:i];
        frame = button.frame;
        frame.origin.y = cY;
        button.frame = frame;
        cY += button.frame.size.height + buttonGap;
    }

    self.scrollView.contentSize = CGSizeMake(320, cY);
```

Build and run. You should now see our note text label sizes to fit the text entered up to a maximum 300 points height. The five buttons also layout neatly under the text, and the scroll view scrolls to the exact height of our content as shown in Figure 9-30.

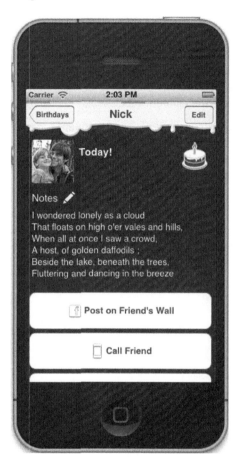

Figure 9-30. Note text height dynamically calculated in code and buttons laid out neatly below the notes text view

Let's examine how the code works. We create a temporary variable named cY to keep track of the current y value as we layout each button below the notes text label. Take a look at our last line of code:

```
self.scrollView.contentSize = CGSizeMake(320, cY);
```

We use the cY value to determine the total height of the content of the scroll view.

We start cY at the top-left point of the notes text label (origin):

```
CGFloat cY = self.notesTextLabel.frame.origin.y;
```

We do this because nothing above the notes text label needs to be laid out dynamically, only everything below it.

There's one bit of skinning left to do: those ugly white buttons need a makeover!

Skinning buttons

Here's the last of my iOS skinning tips. We want to create two button styles for the buttons in our Birthday Detail view: a big blue button style and a big red Delete button style. We can define button styles using the appearance APIs. Great. There's a problem, however: we want buttons in the same container class to have different styles. Apple's appearanceWhenContainedIn: method is not going to work for this scenario. The best solution I've found to this problem is to create multiple subclasses of UIButton and apply different appearance styles to the different subclasses.

In your Xcode project, select the user-interface/components group and create a new Objective-C class file there. Name your class BRBlueButton and subclass UIButton. All done? Great. Now repeat that process and add a new class to the same components group named BRRedButton, but this time subclass your original BRBlueButton. We don't need to add any code to these new classes because we've only created them for skinning purposes.

For each of the buttons in the Birthday Detail view controller scene back in your storyboard, select the button in the document outline pane. Using the identity inspector, change the custom class of the first four buttons to BRBlueButton and the last (Delete) button to BRRedButton (see Figure 9-31).

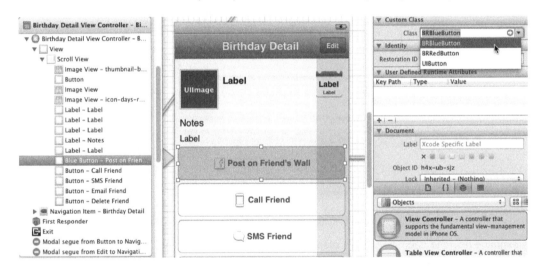

Figure 9-31. Selecting button subclasses in the identity inspector

Open BRStyleSheet.m and, after importing BRBlueButton.h and BRRedButton.h, add the following code to the end of the initStyles method:

```
//BUTTONS
[[BRBlueButton appearance] setBackgroundImage:[UIImage imageNamed:@"button-blue.png"]
forState:UIControlStateNormal];
```

```
    [[BRBlueButton appearance] setTitleColor:kLargeButtonTextColour
forState:UIControlStateNormal];
    [[BRBlueButton appearance] setFont:kFontLarge];

    [[BRRedButton appearance] setBackgroundImage:[UIImage imageNamed:@"button-red.png"]
forState:UIControlStateNormal];
    [[BRRedButton appearance] setTitleColor:kLargeButtonTextColour
forState:UIControlStateNormal];
    [[BRRedButton appearance] setFont:kFontLarge];
```

Build and run. Presto! We now have lickable blue and red buttons, and a very easy way to create new blue or red buttons in any other view in our app (see Figure 9-32)!

Figure 9-32. Lickable blue and red buttons!

In the styling code, notice how we only apply the title color to the blue buttons, yet it still gets inherited by the red button style? Subclasses also inherit appearance styles from their parent class.

One final styling niggle that you may or may not have spotted is that the table view on the home screen has a white background. You'll notice this when the table view bounces at the top and bottom of its scrollable content area. We can fix this and make the table view background color transparent for all table views globally by adding the following code to our `initStyles` method:

```
//TABLE VIEW
[[UITableView appearance] setBackgroundColor:[UIColor clearColor]];
[[UITableViewCell appearance] setSelectionStyle:UITableViewCellSelectionStyleNone];
[[UITableView appearance] setSeparatorStyle:UITableViewCellSeparatorStyleNone];
```

I've also thrown in a couple of lines of code to ensure that we never see Apple's default blue selection style or line separator style in our table view cells, because it doesn't look good with the *Birthday Reminder* design.

Summary

That's Day 3 down. Congratulations! Our iPhone app is really taking form now, looking like the original Photoshop designs. I guess the cake design lends itself well to being considered lickable!

We learned a great deal about how to skin and style an iPhone app this afternoon. *Birthday Reminder* no longer looks like an Apple example test project. It looks like a cool app. Its core functionality is also up and running. We mastered the basics of Core Data this morning and now we can add, edit, and save birthdays or any other type of data entity for that matter.

Tomorrow morning, we'll begin exploring how to populate our app by batch importing birthdays from the user's iPhone Address Book and Facebook. We'll also learn how to schedule local notifications even when our app isn't running.

See you in the morning, bright-eyed and bushy-tailed!

Importing Birthdays from the Address Book and Facebook

Chapter 10

Importing Birthdays from the Address Book

We've passed the halfway mark in our project. It's Day 4 and most of the hard work is now behind us. Today we'll focus on importing friends and family birthdays into *Birthday Reminder*. We'll make this process super easy for our users. In just a few taps, they will have an app full of birthdays.

With any app that you build, designing your user experience to be simple and easy to use is essential. We want to avoid putting our users through the laborious process of manually entering every friend's birthday into the app. They will quickly get very bored! Apple's Phone Contacts app, a.k.a. the Address Book, includes an array of fields for each contact in addition to telephone number, e-mail, and so forth. One of those permits iPhone users to enter a birthday for each contact, as shown in Figure 10-1.

Figure 10-1. Apple's Phone Contacts app: assigning a birthday to a contact

Assigning birthdays to contacts is perhaps the sort of process that some of our users will go through and others won't. So importing directly from the Address Book into *Birthday Reminder* is a feature that only a selection of our users will use.

As developers, we'll need to test that this feature works OK, so at this stage I suggest you add a few birthdays to your iPhone contacts.

Enhancing the home view for an empty database

It's time to say au revoir to our celebrities. We won't be prepopulating our release app with a random list of celebs, so let's kick off by removing that test functionality from our app.

Open the BRHomeViewController.m source file and delete the entire initWithCoder: method. Now delete *Birthday Reminder* from the simulator and your iPhone if you've previously installed it to your device. Build and run. Your app should look just like Figure 10-2. An app screen empty of birthdays when *Birthday Reminder* is first launched is not the most inviting launch screen for new users.

Figure 10-2. The Home view with an empty database of birthdays

When our users first launch *Birthday Reminder* and start with an empty database, we want to invite and encourage them to either add or import some birthdays to get started. Do you remember those nice-looking big blue buttons we skinned yesterday in the Birthday Detail view? I think we should add a couple of those to the center of our empty home screen to invite the user to import birthdays from the Address Book and Facebook.

To do this, we're going to add a subview to our Home view. A subview that displays the text Import Birthdays from... with two big blue buttons, one for importing from the Address Book, and one for importing from Facebook.

Before we start work on modifying our storyboard layout, import a couple more image assets into the `resources/images` group in your Xcode project: `icon-addressbook.png` and `icon-addressbook@2x.png`.

Open your storyboard in Xcode and focus on the Home view controller scene. Ensure the document outline pane is open and then drag a new view instance from the objects library right onto the main home screen view in the document outline pane, as highlighted in Figure 10-3.

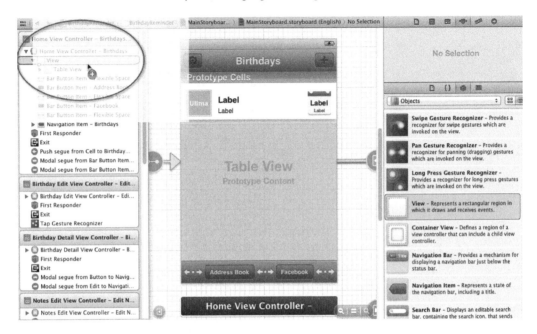

Figure 10-3. Drag and dropping a subview into the Home view

Your new subview should not be a subview of the table view. It should be a subview of the main Home view. It's a little fiddly, but if your subview ended up in the wrong location, then you can relocate it using the document outline pane. Also, move the new subview below the table view in the document outline pane, this will place it in front of the table view and will make it easier for you to work with it.

Keeping your new subview selected, use the size inspector to position, and size the subview (x=0, y=0, width=320, and height=372). We'll also make the background of the subview transparent using the attributes inspector. Open the Background drop-down menu and select Clear Color from the default list of Apple colors (see Figure 10-4).

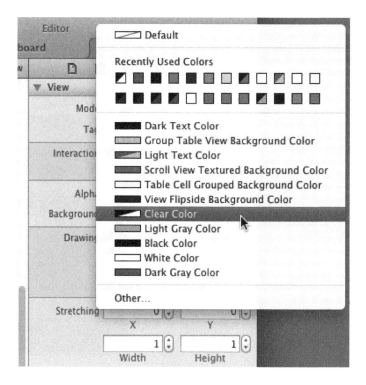

Figure 10-4. Making a view transparent using Apple's Clear color

Next, add one label and two buttons to your subview, and set the position, size, and additional attribute values as listed:

- Label (UILabel): x=14, y=92, width=293, height=21, text aligned: center, font system: 17, text: **Import Birthdays from....**

- Button1 (UIButton): change the text to **Address Book** and then position and size (x=7, y=127, width=307, height=60). Set the Image property to icon-addressbook.png. Using the identity inspector, change the custom class of the button to BRBlueButton just as we did yesterday.

- Button2 (UIButton): change the text to **Facebook** and then position and size (x=7, y=202, width=307, height=60). Set the Image property to icon-facebook.png. Using the identity inspector, change the custom class of the button to BRBlueButton.

Build and run (see Figure 10-5).

Figure 10-5. Creating big blue buttons was a piece of cake thanks to yesterday's style sheet class.

Keeping the Home view controller scene selected in your storyboard, activate the Assistant Editor layout of Xcode. With BRHomeViewController.h visible in the right panel of the assistant layout import BRBlueButton.h and then create new Interface Builder outlets in BRHomeViewController.h for the label, buttons, and holder view, naming them importLabel, addressBookButton, facebookButton, and importView, respectively. We'll need the outlet to the transparent holder view (importView) to hide and show it, depending on whether the birthdays database is empty or populated:

```
#import <UIKit/UIKit.h>
#import "BRCoreViewController.h"
#import "BRBlueButton.h"

@interface BRHomeViewController : BRCoreViewController <UITableViewDelegate,
UITableViewDataSource,NSFetchedResultsControllerDelegate>

-(IBAction)unwindBackToHomeViewController:(UIStoryboardSegue *)segue;
@property (weak, nonatomic) IBOutlet UITableView *tableView;
@property (weak, nonatomic) IBOutlet UILabel *importLabel;
@property (weak, nonatomic) IBOutlet BRBlueButton *addressBookButton;
@property (weak, nonatomic) IBOutlet BRBlueButton *facebookButton;
@property (weak, nonatomic) IBOutlet UIView *importView;

@end
```

In addition to our new outlets, create a Touch Up Inside action from both the Address Book and Facebook buttons to BRHomeViewController.h as follows:

```
- (IBAction)importFromAddressBookTapped:(id)sender;
- (IBAction)importFromFacebookTapped:(id)sender;
```

Notice how we currently have two Import buttons for the Address Book and Facebook in the application toolbar (see Figure 10-5). Duplicate buttons that do the same thing is not good user interface design so we'll fix this so that our users only ever see one Address Book button and one Facebook button. Before we do, add Interface Builder actions to these toolbar buttons by Control-dragging to the importFromAddressBookTapped: and importFromFacebookTapped: actions we've just set up. So both Address Book buttons should be set to invoke the importFromAddressBookTapped: action and both Facebook buttons should be set to invoke the importFromFacebookTapped: action.

We're done with the storyboard for now, so let's move our attention to the BRHomeViewController.m source file. First off, let's apply our style sheet to our Import Birthdays from... label. Import BRStyleSheet.h and then add a viewDidLoad implementation:

```
-(void) viewDidLoad
{
    [super viewDidLoad];
    [BRStyleSheet styleLabel:self.importLabel withType:BRLabelTypeLarge];
}
```

This should result in the cream-colored text and large Helvetica Neue font being applied to our instruction label.

Our new import subview is only intended to display when there are zero birthdays in the Core Data store. Likewise, our toolbar with the Address Book and Facebook bar button items is only intended to display when there are one or more birthdays in the Core Data store. There's a neat way to achieve this in code. We'll add a private Boolean property named hasFriends to our Home view controller. If there are zero birthdays, then we'll set hasFriends to false. If there are one or more birthdays then we'll set hasFriends to true. We'll override the setter for hasFriends, and hide and show the import subview and the toolbar each time our private property is set.

Continuing work on BRHomeViewController.m, let's define our new private property in the private interface:

```
@interface BRHomeViewController()

@property (nonatomic, strong) NSFetchedResultsController *fetchedResultsController;
@property (nonatomic) BOOL hasFriends;

@end
```

We'll now override our hasFriends setter:

```
-(void) setHasFriends:(BOOL)hasFriends
{
    _hasFriends = hasFriends;
```

```
    self.importView.hidden = _hasFriends;
    self.tableView.hidden = !_hasFriends;

    if (self.navigationController.topViewController == self) {
        [self.navigationController setToolbarHidden:!_hasFriends animated:NO];
    }
}
```

We're simply hiding and showing the import view, table view, and toolbar depending on whether hasFriends is set to true or false. But where should we be setting the value of hasFriends?

The simplest solution is just to set hasFriends whenever the Home view controller is about to appear:

```
-(void) viewWillAppear:(BOOL)animated
{
    [super viewWillAppear:animated];
    [self.tableView reloadData];
    self.hasFriends = [self.fetchedResultsController.fetchedObjects count] > 0;
}
```

Build and run. We now have a home screen that updates and renders differently depending on whether our database of birthdays is empty or not. Try tapping the "+" button to add a birthday (see Figure 10-6).

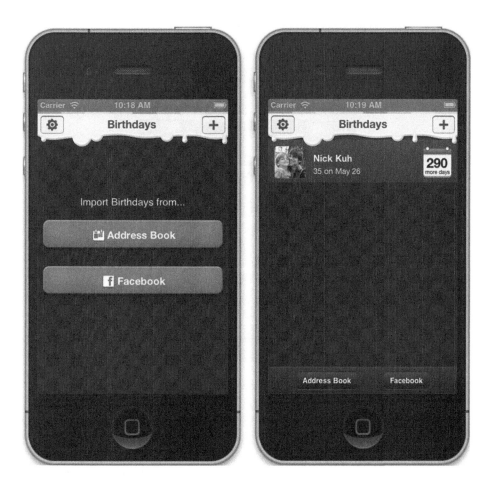

Figure 10-6. Hiding and showing the table view, import view, and toolbar depending on whether we have any saved birthdays

We're going to create a new view and view controller scene to display modally in our app when either of the Address Book buttons are tapped from the Home view. If we cast our memories back to Chapter 1/ Day 1, Figure 10-7 shows us what our import from Facebook view design should end up looking like.

Figure 10-7. The import from Facebook birthdays view we're planning to build

Apart from the title, our import from the Address Book view looks identical to the import from Facebook view. Under the hood, the process to retrieve the list of birthdays to import is very different, but the view rendering is identical.

We've already seen the benefits of creating a core view controller class when we skinned the background of every view in our app in one central superview controller class. It seems logical that both the Address Book and Facebook import screens should also share a superview controller class to centralize shared UI functionality, as they are so similar. So first off, we'll create a core Import view controller.

Select the `view-controllers` group in the Project Navigator and then create a new subclass of `BRCoreViewController` and name it `BRImportViewController`. You can leave Targeted for iPad and With XIB for User Interface deselected.

Back in your storyboard, add a new view controller scene. Because we're going to present the Import Address Book view controller modally, we'll embed it in its own navigation controller as we've done before with other modal view controllers. Select the new view controller and from the menu bar: Editor ➤ Embed In ➤ Navigation Controller. Now title the new Import view controller **Address Book**, and add Cancel and Import buttons, as shown in Figure 10-8.

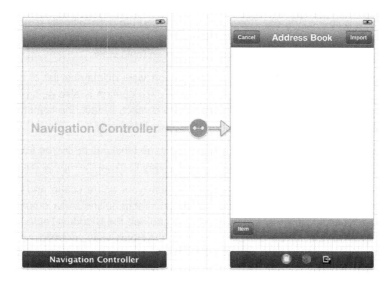

Figure 10-8. Embedding the Address Book view controller in a new navigation controller

Select the parent navigation controller you've just created. Using the attributes inspector, switch on Shows Toolbar under the Bar Visibility options.

A toolbar should be visible in our import Address Book view controller scene and Xcode may have added a single bar button item. Set up the following items in the toolbar in this order: a Flexible Space bar button item, a bar button item titled Select All, and a bar button item titled Select None (see Figure 10-9).

Figure 10-9. Configuring the Address Book import toolbar

Drag a new table view onto the Address Book view. Allow Xcode to automatically resize the table view to fill its parent view before releasing your mouse. With your new table view selected, use the size inspector to modify the row height to 72 points, just like our home screen table view.

When our users import from their Address Book, our import view displays a list of those contacts with assigned birthdays. The table cell that we'll use to display each contact is also going to display the days remaining until a birthday, and a photo if one exists for the contact. In fact, the layout will be virtually the same as the custom table cell we created for our home screen table view.

As the table cell is virtually identical, we're going to duplicate the table cell prototype from the home screen and copy it across to our new import screen table view. It's easy to mess this up, so concentrate. ☺

As shown in Figure 10-10, make sure that you can see both your home scene and new Address Book scene in your storyboard simultaneously. Ensure that the document outline pane is open. In the document outline pane, expand the table view hierarchy so that you can see the Birthday Table View Cell prototype listed. We're going to Alt-drag this table cell prototype from the Home view controller onto the table view in the Address Book scene (see Figure 10-10). The Address Book scene may be located further down the document outline pane, but as you drag, the pane should scroll.

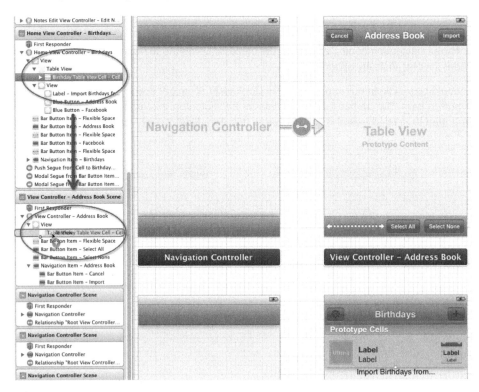

Figure 10-10. Duplicating a prototyped table cell from one table to another

After dropping the custom table cell prototype (keeping Alt selected), a duplicate table cell prototype should appear in our Address Book table view (see Figure 10-11).

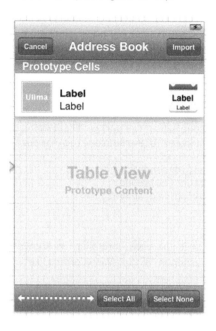

Figure 10-11. Duplicating a prototype table cell in the Address Book scene

We're going to temporarily assign BRImportViewController as the custom class for our Address Book view controller. This enables us to create outlets and actions via drag-and-drop directly to the BRImportViewController class: shared outlets and actions that are eventually used by both the import from Address Book and Facebook view controllers.

Select the Address Book view controller scene and use the identity inspector to change the class to BRImportViewController as shown in Figure 10-12.

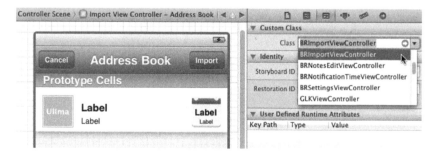

Figure 10-12. Assigning our Import view controller class to our storyboard view controller

With the Address Book view controller selected in your storyboard, activate the Assistant Editor layout of Xcode. With BRImportViewController.h visible in the right panel of the assistant editor, create new outlets for the Import button named importButton and for the table view named tableView.

In addition, create actions for the Import, Select All, and Select None buttons, as shown in the following code:

```
#import "BRCoreViewController.h"

@interface BRImportViewController : BRCoreViewController

@property (weak, nonatomic) IBOutlet UITableView *tableView;
@property (weak, nonatomic) IBOutlet UIBarButtonItem *importButton;

- (IBAction)didTapImportButton:(id)sender;
- (IBAction)didTapSelectAllButton:(id)sender;
- (IBAction)didTapSelectNoneButton:(id)sender;

@end
```

Control-drag from the Cancel button to the view controller, as shown in Figure 10-13, to link the cancel button to the cancelAndDismiss: action in BRCoreViewController.

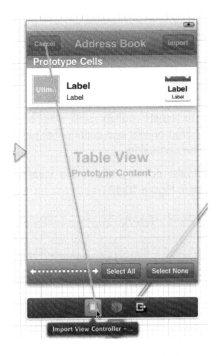

Figure 10-13. Setting up the Cancel button to dismiss the modal view controller

Both of the import screens will display a list of birthdays to import. We'll store the data for this list in an array property of each Import view controller. Let's define that array in the BRImportViewController.h header:

```
@property (strong, nonatomic) NSArray *birthdays;
```

By defining the birthdays array in the public interface of our Import view controller, its subclasses are able to access the array and set its data.

In the BRImportViewController.h header file, our Import view controller implements the UITableViewDelegate and UITableViewDataSource protocols:

```
@interface BRImportViewController : BRCoreViewController<UITableViewDelegate,
UITableViewDataSource>
```

Control-drag from the table view to the view controller in your storyboard to connect up the dataSource and delegate properties of the table view as shown in Figure 10-14.

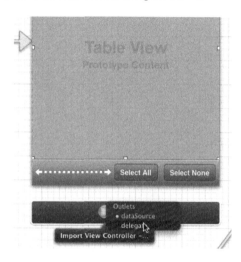

Figure 10-14. Assigning the dataSource and delegate outlets from the table view

We need to add two required methods from the UITableViewDataSource protocol to BRImportViewController.m:

```
#pragma mark UITableViewDataSource

- (NSInteger)tableView:(UITableView *)tableView numberOfRowsInSection:(NSInteger)section
{
    return [self.birthdays count];
}

- (UITableViewCell *)tableView:(UITableView *)tableView cellForRowAtIndexPath:(NSIndexPath
*)indexPath
```

```
{
    UITableViewCell *cell = [self.tableView dequeueReusableCellWithIdentifier:@"Cell"];
    return cell;
}
```

Identifying view controller scenes in a storyboard

We're going to present the Address Book view whenever either of the two Address Book buttons from the Home view are tapped. Rather than create two segues, I'm going to show you an alternative way to access a view controller scene in a storyboard at runtime. We'll add an identifier to the navigation controller parent of our new Address Book view controller. Select the navigation controller. Using the attributes inspector, enter the identifier of the ImportAddressBook scene, as shown in Figure 10-15.

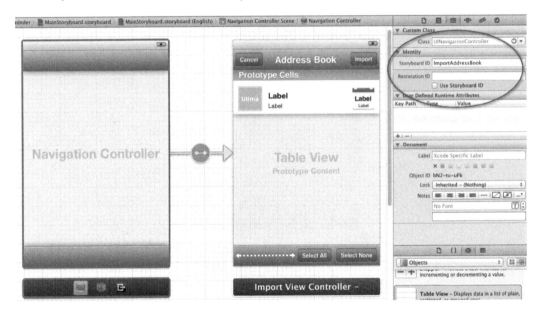

Figure 10-15. Assigning an identifier to a storyboard scene

Switch your attention to BRHomeViewController.m and scroll down to the importFromAddressBookTapped: action method and add the following code:

```
- (IBAction)importFromAddressBookTapped:(id)sender {
    UINavigationController *navigationController = [self.storyboard
instantiateViewControllerWithIdentifier:@"ImportAddressBook"];
    [self.navigationController presentViewController:navigationController animated:YES
completion:nil];
}
```

We're using the identifier ImportAddressBook to instantiate an instance of our navigation controller and Address Book view controller and then presenting it modally sliding over the Home view controller.

Build and run. You should be able to tap the Address Book button to be presented with our new scene, as shown in Figure 10-16. Tapping the Cancel button should dismiss the modal view controller.

Figure 10-16. Modally presented Address Book view controller

At this point, we'll subclass our core Import view controller to create the Address Book Import view controller. Select the `view-controllers` group in the Project Navigator and then create a new subclass of `BRImportViewController` and name it `BRImportAddressBookViewController`. Again, leave Targeted for iPad and With XIB for User Interface deselected.

With your Address Book view controller once again selected in the storyboard use the identity inspector to change its custom class to our new `BRImportAddressBookViewController` class.

Accessing and filtering the address book contacts

We're now going to turn our attention to our data model to access the iPhone Address Book contacts and filter just those contacts with assigned birthdays. As this is a data feature, we'll be adding our Address Book querying code to our main model class `BRDModel`.

Before we write the code, we'll need to add Apple's Address Book framework to our Xcode project. We'll add the new framework just as we did back in Chapter 8 when we added the Core Data framework. Select the BirthdayReminder project in the project navigator, then select the BirthdayReminder target, and finally select the Build Phases tab, as shown in Figure 10-17.

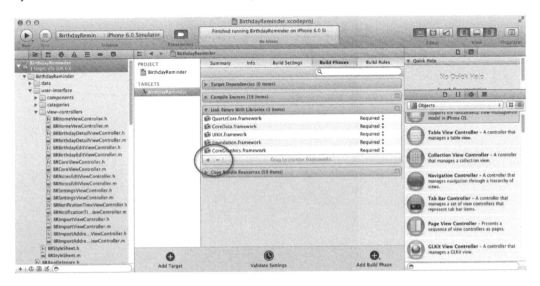

Figure 10-17. Preparing to add a new framework

Tap the "+" button, highlighted in Figure 10-17, and select AddressBook.framework from the list.

Address book data privacy

In iOS 6, Apple tightened up data privacy restrictions. Pre–iOS 6 apps could read and write from/to the users' Address Book without any restriction. Although it's still possible to do this in iOS 6, our app first needs to request access from the user via a system alert view. The alert view only shows the first time an app requests Address Book access, so once our users have authorized our app they will no longer be prompted for renewed authorization.

What this means from an app architectural perspective is that there is a delay the first time we request Address Book access authorization from our user.

Let's write some code to see this in action. Open BRDModel.h and add a new fetching method to our model singleton class:

- (void)fetchAddressBookBirthdays;

Our Address Book Import view controller calls this new method on the model, which in turn checks for Address Book access. Once the user grants access, the model grabs any birthday-compatible Address Book records from the iPhone and dispatches them via a notification that the Address Book view controller will subscribe to and update its view accordingly.

Switch to the BRDModel.m source file. Import the newly added Address Book framework:

```
#import <AddressBook/AddressBook.h>
```

The Address Book framework is written in C and not Objective-C, so there's no ARC (Automatic Reference Counting). That means it's up to us as developers to avoid creating memory leaks, and we need to manually take care of retaining and releasing C objects. Here's the initial fetchAddressBookBirthdays code to add to BRDModel.m:

```
- (void)fetchAddressBookBirthdays
{
    ABAddressBookRef addressBook = ABAddressBookCreateWithOptions(NULL, NULL);

    switch (ABAddressBookGetAuthorizationStatus()) {
        case kABAuthorizationStatusNotDetermined:
        {
            ABAddressBookRequestAccessWithCompletion(addressBook, ^(bool granted, CFErrorRef
error) {
                if (granted) {
                    NSLog(@"Access to the Address Book has been granted");
                }
                else {
                    NSLog(@"Access to the Address Book has been denied");
                }
            });
            break;
        }
        case kABAuthorizationStatusAuthorized:
        {
            NSLog(@"User has already granted access to the Address Book");
            break;
        }
        case kABAuthorizationStatusRestricted:
        {
            NSLog(@"User has restricted access to Address Book possibly due to parental
controls");
            break;
        }
        case kABAuthorizationStatusDenied:
        {
            NSLog(@"User has denied access to the Address Book");
            break;
        }
    }

    CFRelease(addressBook);
}
```

As you can see in the code, there are four possible scenarios for the Address Book authorization status. If the user has not yet permitted or denied access to their Address Book from our app, then the authorization status will be kABAuthorizationStatusNotDetermined, and we'll ask the system for access, which will in turn display an alert to the user to permit or deny access (see Figure 10-18).

In the switch statement, we can also determine whether the user has previously authorized or denied access. There's one further possibility: the user has restricted access to the system (such as when the parental controls are in use) and therefore will not have the authority to provide Address Book access to our app.

Open the BRImportAddressBookViewController.m source file and let's get our Address Book view controller calling the new fetchAddressBookBirthdays method of BRDModel. First, import BRDModel.h and then add a viewWillAppear: method as follows:

```
-(void) viewWillAppear:(BOOL)animated
{
    [super viewWillAppear:animated];
    [[BRDModel sharedInstance] fetchAddressBookBirthdays];
}
```

Build and run. Tap the Address Book Import button from the home screen. You should be prompted to allow/disallow access to your contacts, as shown in Figure 10-18.

Figure 10-18. Requesting Address Book access from the user

Processing address book data

Back to BRDModel.h. Let's begin by declaring a notification name that we'll dispatch from the model singleton when we have successfully processed any friends and family in the user's Address Book with associated birthdays. Add this definition right at the top of BRDModel.h before any other code or import declarations:

```
#define BRNotificationAddressBookBirthdaysDidUpdate
@"BRNotificationAddressBookBirthdaysDidUpdate"
```

Now switch to the BRDModel.m and add a new empty private method, which we'll complete in a moment:

```
-(void) extractBirthdaysFromAddressBook:(ABAddressBookRef)addressBook
{

}
```

We will call the new extractBirthdaysFromAddressBook: method either when our user grants access or immediately when fetchAddressBookBirthdays: is invoked if the user has previously granted access. Update fetchAddressBookBirthdays: with the following two highlighted lines of code:

```
- (void)fetchAddressBookBirthdays
{
    ABAddressBookRef addressBook = ABAddressBookCreateWithOptions(NULL, NULL);

    switch (ABAddressBookGetAuthorizationStatus()) {
        case kABAuthorizationStatusNotDetermined:
        {
            ABAddressBookRequestAccessWithCompletion(addressBook, ^(bool granted, CFErrorRef
error) {
                if (granted) {
                    NSLog(@"Access to the Address Book has been granted");
                    dispatch_async(dispatch_get_main_queue(), ^{
                        // completion handler can occur in a background thread and this
call will update the UI on the main thread
                        [self
extractBirthdaysFromAddressBook:ABAddressBookCreateWithOptions(NULL, NULL)];
                    });
                }
                else {
                    NSLog(@"Access to the Address Book has been denied");
                }
            });
            break;
        }
        case kABAuthorizationStatusAuthorized:
        {
            NSLog(@"User has already granted access to the Address Book");
            [self extractBirthdaysFromAddressBook:addressBook];
            break;
        }
        case kABAuthorizationStatusRestricted:
        {
            NSLog(@"User has restricted access to Address Book possibly due to parental
controls");
            break;
        }
        case kABAuthorizationStatusDenied:
        {
```

```
                NSLog(@"User has denied access to the Address Book");
                break;
        }
    }

    CFRelease(addressBook);
}
```

Here's the initial extractBirthdaysFromAddressBook: method implementation to add to BRDModel.m:

```
-(void) extractBirthdaysFromAddressBook:(ABAddressBookRef)addressBook
{
    NSLog(@"extractBirthdaysFromAddressBook");
    CFArrayRef people = ABAddressBookCopyArrayOfAllPeople(addressBook);

    CFIndex peopleCount = ABAddressBookGetPersonCount(addressBook);

    //this is just a placeholder for now - we'll get the array populated later in the chapter
    NSMutableArray *birthdays = [NSMutableArray array];

    for (int i = 0; i < peopleCount; i++)
    {
        ABRecordRef addressBookRecord = CFArrayGetValueAtIndex(people, i);
        CFDateRef birthdate  = ABRecordCopyValue(addressBookRecord,
kABPersonBirthdayProperty);
        if (birthdate == nil) continue;
        CFStringRef firstName = ABRecordCopyValue(addressBookRecord,
kABPersonFirstNameProperty);
        if (firstName == nil) {
            CFRelease(birthdate);
            continue;
        }
        NSLog(@"Found contact with birthday: %@, %@",firstName,birthdate);
        CFRelease(firstName);
        CFRelease(birthdate);
    }

    CFRelease(people);

    //dispatch a notification with an array of birthday objects
    NSDictionary *userInfo = [NSDictionary
dictionaryWithObjectsAndKeys:birthdays,@"birthdays", nil];

    [[NSNotificationCenter defaultCenter]
postNotificationName:BRNotificationAddressBookBirthdaysDidUpdate object:self
userInfo:userInfo];

}
```

The Address Book framework is part of Core Foundation and any C functions containing the word Copy or Create requires you to release the object reference when you're done with it. Hence, the CFRelease(object) code at the end of the function. The preceding code is incomplete at present, but it shows you how to access the user's Address Book and loop through the contact records. Each contact record has a set of optional properties that we can attempt to access. In our example, the kABPersonBirthdayProperty property refers to any birthday that has been assigned to a contact, so we use this to extract only contacts that have assigned birthdays.

Our code currently dispatches a notification with an empty array even if it finds contacts with assigned birthdays. We'll resolve this later, but for now we're just trying to get this code running and the debugger printing out Found contact with birthday: [Name], [Birthday].

Open the BRImportAddressBookViewController.m source file and let's hook it up to observe and handle the BRNotificationAddressBookBirthdaysDidUpdate notification.

Here's the full BRImportAddressBookViewController.m class code:

```objc
#import "BRImportAddressBookViewController.h"
#import "BRDModel.h"

@interface BRImportAddressBookViewController ()

@end

@implementation BRImportAddressBookViewController

-(void) viewWillAppear:(BOOL)animated
{
    [super viewWillAppear:animated];
    [[NSNotificationCenter defaultCenter] addObserver:self
selector:@selector(handleAddressBookBirthdaysDidUpdate:)
name:BRNotificationAddressBookBirthdaysDidUpdate object:[BRDModel sharedInstance]];
    [[BRDModel sharedInstance] fetchAddressBookBirthdays];
}

- (void) viewWillDisappear:(BOOL)animated
{
    [super viewWillDisappear:animated];
    [[NSNotificationCenter defaultCenter] removeObserver:self
name:BRNotificationAddressBookBirthdaysDidUpdate object:[BRDModel sharedInstance]];
}

-(void)handleAddressBookBirthdaysDidUpdate:(NSNotification *)notification
{
    NSDictionary *userInfo = [notification userInfo];

    self.birthdays = [userInfo objectForKey:@"birthdays"];
    [self.tableView reloadData];

    if ([self.birthdays count] == 0)
    {
        UIAlertView *alert = [[UIAlertView alloc] initWithTitle:nil message:@"Sorry, No
birthdays found in your address book" delegate:nil cancelButtonTitle:nil
otherButtonTitles:@"OK", nil];
        [alert show];
    }
```

```
}

@end
```

Build and run. When you launch the Address Book Import view controller, you should repeatedly see the "Sorry. No birthdays found in your address book" alert because our model is currently dispatching an empty array. However, assuming you provided *Birthday Reminder* with access to your contacts, then the model's `extractBirthdaysFromAddressBook:` method should log any Address Book birthdays to the debugger each time you open the Address Book Import view controller. If you don't see this in the debugger then now's a good time to assign some birthdays to your friends so you can test this code out!

> **Note:** You can reset privacy permissions on your iPhone via Settings ➤ General ➤ Reset ➤ Reset Location & Privacy to test out both permitting and preventing app access to contacts.

Creating a birthday import value object

Our `addressBookBirthdays` method in `BRDModel` loops though the user's Address Book. We need to decide how best to handle and format the returned contact records. Our Address Book view controller will display the table of import birthdays just like the Home view table; that is, the number of days remaining until the friend's birthday, a user-friendly date format, a photo, and so forth.

We're going to create a new `BRDBirthdayImport` class, a subclass of `NSObject`. Select the `data` group in the project navigator, and then create a new subclass of `NSObject` and name it `BRDBirthdayImport`. `BRDBirthdayImport` will be a very similar class to our `BRDBirthday` Core Data managed object. However, we can't just subclass `BRDBirthday` because Core Data's `NSManagedObject` class is a special case class that can only be instantiated by managed object contexts.

Let's add the interface of `BRDBirthdayImport.h`:

```
#import <Foundation/Foundation.h>
#import <AddressBook/AddressBook.h>

@interface BRDBirthdayImport : NSObject

@property (nonatomic, strong) NSNumber *addressBookID;
@property (nonatomic, strong) NSNumber *birthDay;
@property (nonatomic, strong) NSNumber *birthMonth;
@property (nonatomic, strong) NSNumber *birthYear;
@property (nonatomic, strong) NSString *facebookID;
@property (nonatomic, strong) NSData *imageData;
@property (nonatomic, strong) NSString *name;
@property (nonatomic, strong) NSDate *nextBirthday;
@property (nonatomic, strong) NSNumber *nextBirthdayAge;
@property (nonatomic, strong) NSString *picURL;
@property (nonatomic, strong) NSString *uid;
```

```
@property (nonatomic,readonly) int remainingDaysUntilNextBirthday;
@property (nonatomic,readonly) NSString *birthdayTextToDisplay;
@property (nonatomic,readonly) BOOL isBirthdayToday;

-(id)initWithAddressBookRecord:(ABRecordRef)addressBookRecord;

@end
```

With the exception of the notes property, we're creating a group of properties identical to BRDBirthday entity. We're also creating an initializer method initWithAddressBookRecord: so that we can generate and populate an instance of BRDBirthdayImport with an Address Book record initializer.

Now switch to the implementation of BRDBirthdayImport.m and begin by importing the thumbnail category we wrote for UIImage back in Chapter 8:

```
#import "BRDBirthdayImport.h"
#import "UIImage+Thumbnail.h"

@implementation BRDBirthdayImport

@end
```

You can copy and paste the next chunk of code from BRDBirthday.m. Although code duplication is not something to make a habit of, it's hard to avoid in this instance:

```
-(void)updateNextBirthdayAndAge
{
    NSDate *now = [NSDate date];

    NSCalendar *calendar = [NSCalendar currentCalendar];

    NSDateComponents *dateComponents = [[NSCalendar currentCalendar]
components:NSYearCalendarUnit|NSMonthCalendarUnit|NSDayCalendarUnit fromDate:now];
    NSDate *today = [calendar dateFromComponents:dateComponents];

    dateComponents.day = [self.birthDay intValue];
    dateComponents.month = [self.birthMonth intValue];

    NSDate *birthdayThisYear = [calendar dateFromComponents:dateComponents];

    if ([today compare:birthdayThisYear] == NSOrderedDescending) {
        //birthday this year has passed so next birthday will be next year
        dateComponents.year++;
        self.nextBirthday = [calendar dateFromComponents:dateComponents];
    }
    else {
        self.nextBirthday = [birthdayThisYear copy];
    }

    if ([self.birthYear intValue] > 0) {
        self.nextBirthdayAge = [NSNumber numberWithInt:dateComponents.year - [self.birthYear
intValue]];
```

```
        }
        else {
            self.nextBirthdayAge = [NSNumber numberWithInt:0];
        }

}

-(void) updateWithDefaults
{
    NSDateComponents *dateComponents = [[NSCalendar currentCalendar]
components:NSYearCalendarUnit|NSMonthCalendarUnit|NSDayCalendarUnit fromDate:[NSDate date]];

    self.birthDay = @(dateComponents.day);
    self.birthMonth = @(dateComponents.month);
    self.birthYear = @0;

    [self updateNextBirthdayAndAge];
}

-(int) remainingDaysUntilNextBirthday
{
    NSDate *now = [NSDate date];
    NSCalendar *calendar = [NSCalendar currentCalendar];
    NSDateComponents *componentsToday = [calendar
components:NSYearCalendarUnit|NSMonthCalendarUnit|NSDayCalendarUnit fromDate:now];
    NSDate *today = [calendar dateFromComponents:componentsToday];

    NSTimeInterval timeDiffSecs = [self.nextBirthday timeIntervalSinceDate:today];

    int days = floor(timeDiffSecs/(60.f*60.f*24.f));

    return days;
}

-(BOOL) isBirthdayToday
{
    return [self remainingDaysUntilNextBirthday] == 0;
}

-(NSString *) birthdayTextToDisplay {

    NSDate *now = [NSDate date];
    NSCalendar *calendar = [NSCalendar currentCalendar];
    NSDateComponents *componentsToday = [calendar
components:NSYearCalendarUnit|NSMonthCalendarUnit|NSDayCalendarUnit fromDate:now];
    NSDate *today = [calendar dateFromComponents:componentsToday];

    NSDateComponents *components = [calendar components:NSMonthCalendarUnit|NSDayCalendarUnit
fromDate:today toDate:self.nextBirthday options:0];

    if (components.month == 0) {
        if (components.day == 0) {
            //today!
```

```
            if ([self.nextBirthdayAge intValue] > 0) {
                return [NSString stringWithFormat:@"%@ Today!",self.nextBirthdayAge];
            }
            else {
                return @"Today!";
            }
        }
        if (components.day == 1) {
            //tomorrow!
            if ([self.nextBirthdayAge intValue] > 0) {
                return [NSString stringWithFormat:@"%@ Tomorrow!",self.nextBirthdayAge];
            }
            else {
                return @"Tomorrow!";
            }
        }
    }

    NSString *text = @"";

    if ([self.nextBirthdayAge intValue] > 0) {
        text = [NSString stringWithFormat:@"%@ on ",self.nextBirthdayAge];
    }

    static NSDateFormatter *dateFormatterPartial;

    if (dateFormatterPartial == nil) {
        dateFormatterPartial = [[NSDateFormatter alloc] init];
        [dateFormatterPartial setDateFormat:@"MMM d"];
    }

    return [text stringByAppendingFormat:@"%@",[dateFormatterPartial
stringFromDate:self.nextBirthday]];
}

@end
```

Now for something new. We're going to write our new BRDBirthdayImport.m initWithAddressBookRecord: initializer. I've added comments throughout the code to help you to understand the logic:

```
-(id)initWithAddressBookRecord:(ABRecordRef)addressBookRecord
{
    self = [super init];
    if (self) {
        CFStringRef firstName = nil;
        CFStringRef lastName = nil;
        ABRecordID recordID;
        CFDateRef birthdate = nil;
        NSString *name = @"";
```

```
        //Attempt to populate core foundation string and date references
        recordID = ABRecordGetRecordID(addressBookRecord);
        firstName = ABRecordCopyValue(addressBookRecord, kABPersonFirstNameProperty);
        lastName  = ABRecordCopyValue(addressBookRecord, kABPersonLastNameProperty);
        birthdate = ABRecordCopyValue(addressBookRecord, kABPersonBirthdayProperty);

        //combine first and last names into a single string
        if (firstName != nil) {
            name = [name stringByAppendingString:(__bridge NSString *)firstName];
            if (lastName != nil) {
                name = [name stringByAppendingFormat:@" %@",lastName];
            }
        }
        else if (lastName != nil) {
            name = (__bridge NSString *)lastName;
        }

        self.name = name;

        //we'll use this unique id to ensure that we never create duplicate imports in our
Core Data store
        //if the user attempts to re-import this birthday address book contact
        self.uid = [NSString stringWithFormat:@"ab-%d",recordID];
        self.addressBookID = [NSNumber numberWithInt:recordID];

        NSDateComponents *dateComponents = [[NSCalendar currentCalendar]
components:NSYearCalendarUnit|NSMonthCalendarUnit|NSDayCalendarUnit fromDate:(__bridge NSDate
*)birthdate];

        self.birthDay = @(dateComponents.day);
        self.birthMonth = @(dateComponents.month);
        self.birthYear = @(dateComponents.year);

        [self updateNextBirthdayAndAge];

        //just a precautionary measure incase the birthday date has been set more than 150
years ago!
        if ([self.nextBirthdayAge intValue] > 150) {
            self.birthYear = [NSNumber numberWithInt:0];
            self.nextBirthdayAge = [NSNumber numberWithInt:0];
        }


        //Check for Image Data associated with the user
        if (ABPersonHasImageData(addressBookRecord)) {
            CFDataRef imageData = ABPersonCopyImageData(addressBookRecord);

            UIImage *fullSizeImage = [UIImage imageWithData:(__bridge NSData *)imageData];

            CGFloat side = 71.f;
            side *= [[UIScreen mainScreen] scale];
```

```
            UIImage *thumbnail = [fullSizeImage createThumbnailToFillSize:CGSizeMake(side,
side)];

            self.imageData = UIImageJPEGRepresentation(thumbnail, 1.f);

            CFRelease(imageData);
        }

        if (firstName) CFRelease(firstName);
        if (lastName) CFRelease(lastName);
        if (birthdate) CFRelease(birthdate);
    }
    return self;
}
```

Using our new initWithAddressBookRecord: initializer, we'll create BRDBirthdayImport instances from each birthday Address Book record. Our model will generate an array of BRDBirthdayImport instances and dispatch them, in alphabetical order by name in a notification. The Address Book view controller will catch the observed notification and will display the user's contact friends, and easily be able to display calculated birthday data thanks to the code we've just written in our import value object class.

Back to BRDModel.m. First, import the new BRDBirthdayImport.h header and then complete the implementation of extractBirthdaysFromAddressBook: as highlighted in the following:

```
-(void) extractBirthdaysFromAddressBook:(ABAddressBookRef)addressBook
{
    NSLog(@"extractBirthdaysFromAddressBook");
    CFArrayRef people = ABAddressBookCopyArrayOfAllPeople(addressBook);

    CFIndex peopleCount = ABAddressBookGetPersonCount(addressBook);

    BRDBirthdayImport *birthday;

    //this is just a placeholder for now - we'll get the array populated later in the chapter
    NSMutableArray *birthdays = [NSMutableArray array];

    for (int i = 0; i < peopleCount; i++)
    {
        ABRecordRef addressBookRecord = CFArrayGetValueAtIndex(people, i);
        CFDateRef birthdate  = ABRecordCopyValue(addressBookRecord,
kABPersonBirthdayProperty);
        if (birthdate == nil) continue;
        CFStringRef firstName = ABRecordCopyValue(addressBookRecord,
kABPersonFirstNameProperty);
        if (firstName == nil) {
            CFRelease(birthdate);
            continue;
        }
        NSLog(@"Found contact with birthday: %@, %@",firstName,birthdate);

        birthday = [[BRDBirthdayImport alloc]
initWithAddressBookRecord:addressBookRecord];
```

```
        [birthdays addObject: birthday];

        CFRelease(firstName);
        CFRelease(birthdate);
    }

    CFRelease(people);

    //order the birthdays alphabetically by name
    NSSortDescriptor *sortDescriptor = [[NSSortDescriptor alloc] initWithKey:@"name"
ascending:YES];
    NSArray *sortDescriptors = [NSArray arrayWithObject:sortDescriptor];
    [birthdays sortUsingDescriptors:sortDescriptors];


    //dispatch a notification with an array of birthday objects
    NSDictionary *userInfo = [NSDictionary
dictionaryWithObjectsAndKeys:birthdays,@"birthdays", nil];

    [[NSNotificationCenter defaultCenter]
postNotificationName:BRNotificationAddressBookBirthdaysDidUpdate object:self
userInfo:userInfo];
}
```

As BRDModel loops through the birthday Address Book contacts, it creates new instances of BRDBirthdayImport and passes in the C reference to the Address Book contact (ABRecordRef). The result is that extractBirthdaysFromAddressBook builds a mutable array of BRDBirthdayImport instances that will be used by our Address Book view controller when rendering birthday table cells. At the end of the extractBirthdaysFromAddressBook method, we create a sort descriptor and use it to reorder the instances of BRDBirthdayImport using the name property/sort key.

You should be able to build and run your app at this point. If you have any contacts with birthdays in your iPhone, then launching the Import from Address Book view controller should display a table cell representing each of the contacts' birthdays in your iPhone (see Figure 10-19).

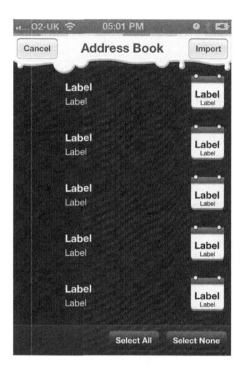

Figure 10-19. Looks like we have some Address Book contacts to import.

Loading contact photos and data into our table view

As you see in Figure 10-19, we need to populate our table cells in our Address Book view controller. We'll populate them in the shared superclass BRImportViewController. Then when we move on to building our import from the Facebook view controller, we'll already have this logic in the superclass, which will be a time-saver.

Each table cell in our table view is an instance of the custom table view cell class BRBirthdayTableViewCell. We've already written the rendering logic for displaying a BRDBirthday entity directly in this class, so begin by opening BRBirthdayTableViewCell.h in Xcode and making the following additions to the interface code:

```
@class BRDBirthday;
@class BRDBirthdayImport;

@interface BRBirthdayTableViewCell : UITableViewCell

@property(nonatomic,strong) BRDBirthday *birthday;
@property(nonatomic,strong) BRDBirthdayImport *birthdayImport;
```

Switch to the BRBirthdayTableViewCell.m source file, import BRDBirthdayImport.h and then override the birthdayImport setter as follows:

```objc
-(void) setBirthdayImport:(BRDBirthdayImport *)birthdayImport
{
    _birthdayImport = birthdayImport;
    self.nameLabel.text = _birthdayImport.name;

    int days = _birthdayImport.remainingDaysUntilNextBirthday;

    if (days == 0) {
        //Birthday is today!
        self.remainingDaysLabel.text = self.remainingDaysSubTextLabel.text = @"";
        self.remainingDaysImageView.image = [UIImage imageNamed:@"icon-birthday-cake.png"];
    }
    else {
        self.remainingDaysLabel.text = [NSString stringWithFormat:@"%d",days];
        self.remainingDaysSubTextLabel.text = (days == 1) ? @"more day" : @"more days";
        self.remainingDaysImageView.image = [UIImage imageNamed:@"icon-days-remaining.png"];
    }

    self.birthdayLabel.text = _birthdayImport.birthdayTextToDisplay;

}
```

The code is again almost identical to the birthday managed object setter.

Back in BRImportViewController.m, import BRBirthdayTableViewCell.h and BRDBirthdayImport.h, and then modify tableView:cellForRowAtIndexPath:

```objc
- (UITableViewCell *)tableView:(UITableView *)tableView cellForRowAtIndexPath:(NSIndexPath *)indexPath
{
    UITableViewCell *cell = [self.tableView dequeueReusableCellWithIdentifier:@"Cell"];

    BRDBirthdayImport *birthdayImport = self.birthdays[indexPath.row];

    BRBirthdayTableViewCell *brTableCell = (BRBirthdayTableViewCell *)cell;

    brTableCell.birthdayImport = birthdayImport;

    if (birthdayImport.imageData == nil)
    {
        brTableCell.iconView.image = [UIImage imageNamed:@"icon-birthday-cake.png"];
    }
    else {
        brTableCell.iconView.image = [UIImage imageWithData:birthdayImport.imageData];
    }

    UIImage *backgroundImage = (indexPath.row == 0) ? [UIImage imageNamed:@"table-row-background.png"] : [UIImage imageNamed:@"table-row-icing-background.png"];
    brTableCell.backgroundView = [[UIImageView alloc] initWithImage:backgroundImage];
```

```
    return cell;
}
```

This is very similar code to the home screen table view cell rendering, so it should all look pretty familiar. Build and run. You should now see the names, birthdays, and photos of your Address Book contacts (see Figure 10-20).

Figure 10-20. There are my Address Book contacts—looking better!

Creating a multiselect table view for importing birthdays

We've got an Import Address Book view with a table view displaying contacts and their birthdays from our Address Book, but how do we multiselect them? Our table view shows either an empty circle or a tick in a circle, depending on whether the contact is currently selected for import or not. Let's add these image assets to the resources/images group of our project: icon-import-not-selected.png, icon-import-not-selected@2x.png, icon-import-selected.png, and icon-import-selected@2x.png.

Let's begin by showing our nonselected circle image on the right side of our custom table view cell. Add the following two lines of code to the tableView:cellForRowAtIndexPath: method of BRImportViewController.m at the end of the method, but just before returning the cell:

```
    UIImageView *imageView = [[UIImageView alloc] initWithImage:[UIImage imageNamed:@"icon-
import-not-selected.png"]];
    brTableCell.accessoryView = imageView;
```

Instances of table view cells have an `accessoryView` property that we can set to any view instance, and our designated view will be displayed to the right of our table cell. Build and run to test if the empty circles appear (see Figure 10-21).

Figure 10-21. The circle appears for each table cell, but it is obscured by the calendar icon.

Although you may not be able to see it clearly in Figure 10-21, the empty circle is visible, but obscured by the calendar icon behind it. We can resolve this problem back in our storyboard. With the prototype cell of our Address Book view controller in focus, multiselect the calendar icon and two labels. Using the size inspector, change the autosizing properties of these subviews so that the only the space to the right is fixed and not to the left, as highlighted in Figure 10-22.

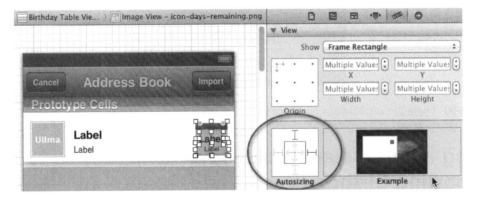

Figure 10-22. Changing the autosize mask of the calendar icon and labels

Build and run. The results should resemble Figure 10-23.

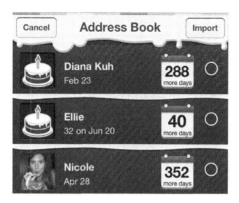

Figure 10-23. Much better!

We can update the accessoryView property of each of our table cells at any time. If a contact has been selected by the user, we'll display a green tick image next in the accessoryView. Otherwise, we'll display an empty circle.

We'll keep track of selected birthdays to import using a mutable dictionary. Ensure you're working on BRImportViewController.m. Begin by adding a new property to the private interface of BRImportViewController just above the class implementation code:

```
@interface BRImportViewController()
```

```
//Keeps track of selected rows
@property (nonatomic, strong) NSMutableDictionary *selectedIndexPathToBirthday;
```

```
@end
```

We'll use this new selectedIndexPathToBirthday dictionary to keep track of which rows are selected and which aren't. As the selection changes, we'll also update the Import button, disabling it if there are zero selected rows.

Now override the getter of your new selectedIndexPathToBirthday property to ensure it is automatically lazy loaded when first accessed:

```
-(NSMutableDictionary *) selectedIndexPathToBirthday
{
    if (_selectedIndexPathToBirthday == nil) {
        _selectedIndexPathToBirthday = [NSMutableDictionary dictionary];
    }
    return _selectedIndexPathToBirthday;
}
```

Next, implement two new private methods: updateImportButton and isSelectedAtIndexPath:

```
//Enables/Disables the import button if there are zero rows selected
- (void) updateImportButton
{
```

```
    self.importButton.enabled = [self.selectedIndexPathToBirthday count] > 0;
}

//Helper method to check whether a row is selected or not
-(BOOL) isSelectedAtIndexPath:(NSIndexPath *)indexPath
{
    return self.selectedIndexPathToBirthday[indexPath] ? YES : NO;
}
```

The `updateImportButton` method checks to see if our selection dictionary has any keys/values. If it does, then the Import button is enabled for the user. Our `isSelectedAtIndexPath:` method checks if we've stored an import birthday object for the index path's row. If we have, then the row has been selected.

To ensure that the Import button is disabled when the view first displays, we'll just call `updateImportButton` in a `viewWillAppear:` implementation:

```
-(void) viewWillAppear:(BOOL)animated
{
    [super viewWillAppear:animated];
    [self updateImportButton];
}
```

Now it's time to make our table cell selection dynamic by setting the accessory view to either our tick or empty circle image. Add one last new private method:

```
//Refreshes the selection tick of a table cell
- (void)updateAccessoryForTableCell:(UITableViewCell *)tableCell atIndexPath:(NSIndexPath
*)indexPath
{
    UIImageView *imageView;
    if ([self isSelectedAtIndexPath:indexPath]) {
        imageView = [[UIImageView alloc] initWithImage:[UIImage imageNamed:@"icon-import-
selected.png"]];
    }
    else {
        imageView = [[UIImageView alloc] initWithImage:[UIImage imageNamed:@"icon-import-not-
selected.png"]];
    }
    tableCell.accessoryView = imageView;
}
```

Revisit the `tableView:cellForRowAtIndexPath:` method and modify your `accessoryView` setting code as follows:

```
    UIImageView *imageView = [[UIImageView alloc] initWithImage:[UIImage imageNamed:@"icon-
import-not-selected.png"]];
      brTableCell.accessoryView = imageView;
    [self updateAccessoryForTableCell:cell atIndexPath:indexPath];
```

To ensure your code is working OK, build and run. Assuming everything compiles OK, the only noticeable change should be that the Import button is disabled. Each table view cell should display an empty circle as its accessory view.

The expected behavior of our import table view is that tapping any row toggles its selection. Our Import view controller is already assigned as the delegate of the table view, so by implementing the `tableView:didSelectRowAtIndexPath:` method of the `UITableViewDelegate` protocol, we'll be able to update the selection whenever a row is tapped:

```
#pragma mark UITableViewDelegate

-(void)tableView:(UITableView *)tableView didSelectRowAtIndexPath:(NSIndexPath *)indexPath
{

    BOOL isSelected = [self isSelectedAtIndexPath:indexPath];

    BRDBirthdayImport *birthdayImport = self.birthdays[indexPath.row];

    if (isSelected) {//already selected, so deselect
        [self.selectedIndexPathToBirthday removeObjectForKey:indexPath];
    }
    else {//not currently selected, so select
        [self.selectedIndexPathToBirthday setObject:birthdayImport forKey:indexPath];
    }

    //update the accessory view image
    [self updateAccessoryForTableCell:[self.tableView cellForRowAtIndexPath:indexPath]
atIndexPath:indexPath];

    //enable/disable the import button
    [self updateImportButton];
}
```

Build and run to test it out.

Next, let's implement our Select All and Select None button actions:

```
- (IBAction)didTapSelectAllButton:(id)sender {

    BRDBirthdayImport *birthdayImport;

    int maxLoop = [self.birthdays count];

    NSIndexPath *indexPath;

    for (int i=0;i<maxLoop;i++) {//loop through all the birthday import objects
        birthdayImport = self.birthdays[i];
        indexPath = [NSIndexPath indexPathForRow:i inSection:0];
        //create the selection reference
        self.selectedIndexPathToBirthday[indexPath] = birthdayImport;
    }
```

```
    [self.tableView reloadData];
    [self updateImportButton];
}

- (IBAction)didTapSelectNoneButton:(id)sender {
    [self.selectedIndexPathToBirthday removeAllObjects];
    [self.tableView reloadData];
    [self updateImportButton];

}
```

Build and run (see Figure 10-24).

Figure 10-24. After tapping Select All.

Importing address book birthdays into the Core Data store

Now that our users are able to multiselect their birthday contacts from the Address Book, the next step is to import the data for those selected contacts into *Birthday Reminder* when the Import button is tapped. Let's turn our attention back to our main model class, BRDModel, and add a method for importing multiple instances of BRDBirthdayImport into BRDBirthday Core Data entities.

Define a new importBirthdays: public method in BRDModel.h:

```
-(void) importBirthdays:(NSArray *)birthdaysToImport;
```

Yesterday, in Chapter 8's "Duplicate Entities and Synchronization of the Core Data Persistence" section, we created a utility method in our model to retrieve all existing birthday entities in our Core Data model with matching unique ids from any list of birthdays ids. We're going to use the same logic in our new importBirthdays: implementation in BRDModel.m:

```
-(void) importBirthdays:(NSArray *)birthdaysToImport
{
    int i;
    int max = [birthdaysToImport count];

    BRDBirthday *importBirthday;
    BRDBirthday *birthday;

    NSString *uid;
    NSMutableArray *newUIDs = [NSMutableArray array];

    for (i=0;i<max;i++)
    {
        importBirthday = birthdaysToImport[i];
        uid = importBirthday.uid;
        [newUIDs addObject:uid];
    }

    //use BRDModel's utility method to retrieve existing birthdays with matching IDs
    //to the array of birthdays to import
    NSMutableDictionary *existingBirthdays = [self getExistingBirthdaysWithUIDs:newUIDs];

    NSManagedObjectContext *context = [BRDModel sharedInstance].managedObjectContext;

    for (i=0;i<max;i++)
    {
        importBirthday = birthdaysToImport[i];
        uid = importBirthday.uid;

        birthday = existingBirthdays[uid];
        if (birthday) {
            //a birthday with this udid already exists in Core Data, don't create a duplicate
        }
        else {
            birthday = [NSEntityDescription insertNewObjectForEntityForName:@"BRDBirthday"
inManagedObjectContext:context];
            birthday.uid = uid;
            existingBirthdays[uid] = birthday;
        }

        //update the new or previously saved birthday entity
        birthday.name = importBirthday.name;
        birthday.uid = importBirthday.uid;
        birthday.picURL = importBirthday.picURL;
        birthday.imageData = importBirthday.imageData;
        birthday.addressBookID = importBirthday.addressBookID;
        birthday.facebookID = importBirthday.facebookID;
```

```
        birthday.birthDay = importBirthday.birthDay;
        birthday.birthMonth = importBirthday.birthMonth;
        birthday.birthYear = importBirthday.birthYear;

        [birthday updateNextBirthdayAndAge];
    }

    //save our new and updated changes to the Core Data store
    [self saveChanges];


}
```

The following is the logic of the import code:

1. Loop through the birthdays to import and collect their unique ids.

2. Pass the unique ids to `getExistingBirthdaysWithUIDs:` to retrieve a mutable dictionary of existing birthday entities with matching ids.

3. Loop through the birthdays to import again, either creating or updating stored Core Data birthday entities.

4. Save our updates.

Let's test out the import code. Back in `BRImportViewController.m`, import `BRDModel.h`, and then implement the `didTapImportButton:` action method:

```
- (IBAction)didTapImportButton:(id)sender {
    NSArray *birthdaysToImport = [self.selectedIndexPathToBirthday allValues];
    [[BRDModel sharedInstance] importBirthdays:birthdaysToImport];
    [self dismissViewControllerAnimated:YES completion:nil];
}
```

Build and run. You should now be able to pick and choose birthdays to import from your iPhone Address Book onto *Birthday Reminder* (see Figure 10-25).

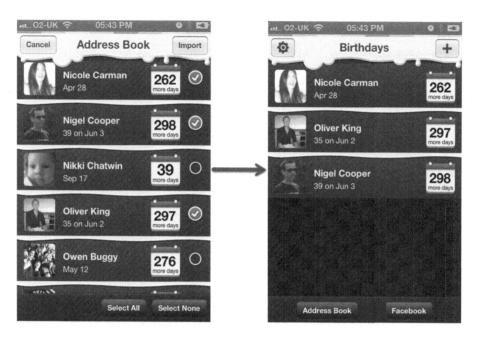

Figure 10-25. Importing birthdays from the Address Book all up and running

Activating phone calls, SMS, and e-mails

Users of *Birthday Reminder* can now import any contact in their Address Book with an assigned birthday. But why stop there? We're already saving the unique ABRecordID property of each imported contact in BRDBirthday.addressBookID. We can use Apple's unique contact record id for each imported birthday to access other information about the contact: information like phone numbers and e-mail addresses.

We'll use this detection code in our Birthday Detail view. If a birthday was imported from the Address Book, then we'll check to see if the iPhone has a phone number for the contact and then Display buttons to call or SMS the friend to wish them a Happy Birthday! Likewise, if we detect an e-mail for the Address Book contact, then we'll present the user with an option to e-mail their friend birthday wishes.

Open BRBirthdayDetailViewController.m source file and begin by importing the AddressBook :

```
#import <AddressBook/AddressBook.h>
```

We're going to create private helper methods in BRBirthdayDetailViewController.m that generate iOS links to initiate phone calls, SMS, and e-mails. We'll begin by adding a telephoneNumber method that retrieves a reference to the Address Book record of the current contact and checks for the existence of the kABPersonPhoneProperty (phone number) property:

```
#pragma mark Address Book contact helper methods
```

```
-(NSString *)telephoneNumber
{
    ABAddressBookRef addressBook = ABAddressBookCreateWithOptions(NULL, NULL);

    ABRecordRef record = ABAddressBookGetPersonWithRecordID
(addressBook,(ABRecordID)[self.birthday.addressBookID intValue]);

    ABMultiValueRef multi = ABRecordCopyValue(record, kABPersonPhoneProperty);

    NSString *telephone = nil;

    if (ABMultiValueGetCount(multi) > 0) {
        telephone = (__bridge_transfer NSString*)ABMultiValueCopyValueAtIndex(multi, 0);
        telephone = [telephone stringByReplacingOccurrencesOfString:@" " withString:@""];
    }
    CFRelease(multi);
    CFRelease(addressBook);

    return telephone;
}
```

If our new method finds a phone number associated to this contact, then it removes any white space in the number because this is a requirement for creating in-app links to Apple's Phone and Messages apps when activating a phone call or SMS. If our method cannot find a phone number associated with the contact, then it returns `nil`.

URL schemes and linking between multitasking apps

There are several URL schemes supported by native iOS applications that enable developers to create buttons or links that open other apps on the user's iPhone, such as the Phone app or Safari. Many apps also include support for passing in additional characters via the URL string, such as an id that the linked app is able to interpret to drill the user straight into a particular piece of content. You can find a list of the URL schemes supported by Apple's own suite of apps on this web page:

`http://developer.apple.com/library/ios/#featuredarticles/iPhoneURLScheme_Reference/Introduction/Introduction.html.`

If you visit this page, you'll discover that the `tel:` URL scheme launches Apple's Phone app on iPhone, and that `sms:` launches the Messages app.

> *Tip:* you can also define a custom URL scheme for your own app (via the info plist) to enable direct linking from other apps to yours.

Next, we create call and SMS link-retrieving methods in `BRBirthdayDetailViewController.m`. These are virtually identical, and both make use of our `telephoneNumber` method:

```
-(NSString *)callLink
{
    if (!self.birthday.addressBookID || [self.birthday.addressBookID intValue]==0) return nil;
```

```
    NSString *telephoneNumber = [self telephoneNumber];
    if (!telephoneNumber) return nil;

    NSString *callLink = [NSString stringWithFormat:@"tel:%@",telephoneNumber];

    if ([[UIApplication sharedApplication] canOpenURL:[NSURL URLWithString:callLink]]) return
callLink;

    return nil;
}

-(NSString *)smsLink
{
    if (!self.birthday.addressBookID || [self.birthday.addressBookID intValue]==0) return nil;
    NSString *telephoneNumber = [self telephoneNumber];
    if (!telephoneNumber) return nil;

    NSString *smsLink = [NSString stringWithFormat:@"sms:%@",telephoneNumber];

    if ([[UIApplication sharedApplication] canOpenURL:[NSURL URLWithString:smsLink]]) return
smsLink;

    return nil;

}
```

Notice how in both methods we can actually check that the system links we're creating are compatible with the device using UIApplication's canOpenURL: method. This is really handy because it enables us to check whether the user has installed other apps with URL schemes that our app knows about and can link to directly.

The emailLink method is very similar to the telephoneNumber method we wrote earlier. Just like telephone numbers, multiple e-mails can be associated with a contact. We'll check if the email property (kABPersonEmailProperty) exists for the contact, and if it does, we'll check that there are one or more e-mails associated with the contact and return the first by default:

```
-(NSString *)emailLink
{
    if (!self.birthday.addressBookID || [self.birthday.addressBookID intValue]==0) return nil;

    ABAddressBookRef addressBook = ABAddressBookCreateWithOptions(NULL, NULL);

    ABRecordRef record =  ABAddressBookGetPersonWithRecordID
(addressBook,(ABRecordID)[self.birthday.addressBookID intValue]);

    ABMultiValueRef multi = ABRecordCopyValue(record, kABPersonEmailProperty);

    NSString *email = nil;
    if (ABMultiValueGetCount(multi) > 0) {//check if the contact has 1 or more emails assigned
        email = (__bridge_transfer NSString*)ABMultiValueCopyValueAtIndex(multi, 0);
    }
    CFRelease(multi);
```

```
    CFRelease(addressBook);

    if (email) {
        NSString *emailLink = [NSString stringWithFormat:@"mailto:%@",email];
        //we can pre-populate the email subject with the words Happy Birthday
        emailLink = [emailLink stringByAppendingString:@"?subject=Happy%20Birthday"];
        if ([[UIApplication sharedApplication] canOpenURL:[NSURL URLWithString:emailLink]])
return emailLink;
    }


    return nil;

}
```

Now that we've created utility methods to detect whether we can call, SMS, or e-mail a birthday contact, we'll check these methods when we layout the list of buttons. We'll display a Call Friend button only if we have a telephone number for the friend and are running on a device that permits us to use the tel: URL scheme. *Birthday Reminder* might be installed on an iPod Touch, for example, where the tel: URL scheme would not be recognized by the operating system; therefore, we won't display a Call Friend button on iPod Touch.

Navigate to the viewWillAppear: method implementation of BRBirthdayDetailViewController.m and modify the last part of the method code with the changes highlighted in the following:

```
NSMutableArray *buttonsToShow = [NSMutableArray
arrayWithObjects:self.facebookButton,self.callButton, self.smsButton, self.emailButton,
self.deleteButton, nil];

    NSMutableArray *buttonsToHide = [NSMutableArray array];

    if (self.birthday.facebookID == nil) {
        [buttonsToShow removeObject:self.facebookButton];
        [buttonsToHide addObject:self.facebookButton];
    }

    if ([self callLink] == nil) {
        [buttonsToShow removeObject:self.callButton];
        [buttonsToHide addObject:self.callButton];
    }

    if ([self smsLink] == nil) {
        [buttonsToShow removeObject:self.smsButton];
        [buttonsToHide addObject:self.smsButton];
    }

    if ([self emailLink] == nil) {
        [buttonsToShow removeObject:self.emailButton];
        [buttonsToHide addObject:self.emailButton];
    }
```

```
UIButton *button;

for (button in buttonsToHide) {
    button.hidden = YES;
}

int i;

for (i=0;i<[buttonsToShow count];i++) {
    button = [buttonsToShow objectAtIndex:i];
    button.hidden = NO;
    frame = button.frame;
    frame.origin.y = cY;
    button.frame = frame;
    cY += button.frame.size.height + buttonGap;
}

self.scrollView.contentSize = CGSizeMake(320, cY);
```

In this code, we now have two arrays: one containing references to the buttons that we should display in the detail view and one containing references to the buttons that we should hide for this birthday. If we can find an e-mail for the birthday contact using the Address Book framework, then we'll show the Email Friend button. If we can't, we won't show the Email button (see Figure 10-26).

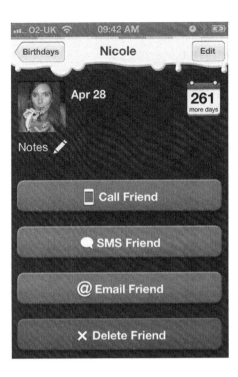

Figure 10-26. Call/SMS/Email buttons are all displayed for this friend, because, believe it or not, I have all my wife's contact details in my phone!

It's all very well knowing that we can e-mail, call, or SMS a contact, but, at the moment, our button actions do nothing at all. Let's implement the action code:

```
- (IBAction)callButtonTapped:(id)sender {
    NSString *link = [self callLink];
    [[UIApplication sharedApplication] openURL:[NSURL URLWithString:link]];
}

- (IBAction)smsButtonTapped:(id)sender {
    NSString *link = [self smsLink];
    [[UIApplication sharedApplication] openURL:[NSURL URLWithString:link]];
}

- (IBAction)emailButtonTapped:(id)sender {
    NSString *link = [self emailLink];
    [[UIApplication sharedApplication] openURL:[NSURL URLWithString:link]];
}
```

Build and run. Awesome, we can make calls, trigger SMS, and send Happy Birthday from our app. ☺

> **Note:** It's also possible to create e-mail and SMS messages directly in our app using Apple's `MessageUI` framework. Personally, I prefer to make the most of multitasking instead, but check out the `MessageUI` framework documentation to handle the whole experience inside your apps.

Deleting birthdays from the data store

While we're implementing button functions in the detail view controller, let's get the Delete Birthday button up and running. Rather than deleting a data item immediately, it's good manners to ask the user to confirm a delete before executing the permanent action. Momentarily switch to the `BRBirthdayDetailViewController.h` header and declare that our Birthday Detail controller implements the `UIActionSheetDelegate` protocol:

`@interface BRBirthdayDetailViewController : BRCoreViewController `**`<UIActionSheetDelegate>`**

Now back in `BRBirthdayDetailViewController.m`, let's implement the `deleteButtonTapped:` action and display a `Delete [Person Name]` action sheet:

```
- (IBAction)deleteButtonTapped:(id)sender {
    UIActionSheet *actionSheet = [[UIActionSheet alloc] initWithTitle:nil delegate:self
cancelButtonTitle:@"Cancel" destructiveButtonTitle:[NSString stringWithFormat:@"Delete
%@",self.birthday.name] otherButtonTitles:nil];
    [actionSheet showInView:self.view];
}
```

The results should look like Figure 10-27 when you build and run.

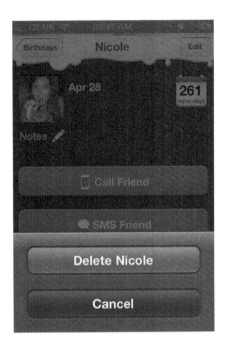

Figure 10-27. I'm deleting the wife, but that's between you and me!

Finally, we'll action the delete instruction if our user presses that big red button. First, import BRDModel.h into BRBirthdayDetailViewController.m.

Now it's time to implement the actionSheet:willDismissWithButtonIndex: method of the UIActionSheetDelegate protocol in BRBirthdayDetailViewController.m:

```
#pragma mark - UIActionSheetDelegate

- (void)actionSheet:(UIActionSheet *)actionSheet
willDismissWithButtonIndex:(NSInteger)buttonIndex
{
    //check whether the user cancelled the delete instruction via the action sheet cancel
button
    if (buttonIndex == actionSheet.cancelButtonIndex) return;

    //grab a reference to the Core Data managed object context
    NSManagedObjectContext *context = [BRDModel sharedInstance].managedObjectContext;
    //delete this birthday entity from the managed object context
    [context deleteObject:self.birthday];
    //save our delete change to the persistent Core Data store
    [[BRDModel sharedInstance] saveChanges];

    //pop this view controller off the stack and slide back to the home screen
    [self.navigationController popViewControllerAnimated:YES];
}
```

Deleting a Core Data entity is pretty simple when it has no relationships to other entities. We just grab a reference to the Core Data managed object context and pass our reference to the birthday entity to the context's `deleteObject:` method. We save our delete change to the Core Data persistent store via `BRDModel`'s `saveChanges` utility method. Finally, we pop the detail view controller off the navigation stack and instruct the navigation controller to slide back to the Home view controller. You'll see the home table view updates automatically.

Summary

What a great start to Day 4! We've explored some of the features of the Address Book framework that Apple provides third-party apps access too.

Being able to access a user's contact list gives our app a lot of responsibility and a trust that we won't share or misuse this sensitive data. Very successful apps like *Path* got a lot of bad press in 2012 when it was discovered that they were passing users' contacts to the their server-side systems. Events like this led to Apple tightening up privacy in iOS 6 and putting users in control of the data they permit or don't permit apps access to. This is a great change to iOS because it puts the power in the hands of the user, solves the abuse of data privacy problem, and makes private data access more transparent to the owners of the data—your users.

As long as the trust is not misused, having this kind of access to the user's contacts can enable us to build really useful features into our apps that facilitate fast and easy personalization and data import that just makes life easier for the app user.

Next up, we'll learn how to work with Apple's new Social Framework in iOS 6 to enable users to import details of their Facebook friend birthdays and before you know it, we'll be presenting import lists of all the user's Facebook friends. The best part is we've already written most of the user interface code for importing from Facebook in this chapter thanks to the wonders of object-oriented code design.

Grab a coffee and I'll see you in five!

Chapter 11

Working with Facebook and the iOS 6 Social Framework

Earlier today, we succeeded in setting up *Birthday Reminder* to batch import birthdays from the iPhone Address Book. But what would really enhance our app for millions of potential users is to enable them to import friends' birthdays from their Facebook account.

In this chapter, we'll take advantage of the new native Facebook integration in iOS 6. Working with Apple's Accounts framework, you'll learn how to enable your users to authenticate *Birthday Reminder* with Facebook. From there, you'll discover how to use the new Social framework to access Facebook's Graph API and enable users to import Facebook friends' birthdays.

But we're not going to stop there. I'll show you how to create your own custom view controller for posting messages directly to friends' Facebook Walls. It's a helpful feature for our users and has the added advantage of autogenerating a link back to the *Birthday Reminder* Facebook page next to every Happy Birthday post shared!

Facebook has its own iOS SDK. But we won't be using that at all. Everything we need for integrating with Facebook's Graph API is built right into iOS 6.

Registering a new app with Facebook.com

In order to create any kind of app, iOS or otherwise, capable of integrating Facebook features such as posting to friend's Facebook Walls, accessing the user's Facebook friends, reading the user's Facebook newsfeed, and so on, you need to have a Facebook.com account of your own. You also need to register as a Facebook developer at www.facebook.com/developer.

Once you become a registered developer and gain access to Facebook's developer web site, you'll be able to navigate to the main Apps section. Click the Create New App button. You are then prompted to enter a new App Name (see Figure 11-1).

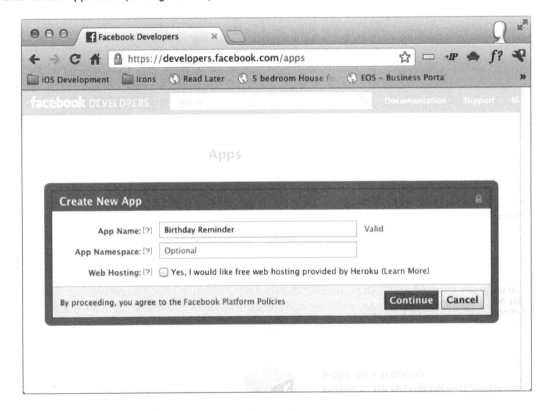

Figure 11-1. Creating a new Facebook app on Facebook.com

The App Namespace is optional, so once you've entered a valid App Display Name that isn't already taken, you're all set. Facebook immediately supplies you with a new app ID for your app.

You don't have to use the name *Birthday Reminder*, but whatever name you use, that is the name that Facebook displays to new users when they go through the authentication process before importing their Facebook friends into your app.

There is one required modification to your new Facebook.com app to enable Apple's native Accounts authentication code to work with Facebook: you need to add your iOS app's bundle identifier to your Facebook app's settings. Tap the Edit Settings link and scroll down to the tab titled Native iOS App. Open the tab and type the bundle identifier of your app into the first text field. In my case, this was com.apress.BirthdayReminder; but in your case, *this needs to match your app's bundle identifier* (see Figure 11-2).

Figure 11-2. Adding an iOS bundle identifier to the Facebook.com settings for our app

It's very important that this bundle identifier matches your app's own native bundle identifier because this is checked and referenced by the Account framework automatically during the single sign-on authentication process.

Creating a Facebook import view controller

Earlier today (in Chapter 10), we put a lot of hard work into creating our Address Book Import view controller. During that process, we created BRImportViewController, a class that both the address book and Facebook import view controllers would subclass. Now we'll see how those development steps will save us a great deal of time creating an Import view controller for Facebook in this stage of the project. Open your storyboard. Use your mouse to multiselect the Address Book view controller and its parent navigation controller scenes, as shown in Figure 11-3.

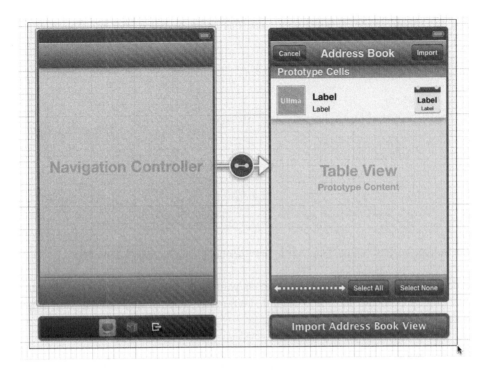

Figure 11-3. Multiselecting storyboard scenes

Using the keyboard, perform a ⌘C shortcut or click Edit ➤ Copy, and then ⌘V or Edit ➤ Paste. You should be able to duplicate the two view controllers in your storyboard. Drag your duplicate view controllers to a new space in the storyboard and change the navigation bar title to **Facebook**. Select the new navigation controller, and using the attributes inspector change, its Identifier property to ImportFacebook.

Open BRHomeViewController.m and just like presenting the Address Book view controller, implement the importFromFacebookTapped: action method:

```
- (IBAction)importFromFacebookTapped:(id)sender {
    UINavigationController *navigationController = [self.storyboard
instantiateViewControllerWithIdentifier:@"ImportFacebook"];
    [self.navigationController presentViewController:navigationController animated:YES
completion:nil];

}
```

Let's now subclass our core Import view controller to create the Facebook import view controller. Select the view-controllers group in the Project Navigator, and then create a new subclass of BRImportViewController and name it BRImportFacebookViewController.

With your Fac[...]rd, use the identity inspector to change
its custom cla[...]lass, as shown in Figure 11-4.

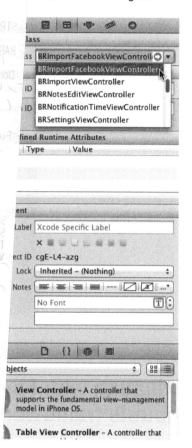

Figure [...] subclass in our storyboard

Build a[...]ss (Cancel) the Facebook view controller in
your app [...]

Figure 11-5. Modally presented empty Facebook import view controller

Authenticating with Facebook using the Accounts framework

In order for *Birthday Reminder* to be permitted to retrieve Facebook friends' birthdays, our user needs to first authorize our app to communicate with Facebook's API on their behalf. We're going to handle all the Facebook authentication process in our model singleton class, BRDModel.

Let's begin by adding the Accounts and Social frameworks to our project. As you've done in previous chapters, select the BirthdayReminder project in the Project Navigator, then select the BirthdayReminder target, and finally select the Build Phases tab. Then tap the Add Framework button under Link Binary with Libraries, and add both the Accounts and Social frameworks. Once you've added both frameworks to your project, drag and drop them both inside the Frameworks group of the Project Navigator, as shown in Figure 11-6.

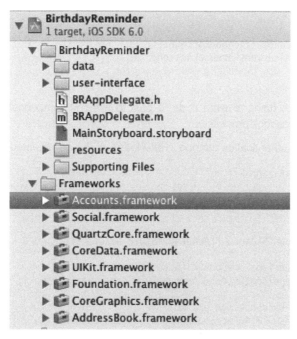

Figure 11-6. Accounts and Social frameworks added to our project

Now open BRDModel.h and declare a new public method, fetchFacebookBirthdays, which our Facebook import view controller will invoke when it appears:

```
- (void)fetchFacebookBirthdays;
```

Switch to the BRDModel.m source file and import the Accounts and Social frameworks:

```
#import <Social/Social.h>
#import <Accounts/Accounts.h>
```

Once our user successfully authenticates with Facebook, we'll have a reference to an authenticated account. By retaining that Facebook account reference in our model, we'll be able to call Facebook's API, post to a Facebook Wall—or any of the other features offered by Facebook's Graph API.

Right at the top of BRDModel.m, before the class implementation, let's now add a new Facebook action enumerator and a private interface for BRDModel that declares two new private properties facebookAccount (our reference to the authenticated Facebook account) and currentFacebookAction (a property to track the current Facebook Graph API action in process):

```
typedef enum : int
{
    FacebookActionGetFriendsBirthdays = 1,
    FacebookActionPostToWall
}FacebookAction;
```

```
@interface BRDModel()

@property (strong) ACAccount *facebookAccount;
@property FacebookAction currentFacebookAction;

@end
```

Later in this chapter, we're going to write code to post to a friend's Facebook Wall; so we're planning ahead here for multiple Facebook processes.

Now to write a Facebook authentication method in BRDModel.m. I've commented the code extensively:

```
- (void)authenticateWithFacebook {

    //Centralized iOS user Twitter, Facebook and Sina Weibo accounts are accessed by apps via
the ACAccountStore

    ACAccountStore *accountStore = [[ACAccountStore alloc] init];

    ACAccountType *accountTypeFacebook = [accountStore
accountTypeWithAccountTypeIdentifier:ACAccountTypeIdentifierFacebook];

    //Replace with your Facebook.com app ID
    NSDictionary *options = @{ACFacebookAppIdKey: @"125381334264255",
ACFacebookPermissionsKey:
@[@"publish_stream",@"friends_birthday"],ACFacebookAudienceKey:ACFacebookAudienceFriends};

    [accountStore requestAccessToAccountsWithType:accountTypeFacebook options:options
completion:^(BOOL granted, NSError *error) {
        if(granted) {
            //The completition handler may not fire in the main thread and as we are going to
            NSLog(@"Facebook Authorized!");
            NSArray *accounts = [accountStore accountsWithAccountType:accountTypeFacebook];
            self.facebookAccount = [accounts lastObject];

            //By checking what Facebook action the user was trying to perform before the
authorization process we can complete the Facebook action when the authorization succeeds
            switch (self.currentFacebookAction) {
                case FacebookActionGetFriendsBirthdays:
                    [self fetchFacebookBirthdays];
                    break;
                case FacebookActionPostToWall:
                    //TODO - post to a friend's Facebook Wall
                    break;
            }
        } else {

            if ([error code] == ACErrorAccountNotFound) {
                NSLog(@"No Facebook Account Found");
            }
            else {
                NSLog(@"Facebook SSO Authentication Failed: %@",error);
            }
```

```
        }
    }];
}
```

In the code above, ensure that you have replaced my Facebook.com app id, 125381334264255, with your own Facebook.com app id.

Apple supports three social network account types natively in iOS 6: Twitter, Facebook, and Sina Weibo. In order to check and access any of these social network accounts, our code queries the ACAccountStore, passing in the social network type of the account we're interested in accessing; in our case, this is an account type with the identifier ACAccountTypeIdentifierFacebook.

Now that we've stated that we're checking for a Facebook account, we also need to let iOS know our intentions for the data we're requesting access to. With Facebook, we need to pass in an options dictionary that includes the Facebook.com app ID and the Facebook permissions that we require access to. For certain Facebook features, it's mandatory to specify an array of *extended permissions*: retrieving friends' birthdays requires the friends_birthday permission. For the full list of extended permissions, visit the following web page: http://developers.facebook.com/docs/reference/api/permissions/.

The ACAccountStore requestAccessToAccountsWithType method requires us to pass in a completion block of code that is invoked when the user taps either Don't Allow or OK in response to the account access request.

Let's now begin implementing fetchFacebookBirthdays in BRDModel.m:

```
- (void)fetchFacebookBirthdays
{
    NSLog(@"fetchFacebookBirthdays");
    if (self.facebookAccount == nil) {
        self.currentFacebookAction = FacebookActionGetFriendsBirthdays;
        [self authenticateWithFacebook];
        return;
    }
    //We've got an authenticated Facebook Account if the code executes here

}
```

Our Facebook import view controller shouldn't need to know anything about the authorization process; it just needs to know which birthdays to import and when that list updates. Each time the Facebook import view controller appears, we'll set it up to call fetchFacebookBirthdays on the model which, in turn, first checks if a self.facebookAccount exists (has been authorized by the user already). If it doesn't, then at this point, our model will start the single sign-on process by executing the authenticateWithFacebook method we've just written.

Open BRImportFacebookViewController.m, import BRDModel, and let's add the fetchFacebookBirthdays method call when the Facebook import view has appeared, as follows:

```
#import "BRImportFacebookViewController.h"
#import "BRDModel.h"
```

```objc
@interface BRImportFacebookViewController ()

@end

@implementation BRImportFacebookViewController

-(void) viewWillAppear:(BOOL)animated
{
    [super viewWillAppear:animated];
    [[BRDModel sharedInstance] fetchFacebookBirthdays];
}

@end
```

Try a build and run. Tap the Facebook button. As long as you have a Facebook account associated to your device or the simulator, then you should see a data privacy alert, as shown in Figure 11-7.

Figure 11-7. Apple's Accounts framework prompts the user to permit access to her Facebook account

The import from Facebook view controller calls the model's fetchFacebookBirthdays method as it appears. BRDModel.m checks for the existence of its private facebookAccount property, and if it's not set, then it calls the authenticateWithFacebook method we wrote earlier.

Clicking OK in the Permissions Alert view triggers the completion block of code in the `authenticateWithFacebook` method to run, which stores `facebookAccount` in the model, and then recalls `fetchFacebookBirthdays` so that our code to fetch the Facebook birthdays can now run with authorization. We haven't yet written the birthday fetching code, so let's get to that now.

Fetching Facebook birthdays

Once our users complete the Facebook single sign-on process and authorize *Birthday Reminder* to communicate with Facebook on their behalf, we can do just that! So let's extend the BRDModel.m's `fetchFacebookBirthdays` method to make a Facebook API request to fetch the birthday details of a user's Facebook friends:

```
- (void)fetchFacebookBirthdays
{
    NSLog(@"fetchFacebookBirthdays");
    if (self.facebookAccount == nil) {
        self.currentFacebookAction = FacebookActionGetFriendsBirthdays;
        [self authenticateWithFacebook];
        return;
    }
    //We've got an authenticated Facebook Account if the code executes here
    NSURL *requestURL = [NSURL URLWithString:@"https://graph.facebook.com/me/friends"];

    NSDictionary *params = @{ @"fields" : @"name,id,birthday"};

    SLRequest *request = [SLRequest requestForServiceType:SLServiceTypeFacebook
requestMethod:SLRequestMethodGET URL:requestURL parameters:params];

    request.account = self.facebookAccount;

    [request performRequestWithHandler:^(NSData *responseData, NSHTTPURLResponse
*urlResponse, NSError *error) {
        if (error != nil) {
            NSLog(@"Error getting my Facebook friend birthdays: %@",error);
        }
        else
        {
            // Facebook's me/friends Graph API returns a root dictionary
            NSDictionary *resultD = (NSDictionary *) [NSJSONSerialization
JSONObjectWithData:responseData options:0 error:nil];
            NSLog(@"Facebook returned friends: %@",resultD);
        }
    }];

}
```

The new code uses the `SLRequest` class from Apple's Social framework to call the `me/friends` path of Facebook's Graph API and requests only the `name`, `id`, and `birthday` fields of the array of friend dictionaries returned. For a full list of user fields, visit the following web page:

http://developers.facebook.com/docs/reference/api/user/.

It's beyond the scope of this book to explore Facebook's Graph API in further detail but if you want to learn about all the Facebook API's your app can access natively then check out Facebook's own API documentation at http://developers.facebook.com/docs/reference/api/.

You should be able to build and run your app. Try to import from Facebook, and the debugger should print all the JSON data returned by the Facebook API request.

Note how we assign the account property of the SLRequest instance to the authorized Facebook ACAccount.

The HTTP request to Facebook is executed by the performRequestWithHandler method of SLRequest that runs in a background thread. When the request returns a response from Facebook, a completion block of code runs.

> *Note: All Apple's user interface code runs on the main thread. By running processes like HTTP requests on background threads, we ensure that our app UI remains responsive, even while requests are still running.*

We're going to process the returned Facebook birthday data next. BRDModel will generate an array of BRDBirthdayImport objects just like in Chapter 10 with importing Address Book birthdays. Once we've created an array of birthday import objects, we'll dispatch a notification from the model that the list of Facebook birthdays was updated. We've looked at the notification/observer feature of Objective-C when we built the blackjack app in Chapter 4 and when we dispatched an array of birthdays imported from the Address Book in the last chapter. Basic MVC rules dictate that our model cannot have direct access to the view. Instead, the model dispatches a notification when its data changes and our Facebook import view controller is able to catch that notification and update its view.

Before processing the data returned by Facebook, let's define a new notification name constant at the top of the BRDModel.h header file, just as we did for the Address Book birthdays:

```
#define BRNotificationFacebookBirthdaysDidUpdate
@"BRNotificationFacebookBirthdaysDidUpdate"
```

Now to continue work on the fetchFacebookBirthdays method for handling, processing, and notifying observers of the full list of Facebook birthdays to display, which our users will be able to pick and choose from.

```
- (void)fetchFacebookBirthdays
{
    NSLog(@"fetchFacebookBirthdays");
    if (self.facebookAccount == nil) {
        self.currentFacebookAction = FacebookActionGetFriendsBirthdays;
        [self authenticateWithFacebook];
        return;
    }
    //We've got an authenticated Facebook Account if the code executes here
    NSURL *requestURL = [NSURL URLWithString:@"https://graph.facebook.com/me/friends"];
```

```objc
    NSDictionary *params = @{ @"fields" : @"name,id,birthday"};

    SLRequest *request = [SLRequest requestForServiceType:SLServiceTypeFacebook
requestMethod:SLRequestMethodGET URL:requestURL parameters:params];

    request.account = self.facebookAccount;

    [request performRequestWithHandler:^(NSData *responseData, NSHTTPURLResponse *urlResponse,
NSError *error) {
        if (error != nil) {
            NSLog(@"Error getting my Facebook friend birthdays: %@",error);
        }
        else
        {
            // Facebook's me/friends Graph API returns a root dictionary
            NSDictionary *resultD = (NSDictionary *) [NSJSONSerialization
JSONObjectWithData:responseData options:0 error:nil];
            NSLog(@"Facebook returned friends: %@",resultD);
            // with a 'data' key - an array of Facebook friend dictionaries
            NSArray *birthdayDictionaries = resultD[@"data"];

            int birthdayCount = [birthdayDictionaries count];
            NSDictionary *facebookDictionary;

            NSMutableArray *birthdays = [NSMutableArray array];
            BRDBirthdayImport *birthday;
            NSString *birthDateS;

            for (int i = 0; i < birthdayCount; i++)
            {
                facebookDictionary = birthdayDictionaries[i];
                birthDateS = facebookDictionary[@"birthday"];
                if (!birthDateS) continue;
                //create an instance of BRDBirthdayImport
                NSLog(@"Found a Facebook Birthday: %@",facebookDictionary);
                //TODO - create instances of BRDBirthdayImport
            }

            //Order the birthdays by name
            NSSortDescriptor *sortDescriptor = [[NSSortDescriptor alloc]
initWithKey:@"name" ascending:YES];
            NSArray *sortDescriptors = [NSArray arrayWithObject:sortDescriptor];
            [birthdays sortUsingDescriptors:sortDescriptors];

            dispatch_sync(dispatch_get_main_queue(), ^{
                //update the view on the main thread
                NSDictionary *userInfo = @{@"birthdays":birthdays};
                [[NSNotificationCenter defaultCenter]
postNotificationName:BRNotificationFacebookBirthdaysDidUpdate object:self
userInfo:userInfo];
            });
        }
```

```
    }];
}
```

The Graph API returns JSON, which we parse using a handy utility class called NSJSONSerialization that Apple added in iOS 5 for JSON reading and serialization. We then extract a data array of Facebook friend dictionaries, loop through the list, and check each for a valid birthday key value. Facebook users select the information they share, so there's no guarantee that we'll find a birthday for each friend in the results set.

There's some new code at the end of the SLRequest response handler, the dispatch_sync function call. The SLRequest instance is optimized to execute the request on a background thread to avoid freezing up the user interface while it runs. However, by dispatching the BRNotificationFacebookBirthdaysDidUpdate notification in this way, we utilize Apple's Grand Central Dispatch, and our notification will fire on the main thread. This is necessary because our Facebook import view controller redraws itself in response to the notification and all user interface rendering must be made on the main thread.

You'll also spot that we've got a TODO comment in the code loop where we'll be creating instances of BRDBirthdayImport. Our birthday import class already has an initWithAddressBookRecord: initializer, so we're now going to write another initializer to handle the creation of BRDBirthdayImport instances from Facebook user dictionaries. Open BRDBirthdayImport.h and add the new initializer signature to the interface:

```
-(id)initWithFacebookDictionary:(NSDictionary *)facebookDictionary;
```

Now switch to BRDBirthdayImport.m and implement the new initializer. I've commented the code throughout:

```
-(id)initWithFacebookDictionary:(NSDictionary *)facebookDictionary
{
    self = [super init];
    if (self) {
        self.name = [facebookDictionary objectForKey:@"name"];
        self.uid = [NSString stringWithFormat:@"fb-%@",facebookDictionary[@"id"]];
        self.facebookID = [NSString stringWithFormat:@"%@",facebookDictionary[@"id"]];

        //Facebook provides a convenience URL for Facebook profile pics as long as you have
the Facebook ID
        self.picURL = [NSString
stringWithFormat:@"http://graph.facebook.com/%@/picture?type=large",self.facebookID];

        // Facebook returns birthdays in the string format [month]/[day]/[year] or
[month]/[day]
        NSString *birthDateString = [facebookDictionary objectForKey:@"birthday"];
        NSArray *birthdaySegments = [birthDateString componentsSeparatedByString:@"/"];

        self.birthDay  = [NSNumber numberWithInt:[birthdaySegments[1] intValue]];
        self.birthMonth = [NSNumber numberWithInt:[birthdaySegments[0] intValue]];

        if ([birthdaySegments count] > 2) {//includes year
```

```
                self.birthYear = [NSNumber numberWithInt:[birthdaySegments[2] intValue]];
            }

        [self updateNextBirthdayAndAge];
    }
    return self;
}
```

Facebook's Graph API request returns Facebook user representations as dictionaries with keys and values matching the Facebook user fields listed in the parameters passed when we initiated the request: name, id, and birthday. As documented in the preceding code comments, Facebook will return birthdays in the [month]/[day]/[year] or [month]/[day] string format, so we don't even need to use NSDateComponents to break up the birthdays; we can just split the string to extract the month, day, and optional year values.

Most Facebook users have a profile photo. We store a reference to each user's profile photo in the picURL of each birthday import object. Thankfully, Facebook provides a handy convenience URL for Facebook profile photos as long as you have the Facebook ID of the user, which of course we do!

Let's head back to BRDModel.m to finish off the fetchFacebookBirthdays method and complete the TODO code comment:

```
        //TODO - create instances of BRDBirthdayImport
        birthday = [[BRDBirthdayImport alloc]
initWithFacebookDictionary:facebookDictionary];
        [birthdays addObject: birthday];
```

Loading Facebook friends into the table view

It's time to display those Facebook friends and their birthdays in our Facebook import table view. The Facebook user birthdays are processed by the model and converted to birthday import instances. The array of birthday import objects is then dispatched via a notification to any observing objects. Therefore, we need to assign our Facebook import view controller as an observer of the BRNotificationFacebookBirthdaysDidUpdate notification. We'll add the Import view controller as an observer when it appears, and we'll remove it when it disappears.

Open BRImportFacebookViewController.m and complete the class with the highlighted new code:

```
#import "BRImportFacebookViewController.h"
#import "BRDModel.h"

@interface BRImportFacebookViewController ()

@end

@implementation BRImportFacebookViewController

-(void) viewWillAppear:(BOOL)animated
```

```
{
    [super viewWillAppear:animated];
    [[NSNotificationCenter defaultCenter] addObserver:self
selector:@selector(handleFacebookBirthdaysDidUpdate:)
name:BRNotificationFacebookBirthdaysDidUpdate object:[BRDModel sharedInstance]];
    [[BRDModel sharedInstance] fetchFacebookBirthdays];
}

- (void) viewWillDisappear:(BOOL)animated
{
    [super viewWillDisappear:animated];
    [[NSNotificationCenter defaultCenter] removeObserver:self
name:BRNotificationFacebookBirthdaysDidUpdate object:[BRDModel sharedInstance]];
}

-(void)handleFacebookBirthdaysDidUpdate:(NSNotification *)notification
{
    NSDictionary *userInfo = [notification userInfo];

    self.birthdays = userInfo[@"birthdays"];
    [self.tableView reloadData];
}
```

@end

When we add the Facebook import view controller as a notification observer, we have to specify a method handler in handleFacebookBirthdaysDidUpdate:—our class for the Facebook birthdays update notification. When BRDModel.m posts the notification, it also packages the birthdays array into the userInfo dictionary of the notification. The following is a recap from the BRDModel code we wrote previously:

```
NSDictionary *userInfo = @{@"birthdays":birthdays};
                [[NSNotificationCenter defaultCenter]
postNotificationName:BRNotificationFacebookBirthdaysDidUpdate object:self userInfo:userInfo];
```

In the view controller, we're able to retrieve the birthdays array from the userInfo dictionary, assign it to the local birthdays array of the controller, and then reload the table view. Then the BRImportViewController superclass does the rest of the work for us!

Build and run. After authorizing with Facebook and returning to the app after a few seconds waiting for the Graph API request to complete, your Facebook friends should appear in the Facebook import table view and you should be able to multiselect them (see Figure 11-8).

Figure 11-8. Facebook import view controller displaying the returned birthdays

Importing Facebook birthdays into the Core Data store

But there's more… Try to import a few Facebook friends… Whoa there, guess what—it just works! The importBirthdays: code we wrote in Chapter 10 was written for importing BRDBirthdayImport instances. We've already converted the Facebook birthday dictionaries to BRDBirthdayImport instances, and all of our import view rendering of birthdays are already taken care of by the BRImportViewController super view controller class. Do you see all the time and effort we saved ourselves just by using a superclass and a generic birthday import class?

The only missing function is that we have remote URLs for the images of our Facebook friends, and currently we've not coded our table views to download and render remote images. So let's do that now!

Loading and displaying remote images

Unfortunately, Apple doesn't include remote image loading as part of the UIImageView or any other class in the iOS SDK. There's a fair amount of hard work and code that's required to implement efficient downloading, caching, and rendering of remote image files. However, we're going to write some reusable image downloading and rendering code, so once we've cracked it here, you should find this code can be used in your other iPhone development projects.

We're going to extend the functionality of Apple's UIImageView to include support for remote image display by creating an Objective-C category and adding a new setImageWithRemoteFileURL:placeholderImage: method on UIImageView.

In the Project Navigator, select the user-interface/categories group and with the ⌘N shortcut or File ➤ New ➤ File, choose the Objective-C Category option from the Cocoa Touch file templates. Create a category on UIImageView named RemoteFile, as shown in Figure 11-9.

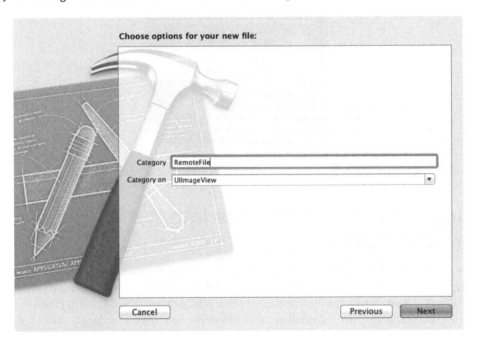

Figure 11-9. Creating a new RemoteFile category on UIImageView

With UIImageView+RemoteFile.h open in Xcode, we're going to add one new method to UIImageView:

```
#import <UIKit/UIKit.h>

@interface UIImageView (RemoteFile)
```

```
- (void)setImageWithRemoteFileURL:(NSString *)urlString placeHolderImage:(UIImage
*)placeholderImage;
```

@end

We're creating a new method for image views, setImageWithRemoteFileURL:placeHolderImage:, which accepts a URL string and a placeholder image instance. The image view will display the placeholder image while it downloads the image data from the remote image URL. When the download completes, the image view will replace the placeholder with the downloaded image.

We also want our image loading to be optimized. If our user has hundreds of Facebook friends and he scrolls through a table view with hundreds of rows, then we must be careful not to attempt to download hundreds of images simultaneously: the result would be that new images would take longer and longer to appear as the download queue enlarges.

Switch to UIImageView+RemoteFile.m. We're going to write about 250 lines of code for the implementation of our new RemoteFile image view category. The reason for this is that we'll be including a few private classes in our category implementation file in addition to the implementation of setImageWithRemoteFileURL:placeHolderImage, our single public method.

To begin, we're going to create a class to cache downloaded images in a mutable dictionary. The cache class will be created as a singleton and accessible by any image view instance.

Add the interface and implementation code for the new ImageCache class above the empty implementation of UIImageView (RemoteFile):

```
//A singleton cache class that will store a mutable dictionary of url keys and UIImage values
for images that have previously been downloaded
@interface ImageCache : NSObject

@property (nonatomic,strong) NSMutableDictionary *cache;

-(UIImage *) cachedImageForURL:(NSString *)url;
-(void) storeCachedImage:(UIImage *)image forURL:(NSString *)url;

@end


@implementation ImageCache

@synthesize cache = _cache;

-(id) init
{
    self = [super init];
    if (self) {
        //the cached dictionary will empty if our app receives a memory warning
        [[NSNotificationCenter defaultCenter] addObserver:self
                                        selector:@selector(clearCache)

name:UIApplicationDidReceiveMemoryWarningNotification
```

```
                                                        object:nil];

    }
    return self;
}

-(void) dealloc
{
    [[NSNotificationCenter defaultCenter] removeObserver:self
name:UIApplicationDidReceiveMemoryWarningNotification object:nil];
}

-(NSMutableDictionary *) cache
{
    if (_cache == nil) {
        _cache = [NSMutableDictionary dictionary];
    }
    return _cache;
}

- (void)clearCache
{
    [self.cache removeAllObjects];
}

-(void) storeCachedImage:(UIImage *)image forURL:(NSString *)url
{
    self.cache[url] = image;
}

-(UIImage *) cachedImageForURL:(NSString *)url
{
    return self.cache[url];
}
```

Our image view category will be able to check for previously cached images by calling cachedImageForURL: with remote URLs. Likewise, when remote images finish downloading, we'll cache them using ImageCache's storeCachedImage:forURL: method.

The next encapsulated class we'll add is a DownloadHelper class and delegate protocol. Again, add this code above the implementation of UIImageView (RemoteFile)—straight after the ImageCache class declaration:

```
//A helper class for handling data download events and storing data progressively as it
downloads for an image file

@protocol DownloadHelperDelegate <NSObject>

-(void)didCompleteDownloadForURL:(NSString *)url withData:(NSMutableData *)data;

@end
```

```objc
@interface DownloadHelper : NSObject

@property (nonatomic,strong) NSString *url;
@property (nonatomic,strong) NSMutableData *data;
@property (nonatomic,strong) NSURLConnection *connection;
@property (nonatomic,assign) id<DownloadHelperDelegate> delegate;

@end

@implementation DownloadHelper

@synthesize url = _url;
@synthesize data = _data;
@synthesize connection = _connection;
@synthesize delegate = _delegate;

- (void) connection: (NSURLConnection*) connection didReceiveData: (NSData*) data
{
    //add the new bytes of data to our existing mutable data container
    [self.data appendData:data];
}

- (void)connectionDidFinishLoading:(NSURLConnection *)connection
{
    //done downloading data - process completed!
    [self.delegate didCompleteDownloadForURL:self.url withData:self.data];
}

-(void) cancelConnection
{
    if (self.connection) {
        [self.connection cancel];
        [self setConnection:nil];
    }
}

-(void) dealloc
{
    [self cancelConnection];
}

@end
```

We're going to create instances of this new DownloadHelper class whenever an image view needs to begin downloading a new remote image file. Each DownloadHelper instance will be owned by a UIImageView instance. The iOS SDK includes a class named NSURLConnection that we'll use to download remote image data from a HTTP request. By subscribing our DownloadHelper instances as the delegates of NSURLConnection instances we'll be able to catch data download updates and completion events via the connection:didReceiveData: and connectionDidFinishLoading: event handlers.

The DownloadHelper will notify its owning image view via a delegate callback method didCompleteDownloadForURL:withData:.

We're now going to add another category on UIImageView. A new category that will be hidden from other classes as it's just for internal use by our remote image downloading and caching logic. As the comments state, the primary reason for creating this UIImageView(RemoteFileHidden) category is to add two additional properties to Apple's UIImageView class: url and downloadHelper. In Objective-C, it's not actually possible to add synthesized properties to a class via a category. Instead, we'll get around this by using dynamic properties that we'll create and add to UIImageView class at runtime. Adding storage properties to the runtime is quite advanced stuff, but for the sake of creating useful reusable code, it's the best way for our requirements. Begin by scrolling up to the top of UIImageView+RemoteFile.m and importing the runtime:

```
#import <objc/runtime.h>
```

Continuing work within UIImageView+RemoteFile.m and before the implementation of UIImageView (RemoteFile), add the hidden UIImageView(RemoteFileHidden) category:

```
//An additional, hidden, dependant category on UIImageView. Primarily for adding 2 dynamic
properties to UIImageView, url and downloadHelper

@interface UIImageView(RemoteFileHidden) <DownloadHelperDelegate>

@property (nonatomic,strong,setter = setUrl:) NSString *url;
@property (nonatomic,strong,setter = setDownloadHelper:) DownloadHelper *downloadHelper;

@end

@implementation UIImageView(RemoteFileHidden)

@dynamic url;
@dynamic downloadHelper;

static char kImageUrlObjectKey;
static char kImageDownloadHelperObjectKey;


+ (ImageCache *)imageCache {
    static ImageCache *_imageCache;

    //return a singleton instance of UIImageCache
    if (_imageCache == nil) {
        _imageCache = [[ImageCache alloc] init];
    }
    return _imageCache;
}

- (NSString *)url {
    return (NSString *)objc_getAssociatedObject(self, &kImageUrlObjectKey);
}

- (void)setUrl:(NSString *)url {
    objc_setAssociatedObject(self, &kImageUrlObjectKey, url,
OBJC_ASSOCIATION_RETAIN_NONATOMIC);
```

```objc
}

- (DownloadHelper *)downloadHelper {

    DownloadHelper *helper = (DownloadHelper *)objc_getAssociatedObject(self,
&kImageDownloadHelperObjectKey);

    if (helper == nil) {//lazy loading of the helper class
        helper = [[DownloadHelper alloc] init];
        //when the helper finishes downloading the remote image data it will call it's
delegate (this image view)
        helper.delegate = self;
        self.downloadHelper = helper;
    }

    return helper;
}

- (void)setDownloadHelper:(DownloadHelper *)downloadHelper {
    objc_setAssociatedObject(self, &kImageDownloadHelperObjectKey, downloadHelper,
OBJC_ASSOCIATION_RETAIN_NONATOMIC);
}

-(void) dealloc
{
    if (self.url != nil) [self.downloadHelper cancelConnection];
}

#pragma mark DownloadHelperDelegate

-(void)didCompleteDownloadForURL:(NSString *)url withData:(NSMutableData *)data
{
    //handles the downloaded image data, turns it into an image instance and saves then it
into the ImageCache singleton.

    UIImage *image = [UIImage imageWithData:data];

    if (image == nil) {//something didn't work out - data may be corrupted or a bad url
        return;
    }

    //cache the image
    ImageCache *imageCache = [UIImageView imageCache];
    [imageCache storeCachedImage:image forURL:url];

    //update the placeholder image display of this UIImageView
    self.image = image;

}

@end
```

Alongside adding the dynamic url and downloadHelper properties to UIImageView, this code adds a new class accessor method, imageCache, to instances of UIImageView. Calling imageCache returns a reference to our singleton instance of our ImageCache class. When the DownloadHelper instance receives the connectionDidFinishLoading: callback from NSURLConnection, it calls its delegate (the image view) via the didCompleteDownloadForURL: withData:, passing the completed data from the server connection. UIImageView's didCompleteDownloadForURL: withData: then creates an image from the data and stores it in the singleton image cache using the remote URL as the access key. The placeholder image is also replaced with the new cached data image.

Finally, let's implement our main category method, setImageWithRemoteFileURL:placeHolderImage:.

```
@implementation UIImageView (RemoteFile)

- (void)setImageWithRemoteFileURL:(NSString *)urlString placeHolderImage:(UIImage
*)placeholderImage
{

    if (self.url != nil && [self.url isEqualToString:urlString]) {
        //if the url matches the existing url then ignore it
        return;
    }

    [self.downloadHelper cancelConnection];

    self.url = urlString;

    //get a reference to the image cache singleton
    ImageCache *imageCache = [UIImageView imageCache];

    UIImage *image = [imageCache cachedImageForURL:urlString];
    //check it we've already got a cached version of the image
    if (image) {
        self.image = image;
        return;
    }

    //no cached version so start downloading the remote file
    self.image = placeholderImage;

    NSURL *url = [NSURL URLWithString:urlString];
    NSURLRequest *request = [NSURLRequest requestWithURL:url];

    self.downloadHelper.url = urlString;
    //set the download helper as the delegate of the data download updates
    self.downloadHelper.connection =(NSURLConnection *)[[NSURLConnection alloc]
initWithRequest:request delegate:self.downloadHelper startImmediately:YES];
    if (self.downloadHelper.connection) {
        //create an empty mutable data container to add the data bytes to
        self.downloadHelper.data = [NSMutableData data];
    }
```

```
}
```

```
@end
```

Imagine that our Facebook friends' table view displays 500 rows of friends and their remote photos. Do you remember how a table view efficiently renders so many rows? It creates only as many table view cells as are required to fill its visible bounds. It then reuses those five or six table cells as the user scrolls downs the table. This means that the `iconView` image view is also being reused. So the first thing we do when the `setImageWithRemoteFileURL:placeHolderImage:` method is called is to cancel any existing file download:

```
[self.downloadHelper cancelConnection];
```

It's this line of code that prevents our application from attempting to download hundreds of Facebook friends' photos simultaneously. Before our method initiates a new file download, it checks to see whether we already have a cached image for the URL:

```
UIImage *image = [imageCache cachedImageForURL:urlString];
```

If we already have a cached version, then rather than attempt to re-download the remote image, we use the existing cached image. If this is the first time our program has attempted to download the remote image then we create a new URL connection and set the download helper instance as the delegate for data connection updates such as the data download completion event:

```
self.downloadHelper.connection =(NSURLConnection *)[[NSURLConnection alloc]
initWithRequest:request delegate:self.downloadHelper startImmediately:YES];
```

We also create a mutable data container to store incremental data downloads for the remote file:

```
self.downloadHelper.data = [NSMutableData data];
```

We've completed the `UIImageView` category, so let's test it out. Open `BRBirthdayTableViewCell.m`, import `UIImageView+RemoteFile.h`, and then add the following code to the end of `setBirthdayImport`:

```
if (_birthdayImport.imageData == nil)
    {
        if ([_birthdayImport.picURL length] > 0) {
            [self.iconView setImageWithRemoteFileURL:birthdayImport.picURL
placeHolderImage:[UIImage imageNamed:@"icon-birthday-cake.png"]];
        }
        else self.iconView.image = [UIImage imageNamed:@"icon-birthday-cake.png"];
}
else {
        self.iconView.image = [UIImage imageWithData:birthdayImport.imageData];
}
```

While we're here, add the following similar code to the end of the `setBirthday:` method:

```
if (_birthday.imageData == nil)
    {
        if ([_birthday.picURL length] > 0) {
```

```
        [self.iconView setImageWithRemoteFileURL:_birthday.picURL
placeHolderImage:[UIImage imageNamed:@"icon-birthday-cake.png"]];
        }
        else self.iconView.image = [UIImage imageNamed:@"icon-birthday-cake.png"];
    }
else {
        self.iconView.image = [UIImage imageWithData:_birthday.imageData];
}
```

The code checks for the existence of a remote image URL (picURL) for birthday entities and birthday imports. If an image URL exists, then the table cell calls our category the setImageWithRemoteFileURL:placeHolderImage: remote image display method.

We've got one last chance to make before testing the code. Open BRImportViewController.m and scroll down to the tableView:cellForRowAtIndexPath: method. Remove the old code for setting the image property of iconView:

```
if (birthdayImport.imageData == nil)
{
        brTableCell.iconView.image = [UIImage imageNamed:@"icon-birthday-cake.png"];
}
else {
        brTableCell.iconView.image = [UIImage imageWithData:birthdayImport.imageData];
}
```

Now do the same thing in the BRHomeViewController.m's tableView:cellForRowAtIndexPath: method:

```
    if (birthday.imageData == nil)
    {
        brTableCell.iconView.image = [UIImage imageNamed:@"icon-birthday-cake.png"];
    }
    else {
        brTableCell.iconView.image = [UIImage imageWithData:birthday.imageData];
    }
```

Build and run. Remote Facebook profile photos should now download and appear in both the home and Facebook import screens (see Figure 11-10).

Figure 11-10. Remote images downloading and rendering thanks to our new UIImageView category

If you ran into any difficulties writing the 250 lines of code for UIImageView+RemoteFile.m, then grab the category files from the source code for this chapter and overwrite your version.

We can also utilize our new category in the birthday detail and birthday edit views. Let's start with BRBirthdayEditViewController.m. Import UIImageView+RemoteFile.h and then update the photoView.image setting code within viewWillAppear:.

```
if (self.birthday.imageData == nil)
{
    self.photoView.image = [UIImage imageNamed:@"icon-birthday-cake.png"];
}
else {
    self.photoView.image = [UIImage imageWithData:self.birthday.imageData];
}

    if (self.birthday.imageData == nil)
    {
        if ([self.birthday.picURL length] > 0) {
```

```
        [self.photoView setImageWithRemoteFileURL:self.birthday.picURL
placeHolderImage:[UIImage imageNamed:@"icon-birthday-cake.png"]];
        }
        else self.photoView.image = [UIImage imageNamed:@"icon-birthday-cake.png"];
    }
    else {
        self.photoView.image = [UIImage imageWithData:_birthday.imageData];
    }
```

Now it's time to make similar changes to the photoView.image setting code within viewWillAppear: of BRBirthdayDetailViewController.m. Be sure to import UIImageView+RemoteFile.h, or the compiler will not recognize setImageWithRemoteFileURL:placeHolderImage: as a method of UIImageView.

```
UIImage *image = [UIImage imageWithData:self.birthday.imageData];
if (image == nil) {
        //default to the birthday cake pic if there's no birthday image
        self.photoView.image = [UIImage imageNamed:@"icon-birthday-cake.png"];
    }
    else {
        self.photoView.image = image;
    }


    if (self.birthday.imageData == nil)
    {
        if ([self.birthday.picURL length] > 0) {
            [self.photoView setImageWithRemoteFileURL:_birthday.picURL
placeHolderImage:[UIImage imageNamed:@"icon-birthday-cake.png"]];
        }
        else self.photoView.image = [UIImage imageNamed:@"icon-birthday-cake.png"];
    }
    else {
        self.photoView.image = [UIImage imageWithData:_birthday.imageData];
    }
```

The Facebook profile photos of friends should now display in both edit and birthday detail views.

Posting to friends' Facebook Walls

Within the birthday detail view controller, we're currently displaying a Post on Friend's Wall button for birthdays imported from Facebook. When a user taps this button, we'll present a modal view controller so that users of our app can post straight to their friends' Walls from *Birthday Reminder*.

As I mentioned at the beginning of the chapter, I'm going to show you how to create your own custom view controller and view for posting messages directly to friend Facebook Walls. Apple does include a more generic view controller class named SLComposeViewController, which you can use to post to your own Wall, as we'll discover in Chapter 13 (see Figure 11-11).

Figure 11-11. Apple's SLComposeViewController class can be used for updating your Facebook status, sending a tweet, or posting to Sina Weibo

However, we want to enable one friend to write directly to another friend's Facebook Wall. Although this may be added to the SLComposeViewController class by Apple in the future, as of the launch of iOS 6.0, you can only write to your own timeline using this class. The Friends button in the bottom right of the modal view in Figure 11-11 allows you to permit which friend groups can see the status update, which isn't enough for our purposes.

Creating a Facebook Wall post view controller

Open your storyboard and begin by adding a new view controller to the storyboard and then embedding it in a new navigation controller: Editor ➤ Embed In ➤ Navigation Controller. Title the new view controller Facebook and add two bar button items to the navigation bar, one named Cancel and one named Post, as shown in Figure 11-12.

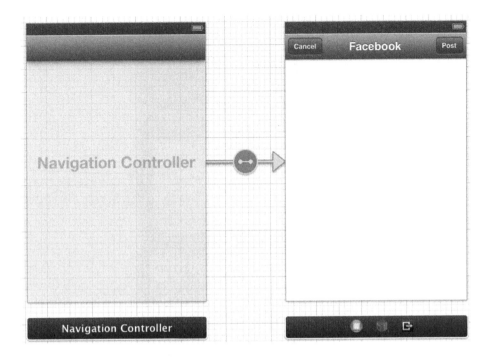

Figure 11-12. Adding a new view controller and bar button items

Select the `user-interface/view-controllers` Xcode group and create a new Objective-C class file within it. Name your class `BRPostToFacebookWallViewController` and enter `BRCoreViewController` into the Subclass Of text field.

Back in your storyboard, select the new navigation controller you just created and using the identity inspector, enter the Storyboard ID `PostToFacebookWall`, as shown in Figure 11-13.

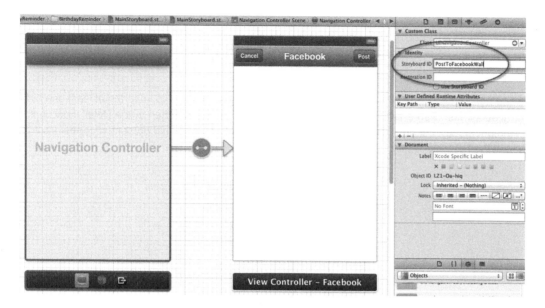

Figure 11-13. Identifying the new navigation controller in the storyboard

Select the new post to Facebook Wall view controller in your storyboard, and using the identity inspector change the custom class of the view controller to your new BRPostToFacebookWallViewController class.

Open BRBirthdayDetailViewController.m and modify the existing facebookButtonTapped: action method as follows:

```
- (IBAction)facebookButtonTapped:(id)sender
{
    UINavigationController *navigationController = [self.storyboard
instantiateViewControllerWithIdentifier:@"PostToFacebookWall"];
    [self.navigationController presentViewController:navigationController animated:YES
completion:nil];
}
```

Back to the storyboard, switch to Assistant Editor mode and ensure that your Post to the Facebook Wall view controller is selected. Control-drag from the Cancel button to the view controller and select the cancelAndDismiss: inherited action method from the contextual menu.

Control-drag from the Post button to the BRPostToFacebookWallViewController.h public interface to add a new action method named postToFacebook. Then Control-drag again from the Post button to create an outlet reference to the button and name it postButton. The resulting header file should match mine, as follows:

```
#import "BRCoreViewController.h"

@interface BRPostToFacebookWallViewController : BRCoreViewController
```

```
- (IBAction)postToFacebook:(id)sender;
@property (weak, nonatomic) IBOutlet UIBarButtonItem *postButton;
```

@end

Build and run. To test the new functionality, you'll need to ensure that you've imported at least one birthday from Facebook first. Tap a birthday from the Home view controller, and then in the Detail view controller, you should find the Post on Friend's Wall button. Tapping the button should present your new Post to the Facebook Wall view controller, as shown in Figure 11-14.

Figure 11-14. The Post to the Facebook Wall view controller presented modally

Back in your storyboard, let's finish our work on the view for the post to Facebook Wall view controller. Add a text view and two images and set them up as follows:

- The text view: x=0, y=10, width=235, height=190

- Both image views: x=238, y=10, width=71, height=71

Set the image attribute of the bottom image view to thumbnail-background.png. The final view should look like Figure 11-15.

Figure 11-15. The Post to the Facebook Wall view with text and image views

Create an outlet for the front image view named photoView and an outlet for the text view named textView. Declare that your BRPostToFacebookWallViewController implements the UITextViewDelegate protocol and then Control-drag from the text view to the view controller to assign the view controller as the delegate of the text view.

BRPostToFacebookWallViewController.h should now read as follows:

```
#import "BRCoreViewController.h"

@interface BRPostToFacebookWallViewController : BRCoreViewController<UITextViewDelegate>

- (IBAction)postToFacebook:(id)sender;
@property (weak, nonatomic) IBOutlet UIBarButtonItem *postButton;
@property (weak, nonatomic) IBOutlet UIImageView *photoView;
@property (weak, nonatomic) IBOutlet UITextView *textView;

@end
```

Before we move our attention to the implementation of BRPostToFacebookWallViewController, let's declare two more public properties in BRPostToFacebookWallViewController.h:

```
@property (strong, nonatomic) NSString *facebookID;
@property (strong, nonatomic) NSString *initialPostText;
```

When we initialize the Post to Facebook Wall view controller, we'll set the initial text to display in the text view and pass a Facebook ID so that our code will know which Facebook Wall to write to and can also display the photo of the Facebook friend using the Facebook ID and standard Facebook profile photo URL format.

Let's set these values from the Birthday Detail view controller now. Open BRBirthdayDetailViewController.m and import BRPostToFacebookWallViewController.h before completing the facebookButtonTapped method:

```
- (IBAction)facebookButtonTapped:(id)sender
{
    UINavigationController *navigationController = [self.storyboard
instantiateViewControllerWithIdentifier:@"PostToFacebookWall"];
    BRPostToFacebookWallViewController *facebookWallViewController =
(BRPostToFacebookWallViewController *) navigationController.topViewController;
    facebookWallViewController.facebookID = self.birthday.facebookID;
    facebookWallViewController.initialPostText = @"Happy Birthday!";
    [self.navigationController presentViewController:navigationController animated:YES
completion:nil];
}
```

You can build and run your app to check that it all compiles OK, however, your Post to Facebook Wall view controller is going to look a little ugly with a nonstyled text view. Let's now implement BRPostToFacebookWallViewController.m:

```
#import "BRPostToFacebookWallViewController.h"
#import "BRStyleSheet.h"
#import "UIImageView+RemoteFile.h"

@interface BRPostToFacebookWallViewController ()

@end

@implementation BRPostToFacebookWallViewController


-(void) viewDidLoad
{
    [super viewDidLoad];

    [BRStyleSheet styleRoundCorneredView:self.photoView];
    [BRStyleSheet styleTextView:self.textView];
}

- (void)viewWillAppear:(BOOL)animated
{
    [super viewWillAppear:animated];

    NSString *facebookPicURL = [NSString
stringWithFormat:@"http://graph.facebook.com/%@/picture?type=large",self.facebookID];

    [self.photoView setImageWithRemoteFileURL:facebookPicURL placeHolderImage:[UIImage
imageNamed:@"icon-birthday-cake.png"]];
```

```
    self.textView.text = self.initialPostText;

    [self.textView becomeFirstResponder];

    [self updatePostButton];
}



- (IBAction)postToFacebook:(id)sender {
}

-(void) updatePostButton
{
    self.postButton.enabled = self.textView.text.length > 0;
}

#pragma mark UITextViewDelegate

- (void)textViewDidChange:(UITextView *)textView
{
    [self updatePostButton];
}

@end
```

There shouldn't be anything unfamiliar in this code because it's really an amalgamation of several coding techniques that you've learned throughout this book. When the view loads our BRStyleSheet class, apply the styling code to the text and image views:

```
[BRStyleSheet styleRoundCorneredView:self.photoView];
[BRStyleSheet styleTextView:self.textView];
```

In the viewWillAppear: method we use the Facebook ID to generate a link to the profile photo for this Facebook user, and then take advantage of our remote image view file loading category method to display the profile pic next to the text view:

```
NSString *facebookPicURL = [NSString
stringWithFormat:@"http://graph.facebook.com/%@/picture?type=large",self.facebookID];

    [self.photoView setImageWithRemoteFileURL:facebookPicURL placeHolderImage:[UIImage
imageNamed:@"icon-birthday-cake.png"]];
```

Just like the edit view controller, we adapt a similar approach to enabling/disabling the Post button with a private updatePostButton method that we invoke when the view appears and whenever the text is edited by the user:

```
-(void) updatePostButton
{
    self.postButton.enabled = self.textView.text.length > 0;
}
```

If you build and run, the results should look like Figure 11-16.

Figure 11-16. Nicely skinned Post to the Facebook Wall view with an enabling/disabling Post button

Great, the UI for our custom Post to the Facebook Wall view and view controller are complete. Now to actually send a post to Facebook!

We'll keep all Facebook API calls centralized in our BRDModel singleton, so open BRDModel.h and declare a new postToFacebookWall:withFacebookID: public method:

```
- (void)postToFacebookWall:(NSString *)message withFacebookID:(NSString *)facebookID;
```

Before implementing the method, jump back to the BRPostToFacebookWallViewController.m file, import BRDModel.h, and complete the postToFacebook action method:

```
- (IBAction)postToFacebook:(id)sender {
    [[BRDModel sharedInstance] postToFacebookWall:self.textView.text
withFacebookID:self.facebookID];
```

```
    [self dismissViewControllerAnimated:YES completion:nil];
}
```

Now to add the posting logic to our model. Open BRDModel.m. We're going to apply very similar logic to the Post to Facebook process as we did with the fetching of Facebook friends' birthdays. That is, we're not going to assume that the user has already authenticated with Facebook. On that basis, that we may need to wait for the authentication process to complete before we can post. So if the authentication process has not completed in the user's current session, we'll store the Facebook ID and message for the post in a couple of new private properties. Add the following private properties to BRDModel.m private interface:

```
@interface BRDModel()

@property (strong) ACAccount *facebookAccount;
@property FacebookAction currentFacebookAction;
@property (nonatomic,strong) NSString *postToFacebookMessage;
@property (nonatomic,strong) NSString *postToFacebookID;

@end
```

Now to implement the first part of the new postToFacebookWall method:

```
- (void)postToFacebookWall:(NSString *)message withFacebookID:(NSString *)facebookID
{
    NSLog(@"postToFacebookWall");

    if (self.facebookAccount == nil) {
        //We're not authorized yet so store the Facebook message and id and start the
authentication flow
        self.postToFacebookMessage = message;
        self.postToFacebookID = facebookID;
        self.currentFacebookAction = FacebookActionPostToWall;
        [self authenticateWithFacebook];
        return;
    }

    NSLog(@"We're authorized so post to Facebook!");

}
```

This code should look pretty similar to the initial fetchFacebookBirthdays code. If we need to authorize the facebookAccount property, then we store the message and Facebook ID, and set the current Facebook action to our FacebookActionPostToWall enumerator value.

Before we complete the postToFacebookWall method, first locate the authenticateWithFacebook method and complete the TODO part of the switch statement for the completion block when the user authenticates:

```
switch (self.currentFacebookAction) {
            case FacebookActionGetFriendsBirthdays:
                [self fetchFacebookBirthdays];
                break;
            case FacebookActionPostToWall:
```

```
                        //TODO - post to a friend's Facebook Wall
                        [self postToFacebookWall:self.postToFacebookMessage
withFacebookID:self.postToFacebookID];
                        break;
                }
```

Great. Let's finish the posting logic back in the postToFacebookWall:withFacebookID method:

```
- (void)postToFacebookWall:(NSString *)message withFacebookID:(NSString *)facebookID
{
    NSLog(@"postToFacebookWall");

    if (self.facebookAccount == nil) {
        //We're not authorized yet so store the Facebook message and id and start the
authentication flow
        self.postToFacebookMessage = message;
        self.postToFacebookID = facebookID;
        self.currentFacebookAction = FacebookActionPostToWall;
        [self authenticateWithFacebook];
        return;
    }

    NSLog(@"We're authorized so post to Facebook!");

    NSDictionary *params = @{@"message":message};

    //Use the user's Facebook ID to call the post to friend feed Graph API path
    NSString *postGraphPath = [NSString
stringWithFormat:@"https://graph.facebook.com/%@/feed",facebookID];

    NSURL *requestURL = [NSURL URLWithString:postGraphPath];

    SLRequest *request = [SLRequest requestForServiceType:SLServiceTypeFacebook
requestMethod:SLRequestMethodPOST URL:requestURL parameters:params];
    request.account = self.facebookAccount;

    [request performRequestWithHandler:^(NSData *responseData, NSHTTPURLResponse
*urlResponse, NSError *error) {
        if (error != nil) {
            NSLog(@"Error posting to Facebook: %@",error);
        }
        else
        {
            //Facebook returns a dictionary with the id of the new post - this might be
useful for other projects
            NSDictionary *dict = (NSDictionary *) [NSJSONSerialization
JSONObjectWithData:responseData options:0 error:nil];
            NSLog(@"Successfully posted to Facebook! Post ID: %@",dict);
        }
    }];

}
```

Build and run. You should be able to post to your friend's Facebook Walls straight from *Birthday Reminder*!

Experiment with the params dictionary that you're passing to the `SLRequest` instance in code. There are additional parameters you can add, such as a link or the URL to a picture to include in the Wall post. Once you get to this point, you have the basis for a very powerful social component. You can read all about the different parameter values that Facebook accepts in the post object at `http://developers.facebook.com/docs/reference/api/post/`.

I would urge you to tread carefully when it comes to enabling friend-to-friend Facebook Wall posts and ensure that the way you using this feature fits with the way your users expect it to work. As we're helping our users to post Happy Birthday messages, I've purposely avoided adding any app advertising in the `post` object, as we don't want our users to accuse us of spamming their friends!

Summary

Today we learned how Facebook's Graph API and Apple's Accounts and new Social framework make a very powerful combination for integrating all kinds of Facebook features natively into your apps. We worked with just two of the Facebook API methods for retrieving friends and for posting to friends' Walls, but there are many other accessible methods to enhance the content and social features for all kinds of iPhone and iPad apps.

For example, one of my apps, *Portfolio Pro for iPad*, is an app for photographers and designers to take their portfolio offline and make available for client presentations. In addition to its core, the offline presentation feature Portfolio Pro allows photographers to sign on to Facebook and upload any of their photos directly to any of their existing Facebook albums. This feature greatly simplifies the workflow for many photographers because they can import photos from Flickr, Dropbox, or their iPad, and easily add and upload them to Facebook albums as well. The benefits are two-fold: the app makes life easier for the photographer and Facebook adds a "via Portfolio Pro for iPad" link next to every photo posted by my users. So I get a subtle promotional link back to my app's Facebook page and more app exposure to the photographer's Facebook friends.

As we developers add Facebook features to our apps, the challenge is to find the right balance between being helpful and taking advantage of social sharing and advertising. The primary focus needs to be to create features that are relevant to our app's primary function and to help our users—rather than get in the way!

Chapter 12

Settings and Local Notifications

We're nearing the end of Day 4. In terms of function and feel, our app is almost complete. However, it is still missing its key feature: birthday reminder notifications! In this chapter, we'll develop our in-app settings functionality so that users can define how many days notice and what time of day they'd like their birthday reminders. We'll then apply those settings to automatically schedule birthday reminder notifications for our user.

Working with static table view controllers

We'll begin by replacing our main settings screen with a table view controller populated with two table cells to enable our user to change the default alert time and number of advance days to get birthday reminder notifications.

Our current implementation of an empty Settings view controller with a lonely Set Alert Time button needs to go. So to begin, we're going to get rid of our current Settings view controller entirely—but don't worry, sometimes you've gotta be cruel to be kind. ☺

Open your storyboard and select the Settings view controller scene (as highlighted in Figure 12-1). Then tap the Backspace key to delete the scene from your storyboard. You should be left with a navigation controller on the left, the Alert Time view controller on the right, and a big space between them! Now multiselect BRSettingsViewController.h and BRSettingsViewController.m in the Project Navigator (also highlighted in Figure 12-1). Delete those files! Be sure to select the Move to Trash option when deleting in order to enable us to re-create files of the same names shortly.

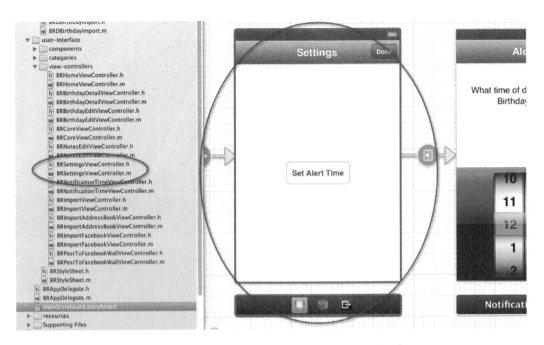

Figure 12-1. Delete the highlighted storyboard scene and Settings view controller class files

Now to replace the old Settings view controller. We're going to build the new Settings view controller using static table cells: table cells that remain in memory and aren't reused by their table view. In order to use static table cells, Xcode requires us to subclass a table view controller rather than the standard view controller to create our new Settings view controller. A table view controller is a view controller with a table view as its main view, and, by default, the controller is set as the delegate and data source of the table view.

Drag a new table view controller (UITableViewController) object onto the storyboard. Control-drag from the Settings navigation controller to the new table view controller in your storyboard, and select the Relationship Root View Controller option from the contextual menu (see Figure 12-2).

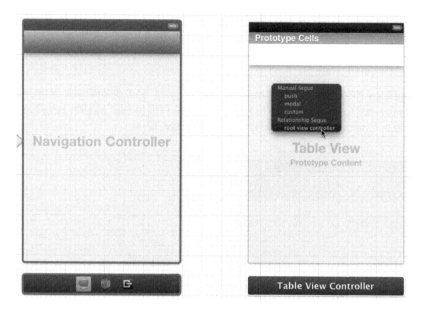

Figure 12-2. Defining a root view controller relationship via the storyboard

A connection between the navigation controller and new setting controller scene should appear. Title the navigation bar of the new settings scene, Settings, and add a bar button item to the right side of the navigation bar. Set its title to Done (see Figure 12-3).

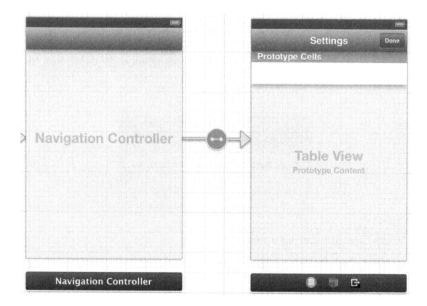

Figure 12-3. Storyboarding the new settings scene

Select the table view in the new settings scene. With the attributes inspector, change the table view style from Plain to Grouped. Change the content setting of the table view from Dynamic Prototypes to Static Cells. Scroll down the attributes inspector to the View attributes, and change the view background color to Clear Color.

Xcode auto generates three static table cells for you. Select and delete two of them. With the one remaining static table cell, change its style to Right Detail (UITableViewCellStyleValue1), enter the title **Days Before**, and set the detail text to On Birthday (see Figure 12-4).

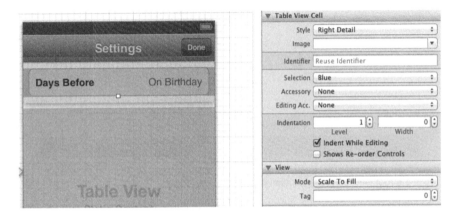

Figure 12-4. Creating a static table cell with the Right Detail (UITableViewCellStyleValue1) style

Now select the Table View Section in the document outline pane of the editor. In the attributes inspector, increment the row count of the table view section to 2. Xcode automatically applies identical style and text from the first static table cell.

Modify the title of the second table cell to Alert Time and change its detail text to 9:00 a.m. (see Figure 12-5).

Figure 12-5. Modifying the rows of a static table view section

Drag another new table view controller onto your storyboard, which will become the Days Before table view controller.

With static table cells, you can create segue connections directly from table cells to other view controller scenes. Control-drag from the first static table cell in the main Settings view to the new Days Before table view controller, and select Push from the selection of segue transition options. Name the new table view controller's navigation bar **Days Before**.

Repeat the segue creation process for the second static table cell, creating a push segue to the Notification Time view controller (see Figure 12-6).

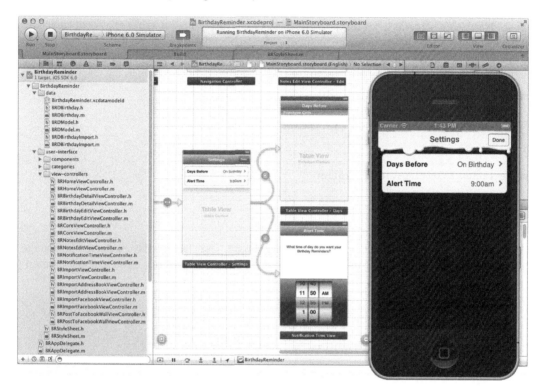

Figure 12-6. Creating segue navigation from static table view cells

You should be able to build and run your app at this point: be able to present the settings table view and navigate between Days Before and Notification Time view controllers.

At the moment, there are a number of problems with the current Settings view:

- It can't be dismissed.

- The Alert Time for in the settings screen does not update when the user changes it in the Notification Time screen.

- The background of the table view is transparent, but still requires the custom-designed screen background for our app.

We're going to have to subclass UITableViewController and fix these issues.

Create a new class named BRSettingsViewController in the settings user-interface/view-controllers group of your Xcode project. From the Cocoa Touch templates, select Objective-C class, and on the next screen type BRSettingsViewController into the Class text field and UITableViewController into the Subclass text field. Ensure that Targeted for iPad and With XIB for User Interface are left deselected, and create the new class.

Because BRSettingsViewController is a subclass of UITableViewController, Xcode automatically adds a bunch of table-controlling delegate methods to the implementation source file. We need to get rid of most of this code because we're building a static table view and most of the UI work is achieved directly in our storyboard. So open BRSettingsViewController.m and strip it right down to the following:

```
#import "BRSettingsViewController.h"

@interface BRSettingsViewController ()

@end

@implementation BRSettingsViewController

@end
```

Just an empty private interface and class implementation.

Select your main Settings view controller in the storyboard. Use the identity inspector to change the custom class of the view controller to the new BRSettingsViewController class you just created (see Figure 12-7).

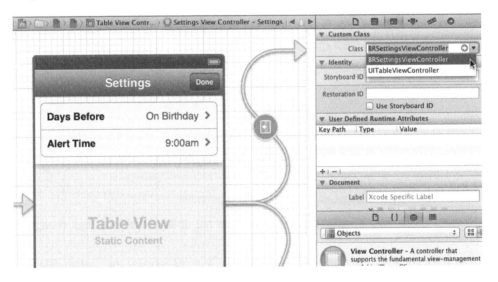

Figure 12-7. Assigning BRSettingsViewController to the main Settings view controller in the storyboard

Using the Assistant Editor layout and by Control-dragging from the cells, hook up outlets for each of the two static table cells:

```
@property (weak, nonatomic) IBOutlet UITableViewCell *tableCellDaysBefore;
@property (weak, nonatomic) IBOutlet UITableViewCell *tableCellNotificationTime;
```

We're also going to create an Interface Builder action for our Done button to dismiss the modal view. To create a new action, Control-drag from your Done button to BRSettingsViewController.h header interface file. Be sure to switch the connection type to Action and name the new action didClickDoneButton:

```
- (IBAction)didClickDoneButton:(id)sender;
```

Let's get to work on the implementation of BRSettingsViewController.m. The implementation for the didClickDoneButton: is simply a call to dismiss the view controller:

```
- (IBAction)didClickDoneButton:(id)sender {
    [self dismissViewControllerAnimated:YES completion:nil];
}
```

BRSettingsViewController can now be dismissed – build and run.

Building the settings singleton class

We're going to build a new abstracted data class that we'll access through a singleton instance. The setting singleton provides a few accessor properties and methods to the user's global birthday reminder notification settings: the number of days in advance to get a birthday notification and the hour and minute of the day for those reminders.

User defaults: iOS cookies

The simplest way to store preference data in iOS is by using Apple's NSUserDefaults class. It's the iOS equivalent of HTML cookies. We can store the data object types such as strings and numbers using NSUserDefaults. The syntax for saving a string looks like the following:

```
NSUserDefaults *userDefaults = [NSUserDefaults standardUserDefaults];
[userDefaults setObject:@"Nick Kuh" forKey:@"name"];
[userDefaults synchronize];
```

Calling synchronize writes your changes to disk, so if you were saving more than one property you would call synchronize once you'd set all the keys and values.

To access and check for properties saved to NSUserDefaults, the code for the preceding example would be as follows:

```
NSUserDefaults *userDefaults = [NSUserDefaults standardUserDefaults];
NSString *name = [userDefaults objectForKey:@"name"];
if (name == nil) {
    NSLog(@"No previous name saved");
}
else {
    NSLog(@"Saved name: %@",name);
}
```

Let's create the new settings singleton class and put this logic into practice for our app. Within the *data* group of your Xcode project, create a new subclass of NSObject named BRDSettings. Let's get to work on the header:

```
#import <Foundation/Foundation.h>

typedef enum : int {
    BRDaysBeforeTypeOnBirthday = 0,
    BRDaysBeforeTypeOneDay,
    BRDaysBeforeTypeTwoDays,
    BRDaysBeforeTypeThreeDays,
    BRDaysBeforeTypeFiveDays,
    BRDaysBeforeTypeOneWeek,
    BRDaysBeforeTypeTwoWeeks,
    BRDaysBeforeTypeThreeWeeks
}BRDaysBeforeType;

#import <Foundation/Foundation.h>

@interface BRDSettings : NSObject

+ (BRDSettings*)sharedInstance;

@property (nonatomic) int notificationHour;
@property (nonatomic) int notificationMinute;
@property (nonatomic) BRDaysBeforeType daysBefore;

-(NSString *) titleForNotificationTime;
-(NSString *) titleForDaysBefore:(BRDaysBeforeType)daysBefore;

@end
```

Just like BRDModel, we'll provide access to the singleton instance of BRDSettings via a sharedInstance class method. The notification hour and minute are returned as integers: within the implementation of our settings data class we'll check if the user has previously set hour/minute notification time for reminders, and if not, we'll return a default time—9:00 a.m. perhaps?

We're going to provide the user with a set of Days Before options ranging from a reminder on the day of to as far back as three weeks before each birthday. We've created a custom enumerator type to provide the different options in this range without creating 0 to 21 days/options that would look messy in our app. The titleForDaysBefore: method returns a human-readable string for each option, such as "On Birthday" or "3 Weeks Before".

Switch to work on the BRDSettings.m source file, and add the implementation of the methods and properties that we've declared in the header:

```
#import "BRDSettings.h"

@implementation BRDSettings

static BRDSettings *_sharedInstance = nil;
```

```
static NSDateFormatter *dateFormatter;

@synthesize notificationHour;
@synthesize notificationMinute;

//accessor method for the singleton instance
+ (BRDSettings*)sharedInstance {
        if( !_sharedInstance ) {
                _sharedInstance = [[BRDSettings alloc] init];
        }
        return _sharedInstance;
}

-(int) notificationHour
{
    //checks if user has saved a notification hour - if not, defaults to 9am
    NSUserDefaults *userDefaults = [NSUserDefaults standardUserDefaults];
    NSNumber *hour = [userDefaults objectForKey:@"notificationHour"];
    if (hour == nil) {
        return 9;
    }
    return [hour intValue];
}

-(void) setNotificationHour:(int)notificationHourNew
{
    NSUserDefaults *userDefaults = [NSUserDefaults standardUserDefaults];
    [userDefaults setObject:[NSNumber numberWithInt:notificationHourNew]
forKey:@"notificationHour"];
    [userDefaults synchronize];
}

-(int) notificationMinute
{
    //checks if user has saved a notification minute - if not, defaults to 0 minutes on the
hour
    NSUserDefaults *userDefaults = [NSUserDefaults standardUserDefaults];
    NSNumber *hour = [userDefaults objectForKey:@"notificationMinute"];
    if (hour == nil) {
        return 0;
    }
    return [hour intValue];
}

-(void) setNotificationMinute:(int)notificationMinuteNew
{
    NSUserDefaults *userDefaults = [NSUserDefaults standardUserDefaults];
    [userDefaults setObject:[NSNumber numberWithInt:notificationMinuteNew]
forKey:@"notificationMinute"];
    [userDefaults synchronize];
}

-(BRDDaysBeforeType) daysBefore
```

```
{
    NSUserDefaults *userDefaults = [NSUserDefaults standardUserDefaults];
    NSNumber *daysBefore = [userDefaults objectForKey:@"daysBefore"];
    if (daysBefore == nil) {
        return BRDaysBeforeTypeOnBirthday;
    }
    return [daysBefore intValue];
}

-(void) setDaysBefore:(BRDaysBeforeType)daysBeforeNew
{
    NSUserDefaults *userDefaults = [NSUserDefaults standardUserDefaults];
    [userDefaults setObject:[NSNumber numberWithInt:daysBeforeNew] forKey:@"daysBefore"];
    [userDefaults synchronize];
}

-(NSString *) titleForDaysBefore:(BRDaysBeforeType)daysBefore
{
    switch (daysBefore) {
        case BRDaysBeforeTypeOnBirthday:
            return @"On Birthday";
        case BRDaysBeforeTypeOneDay:
            return @"1 Day Before";
        case BRDaysBeforeTypeTwoDays:
            return @"2 Days Before";
        case BRDaysBeforeTypeThreeDays:
            return @"3 Days Before";
        case BRDaysBeforeTypeFiveDays:
            return @"5 Days Before";
        case BRDaysBeforeTypeOneWeek:
            return @"1 Week Before";
        case BRDaysBeforeTypeTwoWeeks:
            return @"2 Weeks Before";
        case BRDaysBeforeTypeThreeWeeks:
            return @"3 Weeks Before";
    }
    return @"";
}

-(NSString *) titleForNotificationTime
{
    int hour = [BRDSettings sharedInstance].notificationHour;
    int minute = [BRDSettings sharedInstance].notificationMinute;

    NSDateComponents *components = [[NSCalendar currentCalendar]
components:NSHourCalendarUnit|NSMinuteCalendarUnit fromDate:[NSDate date]];

    components.hour = hour;
    components.minute = minute;

    NSDate *date = [[NSCalendar currentCalendar] dateFromComponents:components];

    if (dateFormatter == nil) {
```

```
        //create a single date formatter to return 9:00am, 2:00pm etc...
        dateFormatter = [[NSDateFormatter alloc] init];
        [dateFormatter setDateFormat:@"h:mm a"];
    }

    return [dateFormatter stringFromDate:date];
}

@end
```

Our BRDSettings class provides an easy-to-use interface for accessing custom user preferences in our app. Not only do we now have a class that can save and read preferences to disk, but it also takes care of the human-readable language, returning a nicely formatted string for the alert times, such as 9:30 a.m. or 2:05 p.m., and so forth.

Jump back to BRSettingsViewController.m. Now we're going to make the right-side values in the two static settings table cells dynamic. First, import BRDSettings.h. Next, add the following viewWillAppear: method:

```
-(void) viewWillAppear:(BOOL)animated
{
    [super viewWillAppear:animated];

    self.tableCellNotificationTime.detailTextLabel.text = [[BRDSettings sharedInstance]
titleForNotificationTime];
    self.tableCellDaysBefore.detailTextLabel.text = [[BRDSettings sharedInstance]
titleForDaysBefore:[BRDSettings sharedInstance].daysBefore];
}
```

Xcode has allowed us to directly access the static table cells we created via the Interface Builder outlets. So, at the moment the Settings view is about to appear, we can update the values of the detailTextLabel for each of the two static cells in order to reflect the current user-setting from the values in the BRDSettings singleton.

The Settings view controller is not a subclass of our core view controller, so it doesn't inherit the viewDidLoad adding a custom background image code. We'll need to add that code directly to display the checkered background:

```
- (void)viewDidLoad
{
    [super viewDidLoad];
    UIImageView *backgroundView = [[UIImageView alloc] initWithImage:[UIImage
imageNamed:@"app-background.png"]];
    self.tableView.backgroundView = backgroundView;
}
```

The Settings view controller is also going to display a stylized cream-colored heading label, Reminders, above the two table rows. We'll use our style sheet class along with a new private method within BRSettingsViewController implementation source code to achieve this. First, import BRStyleSheet.h and then add the following code:

```
-(UIView *) createSectionHeaderWithLabel:(NSString *)text
{
    UIView *view = [[UIView alloc] initWithFrame:CGRectMake(0, 0, 320, 40.f)];
    UILabel *label = [[UILabel alloc] initWithFrame:CGRectMake(10.f, 15.f, 300.f, 20.f)];
    label.backgroundColor = [UIColor clearColor];
    [BRStyleSheet styleLabel:label withType:BRLabelTypeLarge];
    label.text = text;
    [view addSubview:label];
    return view;
}

- (CGFloat)tableView:(UITableView *)tableView heightForHeaderInSection:(NSInteger)section
{
    return 40.f;
}

- (UIView *)tableView:(UITableView *)tableView viewForHeaderInSection:(NSInteger)section
{
    return [self createSectionHeaderWithLabel:@"Reminders"];
}
```

The `tableView:heightForHeaderInSection:` and `tableView:viewForHeaderInSection:` are methods found in `UITableViewDelegate` protocol that enable us to define a custom view and view height for section headers in our table view. The custom `createSectionHeaderWithLabel:` method creates a transparent view to fill the header section and a `UILabel` subview with a transparent background. It sets the label text based on the passed in string parameter. The results should look like Figure 12-8 when run in the simulator.

Figure 12-8. Adding a stylized custom label header to a table view

Let's move over to complete the BRNotificationTimeViewController.m implementation. First, import BRDSettings.h, and then add a new viewWillAppear: implementation:

```
-(void) viewWillAppear:(BOOL)animated
{
    [super viewWillAppear:animated];

    //Retrieve the stored user settings for notification hour and minute
    int hour = [BRDSettings sharedInstance].notificationHour;
    int minute = [BRDSettings sharedInstance].notificationMinute;

    //Use NSDateComponents to create today's date with the hour/minute stored user
notification settings
    NSDateComponents *components = [[NSCalendar currentCalendar]
components:NSHourCalendarUnit|NSMinuteCalendarUnit fromDate:[NSDate date]];
    components.hour = hour;
    components.minute = minute;
    //Update the date/time picker to display the hour/minutes matching the stored user
settings
    self.timePicker.date = [[NSCalendar currentCalendar] dateFromComponents:components];
}
```

Whenever the Notification Time view controller appears, it updates the time it displays based on the stored user-set alert time for birthday notifications. We now need to ensure that when the user changes the time in this view, we in turn update the stored settings. Complete the didChangeTime: method as follows:

```
- (IBAction)didChangeTime:(id)sender {
    NSDateComponents *components = [[NSCalendar currentCalendar]
components:NSHourCalendarUnit|NSMinuteCalendarUnit fromDate:self.timePicker.date];
    NSLog(@"Changed time to: %d:%d",components.hour,components.minute);

    [BRDSettings sharedInstance].notificationHour = components.hour;
    [BRDSettings sharedInstance].notificationMinute = components.minute;
}
```

Build and run. You should not only find that the settings are getting saved when you make changes to the notification alert time, but that the time is also updated in the main Settings view controller, because our Settings view controller updates its static table view cells each time its view appears.

To finish the *Birthday Reminder* settings, we now need to create a class for our Days Before view controller. With the user-interface/view-controllers Xcode group selected in the Project Navigator, create a new Objective-C class named BRDaysBeforeViewController that subclasses Apple's UITableViewController. In your storyboard, select the Days Before table view controller and using the identity inspector, change the custom class to your new BRDaysBeforeViewController class.

While we're working on the storyboard, select the prototype table cell for the Days Before scene, change its style to Basic, and set its reuse identifier to Cell. Finally, select the table view and change its Style to Grouped.

Clear out any Xcode stub code and replace it with the following, commented implementation of BRDaysBeforeViewController.m:

```objc
#import "BRDaysBeforeViewController.h"
#import "BRDSettings.h"

@implementation BRDaysBeforeViewController

-(void) viewDidLoad
{
    [super viewDidLoad];
    UIImageView *backgroundView = [[UIImageView alloc] initWithImage:[UIImage
imageNamed:@"app-background.png"]];
    [self.tableView setBackgroundView:backgroundView];
}

#pragma mark - UITableViewDataSource

-(UITableViewCell *) tableView:(UITableView *)tableView cellForRowAtIndexPath:(NSIndexPath
*)indexPath
{
    UITableViewCell *cell = [tableView dequeueReusableCellWithIdentifier:@"Cell"];
    cell.textLabel.text = [[BRDSettings sharedInstance] titleForDaysBefore:indexPath.row];
    //if this index path row is the stored days before setting then display a checkmark tick
in the table cell
    cell.accessoryType = ([BRDSettings sharedInstance].daysBefore == indexPath.row) ?
UITableViewCellAccessoryCheckmark : UITableViewCellAccessoryNone;
    return cell;
}


- (NSInteger)tableView:(UITableView *)tableView numberOfRowsInSection:(NSInteger)section
{
    //we could alternatively just return a total row count of 8 but this makes use of the last
enumerated value to get the total count
    return BRDaysBeforeTypeThreeWeeks + 1;
}

#pragma mark - UITableViewDelegate

- (void)tableView:(UITableView *)tableView didSelectRowAtIndexPath:(NSIndexPath *)indexPath
{

    if (indexPath.row == [BRDSettings sharedInstance].daysBefore) {
        //if it's the current ticked row then ignore
        [tableView deselectRowAtIndexPath:indexPath animated:YES];
        return;
    }

    NSIndexPath *oldIndexPath = [NSIndexPath indexPathForRow:[BRDSettings
sharedInstance].daysBefore inSection:0];
    //Update the stored days before setting for the user
    [BRDSettings sharedInstance].daysBefore = indexPath.row;
    //The user has changed the selected days before row so we need to reload the table cells
for the old and new rows
    [tableView reloadRowsAtIndexPaths:@[oldIndexPath,indexPath]
withRowAnimation:UITableViewRowAnimationNone];
```

```
}
```

`@end`

Build and run. You should be able to modify the Days Before setting, and again see changes reflected in the main settings screen, as shown in Figure 12-9.

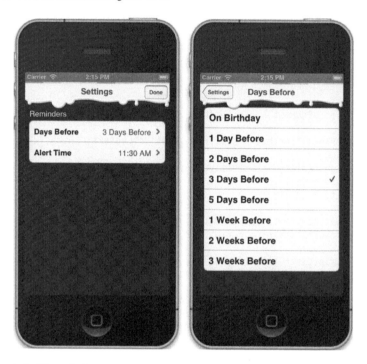

Figure 12-9. User-controlled Days Before settings

Updating birthdays

We're going to move our attention to the data model of our app once more. We're currently storing two persistent properties in our birthday entities that won't remain constant over time: `nextBirthday` and `nextBirthdayAge`. So one task that we will need to address before our app is complete is to regularly update any cached birthdays when the `nextBirthday` property passes and becomes the friend's last birthday!

We're going to create a public method in our model singleton for looping through the database of birthday entities, updating any `nextBirthday` values that are out-of-date.

Open `BRDModel.h` in Xcode and add the new public method declaration to the interface:

`-(void) updateCachedBirthdays;`

Each time the cached birthdays are updated, we'll also dispatch a notification so that any view controller can update its view when the order of the next birthdays changes. At the top of BRDModel.h and above the interface declaration, add a new constant string declaration for this notification name:

```
#define BRNotificationCachedBirthdaysDidUpdate
@"BRNotificationCachedBirthdaysDidUpdate"
```

Switch to the BRDModel.m implementation and add the following birthday entity update code updateCachedBirthdays:

```
-(void) updateCachedBirthdays
{

    NSFetchRequest *fetchRequest = [[NSFetchRequest alloc] init];

    NSManagedObjectContext *context = self.managedObjectContext;

    NSEntityDescription *entity = [NSEntityDescription entityForName:@"BRDBirthday"
inManagedObjectContext:context];
    fetchRequest.entity = entity;

    //Fetch all the birthday entities in order of next birthday
    NSSortDescriptor *sortDescriptor = [[NSSortDescriptor alloc] initWithKey:@"nextBirthday"
ascending:YES];
    NSArray *sortDescriptors = [[NSArray alloc] initWithObjects:sortDescriptor, nil];
    fetchRequest.sortDescriptors = sortDescriptors;

    NSFetchedResultsController *fetchedResultsController = [[NSFetchedResultsController alloc]
initWithFetchRequest:fetchRequest managedObjectContext:context sectionNameKeyPath:nil
cacheName:nil];

    NSError *error = nil;
    if (![fetchedResultsController performFetch:&error]) {

        NSLog(@"Unresolved error %@, %@", error, [error userInfo]);
        abort();
    }

    NSArray *fetchedObjects = fetchedResultsController.fetchedObjects;
    NSInteger resultCount = [fetchedObjects count];

    BRDBirthday *birthday;

    NSDate *now = [NSDate date];
    NSDateComponents *dateComponentsToday = [[NSCalendar currentCalendar]
components:NSYearCalendarUnit|NSMonthCalendarUnit|NSDayCalendarUnit fromDate:now];
    //This creates a date with time 00:00 today
    NSDate *today = [[NSCalendar currentCalendar] dateFromComponents:dateComponentsToday];

    for (int i = 0; i < resultCount; i++) {
        birthday = (BRDBirthday *) fetchedObjects[i];
```

```
        //if next birthday has past then we'll need to update the birthday entity
        if ([today compare:birthday.nextBirthday] == NSOrderedDescending) {
            //next birthday is now incorrect and is in the past...
            [birthday updateNextBirthdayAndAge];
        }
    }

    [self saveChanges];

    //Let any observer's know that the birthdays in our database have been updated
    [[NSNotificationCenter defaultCenter]
postNotificationName:BRNotificationCachedBirthdaysDidUpdate object:self userInfo:nil];
}
```

The method begins by retrieving all Core Data birthday entities in our cached store. The results set is ordered by the nextBirthday property. We loop through the results set, and compare the nextBirthday value to midnight on the start of today's date. If the next birthday is now the user's latest birthday, then we invoke updateNextBirthdayAndAge on the out-of-date birthday entity, and it updates itself accordingly.

Where and when should we call our new updateCachedBirthdays method? At minimum, we should call it each time the *Birthday Reminder* app is brought into the foreground by the user. That would be each time our app becomes the active multitasking app—or whenever the user relaunches our app. Apps can remain in the background for days and weeks, depending on their memory footprint, so we need to cater for that scenario.

Open the BRAppDelegate.m source file. Begin by importing BRDModel.h, and then modify the applicationDidBecomeActive: method to the following:

```
- (void)applicationDidBecomeActive:(UIApplication *)application
{
    [[BRDModel sharedInstance] updateCachedBirthdays];
}
```

One view that we will need to update when the cache updates is our Home view controller table view, if it's currently the foremost view controller. The ordered table of birthdays changes each time the most recent birthday elapses. That birthday will need to be updated and become the furthermost, or last, birthday at the very end of our table. We deal with this scenario by observing the BRNotificationCachedBirthdaysDidUpdate notification and simply reload the table view on the home screen. Open BRHomeViewController.m and add the following highlighted code changes:

```
-(void) viewWillAppear:(BOOL)animated
{
    [super viewWillAppear:animated];
    [self.tableView reloadData];
    self.hasFriends = [self.fetchedResultsController.fetchedObjects count] > 0;
    [[NSNotificationCenter defaultCenter] addObserver:self
selector:@selector(handleCachedBirthdaysDidUpdate:)
name:BRNotificationCachedBirthdaysDidUpdate object:nil];
}

-(void) viewWillDisappear:(BOOL)animated
{
```

```
    [super viewWillDisappear:animated];
    [[NSNotificationCenter defaultCenter] removeObserver:self
name:BRNotificationCachedBirthdaysDidUpdate object:nil];
}

-(void) handleCachedBirthdaysDidUpdate:(NSNotification *)notification
{
    //if the cache updates simply reload the table view
    [self.tableView reloadData];
}
```

We only need to handle the cache update notification when the Home view controller is already displayed because our home table view reloads each time it's about to appear in the existing viewWillAppear: method. So, we add the Home view controller as an observer of the BRNotificationCachedBirthdaysDidUpdate notification when it appears, and we remove it as an observer when it disappears.

Check at this point that your app still compiles OK. Any previously cached birthdays with passed *next birthdays* should update and the Home view controller should now send them to the bottom of the table.

Scheduling and firing reminder local notifications

We're also going to implement scheduled local notification reminders for the soonest upcoming birthdays. Local notifications display just like push notifications in iOS: they are fired by the operating system even when our app isn't running (see Figure 12-10).

Figure 12-10. A scheduled local notification

iOS permits each third-party app to schedule up to 64 local notifications. Go over this limit and additional notifications are ignored. Sixty-four notifications are plenty of birthday reminders for us; in fact, 20 should be more than sufficient. As long as we regularly reset and reschedule the 20 soonest birthdays, that should be enough for *Birthday Reminder* to achieve its core reminder functionality.

Just like push notifications, local notifications can play a custom sound when they fire. I've actually created a HappyBirthday.m4a sound file using Apple's Garage Band software. It's a bit amateur to say the least— but it's kind of fun too. ☺ Add the HappyBirthday.m4a file to your project resources, you'll find it in the assets source for this chapter.

Shortly, we're going to expand the code for our new updateCachedBirthdays method in our model singleton to schedule the next 20 birthday reminders. Before we do this, we're going to add a couple of helper methods to our BRDSettings class for two purposes:

- To calculate the reminder date/time for a birthday based on user preferences.

- To configure the notification text of the reminder based on the difference between the reminder date and the friend's next birthday.

Open BRDSettings.h and add the following modifications to its header:

```
@class BRDBirthday;

@interface BRDSettings : NSObject

+ (BRDSettings*)sharedInstance;

@property (nonatomic) int notificationHour;
@property (nonatomic) int notificationMinute;
@property (nonatomic) BRDaysBeforeType daysBefore;

-(NSString *) titleForNotificationTime;
-(NSString *) titleForDaysBefore:(BRDaysBeforeType)daysBefore;

-(NSDate *) reminderDateForNextBirthday:(NSDate *)nextBirthday;
-(NSString *) reminderTextForNextBirthday:(BRDBirthday *)birthday;

@end
```

We've added a forward class declaration for the BRDBirthday entity class so that we are able to reference a birthday entity in the new reminderTextForNextBirthday: method. Switch to the implementation of these two new public methods. In BRDSettings.m, import BRDBirthday.h, and then implement the reminderDateForNextBirthday: method, commented as follows:

```
-(NSDate *) reminderDateForNextBirthday:(NSDate *)nextBirthday
{
    NSTimeInterval timeInterval;
    NSTimeInterval secondsInOneDay = 60.f * 60.f * 24.f;

    //work out how many days to detract from the friend's next birthday for the reminder date
    switch (self.daysBefore) {
        case BRDaysBeforeTypeOnBirthday:
```

```
            timeInterval = 0.f;
            break;
        case BRDaysBeforeTypeOneDay:
            timeInterval = secondsInOneDay;
            break;
        case BRDaysBeforeTypeTwoDays:
            timeInterval = secondsInOneDay * 2.f;
            break;
        case BRDaysBeforeTypeThreeDays:
            timeInterval = secondsInOneDay * 3.f;
            break;
        case BRDaysBeforeTypeFiveDays:
            timeInterval = secondsInOneDay * 5.f;
            break;
        case BRDaysBeforeTypeOneWeek:
            timeInterval = secondsInOneDay * 7.f;
            break;
        case BRDaysBeforeTypeTwoWeeks:
            timeInterval = secondsInOneDay * 14.f;
            break;
        case BRDaysBeforeTypeThreeWeeks:
            timeInterval = secondsInOneDay * 21.f;
            break;
    }

    //This creates the day of the reminder at time 00:00
    NSDate *reminderDate = [nextBirthday dateByAddingTimeInterval:-timeInterval];

    NSDateComponents *components = [[NSCalendar currentCalendar] components:NSYearCalendarUnit
 | NSMonthCalendarUnit | NSDayCalendarUnit | NSHourCalendarUnit | NSMinuteCalendarUnit
fromDate:reminderDate];

    //update the hour and minute of the reminder time
    components.hour = self.notificationHour;
    components.minute = self.notificationMinute;

    return [[NSCalendar currentCalendar] dateFromComponents:components];

}
```

As an example, if the birthday is Tuesday, June 5, and the user-setting for the Days Before reminder is one day before with an alert time of 9:00 a.m., then this method will return a date of Monday, June 4 at 9:00 a.m., so that the reminder date/time can be scheduled by the model class.

Next, let's add the implementation of reminderTextForNextBirthday:, which returns the birthday reminder message to display for the local notifications we're going to schedule next:

```
-(NSString *) reminderTextForNextBirthday:(BRDBirthday *)birthday
{
    NSString *text;

    if ([birthday.nextBirthdayAge intValue] > 0)
    {
```

```objc
        if (self.daysBefore == BRDaysBeforeTypeOnBirthday) {
            //if the friend's birthday is the same day as the reminder eg. "Joe is 30 today"
            text = [NSString stringWithFormat:@"%@ is %@
",birthday.name,birthday.nextBirthdayAge];
        }
        else {
            //reminder is in advance of the birthday eg. "Joe will be 30 tomorrow"
            text = [NSString stringWithFormat:@"%@ will be %@
",birthday.name,birthday.nextBirthdayAge];
        }
    }
    else {
        text = [NSString stringWithFormat:@"It's %@'s Birthday ",birthday.name];
    }

    switch (self.daysBefore) {
        case BRDaysBeforeTypeOnBirthday:
            return [text stringByAppendingFormat:@"today!"];
        case BRDaysBeforeTypeOneDay:
            return [text stringByAppendingFormat:@"tomorrow!"];
        case BRDaysBeforeTypeTwoDays:
            return [text stringByAppendingFormat:@"in 2 days!"];
        case BRDaysBeforeTypeThreeDays:
            return [text stringByAppendingFormat:@"in 3 days!"];
        case BRDaysBeforeTypeFiveDays:
            return [text stringByAppendingFormat:@"in 5 days!"];
        case BRDaysBeforeTypeOneWeek:
            return [text stringByAppendingFormat:@"in 1 week!"];
        case BRDaysBeforeTypeTwoWeeks:
            return [text stringByAppendingFormat:@"in 2 weeks!"];
        case BRDaysBeforeTypeThreeWeeks:
            return [text stringByAppendingFormat:@"in 3 weeks!"];
    }

    return @"";
}
```

Back to BRDModel.m. Begin by importing BRDSettings.h. We're going to modify updateCachedBirthdays to schedule the first 20 reminder notifications. As this method runs regularly, we need to be careful not to create duplicate local notifications. The easiest way to ensure that doesn't happen is by first clearing all previously scheduled location notifications at the beginning of the updateCachedBirthdays method:

```objc
[[UIApplication sharedApplication] cancelAllLocalNotifications];
```

Now to schedule reminder notifications for the 20 soonest upcoming birthdays. Scroll down to the second half of the updateCachedBirthdays method, and add following highlighted changes:

```objc
    NSDate *now = [NSDate date];
    NSDateComponents *dateComponentsToday = [[NSCalendar currentCalendar]
components:NSYearCalendarUnit|NSMonthCalendarUnit|NSDayCalendarUnit fromDate:now];
    //This creates a date with time 00:00 today
    NSDate *today = [[NSCalendar currentCalendar] dateFromComponents:dateComponentsToday];
```

```objc
UILocalNotification *reminderNotification;
int scheduled = 0;
NSDate *fireDate;

for (int i = 0; i < resultCount; i++) {
    birthday = (BRDBirthday *) fetchedObjects[i];

    //if next birthday has past then we'll need to update the birthday entity
    if ([today compare:birthday.nextBirthday] == NSOrderedDescending) {
        //next birthday is now incorrect and is in the past...
        [birthday updateNextBirthdayAndAge];
    }

    if (scheduled < 20) {
        //get the scheduled reminder date for this birthday from settings
        fireDate = [[BRDSettings sharedInstance]
reminderDateForNextBirthday:birthday.nextBirthday];
        if([now compare:fireDate] != NSOrderedAscending) {
            //this reminder was for today, but the reminder time has now passed -
don't schedule a reminder!
        }
        else {
            //create new new local notification to schedule
            reminderNotification = [[UILocalNotification alloc] init];
            //set the schedule reminder date
            reminderNotification.fireDate = fireDate;
            reminderNotification.timeZone = [NSTimeZone defaultTimeZone];
            reminderNotification.alertAction = @"View Birthdays";
            reminderNotification.alertBody = [[BRDSettings sharedInstance]
reminderTextForNextBirthday:birthday];
            //play a custom sound with a local notification
            reminderNotification.soundName = @"HappyBirthday.m4a";
            //update the badge count on the Birthday Reminder icon
            reminderNotification.applicationIconBadgeNumber = 1;
            //schedule the notification!
            [[UIApplication sharedApplication]
scheduleLocalNotification:reminderNotification];
            scheduled++;

        }
    }
}

[self saveChanges];

//Let any observer's know that the birthdays in our database have been updated
[[NSNotificationCenter defaultCenter]
postNotificationName:BRNotificationCachedBirthdaysDidUpdate object:self userInfo:nil];
```

We generate up to 20 scheduled UILocalNotification instances from the 20 birthdays that are upcoming the soonest. Imagine a scenario where the birthday is today, but the scheduled date for the notification has passed; that is, the user wants reminders at 9:00 a.m. on the day of each friend's birthday—and it's now 10:00 a.m. We don't want to schedule notifications for those birthdays because they've already passed, so we compare the fire date to our now date variable:

```
if([now compare:fireDate] != NSOrderedAscending) {
                //this reminder was for today, but the reminder time has now passed - don't
schedule a reminder!
            }
```

As for the creation of UILocalNotification instances, we schedule the notification date (fireDate), the notification text (alertBody), the number to display on the *Birthday Reminder* home screen icon badge, and even a custom Happy Birthday sound to play when the notification fires.

The app is already calling [[BRDModel sharedInstance] updateCachedBirthdays] each time it launches or comes back into the foreground. However, there are other times when we'll also need to update the scheduled reminders:

- When the user clicks Done and dismisses the setting screen, because they may have updated their birthday reminder time preferences.

- When the user completes the import birthdays process, because we now have new birthdays in the database.

- When the user edits and saves a birthday, because they may have modified the friend's birthday.

Let's add these calls to updateCachedBirthdays now:

In BRDModel.m, add this last line of code to the importBirthdays: implementation:

```
[self updateCachedBirthdays];
```

Open BRSettingsViewController.m, import BRDModel.h, and modify the didClickDoneButton: implementation:

```
- (IBAction)didClickDoneButton:(id)sender {
    [[BRDModel sharedInstance] updateCachedBirthdays];
    [self dismissViewControllerAnimated:YES completion:nil];
}
```

The logic of calling updateCachedBirthdays when Done is tapped on the setting screen is that if a user changes their time of day or number of advance days for birthday notifications, then those changes are applied to the schedule reminders as soon as they dismiss the main settings screen.

Open BRBirthdayEditViewController.m and make the following modification to the saveAndDismiss: method:

```
- (IBAction)saveAndDismiss:(id)sender
{
    [[BRDModel sharedInstance] saveChanges];
    [[BRDModel sharedInstance] updateCachedBirthdays];
    [super saveAndDismiss:sender];
}
```

Resetting the icon badge

On your device, you should be able to test the notification reminders by populating a few birthdays either manually or by importing from Facebook or the Address Book. If the next friend's birthday is tomorrow, for example, then set the Days Before setting to one day before, and then change the alert time to 5 to 10 minutes from now. If all is well, after your first test birthday reminder notification fires, you'll also see an unread badge count of 1 on your *Birthday Reminder* app icon, as shown in Figure 12-11.

Figure 12-11. A badge on the home screen icon

The only problem is that the badge won't go away, even when you enter the *Birthday Reminder* app. This is easily solvable. Open BRAppDelegate.m and tweak the applicationDidBecomeActive: implementation to the following:

```
- (void)applicationDidBecomeActive:(UIApplication *)application
{
    //reset the application badge count
    [[UIApplication sharedApplication] setApplicationIconBadgeNumber:0];
    [[BRDModel sharedInstance] updateCachedBirthdays];
}
```

Now, whenever the app launches, the badge on the home screen should get reset. Job done!

Summary

Congratulations! You have built your first iPhone App! It's only the end of Day 4 and already we have a fully working *Birthday Reminder* app. In this chapter, we discovered how to schedule local notification alerts in iOS that display even when our app isn't running. From a user's perspective, the local notifications look and function identically to push notifications.

We also created an in-app settings screen that enables our users to control when they get their birthday reminder notifications.

But hold on, isn't this book meant to be about how to build an iPhone app in five days, not four?! That's correct, Daniel-san. Although we've built an app, our job as iPhone developers does not stop there. If we are to stand any chance whatsoever of being found in the App Store's hundreds of thousands of iPhone apps, we are going to have to consider our marketing approach very carefully.

Tomorrow we'll primarily focus on how to market our new iPhone app using in-app marketing by empowering our *Birthday Reminder* users to spread the word about our app through social networking. We'll also encourage good App Store reviews and ratings directly from our app. This is going to require additional work on our iPhone app before we submit it to Apple. We're also going to learn about the iTunes Connect submission process and how to ensure our app stands the best possible chance of App Store discovery!

Until tomorrow my friend. I bid you, *adieu*.

Day 5

The Finishing Touches

Chapter 13

Before You Launch: Increasing Your Chances of App Store Success

Congratulations, you've made it to Day 5! In fact, you made it to Day 5 and you've already built a complete iPhone app.

But the work isn't over yet. If, like many other app developers, you make the mistake of thinking that once you've built a good app, submitted it to the App Store, and now you just need to sit back and watch the money roll in—then ,oh boy, you've failed before you've even started.

Your app will be a small fish in the App Store ocean. No matter how great your app may be, if people can't discover it, then you are destined for a very depressing journey ahead! It's not nearly enough to make a great product, you have to spend even more time marketing that product. This is not a unique concept to the App Store, but it's certainly prevalent in Apple's ecosystem.

What can we add to *Birthday Reminder* to take advantage of the millions of potential users of our app? The answer is in-app marketing: encouraging and enabling existing users to spread the word about what a great app discovery they've made.

In a world where communication is powered by the Internet and social networking is king, we'd be fools not to take advantage of Twitter and Facebook integration at minimum to enable our users to share details of *Birthday Reminder* with their friends and followers.

In Chapter 11 yesterday, we learned how to deeply integrate Facebook into our app. There's plenty more that we can do with the powerful Graph API when it comes to sharing. When Chris and I built *Tap to Chat*, an Instant Messenger app for Facebook Chat and Google Talk, we managed to total up over a million downloads in our first year. One of the reasons for the success of *Tap to Chat* (apart from it being an awesome app!) was that we built a custom sharing component into the app that enabled users to post to multiple Friend Walls very, very easily. With a lot of users sharing details of our app directly to Friend Walls, friends of friends were discovering our app and our audience grew very rapidly as a result. This type of in-app marketing can be very powerful if your target audience is power-Facebook users: ours was.

Getting more 5-star App Store ratings

Back in Chapter 1, I also talked about the importance of getting good App Store reviews. The more 5-stars you can get for your app, the better (see Figure 13-1).

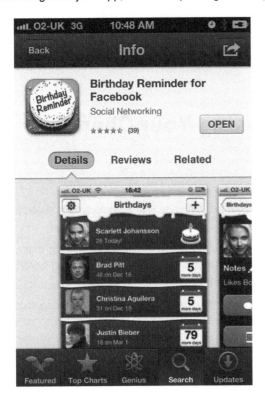

Figure 13-1. The official version of *Birthday Reminder* in the US App Store

Browsing App Store users are more likely to download an app with a lot of good reviews and star ratings than an app with a lot of 1-star ratings and poor reviews. That's just common sense.

However, there are a lot of App Store facts that you need to be aware of. Every country has its own App Store. The App Store version that a user browses is directly related to his Apple account: if a user has registered an Apple account in the United States, then he will browse the US App Store by default. If a user's Apple ID is registered in the UK, then she'll browse the UK App Store. This means that all of the reviews, ratings, and chart positions are all country-specific. Your app may do brilliantly in the UK, but the exact same app is invisible in the United States if you have few US downloads (yep, that's happened to me!). On that point, it's also worth noting that typically an app that rises to the top of its category in the UK, France, Germany, and so forth, is making a great deal less money than an app that rises to the top of the US chart. US iOS users spend more money on paid apps than any other country. That doesn't mean you should target only US users; your target market is going to depend on the type of app that you build.

One thing is for certain though: if your app is getting downloads, you need to ensure that your happy users rate and review your app. In order for a user to rate and review your app, they need to either (a) love (or hate) your app enough to make the effort, and then (b) have to visit the App Store to search and find your app before reviewing it. So why not make their job a little easier by encouraging users to rate your app after they've used it for a number of days—presumably a number of enjoyable days! There's a great open-source Objective-C class for iOS apps called Appirater that will do just that. You can download Appirater from GitHub at `https://github.com/arashpayan/appirater`.

Up until now, we haven't used any third-party code or libraries, but with a tried-and-tested method to encourage users to rate iOS apps, I see no reason to reinvent the wheel for our project.

Create a new folder named `support` at the root level of your project in the Finder. Add a subfolder named `Appirater` and then copy across the files that you've just downloaded from GitHub, as shown in Figure 13-2. It's quite possible that Appirater will have changed since I wrote this chapter, so I've also included the version I worked with in the source code.

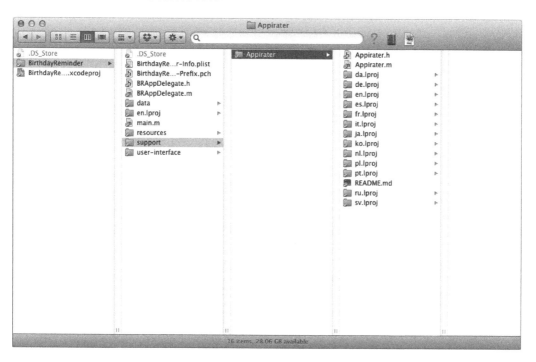

Figure 13-2. Adding Appirater, keeping third-party code separate in a support folder

Now add the support folder and its contents to your *Birthday Reminder* project. At this point, you will probably find that your project will no longer compile and you now have compiler errors. This is because our app uses ARC (Automatic Reference Counting) and Appirater does not. Do not panic young Daniel-san. Luckily, Apple had the foresight to realize that there would be times when ARC-compatible projects might also need to include non-ARC-compatible classes. Here's how to get rid of those compiler errors. Select your *BirthdayReminder* project and then BirthdayReminder target. Select the Build Phases tab and open the Compile Sources section. We are going to add a Compiler Flag for the problem file, Appirater.m, which should be listed at the end of the Compile Sources list. Double-click the class file and type in the fno-objc-arc compiler flag, as shown in Figure 13-3.

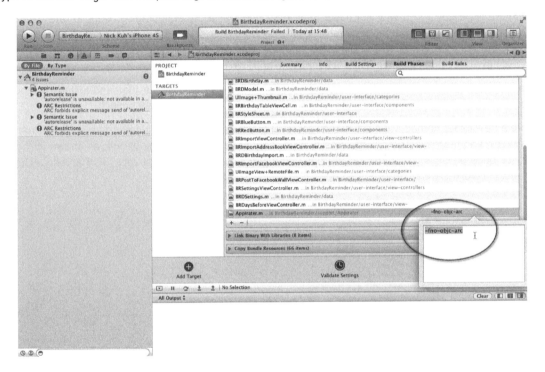

Figure 13-3. Integrating non-ARC files into an ARC project

That should solve the ARC-related errors and generate some new ones. Hurray! The new errors relate to missing frameworks that Appirater is also dependent on. We need to add Apple's CFNetwork and SystemConfiguration frameworks to our project. Do you remember how to do that? Stay in the Build Phases tab of your target's project settings and open the Link Binary Files with Libraries pane. Tap the + button to add CFNetwork.framework and SystemConfiguration.framework, as shown in Figure 13-4.

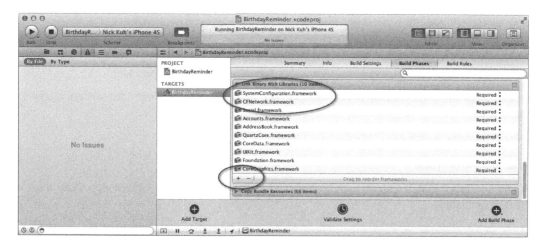

Figure 13-4. Adding CFNetwork.framework and SystemConfiguration.framework to our project

You should now be able to build and run your app without problems.

Following Appirater's *Getting Started* instructions in the README file, we next need to open BRAppDelegate.m and import Appirater.h. Then locate the application:didFinishLaunchingWithOptions: method and modify it to let Appirater know the app has launched:

```
- (BOOL)application:(UIApplication *)application didFinishLaunchingWithOptions:(NSDictionary *)launchOptions
{
    [BRStyleSheet initStyles];
    [Appirater appLaunched:YES];
    return YES;
}
```

Now add the following modification to the delegate's applicationWillEnterForeground: method:

```
- (void)applicationWillEnterForeground:(UIApplication *)application
{
    [Appirater appEnteredForeground:YES];
}
```

Configuring Appirater

To configure Appirater, you have to manually edit the Appirater.h header file.

The first change to make will be to modify the APPIRATER_APP_ID constant declaration to the numeric ID of your app. This is a numeric ID that you can only access once you've created a new app to submit in iTunes Connect. We'll be leaning about iTunes Connect in Chapter 14, so for now, just use *Birthday Reminder*'s live App ID:

```
#define APPIRATER_APP_ID                            489537509
```

Next, change the name that the Alert view will use to reference to our app:

```
#define APPIRATER_APP_NAME                          @"Birthday Reminder"
```

By default, Appirater uses the project name of our app, which is `BirthdayReminder` without a space: not so user-friendly.

If it's not on already, switch `Appirater`'s debug mode on:

```
#define APPIRATER_DEBUG                 YES
```

Build and run *Birthday Reminder* on your iPhone or iPod Touch because links to the App Store won't work on the iOS simulator.

Because we've switched on Appirater's debug mode, we can immediately see what the rating alert will look like when it eventually displays for our users (see Figure 13-5).

Figure 13-5. A user-friendly Appirater alert

Now, it used to be that tapping Rate Birthday Reminder would link users directly into your app's Write Review screen on the App Store. However, in iOS 6, Apple revamped the App Store, and to my knowledge, it's no longer possible to link directly to the write a review screen of an app. Instead, we'll have to opt for the user being taken to our app's main page in the App Store. To fix this in Appirater, switch to Appirater.m and modify the templateReviewURL value to the following:

```
NSString *templateReviewURL =
@"http://itunes.apple.com/WebObjects/MZStore.woa/wa/viewSoftware?id=APP_ID&mt=8";
```

Build and run. Test the Rate Birthday Reminder button link. You should end up on *Birthday Reminder's* main screen in the App Store.

It can be a little disconcerting to use Appirater when you first submit an app because the link won't work when your app isn't live. However, as soon as it gets approved by Apple, the link works—just don't get your App ID wrong! Check, check, and check again.

In Appirater.h, revert the APPIRATER_DEBUG constant back to NO. By default, Appirater won't display the rating request to the user until after at least 30 days have elapsed or the user has run the app 20 times. These are variants that we can change. I tend to go for a rating request after one week's use:

```
#define APPIRATER_DAYS_UNTIL_PROMPT        7              // double

#define APPIRATER_USES_UNTIL_PROMPT        5              // integer
```

It's also worth adding a manual option in our setting screen to encourage the user to rate *Birthday Reminder*. Open your storyboard and select the table view in the main Settings view controller, as shown in Figure 13-6. Using the attributes inspector, increment the Sections value to 2. This should create a duplicate group of table cells in the first section of the table view.

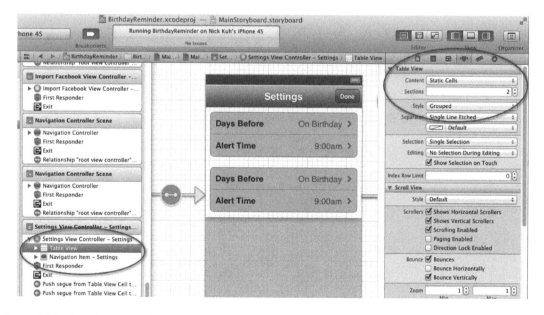

Figure 13-6. Creating a new Static Table section

Delete one of the cells in the second table view section. With the remaining cell, change its style to Basic and change its text to **Add an App Store Review!** (see Figure 13-7).

I've included a bunch of freely-available icons in the assets folder of the source code. Add all these icons to your Xcode project resources/images group. Now select the new table cell and set the image attribute to icon-compose.png. The result should look like Figure 13-7.

Figure 13-7. There's nothing wrong with giving our users a subtle idea...

We need to add the hyperlink to review our app. Open the BRSettingsViewController.m source file, import Appirater.h, and then implement a tableView:didSelectRowAtIndexPath: UITableViewDelegate protocol method:

```
-(void) tableView:(UITableView *)tableView didSelectRowAtIndexPath:(NSIndexPath *)indexPath
{
    //ignore if the user tapped the Day Before or Alert Time table cells
    if (indexPath.section == 0) return;

    //We'll start a switch statement so that we can cater for future row taps in the project
    switch (indexPath.row) {
        case 0: //Add an App Store Review!
            [Appirater rateApp];
            break;
        default:
```

```
            break;
    }
}
```

We've added a second section to our table. At present, we are displaying a section header titled Reminders. In the current implementation, we'll end up with the same header text for both sections, so let's also fix that in `BRSettingsViewController.m`:

```
- (UIView *)tableView:(UITableView *)tableView viewForHeaderInSection:(NSInteger)section
{
    return [self createSectionHeaderWithLabel:@"Reminders"];
    return section == 0 ? [self createSectionHeaderWithLabel:@"Reminders"] : [self
createSectionHeaderWithLabel:@"Share the Love"];
}
```

As before, you'll need to run the app on your iPhone or iPod Touch to see the App Store link working.

Aside from the convenience of calling a simple `rateApp` Appirater method, an additional benefit to linking in this way is that now Appirater won't automatically display a rating alert to the user in this version of your app. You don't want to annoy a happy user who has already rated and reviewed.

Sharing on Facebook, Twitter, and by e-mail

As we've already learned in this book, Apple made some great improvements by deeply integrating social networks into iOS 6. But they've also made it incredibly easy to tweet, post a Facebook status update, or share by e-mail and SMS.

Five-minute sharing integration with the UIActivityViewController

I'll show you just how easy it is to add a single, sharing link that you can include in any iOS 6 app to empower users to share in multiple ways. Using the Document Outline pane, select the second Table View section in your Settings view controller via the storyboard. Increment the row count of the section, as highlighted in Figure 13-8.

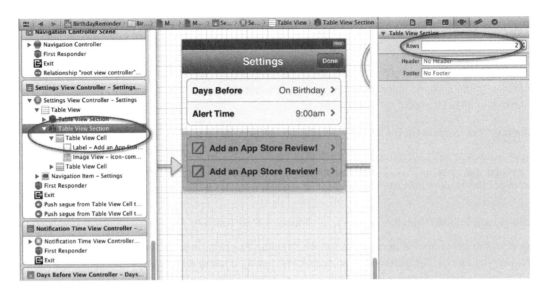

Figure 13-8. Incrementing the row count of a static Table View section

Change the text in the second cell to **Share!**, and then switch back to BRSettingsViewController.m. Next, modify `tableView:didSelectRowAtIndexPath:` method with the highlighted changes:

```
-(void) tableView:(UITableView *)tableView didSelectRowAtIndexPath:(NSIndexPath *)indexPath
{
    //ignore if the user tapped the Day Before or Alert Time table cells
    if (indexPath.section == 0) return;

    NSString *text = @"Check out this iPhone App: Birthday Reminder";
    UIImage *image = [UIImage imageNamed:@"icon300x300.png"];
    NSURL *facebookPageLink = [NSURL
URLWithString:@"http://www.facebook.com/apps/application.php?id=123956661050729"];
    NSURL *appStoreLink = [NSURL
URLWithString:@"http://itunes.apple.com/WebObjects/MZStore.woa/wa/viewSoftware?id=4895375
09&mt=8"];

    switch (indexPath.row) {
        case 0: //Add an App Store Review!
            [Appirater rateApp];
            break;
        case 1: //Share!
        {
            NSArray *activityItems = @[text,image,appStoreLink];

            UIActivityViewController *activityViewController = [[UIActivityViewController
alloc] initWithActivityItems:activityItems applicationActivities:nil];
            [self presentViewController:activityViewController animated:YES
                            completion:nil];
            break;
```

```
        }
    default:
        break;
    }
}
```

Build and run. Try tapping the new Share! table cell in the Settings view. An Activity view controller should appear, as shown in Figure 13-9.

Figure 13-9. An Activity view controller: Apple's go-to component for sharing content

The Activity view controller class was added to UIKit in iOS 6. In just six lines of code, we were able to enable our users to share some text, an image, and a link to our *Birthday Reminder* iTunes page via Twitter, Facebook, e-mail, and SMS. For me, the Contacts, Camera Roll, Print, and Clipboard options in the Activity view controller are overkill for our purposes, but we can easily remove them. Try setting the excludedActivityTypes property of the Activity view controller:

```
        UIActivityViewController *activityViewController = [[UIActivityViewController
alloc] initWithActivityItems:activityItems applicationActivities:nil];
        activityViewController.excludedActivityTypes =
@[UIActivityTypePostToWeibo,UIActivityTypePrint,UIActivityTypeCopyToPasteboard,UIActivity
TypeAssignToContact,UIActivityTypeSaveToCameraRoll];
        [self presentViewController:activityViewController animated:YES
                            completion:nil];
```

Build and run. You should now only see e-mail, SMS, Twitter, and Facebook sharing options. As you can see in Figure 13-10, the Activity view controller provides a very powerful way to add multiple content sharing options of text, links, and images.

Figure 13-10. One Activity view controller, many sharing options

We've seen just how easy it is to integrate the Activity view controller, but what if we want to display our own Facebook, Twitter, e-mail, and SMS links in table cells to launch each of the example sharing modal views individually? We can do that, but it's a bit more work. Tell you what: I'll show you how!

To begin, let's set up a number of new sharing table cells. As you did earlier, select the second Table View section in your Settings view controller via the storyboard. Increment the row count of the Sections to 6, and configure each table cell as follows (see Figure 13-11):

- Second table cell (text: **Share on Facebook**, image: `fbicon24x24.png`)

- Third table cell (text: **Like on Facebook**, image: `like-icon.png`)

- Fourth table cell (text: **Share on Twitter**, image: `icon-twitter.png`)

- Fifth table cell (text: **Email a Friend**, image: `mail-icon.png`)

- Sixth table cell (text: **SMS a Friend**, image: `sms-icon.png`)

Figure 13-11. Setting up table cells with sharing options

Sharing on Facebook with the SLComposeViewController

We're done with the storyboard, so open BRSettingsViewController.m and import the social framework:

```
#import <Social/Social.h>
```

Locate tableView:didSelectRowAtIndexPath: and replace the Activity view controller code with the following highlighted code:

```
-(void) tableView:(UITableView *)tableView didSelectRowAtIndexPath:(NSIndexPath *)indexPath
{
    //ignore if the user tapped the Day Before or Alert Time table cells
    if (indexPath.section == 0) return;

    NSString *text = @"Check out this iPhone App: Birthday Reminder";
    UIImage *image = [UIImage imageNamed:@"icon300x300.png"];
    NSURL *facebookPageLink = [NSURL
URLWithString:@"http://www.facebook.com/apps/application.php?id=123956661050729"];
    NSURL *appStoreLink = [NSURL
URLWithString:@"http://itunes.apple.com/WebObjects/MZStore.woa/wa/viewSoftware?id=489537509&mt
=8"];
```

```
    SLComposeViewController *composeViewController;

    switch (indexPath.row) {
        case 0: //Add an App Store Review!
            [Appirater rateApp];
            break;
        case 1: //Share on Facebook
        {
            if (![SLComposeViewController
isAvailableForServiceType:SLServiceTypeFacebook])
            {
                NSLog(@"No Facebook Account available for user");
                return;
            }
            composeViewController = [SLComposeViewController
composeViewControllerForServiceType:SLServiceTypeFacebook];
            [composeViewController addImage:image];
            [composeViewController setInitialText:text];
            [composeViewController addURL:appStoreLink];
            [self presentViewController:composeViewController animated:YES
                          completion:nil];
            break;
        }
        default:
            break;
    }
}
```

Build and run. Tapping on the Share on Facebook table cell should result in a Compose view controller, as shown in Figure 13-12.

Figure 13-12. Sharing on Facebook with a Compose view controller

As you can see in the new code you just added, we create instances of the SLComposeViewController via the Compose view controller's composeViewControllerForServiceType: class method. It's also important to check that the user has configured a Facebook account by calling another SLComposeViewController class method, isAvailableForServiceType:, where we can pass in Facebook, Twitter, or Sina Weibo social network types.

On to Like on the Facebook call to action. All we're going to do here is link out to our *Birthday Reminder* Facebook page, and then let the user log in and take care of the rest. You might be surprised just how effective this is—we managed to acquire thousands of Facebook Likes on our *Tap to Chat* page in a short space of time simply by linking to the page in-app.

Add a new case to the tableView:didSelectRowAtIndexPath: switch statement:

```
case 2: //Like on Facebook
        [[UIApplication sharedApplication] openURL:facebookPageLink];
        break;
```

Build and run to test out the link. Nice and simple!

Sharing on Twitter with the SLComposeViewController

How complicated do you think it'll be to share on Twitter in the same way as we did with Facebook using the SLComposeViewController? The code is virtually identical, we just need to substitute the two SLServiceTypeFacebook references to SLServiceTypeTwitter. Add another case to your switch statement in tableView:didSelectRowAtIndexPath:

```
case 3://Share on Twitter
    {
        if (![SLComposeViewController isAvailableForServiceType:SLServiceTypeTwitter])
        {
            NSLog(@"No Twitter Account available for user");
            return;
        }
        composeViewController = [SLComposeViewController
composeViewControllerForServiceType:SLServiceTypeTwitter];
        [composeViewController addImage:image];
        [composeViewController setInitialText:text];
        [composeViewController addURL:appStoreLink];
        [self presentViewController:composeViewController animated:YES
                        completion:nil];
        break;
    }
```

Pretty easy, huh? Didn't I tell you Apple has made our lives a lot simpler with iOS 6! Build and run. Tapping the Share on Twitter table cell should result in a modally presented tweet sheet, just like the one shown in Figure 13-13.

Figure 13-13. Sharing on Twitter with a Compose view controller

> **Note:** If you haven't added your Twitter or Facebook account to iOS, then `isAvailableForServiceType:` will return false and no modal view controller will be presented.

Sending e-mail with the MFMailComposeViewController

We've been able to send e-mail in iOS since iOS 3. So in-app e-mail is nothing new to the iOS SDK. However, there are a couple more steps we'll need to follow to send both e-mail and SMS messages. It's a tiny bit more cumbersome than using `SLComposeViewController`.

First, we have to add the MessageUI framework to our project. We've added numerous frameworks throughout the book, so hopefully you're comfortable adding `MessageUI.framework` to begin with.

All set? Then jump over to the `BRSettingsViewController.h` header and import `MessageUI.h`:

```
#import <MessageUI/MessageUI.h>
```

The reason we've imported the framework into the settings header is because our Settings view controller is going to need to subscribe as the delegate of the `MFMailComposeViewController` instance we'll be creating shortly. So do that now:

```
@interface BRSettingsViewController : UITableViewController
<MFMailComposeViewControllerDelegate>
```

Now switch to BRSettingsViewController.m and add another case to your switch statement in tableView:didSelectRowAtIndexPath:

```
case 4://Email a Friend
        {
            if (![MFMailComposeViewController canSendMail]) {
                NSLog(@"Can't send email");
          return;
            }
            MFMailComposeViewController *mailViewController = [[MFMailComposeViewController
alloc] init];

            //When adding attachments we have to convert the image into it's raw NSData
representation
            [mailViewController addAttachmentData:UIImagePNGRepresentation(image)
mimeType:@"image/png" fileName:@"pic.png"];
            [mailViewController setSubject:@"Birthday Reminder"];

            //Combine the text and the app store link to create the email body
            NSString *textWithLink = [NSString
stringWithFormat:@"%@\n\n%@",text,appStoreLink];

            [mailViewController setMessageBody:textWithLink isHTML:NO];
            mailViewController.mailComposeDelegate = self;
            [self presentViewController:mailViewController animated:YES
                        completion:nil];
            break;
        }
```

I mentioned there would be a few extra steps, right? To add our *Birthday Reminder* logo as an e-mail attachment, we have to convert the UIImage instance into an NSData instance. Apple provides UIImagePNGRepresentation and UIImageJPEGRepresentation functions for just this sort of purpose.

As you may have spotted in the code, it's possible to set HTML in your e-mail via the setMessageBody:isHTML: method of the Mail view controller, so you could optionally use HTML to create hyperlinks within your message body.

Try a build and run. You should be able to tap the Email a Friend cell and see a resulting e-mail modal view controller, as shown in Figure 13-14.

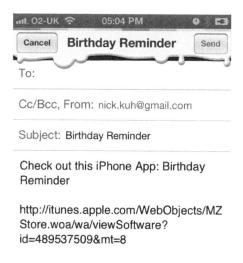

Figure 13-14. Sharing by e-mail with a Mail Compose view controller

While testing the app on your device, try tapping the Cancel button of the Mail Compose view controller. Nothing happened, right? That's because the Mail Compose view controller expects its delegate to deal with dismissing the view controller. This is easy to resolve by adding the `mailComposeController:didFinishWithResult:error:` method of `MFMailComposeViewControllerDelegate` to `BRSettingsViewController.m`:

```
#pragma mark MFMailComposeViewControllerDelegate

- (void)mailComposeController:(MFMailComposeViewController*)controller
didFinishWithResult:(MFMailComposeResult)result error:(NSError*)error
{
	switch (result)
	{
		case MFMailComposeResultCancelled:
			NSLog(@"mail composer cancelled");
			break;
		case MFMailComposeResultSaved:
			NSLog(@"mail composer saved");
			break;
		case MFMailComposeResultSent:
			NSLog(@"mail composer sent");
			break;
		case MFMailComposeResultFailed:
```

```
                    NSLog(@"mail composer failed");
                    break;
    }

    [controller dismissViewControllerAnimated:YES completion:nil];

}
```

That should do the trick!

Sending messages with the MFMessageComposeViewController

Since iOS 4, it's also been possible to create an SMS compose sheet right inside your app. The implementation is very similar to the sending e-mail process we've just stepped through.

Switch to BRSettingsViewController.h and declare that your Settings view controller also implements the MFMessageComposeViewControllerDelegate protocol:

```
@interface BRSettingsViewController : UITableViewController
<MFMailComposeViewControllerDelegate, MFMessageComposeViewControllerDelegate>
```

Now back in BRSettingsViewController.m, add a final case to your switch statement in tableView:didSelectRowAtIndexPath:

```
case 5://SMS a Friend
        {
            if (![MFMessageComposeViewController canSendText]) {
                NSLog(@"Can't send messages");
        return;
            }
            MFMessageComposeViewController *messageViewController =
[[MFMessageComposeViewController alloc] init];

            //Combine the text and the app store link to create the email body
            NSString *textWithLink = [NSString
stringWithFormat:@"%@\n\n%@",text,appStoreLink];

            [messageViewController setBody:textWithLink];
            messageViewController.messageComposeDelegate = self;
            [self presentViewController:messageViewController animated:YES
                        completion:nil];
            break;
        }
```

It's very similar to the MFMailComposeViewController implementation, as you can see from the code. Add the messageComposeViewController:didFinishWithResult: protocol method of MFMessageComposeViewControllerDelegate to BRSettingsViewController.m before testing the new Mail Compose view controller:

```
#pragma mark MFMessageComposeViewControllerDelegate
```

```
- (void)messageComposeViewController:(MFMessageComposeViewController *)controller
didFinishWithResult:(MessageComposeResult)result
{
    switch (result)
        {
                case MessageComposeResultCancelled:
                        NSLog(@"message composer cancelled");
                        break;
                case MessageComposeResultFailed:
                        NSLog(@"message composer saved");
                        break;
                case MessageComposeResultSent:
                        NSLog(@"message composer sent");
                        break;
        }

    [controller dismissViewControllerAnimated:YES completion:nil];

}
```

Build and run. The results should look like Figure 13-15.

Figure 13-15. Sharing by SMS with a Message Compose view controller

It may be becoming clear to you now that the five-minute process to add an Activity view controller that you went through earlier brings with it all of the other sharing content view controllers we've implemented through this chapter. The difference is that we can retain a finer level of control over the content we share based on the type of sharing. When sharing by e-mail, for example, I'd want to take advantage of the HTML compatibility in the body text and add multiple hyperlinks throughout my content. Likewise, when sharing by Twitter, we have to be careful about character numbers.

It's wonderful to have the new Activity view controller that Apple built in iOS 6, but there are times when abstracting all sharing functionality into just a paragraph of text and an image or two is not enough, and finer control is necessary.

Summary

Developing social sharing features this morning has been time well spent. The sharing and app rating code I've shown you can be applied to any project (just make sure that you update the text, image and links!). If you leave the in-app marketing work until version 1.1 or version 2 of your app, you've made a real schoolboy error! Apple just keeps making it increasingly simple to be social with iOS apps. You really have no excuse not to take advantage of their simple-to-implement features.

You've finished your iPhone app development phase! What a momentous journey you've travelled.

We've covered a great deal of the iOS SDK in the last four and a half days. You've absorbed the skills and code required for many everyday tasks as an iOS Developer. Although *Birthday Reminder* is a small five-day app, so many of the techniques I've introduced to you to during the course can be applied to far bigger projects.

So what's left to do? Submit our app, of course! In the final chapter of our journey, I'll take you on a tour of iTunes Connect, and guide you through the steps of submitting an app to the App Store. See you shortly.

Chapter 14

Submitting Our App

You've built your iPhone app and you're ready to go live! So erm … how do you do that exactly? Using iTunes Connect, that's how. iTunes Connect is a web-based tool that Apple provides for iOS and Mac developers to submit and distribute their apps via the App Store.

There are two main steps to the app submission process:

1. Create a new app submission via the iTunes Connect web site.

2. Build and upload a release binary of your app directly from Xcode to iTunes Connect.

After you complete step one, you'll have immediate access to your app's iTunes Apple ID, which, as we learned in Chapter 13, can be used to link directly to your app in the App Store.

Apple gives you up to six months to upload your app binary after completing the initial iTunes Connect app submission forms. So it is possible to reserve an App Store name well in advance of completing the final build of your app.

Creating a new app submission with iTunes Connect

Only paid-up, enrolled iOS developers can access iTunes Connect. As I mentioned back in Chapter 2, there's quite a bit of red tape to get through to become an enrolled iOS developer in the first place, so if you haven't already gone through that first stage—then back to Chapter 2 you go!

So, are just the enrolled iOS developers left in the room? Fire up Safari and point your browser to iTunes Connect at `http://itunesconnect.apple.com`.

Begin by logging in with your iOS developer Apple ID and password (see Figure 14-1).

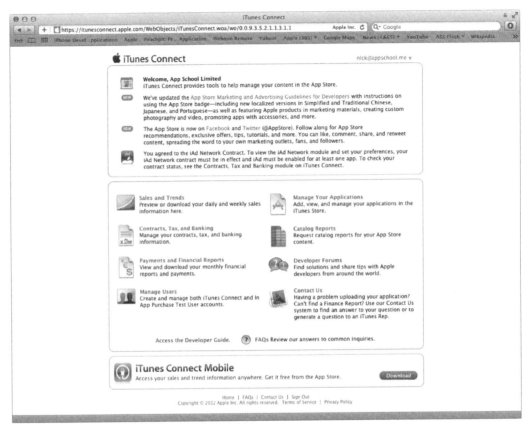

Figure 14-1. The iTunes Connect home screen

In addition to submitting new apps and app updates to Apple, you'll use iTunes Connect to view your sales and download stats; complete contract, tax, and billing forms; and manage and track advertising earnings if you use Apple's iAd platform.

We're going to focus on the submission process, so click the Manage Your Applications link to get started. Next, click the big blue Add New App button.

As you see in Figure 14-2, the next step is to add some basic app information.

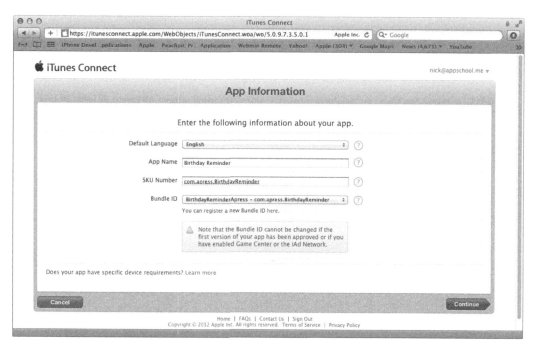

Figure 14-2. Setting up basic app information, such as the App Store name

Setting a default language

If the base language for your app is French, then here's the time to let Apple know! Whatever language you choose, it will become the primary language that the App Store associates with your app. It's also worth noting that you can add additional localized App Store descriptions and even a localized name at a later point.

Entering an app name

The App Name is the name displayed next to your app icon, which users see when browsing the App Store. It is not to be confused with your app display name—the name that displays under your app on the iPhone home screen. Unlike the display name, the App Store name can be quite long—up to 255 bytes, which is about the same number of regular characters. In terms of App Store search optimization, I'd recommend taking advantage of those additional characters and including relevant keywords in your App Store title. This improves the chances of your app being found or displayed in the App Store's regular and predictive search results.

You can wait until you've filled in all four fields in this form before submitting, or you can tap Continue to check whether the App Name you've entered is already taken in the App Store (see Figure 14-3).

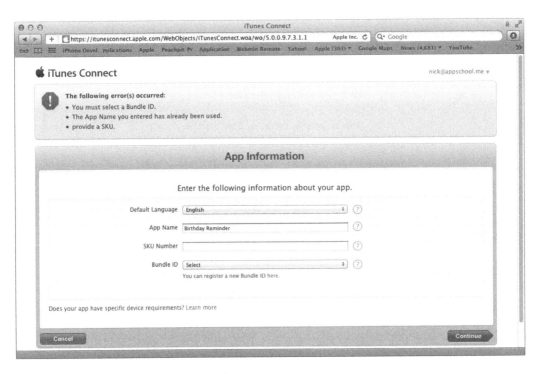

Figure 14-3. Checking if an App Name already exists

In Figure 14-3, spot the error in "The App Name you entered has already been used." Keep trying different names until you get rid of this error, which is when you'll know that you have chosen a unique App Store name.

Entering the SKU number

Apple's online documentation on handling the SKU field reads as follows:

In the SKU field, put the unique UTF-8 alphanumeric identifier for your app. The SKU is any alphanumeric sequence of letters and numbers you'd like to use to be uniquely identified in our system. You may create any string of UTF-8 letters and numbers, as long as it is unique to your developer account. This SKU is internal only and is not seen by users at any time. After you have submitted your metadata, this SKU is not editable.

I tend to simply use the bundle identifier for my apps as the SKU number (see Figure 14-2).

Connecting a bundle identifier

In the provisioning portal, iTunes Connect automatically detects all of your valid bundle identifiers that aren't already in use by your live App Store apps. You set up a bundle identifier back in Chapter 2, so using the drop-down, you should be able to select your bundle identifier. When you've selected a valid bundle identifier, iTunes Connect will alert you that "the Bundle ID cannot be changed if the first version of your app has been approved"—so make sure that you've picked the correct bundle identifier before tapping the Continue button.

Scheduling and pricing your app

On the next page of the app submission form, you set your app's availability date and price (see Figure 14-4).

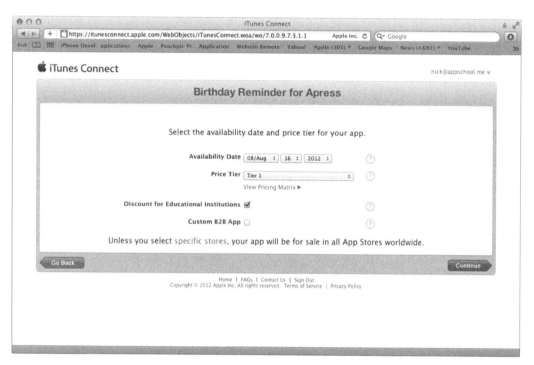

Figure 14-4. Setting the availability date and price of your app

Delaying the launch of your app

If you want your app to go live the moment that Apple approves it, then just leave the availability date set to its default (today's date). However, this is another great chance to market your app. Before it launches, no one can fairly deem your app a success or failure. Once you've uploaded your binary, in my experience, it typically takes Apple about seven days until they review and then approve or reject an app. If you schedule your app's availability date for two weeks after submission, then once your app gets approved, you then hold the power to make it live in the App Store. Make the most of this power! Once I know an app has already been approved by Apple, I start e-mailing journalists about the launch of my app. At this point, I know exactly when my app will be live in the App Store: there is zero uncertainty because Apple has already approved the submission. So I can provide journalists with a tip that My Cool App will be launching on Friday August 24th or whatever date I choose. Do you see the advantage to launching this way? Stay in control and delay the launch of your app. Launch on *your* terms, not Apple's!

Pricing your app

Pricing an app for sale via the App Store is achieved either by choosing to distribute your app for free or by selecting a pricing tier. The pricing tiers are based on dollars. Tier 1 is $0.99, Tier 2 is $1.99, Tier 3 is $2.99, and so on. Each tier has a corresponding tier price on a currency-by-currency basis, which you can look up via the Pricing Matrix link. I've taken a snapshot of the current pricing matrix (see Figure 14-5). Apple updates the pricing matrix every once in a while, particularly after significant currency exchange rate fluctuation.

App Store Pricing Matrix

Tier	U.S. - US$		Canada - CAD		Mexico - MXP		Australia - AUD		New Zealand - NZD		Japan - Yen		Europe - Euro		Switzerland - CHF		Norway - NOK		U.K. - GBP	
	Customer Price	Your Proceeds	Customer Price	Your Proceeds	Customer Price	Your Proceeds	Customer Price	Your Proceeds	Customer Price	Your Proceeds	Customer Price	Your Proceeds	Customer Price	Your Proceeds	Customer Price	Your Proceeds	Customer Price	Your Proceeds	Customer Price	Your Proceeds
Tier 1	0.99	0.70	0.99	0.70	12.00	8.40	0.99	0.63	1.29	0.90	85	60	0.79	0.48	1.00	0.65	7.00	3.92	0.69	0.42
Tier 2	1.99	1.40	1.99	1.40	24	16.80	1.99	1.27	2.59	1.81	170	119	1.59	0.97	2.00	1.30	14.00	7.84	1.49	0.91
Tier 3	2.99	2.10	2.99	2.10	36	25.20	2.99	1.90	4.19	2.93	250	175	2.39	1.45	3.00	1.94	21.00	11.76	1.99	1.21
Tier 4	3.99	2.80	3.99	2.80	48	33.60	4.49	2.86	5.29	3.70	350	245	2.99	1.82	4.00	2.59	28.00	15.68	2.49	1.52
Tier 5	4.99	3.50	4.99	3.50	60	42.00	5.49	3.49	6.49	4.54	450	315	3.99	2.41	5.00	3.24	35.00	19.60	2.99	1.82
Tier 6	5.99	4.20	5.99	4.20	72	50.40	6.49	4.13	8.29	5.80	500	350	4.99	3.04	6.00	3.89	42.00	23.52	3.99	2.43
Tier 7	6.99	4.90	6.99	4.90	84	58.80	7.49	4.77	9.99	6.99	600	420	5.49	3.34	7.00	4.54	49.00	27.44	4.99	3.04
Tier 8	7.99	5.60	7.99	5.60	96	67.20	8.49	5.40	10.99	7.69	700	490	5.99	3.65	8.00	5.19	56.00	31.36	5.49	3.34
Tier 9	8.99	6.30	8.99	6.30	108	75.60	9.49	6.04	12.99	9.09	800	560	6.99	4.25	9.00	5.83	63.00	35.28	5.99	3.65
Tier 10	9.99	7.00	9.99	7.00	120	84.00	10.49	6.68	13.99	9.79	850	595	7.99	4.86	10.00	6.48	70.00	39.20	6.99	4.25
Tier 11	10.99	7.70	10.99	7.70	130	91.00	11.49	7.31	14.99	10.49	900	630	8.99	5.47	11.00	7.13	77.00	43.12	7.49	4.56
Tier 12	11.99	8.40	11.99	8.40	140	98.00	12.99	8.27	15.99	11.19	1000	700	9.99	6.08	12.00	7.78	84.00	47.04	7.99	4.86
Tier 13	12.99	9.10	12.99	9.10	160	112.00	13.99	8.90	16.99	11.89	1100	770	10.49	6.39	13.00	8.43	91.00	50.96	8.99	5.47
Tier 14	13.99	9.80	13.99	9.80	170	119.00	14.99	9.54	17.99	12.59	1200	840	10.99	6.69	14.00	9.07	98.00	54.88	9.99	6.08

Figure 14-5. Apple's App Store Pricing Matrix

Based on the current pricing matrix, if a customer buys an app for $0.99 in the United States, then the same app will sell for £0.69 to UK customers or €0.79 when purchased through a European App Store.

The pricing matrix also shows you the sales proceeds value you'll receive from Apple for each app sale (the amount in each country's currency). For each sale of a $0.99 app in the United States, for example, you'll receive $0.70 from Apple.

Limiting your app to specific countries

By default, Apple distributes your app through all of its App Stores, but you can change that if you wish. Tapping the Specific Stores link enables you to pick and choose the countries to sell your app in (see Figure 14-6).

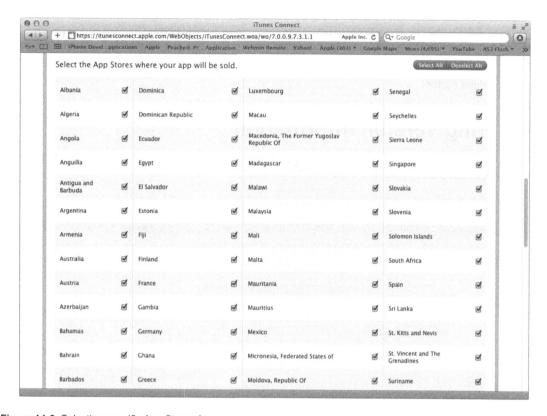

Figure 14-6. Selecting specific App Stores for your app

> *Tip: If, for any reason, you have to take your app offline temporarily, you can do so without deleting it from the store. Simply tap the Rights and Pricing link to edit your app, and you'll return to the availability and pricing screen. Deselect all stores and save. This simply removes your app from all App Stores until you return to this screen to switch your app back on for sale.*

There are many horror stories from developers who submitted a fantastic update to their app, and only when it was approved by Apple and live in the store did they discover that they'd neglected to test the migration process of users updating from older versions of the app. Crash City ensued. Once an app update gets approved, there's no way to revert it back to an older version. The best solution in my book is to switch your app off temporarily and submit another update. Well, no, actually the best solution is to test thoroughly with new users and existing users updating their apps. Just never make a mistake, OK? ☺

Let's assume that we're happy selling our app in all global App Stores.

Have you selected a price tier for your app? You can change this later.

I also recommend leaving the Discount for Educational Institutions ticked. Apple provide schools and universities bulk purchase discounts. If there are educational institutions purchasing 30 or more copies of your app in one go, then they deserve a discount, don't they?

Tap the Continue button.

Configuring version information

The next details we have to supply for our app are version numbers, copyright text, and primary and secondary App Store categories (see Figure 14-7).

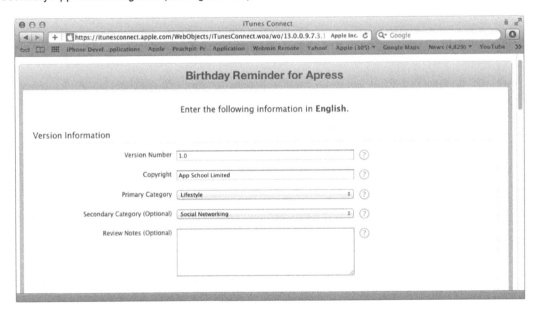

Figure 14-7. Setting a version number, copyright information, and categories for our app

Use a conventional version-number format when submitting your apps. Avoid using words like alpha, beta, and the like; instead, stick to 1.0, 1.20, 2.0, and so on. Because this is the first submission of our release app, I recommend using 1.0. The version number we set in iTunes Connect needs to match the `Bundle versions string, short` value in the `Info.plist` of our Xcode project, which by default is also 1.0.

Selecting an App Store category

You must select a primary category for your app, and you can optionally select a second category. If your app can be fairly placed within multiple categories, then I recommend looking at the latest App Store metrics by 148Apps at `http://148apps.biz/app-store-metrics`.

Among many other useful statistics, the 148Apps App Store metrics include a category-by-category app count (see Figure 14-8).

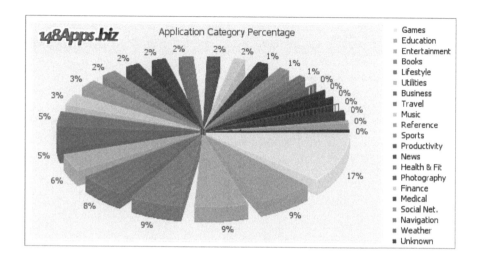

Current Active Application Count By Category

Games	124,628 (17.62%)
Education	70,606 (9.98%)
Entertainment	68,002 (9.62%)
Books	64,922 (9.18%)
Lifestyle	59,836 (8.46%)

Figure 14-8. App Store metrics by 148Apps provide insight into the most popular, competitive categories

We can see in Figure 14-8 that after Games, the second most popular (and therefore competitive) category is Education, and third most popular is Entertainment. This is incredibly valuable information because the higher we can climb in our category, the better App Store–visibility we get. So if you can pick a less busy category, do so!

148Apps App Store metrics include app price distribution. Did you know that about 50 percent of the apps in the App Store are free? Many of the free apps monetize via in-app purchase and advertising, but it's very useful to know that there's a lot of competition—even if you choose to distribute your app for free!

You can leave the Review Notes section of the submission process blank, but if, for example, your app required that users have an account with a third-party web site, then you should help out the Apple reviewer by including a test-account username and password in the review notes.

Setting up an app rating

The next set of choices to make relate to your app content. Select the most applicable radio button choice for each, and the form will automatically generate an app age rating that Apple deems applicable to your app (see Figure14-9).

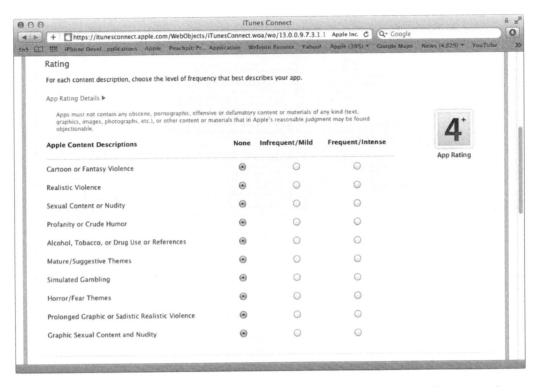

Figure 14-9. I don't think our Apple audience will find anything too controversial in our *Birthday Reminder* app!

Adding a description and metadata

At the point that a user first reads your app's description, you have already got him through the door, enticing him to learn more about your app thanks to a beautiful icon and a strong and informative app name. You are now close to a sale, so be sure that your description clearly and concisely summarizes what your app does (see Figure 14-10).

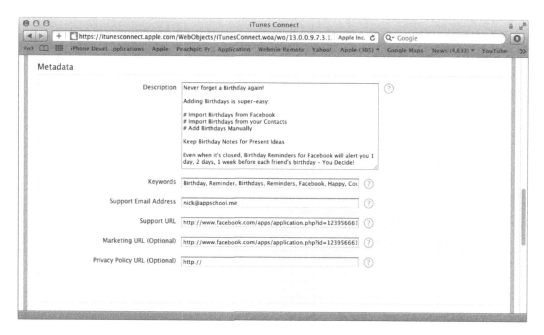

Figure 14-10. Entering descriptive text, keywords, and other metadata

The very first line of your description is the most important. The App Store description is shown on iPhones, iPads, in iTunes, and on the Web. In many cases, it also gets truncated to just the first couple of lines, so be sure that you summarize your app in your first sentence.

Also note that your descriptive text and screen grabs will be aggregated by sites like App Shopper (www.appshopper.com) as soon as your app goes live, so don't write anything dumb like "Description to be added at a later point" and forget to fill in some useful details about your app before launch!

Adding keywords

You've got a maximum of 100 bytes for your keywords (about 100 characters)—use them all. Apple's search algorithm checks your app title, keywords, and description to find search results. Keywords take more importance than the description, so choose them wisely! Separate your keywords with commas.

Note that once Apple has approved your app submission, then you will no longer be able to edit your app's keywords. The same applies to your App Store title. You can only edit these details when you submit future updates of your app.

Uploading screenshots and iTunes artwork

In order to complete the first step of our App Store submission, we need to upload a large version of our app icon and at least one screenshot for our app (see Figure 14-11).

Figure 14-11. A large app icon and up to five screenshots per device uploaded

Apple specifies that the large app icon for iTunes now needs to be 1024×1024 pixels. Your very large icon will pop on the retina iPad and iOS 6 App Store.

Just like the app icons in your app binary, ensure the corners of your iTunes icon bleed all the way to the edge, and don't add your own round corners—Apple does this for you.

You have the choice of uploading iPhone/iPod Touch, iPhone 5/iPod Touch (5th generation) and iPad screenshots. In *Birthday Reminder*, we're only targeting the iPhone and iPod Touch devices, so we should only upload screenshots for the iPhone. iPhone and iPod Touch screenshots should be targeted at the following retina sizes: 640×960 pixels for portrait-oriented screenshots and 960×640 pixels for landscape-oriented screenshots. The 20-point iOS status bar is optional, so you can also upload 640×920 or 960×600 pixel screenshots. We're supporting the iPhone 5's 4 inch display so we must also upload native 640x1136 pixel iPhone 5 screenshots (see Figure 14-11).

If you were uploading an iPad-only app or a universal app (one app with a native UI for both iPhone and iPad), then you'd also be required to upload at least one screenshot for iPad.

You can actually change your screenshots and edit your description text at any point—even when your app is live; you won't need to wait for Apple to approve your changes.

Save your App Store submission. Don't worry, it won't actually start the App Store submission process yet. After all, you haven't uploaded an app yet.

App name secured and we have an iTunes App ID

Having completed Apple's submission form, you should receive an automated e-mail from Apple confirming your submission and letting you know that your app status is Waiting for Upload.

At this point, you'll also have access to our app's Apple ID, as highlighted in Figure 14-12.

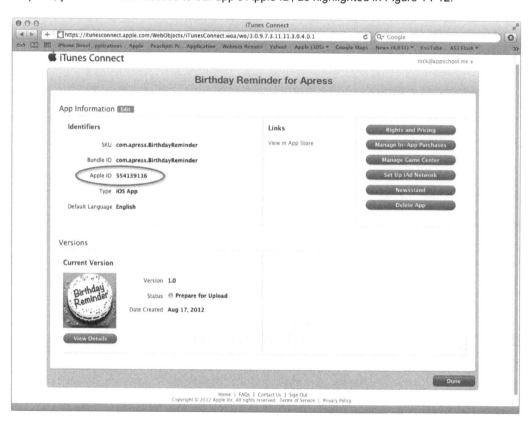

Figure 14-12. Our app now has an Apple ID and our app submission is in a Prepare for Upload state

We still have some work to do before we can sit back and wait for our app to reach Apple's reviewers. Tapping the View Details button, shown in Figure 14-12, takes you to the all the details you entered in the app submission form (see Figure 14-13).

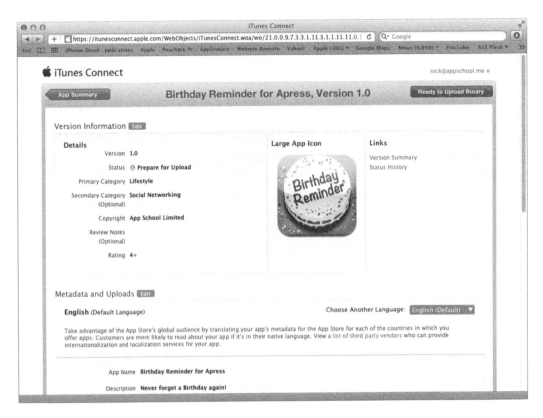

Figure 14-13. Details about version 1.0 of our app

Now click the Read to Upload Binary button. You'll have to first answer No to our app incorporating or containing cryptography, but once you click the Save button, you have completed all the steps required in iTunes Connect prior to uploading your app to Apple's submission queue. Your app's status will have changed to Waiting For Upload.

Preparing our app for App Store submission

In order to compile an App Store–ready app for distribution, you'll need to first visit Apple's provisioning portal just as you did in Chapter 2 (https://developer.apple.com/ios/manage/overview/index.action).

In Chapter 2, we created a **development certificate** and a **development provisioning profile**. Now that we're ready to submit our app to the App Store, if you haven't already then now you'll need to repeat the exact same process but this time generate a **distribution certificate** and a **distribution provisioning profile** for App Store submission. In the provisioning portal, you'll find that both the Certificates and Provisioning sections both have a Distribution tabs. The process to generate the distribution certificate and App Store provision profile is virtually identical to the process described in Chapter 2, apart from device selection that is disabled for App Store provisioning profiles (see Figure 14-14).

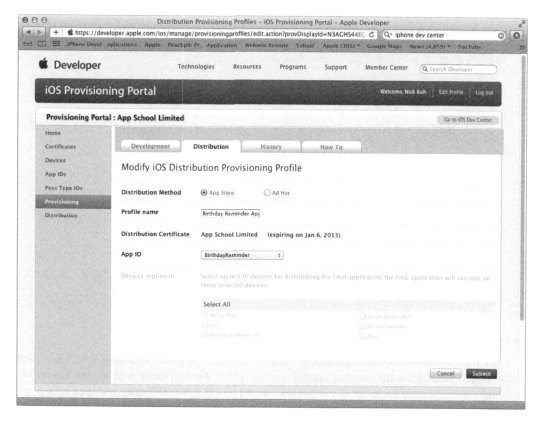

Figure 14-14. Creating an App Store provisioning profile for our app

Have you created your distribution certificate and App Store provisioning profile? Ensure that you've downloaded and double-clicked both of these files to install them.

The process of submitting an app binary to the App Store requires us to archive our *Birthday Reminder* project before signing the archive build with our distribution certificate and App Store provisioning profile. All archive builds remain accessible though Xcode's Organizer window.

Unfortunately, Xcode's Organizer will only recognize and display our app icon alongside our app archive if we add a reference to the icon via the `BirthdayReminder-Info.plist` file. So we're going to make a minor change to our project to reference the icons via the `plist`. The simplest way to do this is to let Xcode do it for us. First, open the `resources/images` Xcode group and scroll to the bottom of the list of image assets in our project. Multiselect `Icon.png` and `Icon@2x.png`, and hit the Delete key on your keyboard. Select the Move to Trash option from the dialog box, as shown in Figure 14-15.

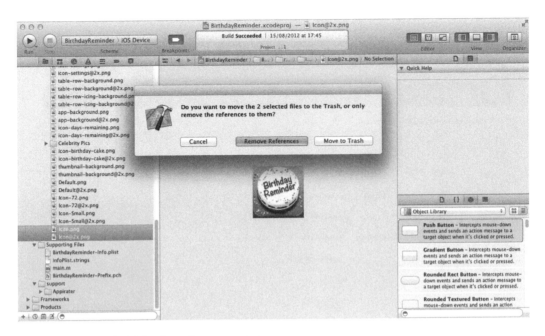

Figure 14-15. Temporarily deleting icons from our project

Now select your *Birthday Reminder* project in Xcode's project navigator, and then select the *Birthday Reminder* target. Scroll down the summary panel until you reach the App Icons section (see Figure 14-16). In the Finder, open the `assets` folder of the source files for this chapter, and drag-and-drop Icon.png onto the first icon tray, and `Icon@2x.png` onto the second icon tray, as shown in Figure 14-16.

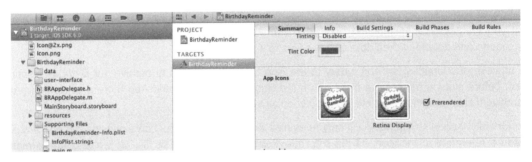

Figure 14-16. Importing icons into our project that will appear in the info plist

As you see in Figure 14-17, this import process has automatically generated some new data entries in our project's info plist, referencing the two main icons.

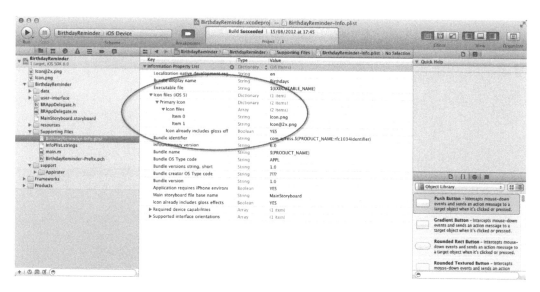

Figure 14-17. *Primary icon file references have automatically been added to BirthdayReminder-Info.plist*

Creating an archive build of our project

In order to create an archive build of your *Birthday Reminder* project, you'll need to set the active scheme to your iPhone device and not the simulator, as shown in Figure 14-18.

Figure 14-18. *Setting the active scheme to "iOS Device" or your iPhone/iPod, if it's connected to your Mac*

Now create an archive build with the menu command Product   Archive. When the build of your archive completes, Xcode automatically opens the Organizer window on the Archives tab (see Figure 14-19).

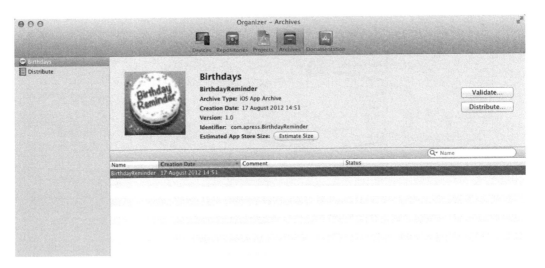

Figure 14-19. The project archives in Xcode's Organizer window

Xcode stores all of your archived projects. This means that if you ever need access to an older build of a project for testing purposes, you can access it through the Organizer.

Ready to upload and submit your app? There's one last step to take!

Signing and uploading the build

With your *Birthday Reminder* app selected in the archive builds window, tap the Distribute button. You'll be presented with three options, as shown in Figure 14-20.

Figure 14-20. Export App Store, Ad-Hoc builds, or an Xcode Archive

There are three distribution options for your project:

- **Submit to the iOS App Store**: We'll learn how this process works next.

- **Save for Enterprise or Ad-Hoc Deployment**: You can create and distribute release builds of your app that you can distribute without having to go through the App Store. Enterprise apps can be installed to any iOS device, but need to be signed with an iOS Enterprise license certificate. An Ad-Hoc build is a release build intended for distribution to any of the devices already added to your Ad-Hoc distribution provisioning profile. You might have a group of beta testers to distribute your app to in advance of App Store submission.

- **Export as Xcode Archive**: Exporting an Xcode archive packages up your app along with a dSYM file that enables other developers in a team to test your app, gain debug access to your app, and the ability to analyze detailed crash reports. There are third-party systems like Test Flight that require you to export and upload your Ad-Hoc app's dSYM file in order to remotely debug your app while it's being run by all of your beta testers.

We'll stick with the Submit to the iOS App Store default selection and tap the Next button. Xcode will ask you to sign-in to your iOS developer account. Do so and tap Next again.

As long as you've successfully installed a valid iOS distribution certificate and App Store provisioning profile from the provisioning portal, then at this point you should see a similar screen to Figure 14-21.

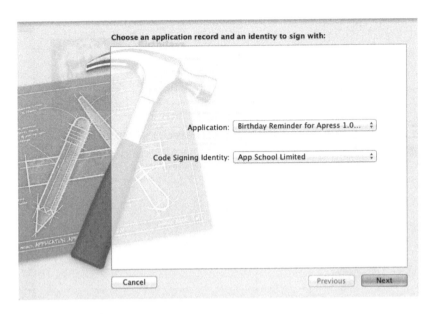

Figure 14-21. Preparing our archive build for signature

The first drop-down menu lists pending iTunes Connect app submissions that match the bundle identifier and bundle version of our app. Great! There's our *Birthday Reminder* 1.0 submission!

The second drop-down should automatically find and autoselect your distribution certificate.

Tap Next to submit.

Our app bundle will first go through a validation process, checking that the provisioning profile and signing certificate validate, and that we've included valid app icons. Should validation fail, then Xcode will supply errors and suggestions to remedy the problems.

Assuming that all is well, Xcode then begins to upload your app to iTunes Connect directly from the Organizer window (see Figure 14-22).

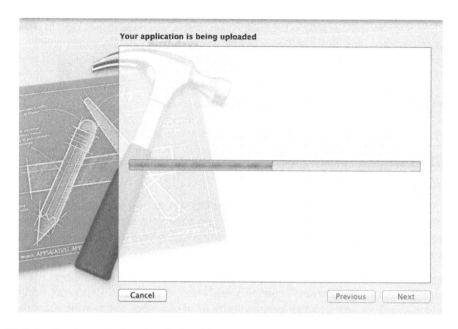

Figure 14-22. Uploading the verified app bundle from Xcode to iTunes Connect

After a few minutes, depending on the file size of your app, the upload should complete, and shortly afterward, you'll receive an automated e-mail from iTunes Connect with the subject: Your App Status is Waiting for Review.

At this point, your app is now in the App Store submission queue. In my experience, the waiting time until each new app submission and update gets to be reviewed by Apple and approved or rejected, is typically seven consecutive days. Sometimes I get lucky and the wait is shorter, and occasionally the wait slips past the seventh day.

Beware of submitting apps in the run-up to Christmas—expect to wait a little longer, possibly 14 days—as Apple gets inundated with new apps and app updates just before the festive season. Developers are trying to cash in on the influx of new iOS device owners on Christmas Day!

But what if I spot a bug in my pending app?

This happens quite a lot. Especially if, like me, you're a bit of a perfectionist. You've been waiting in the submission queue for three days but you're still testing your app, of course. Suddenly, you spot a bug you hadn't spotted before. You fix the bug in your Xcode project. Great.

But now you have a dilemma: in order to submit a replacement binary, you have to reject your existing binary, upload the new version, and unfortunately, move right to the back to the beginning of the App Store submission queue once more.

To replace a binary for an app currently in the submission queue, you have to first login to iTunes Connect, visit your app details page, and click the Binary Details link. The binary details page provides a Reject this Binary button link, enabling you to delete the app binary with the bug and then upload your new, fixed app.

Summary

Although we've now reached the end of the five-day course, this is the point where the excitement really begins for an app developer. You've built a great app. You've submitted your app. In about a week, your app should be live in the App Store—available for download to millions of potential iPhone owners. What an exciting prospect that is!

In Chapter 13, we added a number of in-app marketing features to help spread the word about our app. But there's plenty more you can do and will be able to do once your app is publically available: contact journalists, tell all your friends, start a Facebook page, and create a Twitter account for your app—to name but a few marketing strategies.

Once your app goes live, you'll also want to keep track of your app downloads, ratings, reviews, and any potential features by Apple if you create something really cool and original. Check out AppAnnie.com, a wonderful tool for App Store analytics that keeps track of all of your apps and e-mails you daily reports. Or if you're the kind of developer that likes to check out your App Store category ranking on an up-to-the-minute basis, then try out AppViz, a great desktop tool for tracking and caching all of your app sales reports, stats, and reviews.

At this point, I'm going to bid you good-bye and wish you good luck with your future iPhone developer career. I hope you've enjoyed the book. You can find me on Twitter at @nickkuh or via my web site www.nickkuh.com.

Index

A

App development, 21
  Apple Developer Forums, 24
  Apple developer registration, 22–24
  designing and planning
    app idea, 4–5
    App Store title, 6–7
    competitor apps, 5–6
    icon design, 7–8
    user interface design, 8–18
  iOS Developer Program
    enrollment, 24–25
  iOS Provisioning Portal, 26
    App ID creation, 34–35
    certificates generation, 27–32
    provisioning profiles generation, 36–39
    provisioning stage, 26–27
    UDID, 32–34
  iTunes Connect, 24
  Xcode, 21–22
App Store, 395

Appirater configuration, 399
  numeric ID, 399
  Static Table section creation, 401
  tableView:didSelectRowAtIndexPath: UITableViewDelegate protocol method, 402–403
  user-friendly Appirater alert, 400
ratings, 396
  Appirater insertion, 397
  Automatic Reference Counting, 398
  Birthday Reminder official version, 396
  CFNetwork.framework and SystemConfiguration.framework, 399
sending e-mail, with MFMailComposeViewController, 411–414

X, Y, Z

CPSIA information can be obtained at www.ICGtesting.com
Printed in the USA
LVOW012158051112

305941LV00001B/1/P